LABOR RELATIONS

Arthur A. Sloane
Associate Professor of Business Administration
University of Delaware

Fred Witney
Professor of Economics
Indiana University

LABOR RELATIONS

PRENTICE-HALL, INC., *Englewood Cliffs, New Jersey*

Library of Congress Catalog Card Number: 67–15181

Printed in the United States of America

Current Printing (last digit):
10   9   8   7   6

PRENTICE-HALL INTERNATIONAL, INC., *London*
PRENTICE-HALL OF AUSTRALIA, PTY. LTD., *Sydney*
PRENTICE-HALL OF CANADA, LTD., *Toronto*
PRENTICE-HALL OF INDIA (PRIVATE) LTD., *New Delhi*
PRENTICE-HALL OF JAPAN, INC., *Tokyo*

To
Louise and Amy
and
Judy, Eileen and Frank

Although it is our hope that this book will aid all readers who desire a deeper understanding of union-management relations, we have specifically designed it for business school students who seek a one-semester introduction to the field. As such, it contains certain areas of focus, and certain ones which must necessarily be minimized in treatment.

On the side of relative omission, the book does not attempt to be both a labor economics and a labor relations text. Rather, it brings in what we believe is sufficient economic material to allow a basic appreciation of the labor relations process and stops at that point.

On the other hand, it in no way *restricts* itself to what is commonly described as "collective bargaining." Although the focus of this volume is on the negotiation and administration of labor agreements, with emphasis on the development and application of the more significant bargaining issues as these now appear between the covers of the contracts, our own teaching experiences have taught us that these topics cannot profitably be studied in isolation. Labor relations, in the sense in which we shall use the term, can best be

Preface

viewed as an interaction between two organizations, management and the labor union; and the parties to this interaction are always subject to various, often complex, environmental influences. Only after the student gains an understanding of the evolving management and labor institutions, and only after he has come to appreciate the environment surrounding their interactional process, can he attempt to understand bargaining itself in any meaningful way.

The direction which this book will take is consequently an obvious one: downward, from a broad overview of the general nature of the labor-management relationship as it currently exists in the United States (Part I), through a survey of the historical, legal, and structural environments which so greatly influence contractual contents and labor relations behavior (Part II), to a close examination of the negotiation, administration, and major contents of the labor contract itself (Part III). Through description, analysis, discussion questions, and, in the later stages of this volume, selected arbitration cases drawn from our own experience, we hope to impart understanding of all these labor relations aspects to the future business practitioner.

This book is no exception to the rule that such a project is inevitably the result of the efforts of many people. Above all, we are indebted to Professor E. Robert Livernash of the Graduate School of Business Administration, Harvard University; Professor Abraham J. Siegel of the Massachusetts Institute of Technology's Sloan School of Management; and Professor E. B. McNatt of the School of Commerce, University of Illinois: Through the encouragement and constructive suggestions of each of these three scholars, *Labor Relations* has undoubtedly been substantially improved. Mr. John F. Pritchard of Prentice-Hall also bears our considerable gratitude for his understanding and cooperation. Nor can Miss Janet Dalton of Indiana University, who painstakingly typed every word of the manuscript as well as its multitudinous changes, be exempted from the list of those receiving credit.

For all these entirely deserved acknowledgments, however, we alone stand responsible for the final product.

ARTHUR A. SLOANE
FRED WITNEY

Contents

part one

SETTING
THE STAGE

Our society has historically placed a high premium on property rights. Because of this, and perhaps also because the American soil has nurtured a breed of highly individualistic and aggressive businessmen, employers in this country have accepted unionism through the years approximately as well as nature tolerates a vacuum.

The evidence for this phenomenon is not in short supply. Symbolic of management sentiments in the mid-nineteenth century were, for example, the comments of the editors of the *New York Journal of Commerce* relating to current demands of the printers in that locality:

> Who but a miserable craven-hearted man, would permit himself to be subjected to such rules, extending even to the number of apprentices he may employ, and the manner in which they shall be bound to him, to the kind of work which shall be performed in his own office at particular hours of the day, and to the sex of the persons employed, however separated into different apartments or buildings? For ourselves, we never employed a female as a compositor and have no great

1

Organized labor and the

management community:

an overview

opinion of apprentices, but sooner than be restricted on these points, or any other, by a self-constituted tribunal outside of the office, we would go back to the employment of our boyhood, and dig potatoes, pull flax, and do everything else that a plain, honest farmer may properly do on his own territory. It is marvelous to us how any employer, having the soul of a man within him, can submit to such degradation.[1]

Five decades later, President George F. Baer of the Philadelphia and Reading Railroad relied on God, rather than ridicule, in setting forth views which were no less representative of many employers of *his* time. In a 1903 letter, Baer replied to a citizen who had requested him "as a Christian gentleman" to make concessions to the striking workers on his railroad, as follows:

I see you are evidently biased in your religious views in favor of the right of the working man to control a business in which he has no other interest than to secure fair wages for the work he does. I beg of you not to be discouraged. The rights and interests of the laboring man will be protected and cared for, not by the labor agitators, but by the Christian men to whom God in His infinite wisdom has given control of the property interests of the country. Pray earnestly that the right may triumph, always remembering that the Lord God Omnipotent still reigns and that His reign is one of law and order, and not of violence and crime.[2]

Sinclair Lewis used the medium of fictional satire to make his points, but real-life counterparts of his small-town businessman George F. Babbitt were sufficiently in supply to make *Babbitt* an instant success when it was published in 1922. Babbitt's opinions on the subject of organized labor were quite forthright, if not entirely consistent:

A good labor union is of value because it keeps out radical unions, which would destroy property. No one ought to be forced to belong to a union, however. All labor agitators who try to force men to join a union should be hanged. In fact, just between ourselves, there oughtn't to be any unions allowed at all; and as it's the best way of fighting the unions, every businessman ought to belong to an employer's association and to the Chamber of Commerce. In union there is strength. So any selfish hog who doesn't join the Chamber of Commerce ought to be forced to.[3]

In our own day, management views on the subject are considerably more sophisticated and far less emotion-laden. Over the past few decades,

---

[1]*New York Journal of Commerce*, February 7, 1851. As quoted in Neil W. Chamberlain, *The Labor Sector* (New York: McGraw-Hill Book Company, 1965), p. 341.

[2]Herbert Harris, *American Labor* (New Haven: Yale University Press, 1939), pp. 126–27.

[3]Sinclair Lewis, *Babbitt* (New York: Harcourt, Brace & World, Inc., 1922), p. 44. (Rights for the British Commonwealth excluding Canada have been granted by Jonathan Cape Limited, Publishers, London, England.)

major changes have affected the employment relationship and contributed to the lessening of overt anti-unionism. The findings of the behavioral sciences, particularly industrial sociology and applied psychology, have led to an employee-centered management approach which was unknown to an earlier era. Far greater worker expectations have been fostered by a new social climate derived from the ending of mass immigration, growing levels of education, and the spread of the world's most ambitious communications network. Moreover, the old-time owner-manager, holding a major or exclusive proprietary interest in his business, has now been substantially displaced. He has been succeeded by the hired administrator, oriented toward management as a profession, as much an employee as the people far below him in the company hierarchy, and increasingly aware that profitability is not the only test of his company's performance today (and that *community* responsibilities are also prime considerations). Finally, the right of workers to organize and bargain collectively, free of employer restraint or coercion, has been protected by statute since the early 1930's.

In this new setting, progress in union-management relations has undeniably been made. Considerably more enlightened management policies toward organized labor are in effect today than was the case even twenty years ago. A large measure of contractual stability has been achieved in many situations. Violence in labor disputes has all but disappeared. The incidence of strikes has been steadily decreasing, and strikes now consume a minuscule portion of total working time, less than 0.18 per cent in most recent years. A greater willingness by both parties to resort to facts rather than to power or emotion as a basis for bargaining is in evidence. And, indeed, unions have now been completely accepted by some managers, with outspoken attacks on organized labor, in general, being relatively rare from *any* employer quarter.

For all these sanguine developments, however, the fact remains that unions are still far from welcome in the eyes of the employer community. If the attacks on unionism are more muted and less belligerent than they were in the past, they nonetheless exist on a wide scale. Professor Albert Blum, an eminent observer of present-day management thinking, sums up what is perhaps the current modal situation in words which the authors believe to be wholly appropriate:

> . . . Even if the manager does not view the union as a gang, he often still feels that they strike a discordant note in the happy home. Once there, unrest develops. A peer group outside the home becomes more important to the children than the parents; the father's powers are challenged; the child begins to think his goals are not synonymous with those of the parents (he may even want his allowance raised); and, perhaps

worst of all, he wants to have his voice heard in how the home should be run . . .[4]

In the face of this management enmity, on the other hand, unionism has shown absolutely no tendency to retreat. Owing primarily to the inroads of automation and its resulting employment decline as well as to changing market demands affecting the manufacturing sector, organized labor *has*, it is true, failed to expand its membership in the past few years. And, despite some claims by labor relations analysts that the fast-growing white-collar worker sector will soon become more hospitable to collective bargaining, it is equally true that union penetration in this area thus far has been anything but impressive. But it is no less a matter of record that six times as many workers are union members today as was the case in 1932, and it is quite apparent that the 18 million employees who currently constitute the labor movement in this country exhibit no notable signs of disenchantment with it. Whatever one's speculation about the problems awaiting unionism as the nature of our labor force changes (and, as will be shown, the speculation is both optimistic and pessimistic from the union viewpoint), the labor union seems to be very much here to stay.

In this introductory chapter, then, we shall want to examine several questions. Why do workers, apparently in complete disregard of their employers' wishes, join and remain in unions? Why, for that matter, do employers so steadfastly continue to oppose the concept of unionism (beyond the extremely general reasons suggested by the preceding paragraphs)? Assuming that managers have no choice other than to deal with a labor organization, what alternative methods for this collective bargaining are open to them? And what, if any, trends in their concrete dealings with unions have managements exhibited in recent years? Before we discuss these questions, however, we must assess the current status and strategic power of the American labor movement itself.

The State of the Unions Today

Completely reliable statistics relating to union membership in this country have never been available. Some unions in reporting their figures have traditionally exaggerated, to gain respect and influence for the union itself within the total labor movement, to make the union officers look better by showing a rise in enrollments during their term of office,

[4]Albert A. Blum, "Management Paternalism and Collective Bargaining," *Personnel Administration*, XXVI (January–February, 1963), 38.

or merely to hide a loss of membership. Other unions have been known to report *fewer* members than they actually have, for financial reasons (for example, to avoid paying per capita taxes to labor federations to which they may belong, particularly the AFL–CIO), or because of book-keeping practices which exclude workers currently on strike (or those on layoff from work) from the list of present members.

The figure of 18 million workers, offered above as constituting the present extent of union organization, is commonly accepted as an appropriate one, however. This total includes some 16.5 million United States members of national and international unions[5] and roughly 1.5 million American members of independent local unions (those not affiliated with any national or international).[6] It excludes the approximately 1.2 million Canadians who belong to internationals with headquarters in the United States.

In 1966, in terms of relative labor force penetration, the 18 million in the unionized work force represented approximately 22 per cent of all civilian members of the labor force in the country and accounted for three out of every ten employees in nonagricultural establishments (where union organizing has historically been concentrated). They also constituted somewhat less than 37 per cent of "organizable" American industrial employees (our nonprofessional and nonsupervisory employees, although some union representation from both the professional and supervisory sectors does exist).[7]

More specifically, just about one-half of the nation's 31 million blue-collar workers (craftsmen, operatives and kindred workers) are now in unions. These include at least 80 per cent of such workers in transportation, mining, construction, and municipal utilities and somewhat over two-thirds of all blue-collar employees in manufacturing. Almost all manual workers in many manufacturing industries—steel, automobile, rubber, aerospace, meat packing, agricultural implements, brewing, paper, the needle trades, and a few others—have now been organized. So, too, has a substantial percentage of the blue-collar employees in the printing, oil, chemical, shoe, electrical, electronic, and pharmaceutical industries.

[5]The terms "national" and "international" will be used interchangeably in this volume as, indeed, they are used in practice.

[6]Unfortunately, no completely satisfactory current figures are available, but the reader is referred to two competent articles by Leo Troy which are only slightly outdated: "Local Independent and National Unions: Competitive Labor Organizations," *Journal of Political Economy* (October, 1960); and "Local Independent Unions and the American Labor Movement," *Industrial and Labor Relations Review* (April, 1961).

[7]Unofficial data furnished by United States Department of Labor, Bureau of Labor Statistics.

States and cities with a high percentage of their workers in these industries show (not surprisingly) a high proportion of unionized employees. The United States Bureau of Labor Statistics revealed in 1960, in the most recent authoritative survey on the subject, ratios of union membership to nonagricultural employment which were well above the national average of 30 per cent in such states as Washington, Pennsylvania, Illinois, Ohio, New York, Massachusetts, and Michigan. South Carolina, Florida, Georgia, and Mississippi, on the other hand, had ratios running only between 6 and 11 per cent. Several major cities, too, which are heavily dependent on the industries cited—Pittsburgh, Detroit, and Seattle, among others—presently have at least 90 per cent of their manufacturing plant workers covered by union contract. Cities without large representation from these industries tend to show considerably lower figures.

Union strength, then, is highly concentrated—in areas which are strategic to our economy. If organized labor has thus far been notably unsuccessful in its attempt to organize such white-collar (and fast-growing) sectors as trade, services, and finance, and such remaining great pockets of nonunionism in manufacturing as the textile industry, unions *have* been cordially greeted by the workers in much of large-scale industry. Indeed, the labor movement today bargains with many of the most influential managements in the country, those which regularly take the lead in price and wage movements. By and large, as Slichter, Healy, and Livernash have pointed out, trade unions have dominant representation "where technology is most advanced, where capital is used most abundantly, where the productivity of labor is highest, and where technological progress is most rapid. . . . In other words, trade union membership is concentrated and strongest where strength counts most of all."[8]

Table 1 shows the distribution of national and international unions by industry group in 1962. Even at a cursory glance, the reader cannot easily avoid noting the high percentage of union organization accounted for by the groups cited above. Manufacturing, transportation, mining, construction, and utilities account for 80.5 per cent of the total. The ratio is believed to have changed only slightly, if at all, since 1962.

Further evidence of the importance of these industry groups to the labor movement is given in Table 2's listing of the largest unions. Ranked according to their size in 1965, the seven largest internationals show their heavy dependence on blue-collar workers even in their titles.

[8]Sumner H. Slichter, James J. Healy, and E. Robert Livernash, *The Impact of Collective Bargaining on Management* (Washington, D.C.: The Brookings Institution, 1960), p. 2.

Table 1

DISTRIBUTION OF NATIONAL AND INTERNATIONAL UNIONS AND THEIR MEMBERSHIP, BY INDUSTRY GROUP AND AFFILIATION, 1962

| | All Unions | | |
Industry Group	Number[1]	Members[2] Number (thousands)	Per cent
All unions	181	17,564	100.0
Manufacturing	107	8,050	45.8
Food, beverages, and tobacco	28	1,045	6.0
Clothing, textiles, and leather products	24	1,226	7.0
Furniture, lumber, wood products, and paper	23	766	4.4
Printing and publishing	15	359	2.0
Petroleum, chemicals, and rubber	20	491	2.8
Stone, clay, and glass	18	269	1.5
Metals, machinery, and equipment, except transportation equipment	38	2,583	14.7
Transportation equipment	16	1,187	6.8
Manufacturing (not classifiable)	23	123	.7
Nonmanufacturing	103	8,289	47.2
Mining and quarrying	11	352	2.0
Contract construction	28	2,417	13.8
Transportation	47	2,572	14.6
Telephone and telegraph	6	416	2.4
Electric and gas utilities	16	327	1.9
Trade	19	1,129	6.4
Finance and insurance	5	31	.2
Service industries	33	996	5.7
Agriculture and fishing	7	36	.2
Nonmanufacturing (not classifiable)	8	14	.1
Government: Federal, State and local	41	1,225	7.0

[1]These columns are nonadditive; many unions have membership in more than one industrial classification.

[2]Number of members computed by applying reported percentage figures to total membership outside the United States. Total membership, moreover, may include retired and unemployed workers.

Source: Monthly Labor Review (May, 1964), p. 507.

Accounting for somewhat over one-third of all union members, these internationals are:

Table 2

THE SEVEN LARGEST INTERNATIONAL UNIONS, 1965

Union	Members
Teamsters (Independent)	1,600,000
Automobile Workers (AFL-CIO)	1,120,000
Steelworkers (AFL-CIO)	910,000
Machinists (AFL-CIO)	900,000
Electrical Workers (AFL-CIO)*	850,000
Carpenters (AFL-CIO)	800,000
Mine Workers (Independent)	450,000

*International Brotherhood of Electrical Workers.

Source: Authors' estimates based on data published by the U.S. Department of Labor.

If the labor movement is predominantly a blue-collar one, however, this is no longer true of the United States labor force itself. In 1956, the number of white-collar workers exceeded that of blue-collar workers in this country for the first time in our nation's history. The gap, moreover, has been steadily widening ever since: Such sectors as trade, services, finance, and government have continued to expand, while the blue-collar sectors—particularly manufacturing, mining, and transportation—have actually, in the face of improved technologies and changing consumer demands, shown employment declines.

More than any other factor, this changing complexion of the labor force has given organized labor cause for concern. Over the past decade, its inability to recruit white-collar workers on any significant scale has forced it to watch the unionized percentage of the total civilian work force slip somewhat, from over 24 per cent to the 22 per cent figure noted above. And even in terms of *absolute* numbers, the adverse employment changes in the traditionally unionized sectors has caused union membership to drop in this time period, from a 1958 high of roughly 18.4 million members to the present 18 million approximate total.

This is not to say, of course, that unions do not exert a major collective-bargaining influence on behalf of some groups of white-collar workers. Such white-collar types as musicians (who frequently wear not only white collars but also, full tuxedo dress) and barbers have for years been willing joiners of labor organizations. In recent years, the Retail Clerks (with an estimated 400,000 members in 1965), State, County, and Municipal Employees (250,000), and Retail, Wholesale, and Department Store Employees (175,000) have significantly increased their memberships. So, too, have somewhat smaller white-collar internationals such as the Letter Carriers (155,000), Postal Clerks (150,000), and American Federation of Teachers (120,000). And although substantial numbers of workers within some of these unions (in particular, the Retail Clerks and the Letter Carriers) perform such clearly blue-collar assignments as stock-handling, the percentage of pure white-collar types in each of them appears to have been rapidly climbing in the 1960's. In addition, many of labor's largest internationals—most notably the Teamsters and the Electrical Workers—do represent large numbers of white-collar workers in addition to their traditional types of constituents.

Nonetheless, there has been virtually no change in total union penetration of the white-collar field during the past decade. In 1956, about 2.5 million white-collar workers were in unions; in the mid-1960's, the figure was approximately the same despite the growth of this area by several million more jobs, to roughly 25 million by 1966. Even these very general statistics show a standstill in terms of absolute white-collar unionization and a definite decline in terms of relative union penetration of this sector.

Why have these employees been so relatively unreceptive to the union organizer when their blue-collar counterparts have been so hospitable to him? Many theories have been advanced by almost as many theorists. But above all, as has been suggested by Strauss and Sayles,[9] the reluctance stems from four factors: (1) white-collar workers feel superior to blue-collar employees and tend to believe that joining a "union" (an institution historically associated with manual workers) would lower their social status; (2) many white-collar employees are geographically close to members of management and themselves aspire to promotions into management circles; (3) such workers are often broken down, for purposes of efficient work performance, into small, heterogeneous groups, depriving them of the consensus needed for union organization; and (4) many white-collar workers with professional identifications—engineers, for example—continue to feel that for them there is still more to be gained in the way of tangible benefits from individual negotiations with their employer than from any form of collective bargaining.

Some qualified observers, on the other hand, are quite *optimistic*, from the union point of view, on the white-collar question. They feel that labor's lack of membership success is due primarily to *temporary* obstacles which will vanish in the years ahead. By way of example, they point to currently unimaginative and tradition-anchored labor leadership, the presently adverse public reaction (a reaction which, these observers say, can be expected gradually to fade away) to *all* unions because of Congressional revelations of the corrupt practices of a few unions in the late 1950's and the present success of management attention to personnel policies which may, in the face of accelerating foreign and domestic competition, ultimately have to be sacrificed by employers. Levine and Karsh, two of the more vocal analysts in the camp of the labor "optimists," also feel that unions will become considerably more attractive to white-collar workers as the size of office, sales, and technical work forces continues to grow and as the white-collar workers' feelings of "colleagueship" with management and, indeed, their sense of "fulfillment" on the job evaporates.[10]

A case can thus be erected in either direction, although few would

[9]George Strauss and Leonard R. Sayles, *Personnel: The Human Problems of Management* (Englewood Cliffs, N. J.: Prentice-Hall, Inc., 1960), p. 88.

[10]Solomon B. Levine and Bernard Karsh, "Industrial Relations for the Next Generation," *The Quarterly Review of Economics and Business* (February, 1961), pp. 18–29.

deny that greater union penetration of the white-collar sector does face formidable obstacles.

The same can be said of other issues which confront organized labor today. It is undeniable that unions *have* in recent years fallen from public favor, owing above all to the McClellan Committee Congressional hearings, but also to their own bargaining excesses. These latter topics will be discussed on subsequent pages. Here, it is relevant to note that the publicity involved, temporarily or not, has cost the labor movement thousands of friends among both the general public and, presumably, the ranks of potential union members. It has also led to restrictive federal and state legislation (summarized in Chapter 3) which in some ways can be construed as "antilabor." And, finally, labor has been handicapped to some extent by such current factors as: the national trend to smaller, decentralized plants, resulting in more personalized worker treatment; industry's present tendency to locate new plants in smaller, semi-rural and often Southern communities, climates not conducive to a hearty reception for the union; and the growing levels of income across the nation, stripping union promises of a "living wage" of some of their effect.

Yet, for all these adverse factors, it is still of some relevance for anyone who attempts to predict the labor movement's future that in their century and one-half on the American scene unions have faced even greater obstacles than these and have ultimately surmounted them. As Chapter 2 relates, the history of United States labor is in many ways a study of triumph over economic, social, and political adversity.

However one views organized labor's future, its present strategic power cannot be denied. The labor movement's concentration of membership in the economy's most vital sectors has meant that the 22 per cent of the labor force that bargains collectively has been an extremely influential minority. One may not agree with the newspaper headlines that a particular strike has "paralyzed the economy," but it appears to be an acceptable generalization that the wages or salaries and other conditions of employment for much of the remaining 78 per cent of the labor force are regularly affected to some degree by the unionized segment.

Thus, if the exact future dimensions and membership totals of organized labor are today in some doubt, the importance of collective bargaining is not. Neither can one dispute labor's staying-power, given the labor movement's deep penetration into virtually all the traditional parts of our economy and its continuing hold upon these areas. The reports of collective bargaining's death are, as Mark Twain cabled from Europe following reports of his own demise, "greatly exaggerated." And, if the modern manager is unhappy with unionism, realism dictates not that he wait for it to vanish from the scene, but that he apply his efforts toward improving the collective bargaining process by which he is so likely to be directly affected.

Why Workers Join Unions

Questions concerning human behavior do not lend themselves to simple answers, for the subject itself is a highly complex one. "Why do workers join unions?" clearly falls within this category.

In his widely-accepted theory of motivation,[11] however, psychologist A. H. Maslow has provided us with many helpful hints, although the theory itself relates to the whole population of human beings rather than merely to those who have seen fit to take out union membership.

Maslow portrays man as a "perpetually wanting animal," driven to put forth effort (in other words, to work) by his desire to satisfy certain of his needs. To Maslow, these needs or wants can logically be thought of in terms of a hierarchy, for only one type of need is active at any given time. Only when the lowest and most basic of the needs in this hierarchy has been relatively well satisfied will each higher need become, in turn, operative. Thus, it is the *unsatisfied* need which actively motivates man's behavior. Once a need is more or less gratified, man's conduct is determined by new, higher needs which up until then have failed to motivate simply because man's attention has been devoted to satisfying his more pressing, lower needs. And the process is for most men (and, needless to say, women) unending, since few people can ever expect to satisfy, even minimally, *all* their needs.

At the lowest level in this Need Hierarchy, but paramount in importance until they are satisfied, are the *physiological* needs, particularly those for food, water, clothing and shelter. "Man lives by bread alone, when there is no bread"; in other words, any higher needs which he may have are inoperative when he is suffering from extreme hunger, for man's full attention must then necessarily be focused on this single need. But when the need for food and the other physiological essentials *is* fairly well satisfied, less basic or higher needs in the hierarchy start to dominate man's behavior, or to motivate him.

Thus, needs for *safety*—for protection against arbitrary deprivation, danger, and threat—take over as prime human motivators once man is

11A. H. Maslow, *Motivation and Personality* (New York: Harper & Row, Publishers, 1954). Much of Maslow's concept was originally presented in his article "A Theory of Human Motivation," *Psychological Review*, 50 (1943), 370–96. See also Douglas Mc-Gregor, *The Human Side of Enterprise* (New York: McGraw-Hill Book Company, 1960), pp. 36–39, for an excellent restatement of Maslow's theory.

eating regularly and sufficiently and is adequately clothed and sheltered. This is true because (1) a satisfied need is no longer a motivator of behavior, yet (2) man continues to be driven by needs, and (3) the safety needs are the next most logical candidates, beyond the physiological ones, to do this driving.

What happens when the safety needs have also been relatively satisfied, so that both of the lowest need levels no longer require man's attention? In Maslow's scheme of things, the *social* needs—for belonging, association, and acceptance by one's fellows—now are dominant, and man puts forth effort to satisfy *this* newly activated type of want.

Still higher needs which ultimately emerge to dominate man's consciousness, always assuming that the needs below them have been gratified, are in turn: *self-esteem* needs, especially for self-respect and self-confidence; *status* needs, for recognition, approval, and prestige; and, finally, *self-fulfillment* needs, for realization of one's own potential and for being as creative as possible.

All of this constitutes an oversimplification of Maslow's Need Hierarchy. Maslow himself qualified his concept in several ways, although only one of his reservations is important enough for our purposes to warrant inclusion here: he recognized that not all people follow the pattern depicted, and that both desires and satisfactions vary with the individual.

Even in the capsule form presented above, however, Maslow's contribution is of aid in explaining why workers join unions. The many research findings which now exist on this latter topic[12] basically agree that all employees endeavor to gratify needs and wants that are important to them, because of dissatisfaction with the extent to which these needs and desires have been met. They also agree that, while what is "important" among these needs and wants varies with the individual employee, much of the answer depends upon what has already been satisfied either within the working environment or outside of it. Many of these studies also support Maslow's hierarchy for the majority of workers in approximately the order of needs indicated by Maslow.

It should not be surprising that dissatisfaction with the extent of physiological need gratification is no longer a dominant reason for joining unions in this country. In our relatively affluent economy, few people who are working have any great difficulty in satisfying at least the most

[12]Perhaps the best of these studies are: E. Wight Bakke, "To Join or Not to Join," in E. Wight Bakke, Clark Kerr, and Charles W. Anrod, eds., *Unions, Management and the Public* (New York: Harcourt, Brace & World, Inc., 1960), pp. 79–85; Joel Seidman, Jack London, and Bernard Karsh, "Why Workers Join Unions," in *The Annals of the American Academy of Political and Social Science*, 274:84 (March, 1951); and Ross Stagner, ed., *Psychology of Industrial Conflict* (New York: John Wiley & Sons, Inc., 1956).

basic of these needs. In an earlier day, before the advent of minimum wage laws and other forms of legal protection, this was not as true and, as has already been suggested, union promises of a "living wage" were of great appeal to many workers. However, those members of the labor force who today are frustrated in trying to satisfy their minimal needs for food, clothing, and shelter are those who are *unemployed*, not the most logical candidates for union membership. The research substantiates this down-playing of the role of physiological needs rather conclusively. Significantly, one of the most thorough of the recent studies found that not one employee out of 114 workers in a large industrial local union became a union member primarily for this purpose.[13] (This is hardly to say that union members have lost interest in higher wages and other economic improvements. As will be shown later, the desire for these benefits persists as strongly as ever. The point is, however, that this desire now stems from *higher* need activation. Money can satisfy more than just the physiological needs.)

On the other hand, research suggests that dissatisfaction with the extent of gratification of (1) safety, (2) social, and (3) self-esteem needs—in approximately that order—has motivated many workers to join unions. To a lesser extent, status and self-fulfillment needs have also led to union membership.

Unions are uniquely equipped, in the eyes of thousands of workers, to gratify safety needs. If very few of the 150,000 labor-management contracts currently in force in the United States are identical, at least this much can be said for virtually all of them: they are generally arrived at through *compromise,* and they define in writing the "rules of the game" which have been *mutually agreed upon* to cover the terms and conditions of employment of *all* represented workers for a specific future period of time. The union thus acts as an equal partner in the bilateral establishment of what the late Sumner H. Slichter called the "system of industrial jurisprudence." And, in the interests of minimizing conflict among the workers it represents, it strives to inject uniformity of treatment—particularly in the area of job protection—into the contract.

Union membership can consequently provide workers with some assurance against arbitrary management actions. The union can be expected to push for curbs against what it calls "management discrimination and favoritism" in, for example, job assignment, promotional opportunity, and even continued employment with the company. However well-meaning are a management's intentions, the company cannot guarantee that it will *not* at times act arbitrarily, for in the absence of such checks as the union places on its actions it is always acting uni-

13Seidman, London and Karsh, *op. cit.*

laterally. Satisfaction of the safety needs—in the form of considerable protection against arbitrary deprivation, danger, and threat—is thus offered by the union in its stress on uniformity of treatment for all workers. Many employees, particularly after they have perceived "arbitrary" action by management representatives, have found the appeal irresistible.

The social needs are also known to be important, if secondary, motivators of union membership. Especially where the work itself must be performed in geographically scattered locations (as in many forms of railroad employment, truck-driving, or letter-carrying) or where the technology of the work minimizes on-the-job social interaction (as on the automobile assembly line), the local union can serve the function of a club, allowing the formation of close friendships built around a common purpose. But even when the work is not so structured, local unions foster a feeling of identification with those of like interests, often in pronounced contrast to the impersonality of the large organization in which the worker may be employed. Increasingly, unions have capitalized upon their ability to help satisfy social needs. As the latter have become more important to members of the labor force (not only because of the declining frustration of the lower needs but also because general leisure time has increased) unions have become increasingly ambitious in sponsoring such activities as vacation retreats, athletic facilities, and adult education programs for "members only." But unions have never been reluctant to publicize the social bonds which they allow: It is not by accident that internal union correspondence has traditionally been closed by the greeting "Fraternally yours," that the official titles of many unions have always included the word "Brotherhood," and that several labor organizations continue to refer to their local unions as "lodges."

Social *pressure* has also been instrumental in workers joining unions. Employees often admit that the disapproval of their colleagues would result from their not signing union application cards. Normally, the disapproval is only implied. The Seidman, London, and Karsh study, for example, unearthed such explanations from workers who had joined unions as "I can't think of a good reason except everybody else was in it" and "I suppose I joined in order to jump in line with the majority." On occasion, however, the pressure has been considerably more visible, as witness this quotation from the same study: "They approached you, kept after you, hounded you. To get them off my neck, I joined."

Other workers, at higher levels, have explained their union membership as being attributable mainly to their desire to ensure that they will have a direct voice, through union election procedures, in decisions which affect them in their working environments. Such employees tend to participate actively in union affairs and to use such phrases as "I wanted to have a voice in the system" rather freely. The underlying rationale of this behavior is a clear one: Managements do not normally put questions relating to employment conditions to worker vote; unions, however imperfectly, purport to be democratic institutions. To these workers, representation by a labor organization has appeared to offer the best hope in our complex, interdependent, and ever-larger-unit industrial society that their human dignity will not be completely crushed. On this basis, self-esteem needs can, at least to some extent, be appeased.

Finally, a relatively few other employees have found in the union an opportunity for realization of their highest needs, for status and self-fulfillment. They have joined with the hope of gaining and retaining positions of authority within the union officer hierarchy. For the employee with leadership ambitions, but with educational or other deficiencies which would otherwise condemn him to a life of prestige-lacking and unchallenging work, opportunities for further need satisfaction are thus provided.

Unionization, then, results from a broad network of worker needs. The needs for safety, social affiliation, and to a lesser extent self-esteem appear to be of primary importance to employees in contemporary America. And it would appear that these needs are being relatively well met by unions, or workers would have exercised their legally granted option of voting out unions in far greater measure than they have done.

This in no way minimizes the role of money and other economic benefits, for these emoluments—which unions have not been reluctant to seek even with their members' incomes at today's high levels—are clearly related to needs beyond the physiological. Health insurance and pensions lend protection against deprivation, for example, and wages themselves can increase not only safety but status. But it does emphasize the roles of protection against arbitrary treatment, formal group affiliation beyond the framework of the company, and—for some workers—an opportunity for participation in "the system." By definition, management can never itself satisfy either of the first two worker needs. Thus far, in unionized establishments, it has failed to satisfy employees on the last ground.

Two final remarks are in order. First, it has often been hypothesized that many workers join unions for *none* of the reasons cited above, but simply because they work where union membership is required for continued employment after their probationary period (the so-called "union shop" arrangement). While it is undeniable that some workers *do* join for this reason, the facts do not support the belief that they are numerous. Beginning in 1947, the American labor laws provided that only if a majority of workers in the bargaining unit voted for the union shop in a secret-ballot election supervised by the government would such a shop be permitted in a labor contract. In the next four years,

46,000 elections were held: 97 per cent of them favored the union shop and 91 per cent of the workers eligible to vote voted in favor of the arrangement. In 1951, the election provision was repealed as a waste of the taxpayer's money.

Second, although an explanation of "why workers join unions" can be reduced (as was done here) to relatively uncomplicated statements, for a specific worker the motivations may be considerably more involved, even encompassing several levels of need satisfaction at once. The summary offered is, if the research on which it is based is valid, sufficiently accurate to meet our own needs. By the same token, however, unionization is at times derived from a variety of complex variables and complete understanding of it must therefore necessarily rest on a situational foundation.

Why Managers Resist Unions

Some time ago, after years of successfully withstanding union organization attempts, a small-scale New York City dress manufacturer discovered that a majority of his workers had finally become union members. Immediately thereafter, these employees struck for increased job security and improved pension benefits. On the very first morning of the strike, the manufacturer's wife—who was also the firm's bookkeeper—reported to work at her customary hour of 8 A.M. She was amazed to see her husband out on the picket line, addressing the strikers as follows: "Sam, you stand over there; Harry, you stand eight yards in back of Sam; and Leo, you come over here, eight yards behind Harry." The puzzled woman posed the natural question, "Jack, what on earth are you doing?" And the manufacturer replied, "I want they should right away know who's boss!"

The outcome of this particular labor-management struggle is unknown. But the episode nonetheless furnishes a clue as to one reason why managers are considerably less than enthusiastic about unions. As we have already seen, collective bargaining necessarily decreases the area of management discretion. Every contractual concession to the union subtracts from the scope that the company has for taking action on its own. As Bakke has put it, "A union is an employer-regulating device. It seeks to regulate the discretion of employers . . . at every point where their action affects the welfare of the men."[14] Yet it is the *manager* who

[14]E. Wight Bakke, *Mutual Survival: The Goal of Unions and Management* (New York: Harper and Row, Publishers, 1946), p. 7.

tends ultimately to be held responsible for the success or failure of the business, and not the union. Hence company representatives feel that it is essential that they reserve *for themselves* the authority to make all major decisions, including those which the union might construe to be "affecting the welfare of the men." In short, they feel that they must still be allowed to remain, on all counts, "the boss."

Managers tend to be quite adamant on the subject. One company representative's thoughts are illustrative:

> Restriction on management freedom is a big issue . . . We've got heavy responsibilities for making quick, accurate and effective decisions. Sometimes there are considerations that we can't divulge or that wouldn't be understood if we did. We're held responsible for the success of them, but the union isn't. It takes complicated maneuvering to run a business and all the parts have to be kept working together. You have to have a good deal of free play in the rope for that. Sometimes there is a particular restriction that gets your goat, but on the whole it's the over-all sense of being closed in on . . . that gets you. It's the cumulative effect of one area of freedom after another being reduced and the promise of still more that gives us real concern, but you make adjustments and go on to every particular one. It's not impossible, but you wonder how long it can go on and leave you able to meet your responsibilities.[15]

Behind such remarks as these is a managerial awareness, continuously reinforced for all administrators of profit-making institutions by day-to-day realities, that management hardly owes its exclusive allegiance to its employees. Clearly, employee needs are important and, for that matter, can be ignored for any length of time only with complete disregard for the continued solvency of the enterprise. But exactly the same can be said of the pressures exerted on management by the firm's customers, stockholders, competitors, and suppliers. Were those pressures not *opposing* ones management's job would be far easier than it is. Because there *are* so many points of conflict, an aggressive union can make the managerial role a highly difficult one.

The desire to retain decision-making authority is by no means, however, strictly attributable to a managerial desire for peace of mind. Unions undoubtedly do add to the personal unhappiness and consequent morale problems of managers, but the resistance to unionism is also often based on a genuine and deep concern for the welfare of *society*. Countless managers believe that only if management remains free to operate without union-imposed restrictions can American business continue to advance. And only through such progress, they believe, can it provide employment for our rapidly growing labor force, let this nation compete successfully

[15]*Ibid.*, p. 29.

in world markets, and increase general living standards. By decreasing company flexibility (in the form of work method controls, decreased work loads, increased stress on the seniority criterion in the allocation of manpower, and various other ways), it is argued, unions endanger the efficiency upon which continued industrial progress depends. And this is no less true, managers contend, just because these union demands are made in the name of such euphemistic goals as "job security," "equitability," and "democracy in the workplace."

A related employer fear is also held by many managers, although it is understandably given somewhat less publicity by them than is the previous argument. Such company representatives feel that in the absence of management's unhampered freedom to manage the optimum utilization of manpower will be lost to society. This argument assumes that there are strong elements of a process of natural selection at work in the industrial world and that, admittedly with some exceptions, those who rise to levels of great authority within it are those who have proven that they are best equipped to hold such places. Any attempt to undercut this authority—on the part of, for example, labor unions—consquently makes society the poorer.

On four different grounds, then—(1) that the manager must be allowed authority commensurate with his responsibility, (2) that unchecked union pressures may totally frustrate the manager in his role as the recipient of cross-pressures from many other institutional and market forces, (3) that unions limit company flexibility and thus endanger economic progress, and (4) that only by allowing managers maximum opportunity to manage is society furnished with an optimum allocation of manpower—union inroads are typically resisted by managements. There is, however, a common denominator to all four: Each argument seeks to ward off encroachments on management's *decision-making* powers.

Admittedly, even in the absence of unionism management's ability to make decisions in the employee relations area is not an unlimited one. A widespread network of federal, state, and community legislation now governs minimum wages, hours of work, safety and health, and a host of other aspects of employee life with complete impartiality as to whether or not the regulated firms are organized or nonunion. Moreover, where employers encounter tight labor markets (those in which new employees are difficult to recruit) they tend to accommodate at least their more visible personnel practices—wages and other economic benefits, in particular—to what the market demands. Finally, the prevalent values of our times must always be considered: The mores of society have an important influence on employers. And it is a hallmark of our ever more sophisticated society that workers expect to be governed by progressive personnel policies which are based on objective standards whenever possible. Most nonunion firms have attempted to conform to these values no less actively than have most unionized enterprises.

The fact remains, however, that managers who are not bound by the restrictions of labor agreements and who do not have to anticipate the possibility of their every action in the employee relations sphere being challenged by worker representatives through the grievance procedure have considerably more latitude for decision making than do their counterparts at unionized companies. One need not in any way sympathize with the management fear of unionism to *understand* this fear. Given the importance of the decision-making prerogative to managements, the managerial resistance to labor organizations—whether it stems directly from management self-interest or from a concern for the welfare of society—can at least be appreciated.

If the previous paragraphs help to explain the major reasons for management's jaundiced view of the labor union, they do not acknowledge other reasons which frequently *bolster* this view. There are, undoubtedly, several such reasons.

In the first place, many employers tend to look upon the union as an *outsider*, with no justifiable basis for interfering in the relationship between the company and its employees. The local union, with which the firm is most apt to engage in direct dealings, typically represents workers of many competitive companies, and hence by definition it cannot have the best interests of any particular firm at heart. Worse yet, runs this charge, the local is often part of a large, geographically distant international union, is closely controlled by the latter, and thus is not allowed to give adequate consideration to unique problems within its locality.[16] Beyond this, the union (whether local, international, or some intermediate body) has objectives and aspirations which are very different from those of the particular company: Where the company seeks to maximize profits within certain limits, the union seeks such goals as the maximization of its own membership and of its general bargaining power. These are objectives which the company can at best greet with apathy and at worst (when the pursuit of such goals is "subsidized" by the company in the form of its own concessions to the union) can view only with unhappiness.

Second, the manager may look upon the union as a *trouble-maker*, bent upon building cleavages between management and workers where

[16]Not all employers lament the "outside" aspects of unionization. Many prefer the more detached viewpoints of international union representatives who *are* removed from the tensions and political considerations involved in day-by-day local labor relations. Some managers welcome, in addition, the stabilization of labor terms among otherwise competitive employers that frequently accompanies wider-scale bargaining.

none would otherwise exist. Even aside from the previously noted fact that the union grievance procedure allows all management actions which affect areas delineated in the labor contract to be challenged, and therefore regularly provides an opportunity for controversy which is normally absent in nonunion situations, there is some truth in this charge. Particularly where the union occupies an insecure status in the plant (possibly in the absence, for example, of the union shop), its leaders may find it essential to solicit grievances in order to keep the employees willing to pay union dues. But even where the labor organization does have such security, grievances may still be encouraged by union officials. Slichter, Healy, and Livernash pinpoint several possibilities:

> The purpose may be to harass management into accepting interpretations of the agreement that the union wants; or the purpose may be to develop a militant attitude among the members to help the union in negotiating new contracts. Some union representatives may stir up grievances . . . in an effort to advance their political fortunes within the union or to build up interest in it. Finally, elected stewards or committeemen may lack the independence to handle weak cases.[17]

Third, many managers view unions as *underminers of employee loyalty* to the company. In order to understand this point of view one does not have to fully embrace the philosophy that high worker motivation levels depend upon appreciative employees who view the employer as a benefactor and work for him to a great extent out of gratitude. It is sufficient for the reader to imagine the reactions of any employer who has prided himself on providing good wages and working conditions and showing a personal concern for the individual problems of his employees (perhaps tangibly evidenced by the voluntary payment of medical expenses to meet health emergencies and unsolicited loans to meet other financial crises) upon learning that a majority of his work force has suddenly decided to "go union." While this employer may use such epithets as "ingrates" in speaking of his *own* employees, it is more likely that the union itself will bear the brunt of his censure. It is human nature to attribute one's defeats to forces beyond one's own control ("an irresponsible union misleading our employees and turning them against the company") rather than to factors looked upon as controllable ("employee attitudes"). The previously cited facts that management can *never* itself provide either full protection against arbitrary treatment or formal group affiliation independent of the company are overlooked by company representatives at such moments. So, too, is a silver lining in the situation, namely that it is entirely possible for workers to have dual

---

[17]Slichter, Healy, and Livernash, *op. cit.*, p. 40.

loyalties, to the union *and* to the company.[18] In at least the early stages of the union-management relationship unions may be resisted for having subverted employee allegiance fully as much as they are opposed on the other grounds which have been noted.

A fourth root of tension, although it is applicable only to a minority of company executives, may arise simply because the *reputation* of the labor movement has *preceded* the arrival of unionism in the plant. This has been a particularly influential factor in the resistance of some managers to collective bargaining in the recent past. Not being forced to deal with a union until now, and primarily because of this freedom knowing little more about labor unions than they have been informed by the mass media, such relatively unsophisticated employers have been alarmed by the widely publicized reports of irresponsible union strikes, union leader criminality, and featherbedding charges which have found their way onto newspaper front pages and through television antennae over the past decade. These managers have asked, in effect, "How can you expect us to welcome an institution whose representatives engage in such activities?"

The dilemma here is an obvious one. It is *conflict,* as more than one journalist has observed, which makes news. The large majority of labor agreements which are peacefully renegotiated year after year go virtually unnoticed in the press, as does the steadily declining incidence of strikes for the over-all economy, but the few strikes of any dimensions are treated with the journalistic zeal of a Dostoevski. The overwhelming proportion of union officials continue to lead their lives in full compliance with the laws, but this seems insignificant to the mass media in the face of the conviction of a single Jimmy Hoffa or Dave Beck, both of whose court appearances received wide publicity. And charges that unions demand pay for work which is not performed totally dwarf the large body of evidence that featherbedding is engaged in by only a small segment of unionized employees. Yet what editor can justify headlines proclaiming that "Local 28 of the Hatters is a Very Statesmanlike Local," that "Business Agent Duffy Gabrilowitz of the Plumbers Union is One Hundred Per Cent Honest," or that "Management Says that Retail Clerks are Giving a Fair Day's Work for a Fair Day's Pay?" Only, it is

---

[18]The most exhaustive study on the subject of "dual loyalties" is that of Father Theodore Purcell, conducted in the mid-1950's. Interviewing 202 workers in various departments at Swift and Company, he discovered that while at least 79 per cent felt a definite allegiance to the union as an institution, 92 per cent felt allegiance to the company. "Allegiance" was construed as an attitude of approval of the over-all objectives of each institution, rather than strict loyalty. See Theodore V. Purcell, *Blue Collar Man* (Cambridge: Harvard University Press, 1960) ; and also *The Worker Speaks His Mind on Company and Union* (Cambridge: Harvard University Press, 1953), by the same author.

to be suspected, a newsman with a deeply rooted suicidal urge. Accordingly, managers who allow their opinions of unionism to be molded only by that portion of labor relations which receives wide publicity invariably have one further reason for resisting their own employees' union when it is formed.

Fifth, and rounding out the list of major causes of the corporate executive's opposition to organized labor, are the *major values of the labor movement* as these are perceived by management. Some of these values—a stress on seniority, work method controls, and decreased work loads—have already been mentioned in the context of "threats to decision making." There are, however, many other such shared union values which rankle management at least as much.

"Security," for example, has far more favorable connotations to unionists than it does to company representatives. Higher managers, as Ross Stagner has noted, have a history of successful achievement behind them in their rise through the company ranks, and hence are willing to take chances because they are relatively optimistic as to the outcome. The average union member, feeling that the probabilities of his success in risk-taking are low and, indeed, often believing that he is running in a race that is fixed, presses the union leadership to obtain even greater protection for him in his *current* job.

"Democracy" is a hallmark of the union value structure, and union representatives who bargain with managements are usually elected through a process which at least claims to be democratic. Managers, whose hierarchy is based on merit and experience, are thus forced to bargain, often on issues with major ramifications for the company, with unionists who may have no better credentials for their role than the possession of a plurality of votes in a popularity poll.

And where the company representative speaks glowingly of "individualism" and declares that America's economic triumphs have been based upon it, the union sees itself as part of a social movement and places a premium on "group consciousness."

As for "efficiency," which scores high on the management scale of values, to the union it smacks of a callous disregard for worker dignity and even worker health. Accordingly, it is something to be regarded with deep suspicion by employee representatives and to be resisted whenever resistance is practicable.

Such comments as the above can, as was true of this chapter's treatment of "Why Workers Join Unions," be offered only as generalizations. For a specific union-management relationship, the value differences may hardly be as pronounced: One of the writers is personally familiar, for that matter, with several relationships where the *unions* seem to place far higher values on ability and efficiency than do the *managements*. Such value conflicts as the ones enumerated are, however, quite genuine in many union-management situations, and thus represent the realities of labor relations rather than its stereotypes. As such, they serve to reinforce management's opposition to unionism, however much this opposition may be anchored to such other reasons as the decision-making issue.[19]

Management Philosophies Toward Unions

Given the many different roots of management opposition, and the pervasiveness of so many of these, it is tempting to speculate that deep in their corporate hearts the basic attitude of most business enterprises must be one of intransigent hostility. Were this presumed attitude, in other words, to be stated as an official policy, it would read approximately, "We seek to weaken organized labor by any and all means at our command, to frustrate it in its demands, to grant it nothing which is not absolutely necessary, and—under no circumstances—to make any attempt at accepting the union as a permanent part of our employee relations. If we adhere to this approach consistently and with sufficient patience, our workers will see that the union offers them nothing. And they will ultimately arise and vote the union out at least as enthusiastically as they have voted it in."

There can be no denying that some executives do espouse this policy, and that at an earlier time in American labor history many managers did so. The irony of contemporary labor relations, however, is that despite management's continuing opposition to unionism and its constant resistance of new labor inroads, much of the employer community has substantially departed from such a provocative stance. It has moved instead to what Professor Lloyd Reynolds of Yale calls a "defensive endurance" philosophy: "If this is what our workers want, I guess we'll have to go along with it." In a word, the union is *accommodated*, however unwelcome and even unpalatable its presence may be. Management remains ever on guard as to "matters of principle," seeks to prevent the union from "intruding" in areas which are "the proper function of management," and frequently is highly critical of certain union actions. *But* the labor organization is taken for granted, harmony with it is sought wherever possible, and the employer can deal with the union on a day-by-day basis without feeling that conciliation has made him a

---

[19]To this list of why employers resist unionization, some managers would probably add "status": It is, in certain management circles, quite a mark of distinction to be able to keep a union out. Such a reason is, however, somewhat less visible than are the ones outlined in the body of this section.

traitor to his class. When one speaks of "maturity" in labor relations he is frequently thinking of this rapidly growing managerial posture—and organized labor's reciprocation of it.

A specific union-management relationship even in the late 1960's, however, need not necessarily be marked by *either* employer attitude depicted above. Variety is still the essence of our labor relations system and so many variables can influence management policies that it is unrealistic to assume that the only possibilities are (1) intransigence and (2) accommodation. Variations in the abilities of managers to accurately understand the membership goals and leadership desires of the unions with which they are dealing, and in the statesmanship with which companies have met these union aspirations—to say nothing of the nature of these goals and desires themselves—have led to a wide diversity of management positions. So, too, have variations in the managers' own relative degree of security within the corporate framework, and the economic healths of the companies involved. Obviously, variations in union attitudes may be highly relevant. And the same can be said of such other variables as the past labor relationships between the parties, the technological environments of both the industry and the employer, and even the role of the government, where this is a factor. Most of these topics will receive fuller treatment in later chapters of this book. Here, it is pertinent to note the many grounds for differing attitudes towards unions among managerial groups.

Thus, although accommodation today is the dominant attitude, in many relationships having followed an era of intransigence, there are many variations on the theme of "management–labor relations philosophies." And even among the more general of these different philosophies at least six separate types (including the two above) can be distinguished.[20]

In reviewing these different possibilities for management policy let it be clearly understood that in each case the company's ability to adopt the avenue under description depends upon a factor which is beyond its direct control: The union's own basic policy for *its* dealings with management. The labor organization, obviously, must reciprocate in kind

[20]The late Benjamin M. Selekman was justifiably considered one of the foremost theoreticians in this field, although he generally portrayed "bargaining relationships" and not merely the management "portion" of these relationships. The exposition which follows bears a strong indebtedness to his work (although it departs from it on several major points), and particularly to his *Labor Relations and Human Relations* (New York: McGraw-Hill Book Company, 1947), his "Varieties of Labor Relations," *Harvard Business Review*, 27 (March, 1949), 177–85, and his "Framework for Study of Cases in Labor Relations," in *Problems in Labor Relations*, 3rd ed., co-authored with S. H. Fuller, T. Kennedy, and J. M. Baitsell (New York: McGraw-Hill Book Company, 1964), pp. 1–11. See also Frederick H. Harbison and John R. Coleman, *Goals and Strategy in Collective Bargaining*, (New York: Harper & Row, Publishers, 1951).

and in the absence of such reciprocation, at least in the long run, management's chosen approach becomes a completely fruitless one. In short, the company can *work toward* each of the following approaches, but this managerial project will always be subject to some modification depending upon the union's response.

1. *Conflict*, or the intransigent, uncompromising attitude depicted previously, is now fast fading from the labor relations scene. Nonetheless, this attitude existed on a wide scale prior to World War II. Such a managerial stance arose to a great extent because many companies were newly organized before that time, and because union organizational campaigns have never been notable for their sensitivities to personal feelings. As Selekman has stated:

> . . . The [union] organizers dramatize and make tangible [their] appeals . . . by personifying whatever stands in the way of these objectives as enemies who must be fought . . .
>
> The organizer will of course make full use of the actual executives and supervisors in the plant if their past behavior affords substance for the antagonism he is mobilizing. But he will also evoke hostility by stereotyped images of "the other side." Behind any employer, for instance, the average worker is made to see the so-called "profit maker" . . . , the inhuman corporate "interests" generally, or just the harsh figure of authority . . . Employers who have long prided themselves upon fair dealing with their men only to be shaken by hostility thus unexpectedly turned toward them should probably realize that they too have been temporarily assimilated into these hate images or symbols.[21]

The union, consequently, does more than "undermine employee loyalty to the company" at such a time: It frequently goes well beyond the borders of the factual and bruises management egos in the process. Add managerial fears of decision-making encroachments and of union values which are antithetical to those of management, as well as the other grounds for managment's opposition to unionism on top of such an emotion-charged atmosphere, and it should not be surprising that many companies in the period immediately following their unionization embraced a philosophy of "no acceptance" of the union. Only in the face of the law and union power could unions extract concessions from such managements, and then only quite begrudgingly and on as temporary a basis as possible.

Some companies are, of course, even today among the newly organized, since new union conquests hardly ended with the unionization of the major mass-production industries in the 1933–1941 period. And it is in the labor relations of these enterprises, indeed, that one is most apt

---

[21]Benjamin M. Selekman, *Labor Relations and Human Relations*, p. 20.

today to encounter the conflict philosophy. But this managerial attitude is not *confined* to new bargaining relationships: A minority of long-organized companies also currently adheres to it, owing to changes in management personnel, changes in union personnel, or various other factors—including the particular management's sheer refusal to abandon the hope that if unions are never really accepted by their companies they will eventually also lose acceptance from their worker-members. In recent years, the Kohler Company of Sheboygan, Wisconsin has seemed to many observers to have epitomized this latter situation, as have various newspaper publishers in the Midwest.

Such an attitude does not lead to amicable labor relations. It can also be expected to foster union militancy, as the union reacts by engaging in various pressure tactics (often including slowdowns of production and sudden "wildcat" strikes) to gain through these means what it cannot hope to procure at the bargaining table. Finally, managements embracing a "conflict" philosophy run a decided risk of being found in violation of the labor laws, particularly those involving "refusal to bargain" and discrimination against employees for the purpose of discouraging membership in a union.

It is primarily for these reasons that many conflict philosophies have either been dismissed as realistic management alternatives in the first place, or given way to:

2. An *Armed Truce* attitude. Here company representatives are motivated by approximately the following logic: "We are well aware that the vital interests of the company and the union are poles apart, and that they always will be. But this doesn't mean that every action we take in our labor relations should be geared to weakening the union and thus forcing head-on conflict with it. Instead, since we can expect the union to firmly press to extend its fields of interest, our basic mission is to press, just as ambitiously, toward containing it *within* limits. We will honor the law immaculately, and therefore deal with the union without any subterfuges on the subjects of wages, hours, and conditions of employment; but we will hold our bargaining practice strictly within the *boundaries* of these legal obligations, and thus define our negotiation scope as rigidly as possible. Moreover, we will *strictly* interpret any agreements which emerge from these negotiations and insist upon the union observing, in its day-to-day conduct, its contractual obligations 100 per cent."

Even today, many union-management relationships have made no more progress than this. The union representatives return the feelings of their management counterparts and the struggle for power goes on indefinitely. Wages, hours, and other rigidly construed employee relations areas are dealt with as their issues arise, but the more crucial question of union security versus management rights, being insoluble in such an atmosphere, continually blocks more constructive dealings. With some justification, the General Electric Company is frequently regarded as an excellent example of a company which has espoused this Armed Truce philosophy.

3. *Power Bargaining*, as an alternative, is only slightly more conducive to solving labor relations problems than is the Armed Truce approach. As is *not* the case under either Conflict or Armed Truce, managers in power bargaining can "accept" the union and, in fact, tend to pride themselves on their sense of "realism" which leaves them no choice but to acknowledge the union's power. (A prerequisite for this philosophy, obviously, is that the union *has* significant power.) By the same token, such executives press their own company's bargaining power to the maximum that economic and other conditions at any one time allow. To paraphrase Selekman, the managerial rationale is: "We face strong and deeply entrenched unions squarely and with an accurate perception of their power—and we accept them as sovereign spokesmen for their side. We are practical men and economic realists, not crusaders with a naïve faith in idealistic trimmings. Our task is not to pursue the fruitless approach of directly opposing and limiting the union, but to increase and then use our *own* power to offset that of the other side where we can."

Might does not necessarily make right, but it can lead to agreement at the bargaining table. And on this basis it can be argued that continued controversy is minimized in power bargaining. However unenthusiastically, managements in such a relationship can live with their unions, for at least the short run, in most areas affecting employee relations.

On the other hand, any relationship focused upon a balance of power is a highly tenuous one. It always contains the danger of regression to one of the earlier approaches when the power ratios change. As such, power bargaining has not been widespread at any one time in American labor relations, although many industries marked by small employers and highly centralized unions have at one time or another seen it. In such cases, the employers have typically associated in an attempt at a united front to counter the union's strength.

In short, for the reasons indicated, most managements in the current economy view all three previous alternatives as unsatisfactory. Since, needless to say, their unions wholeheartedly agree with them on this point, the climate for a more harmonious relationship—in the form of accommodation—exists.

4. *Accommodation*, however, is hardly the same as "cooperation." As pointed out earlier, management remains constantly vigilant as to "principle" and, as does the union, clings to such values as "orbits of respective equities and privileges." In this regard, Accommodation differs little from Armed Truce. Moreover, the management gaze is still riveted upon the traditional agenda of collective bargaining—wages, hours, and conditions of employment—and there is a self-conscious employer unwillingness to *officially* discuss anything which cannot rather rigidly be construed as falling within these topics.

The property of Accommodation which makes it unique lies in the area of everyday *practice* rather than in formal declarations. Once again, Dr. Selekman has provided a definitive description,—in this case of what results in daily affairs when a management philosophy of "meeting the union halfway" is reciprocated by the labor organization:

> . . . within these bounds (of "principles," "equities" and "privileges") the leaders, the ranks, and the organizations . . . interact within comfortable "customary," familiar patterns of behavior. They have evolved their routines of recognizing functions and settling differences. They have learned how to adjust one to another . . . , to accept the reduction of conflict as an accomplishment without demanding its total elimination. They have proved themselves willing to . . . conciliate whenever necessary, and to tolerate at all times.[22]

Note that such a definition in no way implies that the company need go out of its way to *help* organized labor. For that matter, opposition to the concept of unionism in general may still remain the hallmark of management's philosophy, as it frequently does. In an atmosphere of accommodation, however, the roles of both emotion and raw power are minimized, in favor of the company's *adjusting* to the union *as it is*. Extreme legalism in at least the basic areas of wages, hours, and conditions is supplanted by compromise, flexibility, and "toleration." As such, accommodation constitutes a considerably more positive approach to labor relations than do any of the previous alternatives.

There is ample evidence that the mainstream of American management has today entered the accommodation stage in its dealings with unions. The process of adjustment is still, as Slichter, Healy, and Livernash point out in their authoritative study, "neither complete nor uniform": Mutual accommodation of the parties' goals and policies has gone farthest in such areas as employee benefits, discipline, work scheduling, and development of grievance procedures, and least far in the areas of production standards, promotion principles, work assignment,

22Benjamin M. Selekman, S. H. Fuller, T. Kennedy, and J. M. Baitsell, *Problems in Labor Relations*, p. 7.

and subcontracting.[23] And not surprisingly, there is still wide variation in the nature and quality of contract administration among companies and even among plants within the same company. But the growth of accommodation has quite visibly resulted in the significant development of mutually acceptable policy and in more orderly day-to-day union-management relations, results which even the great diversity of labor relations cannot obscure.

5. *Cooperation*, involving full acceptance of the union as an active partner in a formal plan, is for exactly that reason decidedly rare. It necessitates a management (as well as a union) which is willing to extend matters of everyday union-management relations beyond the traditional areas to such broader fields as technological change, waste, and business solvency. And this, in turn, calls for corporate executives who genuinely believe that unions can make definite and positive contributions to the success of the firm, through furnishing management with information which it would not otherwise have, through winning over worker support for management goals, and in various other ways.

In a formal plan for cooperation, the management supports not only the right but the *desirability* of union participation, and the union reciprocates by actively endorsing the company's right and need for an adequate return on its investment. The two labor relations parties *jointly* deal with both personnel and production problems as they occur. Suggestions pertaining to cost reduction and productivity improvement are typically solicited from all worker levels. And whatever economic gains in increased efficiency may be realized from such cooperative projects are normally shared by the company with the work force.

Most companies which have adopted this approach to labor relations have, by and large, been well publicized, either as participants in rather formalized "Scanlon Plans" or, as in the case of the Kaiser Steel Corporation, independently. But the very fact that so much publicity *has* been given to these plans based on the cooperative approach graphically symbolizes how few in number they have been thus far. Moreover, the approach is still so incompatible with present-day management (and, often, union) value systems that to date most such plans have been implemented only as a last resort, when the company was faced with a severe financial crisis. The word "cooperation" is frequently used in management addresses to worker groups, but in the managers' lexicon of the late 1960's it obviously has a meaning which is considerably more restricted than the one depicted here.

As different as each of the previous five approaches to labor relations is from the four others, there is a common denominator: Whichever

23Slichter, Healy, and Livernash, *op. cit.*, p. 958.

one is selected is, subject to its ability to meet management goals, at the outset strictly the company's business. Ultimately, a conflict approach may lead to a strike involving government intervention, or an amassing of strength in a Power Bargaining situation may have other legal ramifications, and in any of the five cases the *union* may, of course, react in such a way to make the approach unsuitable. The company can hardly do much with Accommodation if the union is Conflict oriented. But at least at the outset the company is perfectly free to experiment with any of the various approaches.

The same *cannot* be said of one other approach, *Collusion*. If, up until now, the enumerated management alternatives can be viewed as leading to successively more union-management harmony (from conflict on the one hand to cooperation on the other), this one can be looked upon as generating "too much harmony." Our public policy, needless to say, is designed to prevent it from serving as a workable labor relations alternative.

To Selekman, alternative (6), *Collusion*, constitutes:

> . . . "cooperation" (which) generates problems that extend beyond the specific structure of relationship to affect adversely the legitimate interests of other employers, other workers, and the consuming public. For the collusive parties to collective bargaining connive to control their market, supplies, or prices, or to engage in practices of mutual interest to serve their exclusive advantage. They cooperate but through a form of jointly established monopoly which is frankly unconcerned with every legitimate interest except their own. The courts . . . and the watchfulness of competitors, rival unions, and public representatives no doubt will continue to curb these questionable deals.[24]

To such curbs might be added the sheer unwillingness of both companies and their unions, in all but a relatively few black-mark situations, to attempt such arrangements in the first place. Employer bribes to union officials to agree to substandard or "sweetheart" labor contracts and various other illegal pursuits have hardly been unknown to American labor history. But such collusion has been almost exclusively confined to narrow sectors of local market industries, with marginal and intensely competitive employers for whom a small difference in labor cost can mean the difference between solvency and insolvency and where visibility to the public law-enforcement agencies is relatively slight. Having named the least ethical sectors of the garment trades, building trades, trucking, waterfront, and entertainment industries, one has almost exhausted the list.

[24]Benjamin M. Selekman, S. H. Fuller, T. Kennedy, and J. M. Baitsell, *Problems in Labor Relations*, p. 8.

Some Concluding Remarks on the Current Qualities
of Labor-Management Relationships

"Anyone," says Kheel, "who starts a sentence by saying that 'the trouble with labor or management is' is bound to be partially right but mostly wrong."[25] Such sweeping generalizations as the one cited are highly hazardous in most areas of life, but in a field which is as varied as labor relations they are wholly unwarranted.

It is hoped that in pointing up the various "multiplicities"—of causes for workers joining unions, of reasons why managers resist unions, and of employer philosophies themselves—the dangers of being overly cavalier in *interpretation* have also been implied. Maslow's Need Hierarchy does not always fall neatly into place in linking Specific Employee X to his labor organization. And when one analyzes the motivations of "workers" as a general grouping he may be equally far off base unless he recognizes that a variety of *different* need-motivated reasons may be *simultaneously* at play. The management resistance to union inroads is, in turn, also derived from a wide array of specific causes, even though the desire to retain decision-making authority in managerial hands lies at the heart of most of them. And employer *philosophies* concerning unionism can run a gamut from intransigent hostility on the one hand to complete "togetherness' in the form of collusion on the other, although neither of these extremes is common. The various frameworks presented in this chapter can serve as useful guides for specific analyses, but a little knowledge has at times been known to be a dangerous thing. Let the student beware!

Moreover, if variations in (1) worker expectations from their unions, (2) employer grounds for resisting unionism, and (3) company attitudes in implementing this resistance account *by themselves* for much present-day diversity in labor relationships, *other* factors augment this diversity. To recall only a few which were cited in this chapter, the current financial states of the individual companies (and industries) may serve as an influential variable. So, too, may technological change confronting both the industry and the employer, *past* relationships between the parties, the goals of the leaders themselves on both sides of the bargaining table, management's degree of perception regarding labor situations; and, of relevance for some relationships, the prospects for governmental intervention, including an assessment of the form which this is likely to take.

And this is to say nothing of the differences between one union *as an institution* and another, a topic which has been intentionally deferred

25Theodore W. Kheel, "A Labor Relations Policy for 1964," *Personnel Journal* (April, 1964) , p. 181.

for extensive treatment in Chapter 4. Let it suffice to state here that unions exhibit a heterogeneity all their own. In a very important sense, indeed, there has never been a literal "labor movement" in this country. The AFL-CIO is a loose federation with very limited power. Bargaining is carried out by the highly diverse international unions, each with its particular traditions, structure, and government, and by the constituent locals and other subgroups of the internationals. Even today, despite a strong trend toward international union control over local union activities, a few international unions perform little more than bookkeeping functions, with the locals exercising almost complete autonomy. Other internationals are highly centralized and local independence in any sphere is virtually nonexistent. Organized labor is broad enough, too, to contain: (1) the Teamsters Union, which represents to many people a prime form of "business unionism," with its leaders utilizing the union as "a marketing cooperative to sell so many head of labor to employers at the highest market price"[26] and in no way being concerned with general social reform; (2) the United Automobile Workers, whose president Walter P. Reuther is frequently thought of as the nation's foremost "social unionist"; and (3) the garment unions, which have—through ambitious union-financed projects ranging from cooperative housing to adult education programs—made unionism for *their* constituents a "way of life." In short, there are unions and there are unions.

Any of the variables enumerated above can be crucial to the molding of a specific labor-management relationship. At any one time, several of them are apt to be at work in influencing the nature of this relationship. And, given this situation, the great variety in the subject areas, wordings, and lengths of the nation's 150,000 labor-management contracts, which serve as tangible (if, as will be seen, not always completely accurate) symbols of labor relationships, is understandable.

Certainly, there is no reason to expect a contract for the five waitresses in a New Hampshire restaurant to bear any resemblance to the International Brotherhood of Teamsters' nationwide trucking agreement. Any great similarity between the General Electric Company–International Union of Electrical Workers document and that negotiated by the Lace Workers and their marginal employer in Honeysuckle, Mississippi, would likewise constitute a striking coincidence.

Can *any* remarks, then, in the face of all of these variables, be applied even to merely the "majority" of the contracts in this country? Some statements can *still* be made, and even as ambitious a phrase as "the *vast* majority of all agreements" will support them.

For all their variations, almost all labor contracts today validate a

26Lester Velie, *Labor U.S.A.* (New York: Harper & Row, Publishers, 1959), p. 14.

particular institutional status for the union and well over two-thirds of them incorporate the union shop arrangement, requiring union membership for continued employment. The vast majority of the agreements reveal what the parties have agreed to as being "vested exclusively in the company," either explicitly (in a so-called "management rights" article) or implicitly (in indirect language which is scattered throughout the contract). They announce, in more or less detail, the increasingly broad range of wage, hour, and other economic-related employment conditions under which the employees have agreed to be governed. They incorporate a variety of administrative clauses dealing with work rules and job tenure. And they outline the procedures for settling the disputes that will inevitably arise during the life of the agreement, as well as providing for a renegotiation of the contract when its duration has been exhausted.

These are no small accomplishments. Real or imaginary threats to job security, to the union's existence, to what managers deem their "freedom to run" their own businesses, and to what employees refer to as "fair" conditions are regularly involved. Yet the signing of any contract requires some form of mutual agreement and, most often, some major concessions by both the management and the union. It is a tribute to the increasing maturity of both parties that so much progress has been made in this direction over the past three decades. This is particularly true when one considers not only the drastic technological and economic changes that have taken place in our society since the Great Depression but also the many direct grounds for open conflict between labor and management which have existed ever since.

A host of other accomplishments, which will be given liberal treatment in the pages that follow, also bears testimony to the ability of the labor relations system to adjust itself to accommodate new needs and desires. The spread of the seniority principle, under which the employee with the longest service receives preference in various employment matters, has minimized employee demands for both "justice" and "objective personnel management." On these morale-building grounds it has also had considerable appeal—when used in moderation—to many managements. Moreover, the almost complete acceptance by the parties of binding arbitration by a neutral as the final step in the grievance procedure, thus normally ruling out work stoppages during the term of the agreement, has also injected much stability into labor relations. And the same can be said of the growth of long-term contracts—now commonly two and three years in duration instead of the traditional one-year basis. Nor can one overlook the contractual adjustments to the spread of the many new employee "fringe" benefits which have arisen in this period. Bilateral statesmanship must receive some credit, too, for the satisfactory contractual resolution, at least over time, of many knotty problems involving technological change and unionized workers.

The labor contract, admittedly, forms only the bare skeleton of the total relationship between a union and a management. As is also true of both the marriage contract and the citizen's income tax report, it is little more than a legal prerequisite to harmony: By itself it does not produce rapport. To evaluate accurately any labor relationship, one must know the degree of mutual trust and good will that lies in back of the written agreement, to say nothing of the extent to which supplementary documents and verbal understandings may affect the wording printed on the contract pages. Finally, no contract is any better than its *administration*: The contract incorporates a body of rules, but this does not guarantee that both parties will always interpret these rules in the same way. Moreover, the fact that agreements can never hope to explicitly cover all contingencies means that there will always be at least the chance for future disagreement. In short, a variety of problems affecting the relationship can surround even the most harmonious appearing labor contract.

Judged by any available standard, however, the considerable progress and increasing maturity which is at least *symbolized* by the contractual contents has marked *all* portions of union–management relations over the past very few decades. One can accept the Slichter, Healy, and Livernash verdict that the process of accommodation is "neither complete nor uniform" without in any way negating the more basic conclusions of these three scholars that

> . . . The American collective bargaining system must be regarded as one of the most successful economic institutions in the country. In the great majority of plants it has produced rules and policies that are fair to both sides and that permit managements to conduct operations efficiently. Although there is wide variation in the results of bargaining, the concentration of settlements that are good compromises is large . . . (and) experience to date evidences a degree of social progress that few would have predicted (at the end of the 1930's) .[27]

The reader is invited to postpone his own agreement (or disagreement) with these opinions until the contents of the various areas cited in the preceding paragraphs are treated more fully. Part III's six chapters are totally reserved for this latter purpose: Chapter 5, for an examination of management and union behavior at the bargaining table; Chapter 6, for the treatment of contract administration; Chapters 7 and 8, for description and analysis of the major economic issues with which collective bargaining is now involved; and Chapters 9 and 10, for a

[27]Slichter, Healy, and Livernash, *op. cit.*, pp. 960–1.

relatively detailed inspection of the basic institutional and administrative issues in the current labor-management sphere.

If one does acquiesce at this early point, however, is there also justification for assuming that the mainstream of our labor relations system today stands on the threshold of a great new era to which strikes will be entirely foreign and where "harmony" will be the universal guiding rule?

Despite all the progress to date, such a prophecy would, we think, be extremely naïve. It can be expected that managements will continue to oppose the concept of unionism and to resist new union inroads as energetically as ever, for the roots of this opposition are essentially rational ones *as judged by management values*. By the same token, there is little reason to believe that unions will not continue to press for an ever-greater narrowing of the scope of management discretion, in the interests of obliging worker wants and needs as *they* view these. Indeed, in the years immediately ahead the stresses between the parties seem destined to *grow*: The recent intensification of industrial price and technological competition has already pitted an accelerated employer search for greater efficiency against an equally determined union campaign for increased job security.

Since a labor relations millennium *is* far distant, it seems a safe prediction that occasional impasses will continue to be reached by labor and management, and that these will result in strike actions, as they have in the past.

There is both an irony and a serious threat for our system of free collective bargaining in the inevitability of future strikes. If labor relations progress has clearly been evident, the community has also increased its expectations from union-management relations. Indeed, as Livernash has pointed out, "Our level of aspiration rises perhaps more rapidly than realized progress. In this situation, there is always some feeling of impatience with the degree of progress of private institutions and a desire for increased governmental control."[28]

Our system of industrial jurisprudence has thus far remained essentially in private hands despite an ever deeper penetration of government regulations (described in Chapter 3). This toleration for private decision making is consistent with the dominant values of our society, particularly with its premium on maximum freedom of action for both individuals and organizations. But the possibility that a tripartite labor relations system, with the government as a full-fledged participant, will ultimately supplant the present bipartite system can never be overlooked. Whether or not what is still "free collective bargaining" will be allowed

28Arthur A. Sloane and E. Robert Livernash, *Note on Collective Bargaining in the United States* (Cambridge: Harvard University Press, 1961), p. 35.

to continue will depend to no small degree on the ability of the current system to continue its progress sufficiently and in time to satisfy the increasingly high level of public expectation. Unions may be here to stay, as all evidence indicates that they are. But the fact that there is still much room for improvement in labor-management relations makes the entire system as it currently exists a vulnerable one.

DISCUSSION QUESTIONS

1. George P. Schultz and John R. Coleman have argued that "there is at least some excuse for the inability of all of us to understand unionism as fully as we might like to: There is just too much to understand." How much knowledge and understanding of labor-management relations *does* it appear realistic to expect from the course in which this book is currently being used, and *why?*
2. "Unions have outlived their usefulness, if indeed they ever had any, for at least the many employees whose managements deal with them on the basis of enlightened, worker-oriented policies." Discuss.
3. From your own experience (first- or second-hand), which case regarding future union penetration of the white-collar field is more persuasive with you: the relatively "pessimistic" one (as advanced in this chapter by Strauss and Sayles) or the more "optimistic" one which has also been presented on the previous pages?
4. The authors' own qualified endorsement of A. H. Maslow's theory of motivation notwithstanding, how valuable do you personally view this theory in understanding "why workers join unions"?
5. From the viewpoint of *society*, is there anything to be said for the union's role as an "employer-regulating device," seeking (in Bakke's words) "to regulate the discretion of employers . . . at every point where their action affects the welfare of the men"?
6. "Even if some of the day-by-day values of management and labor are not fully compatible, in the last analysis the *basic goals* of the two parties are identical." Evaluate.
7. What *primary* standards do you feel should be adopted by anyone attempting to evaluate the current performance of labor-management relations in this country, and why?
8. Reflecting upon his distinguished career as vice-president and general counsel of the Pittsburgh Plate Glass Corporation, Leland Hazard once wrote: ". . . I have rarely had occasion to modify the axiom: scratch a labor problem, and you will find a management problem." What considerations might have led to this observation?

SELECTED REFERENCES

Bakke, E. Wight, *Mutual Survival: The Goal of Unions and Management.* New York: Harper & Row, Publishers, 1946.

Cole, David L., *The Quest for Industrial Peace.* New York: McGraw-Hill Book Company, 1963.

Davey, Harold W., "The Continuing Viability of Collective Bargaining." *Labor Law Journal,* Vol. 16, No. 2 (February, 1965) .

Harbison, Frederick H., and John R. Coleman, *Goals and Strategy in Collective Bargaining.* New York: Harper & Row, Publishers, 1951.

Maslow, A. H., *Motivation and Personality.* New York: Harper & Row, Publishers, 1954.

Northrup, Herbert R., *Boulwarism.* Ann Arbor, Michigan: Bureau of Industrial Relations, University of Michigan, 1964.

Reynolds, Lloyd G., *Labor Economics and Labor Relations,* 4th ed. Englewood Cliffs, New Jersey: Prentice-Hall, Inc., 1964, pp. 141–58.

Sayles, Leonard R., *Managerial Behavior.* New York: McGraw-Hill Book Company, 1964.

Selekman, Benjamin M., *Labor Relations and Human Relations.* New York: McGraw-Hill Book Company, 1947.

Slichter, Sumner H., James J. Healy, and E. Robert Livernash, *The Impact of Collective Bargaining on Management.* Washington, D.C.: The Brookings Institution, 1960, pp. 1–26.

part two

THE ENVIRONMENTAL
FRAMEWORK

As is true of other established disciplines, there is still some controversy as to the returns inherent in the study of history. For every Shakespeare asserting that "what is past is prologue" or a Santayana who proclaims that "those who do not understand history are condemned to repeat its mistakes," there is a Henry Ford declaring that "history is a pack of tricks that we play on the dead," and that the field is, in fact, "bunk."

No one can claim to understand present-day institutions, however, unless he has at least some basic knowledge of their roots. It would make a considerable difference to those who are either hopeful or fearful that labor unions will ultimately fade from the industrial scene, for example, if unions were purely a phenomenon of the last few years (and thus potentially destined for extinction when environmental conditions change), rather than being—as they are—organizations of relatively long standing in the economy. Similarly, only by recognizing what workers have expected of their unions in the past is one entitled even to begin to pass judgment on the present performance of organized labor. This chapter

2

The historical framework

thus attempts to provide the reader with a necessary working knowledge of American labor history.

The Eighteenth Century: Genesis of the American Labor Movement

If labor unions connote *permanent* employee associations which have as their primary goal the preservation or improvement of employment conditions, there were no such institutions in America until the closing years of the eighteenth century. Concerted actions of workingmen in the form of strikes and slowdowns were not unknown to the colonial period, and a few such actions—those of the Boston caulkers (1741), New York City tailors (1768), and New Jersey carpenters (1774)—attracted widespread attention. But these and similar disturbances were, without exception, spontaneous efforts. They were conducted on the spur of the moment over temporary grievances, such as withholding of wages. Generally unsuccessful, they were never undertaken by anything resembling "permanent" organizations.

Given the dimensions of the labor movement today and the variety of seemingly compelling reasons why workers have attached themselves to it, this total absence of labor unions for well over a century calls for an immediate explanation.

In these years of simple handicraft organization there were, in fact, at least *four* forces at work which served to weaken any motivation that workers might otherwise have had for joining together on a long-term basis.

In the first place, the market for the employer's product was both local and essentially noncompetitive. Workingmen were thus allowed close social ties with the owner, often performing their work in the owner's home. In addition, they could maintain a comparatively relaxed pace of production in such an atmosphere.

Second, both the laws of supply and demand and government regulations allowed employees a large measure of job security at this time. Labor of all kinds, and particularly skilled craft labor, was in short supply in the colonies. In addition, a series of colonial labor laws calling for apprenticeship service prior to many kinds of employment and carefully circumscribing the conditions under which employees could be discharged offered further protection to jobholders.

Third, the existence of ample cheap land in the West meant that the dissatisfied artisan or mechanic could always move on should either local adversity or the spirit of adventure strike him. Many workers did migrate to the ever-expanding frontier, allowing even more advantageous employment conditions for those who remained: Incomes increased all the more in the East, to the point where by some estimates wages were twice those paid to workers in Britain.

Finally, the low ratio of labor to natural resources in the frontier nation helped ensure that price rises would lag behind the wage increases. Assistant Secretary of the Treasury Coxe, sounding very much like a twentieth-century Chamber of Commerce manager, could—even as late as 1790—assert with considerable justification that "though the wages of the industrious poor are very good, yet the necessaries of life are cheaper than in Europe, and the articles used are more comfortable and pleasing."[1]

Ironically, however, the development of the frontier laid the groundwork for the birth of *bona fide* labor organizations. An expanded system of transportation built around canals and turnpikes was simultaneously linking the new nation's communities and allowing the capitalists of the late eighteenth century to enlarge their product markets into the beginnings of "nationwide" ones. The merchant who was unwilling or unable to respond to the challenge was left by the wayside as competitive pressures forced each businessman to find cost-cutting devices in the newly unsheltered atmosphere. The more imaginative employers located such devices: To decrease labor costs, they introduced women and children to their workplaces, farmed out work to prison inmates, and generally cut the wages of males who remained in their employ. For good measure, they frequently increased the hours in the work day (at no increase in pay), minutely subdivided the work into more easily assimilated (but commensurately more repetitive and monotonous) operations, and hired aggressive overseers to enforce newly tightened work standards.

The less-skilled workingman could react to these unwelome changes by moving to the frontier. Not having invested much in the way of time or education in learning his current job, he might also attempt to move occupationally to more desirable kinds of work. The skilled worker, on the other hand, had mastered his craft through years of apprenticeship and was no longer occupationally mobile.

Some skilled craftsmen did move to the frontier. But the extension of the product market meant that their new masters were still not free to ignore labor cost-cutting methods: Suits tailored in Ohio competed now with those made in Boston. Nor could the craftsmen count any longer on advancing into the class of masters themselves: The scope of manufacturing was necessarily greater and to enter the employer ranks it now took capital on a scale not ordinarily available to most wage-earners. Basically, the skilled workers' alternatives were to passively accept the wage cuts, the competition of nonapprenticed labor, and the harsh

[1] Lloyd Ulman, *American Trade Unionism—Past and Present* (Berkeley, California: Institute of Industrial Relations, 1961), p. 367.

working conditions, or to join in collective action against such employer innovations. Increasingly, by the end of the eighteenth century, they chose the latter course of action.

The First Unions and Their Limited Successes

These early trade unions—individually encompassing shoemakers, printers, carpenters, tailors, and artisans of similar skill levels—waged blunt attacks on the changes brought about by the extension of markets. Their members agreed upon a wage level and pledged not to work for any employer who refused to pay this amount. They also bound themselves not to work alongside of any employee who did not receive the basic minimum or who had not served the customary period of apprenticeship for the trade. In addition, most of these craft unions attempted to negotiate closed shop agreements, whereby only those who were union members in the first place would be employed at all. Whatever agreement was subsequently struck with the employer, little trust was placed in him by the representatives of his workers: The union sent a "walking delegate" to walk around from shop to shop on a regular basis and thus ensure that the wages and conditions of the contract were being honored. Later, "tramping committees" of union delegates performed the same function.

Generally proving themselves willing to strike, if need be, in support of their demands, the early unions were at times surprisingly successful in achieving them. And although work stoppages of the day were typically both peaceful and short in duration, the new worker aggressiveness which they symbolized was sufficient to bring on considerable countervailing action from the employers.

The masters turned to two sources: organization in employers' associations and aid from the courts. Societies of otherwise competitive master masons, carpenters, shoemakers, printers, and other employers of skilled labor were quickly established in most urban areas where union activity was pronounced, for the purposes of holding down wages and destroying labor combinations wherever these existed. Attacking on a second front, the masters also turned to the judges and urged prosecution of their workers' organizations as illegal conspiracies in restraint of trade. The jurists were quickly convinced: The Journeyman Cordwainers (shoemakers) of Philadelphia were found guilty of joining in such a conspiracy by striking in 1806, and within the next decade a variety of similar court cases had also resulted in shattering defeats for the worker organizations. Not until 1842, indeed, with the famous *Commonwealth vs. Hunt* decision in Massachusetts that strikes could be legal if they were undertaken for legal purposes, did the judges even begin to modify the harsh tenets of the *Cordwainer* doctrine when requested to rule on union affairs by employers.

If the criminal conspiracy doctrine and the varying successes of the employer associations crimped the growth of the incipient labor movement, moreover, an economic event temporarily sent unionism into almost total collapse. In 1819 a major nationwide depression occurred and, as was to be no less the case in later nineteenth century periods of economic reversal, labor organizations could not withstand its effects. Union demands which might be translated into employer concessions when the demand for labor was high could be safely dismissed by the masters with jobs now at a premium. Employers once again cut rates with impunity and showed little hesitation in dismissing workers who had joined unions in earlier years. Under the circumstances, the worker cry was "Every man for himself" rather than "In union there is strength," and virtually no union could, or did, survive such mass desertion.

Revival, Innovation and Disillusionment

The return of economic health to the country by late 1822 was paralleled by a revival in unionism. Their bargaining power restored, skilled employees in the trades which had previously been organized once again turned to union activity.

More significantly, the process of unionization now spread to new frontiers, both geographic and . occupational. Aroused by the same merchant-capitalist threats to living standards and status which had previously given incentive for collective bargaining to their East Coast counterparts, craftsmen in such newly developed cities as Buffalo, Pittsburgh, Cincinnati, and Louisville established trade union locals at this time. And new (and widely publicized) victories of the skilled worker unions both in the older and newer cities had by the mid-1830's generated the formation of unions among such previously nonunion groups as stonecutters, hatters, and painters. By 1836, there were fifty-eight different local trade unions in Philadelphia, fifty-two in New York, twenty-four in Baltimore, fifteen in Boston, and fourteen in Cincinnati.

These years also saw other innovations made by organized labor. Prior to 1827, each local craft union had operated on its own as a totally separate organization. In that year, however, representatives of fifteen different trades in the city of Philadelphia formed the country's first central labor union, for joint action on a citywide basis. The original goal of the Philadelphia group was a ten-hour day for its trade union members, but this was soon displaced as a major demand: In 1828 the organization converted itself into a political party, endorsing "workingmen's candidates"—with only limited success—for public office.

Workingmen's parties were also organized in other Eastern states in this period of Jacksonian democracy. Political associations of workers seeking such goals as universal free education and the abolition of imprisonment for debt arose in New York, Massachusetts, and Delaware. Most of their objectives were soon realized, but the workingmen's parties themselves—often torn by internal dissension and always confronted by competition from the two major national parties—were generally short-lived.

The original form which the Philadelphia "city central" had taken—as a purely economic joint undertaking of several trade unions in a single city—had a more lasting influence on workers in other locations. Similar bodies were quickly set up throughout the East and, despite the frequent divergence of opinion among the various trades represented, showed remarkable staying-power. By the mid-1830's, at least twelve cities had such "city centrals," most of which provided their affiliated local unions with financial and moral encouragement in times of strikes and coordinated such ancillary activities as the promotion of union-made goods.

Even the beginnings of national worker organization were attempted at this time. In 1834, delegates from the city centrals of several Eastern cities met in New York to form the National Trades' Union. This pioneering workers' project quickly proved fruitless—industry had not yet itself significantly organized on a national basis, and would not for three more decades—but the scope of the NTU's activities nonetheless symbolizes the ambitiousness of the worker representatives involved.

Indeed, the initiative displayed by leaders of both the city centrals and the local unions had led to impressive union membership totals by 1836. It has been estimated that there were in the country as a whole in that year 300,000 unionized workers,[2] constituting 6.5 per cent of the labor force. One can only guess as to what heights the total figures would have risen had not the following year brought a national economic depression which was even more severe than the business slump of 1819.

The hard times which began in 1837 were to last for almost thirteen years. In the face of them, trade union activity vanished almost as completely as it had two decades earlier. Moreover, a new factor now arose to compound union ills: The 1840's saw waves of immigrants—themselves often the victims of economic adversity in such countries as Ireland, Germany, and England—enter the United States. American business con-

[2]Foster Rhea Dulles, *Labor in America*, 2d rev. ed. (New York: Thomas Y. Crowell Company, 1960), p. 59.

ditions by themselves had been sufficient to wipe out most unions of the day, but this new source of job competition and low wages ensured that not even the strongest of unions could endure.

Now so severely frustrated in their economic actions and distrustful of the free enterprise system for having failed to safeguard their interests, some workers transferred their energies to a series of ambitious political schemes for redesigning the economy. "Associationists" set up socialistic agricultural communities; George Henry Evans preached the virtues of "land reform" through direct political action by workingmen ("Vote Yourself a Farm"); and still other advocates of a new social order promulgated producers' cooperatives—employee-owned industrial institutions—as the workingman's salvation.

None of these programs succeeded, however. As Dulles has astutely observed, they did not "in any way meet the needs of labor. In spite of the enthusiastic propaganda, the answer to industrialization did not lie in an attempt to escape from it."[3]

The Laying of the Foundation for Modern Unionism and Some Mixed Performances With It

With the return of prosperity in 1850, unions once again became a factor to be reckoned with. Profiting from the past, they eschewed political diversions, concentrated on such now traditional goals as higher wages, shorter work days, and increased job security, and regained much of their former membership.

The first major national unions, often superseding the economic functions of the city centrals, were also established at this time. Although the "Golden Age" of American railroading still lay ahead, the construction of the first complex rail systems was now accelerating. As a result, not only were product markets once more widening, but so too were labor markets, bringing workers within the same crafts and industries into direct economic competition with each other. National coordination to standardize wages, working conditions, membership rules, and bargaining demands was deemed necessary by labor leaders: The alternative was cutthroat competition among individual local unions, eager for new members and expanded work opportunities and therefore willing to undercut the terms of other locals (to the employer's distinct advantage). The National Typographical Union, the country's oldest permanent national, dates from 1850. By 1860, at least fifteen other crafts had organized on a national basis. In addition to the Typographers, the Machinists and the Iron Molders have continued as labor organizations to

[3]*Ibid.*, p. 81.

this day, although the last-named is currently anything but a giant in labor circles.

The 1861 advent of the Civil War brought a new spurt in union membership growth to a post-1836 high of over 200,000 unionists by the end of hostilities in 1865. Some of this organizational success was due to the labor shortages brought on by military mobilization: The economy's demand for labor commensurately increased, thus enlarging labor's bargaining power and union economic gains. There were undoubtedly at least two other reasons, however: (1) wartime inflation always threatened to counteract the wage increases achieved by unions, and many workers (somewhat unsuccessfully) looked to collective bargaining as a force for staving off this menace; and (2) organized labor was further helped by the pro-labor sentiments of President Lincoln, who firmly resisted employer and public pressure to intervene in the occasional wartime strikes and instead offered as his opinion that "Labor is the superior of capital and deserves much the higher consideration."

At war's end, the labor movement still enrolled less than 2 per cent of the country's labor force (as against 6.5 per cent in 1836) and had yet to make any real penetration into the factories of the land and their huge organizing potential. But the foundation for the unionism of the next seventy years had now been laid. Few skilled worker types were totally unrepresented by unions in 1865: Over 200 local unions, individually encompassing such widely divergent craftsmen as cigar-makers, plumbers, and barrel-makers, were founded in the war years alone. In addition, the logical necessity of forming *national* unions had now been almost universally recognized by labor leaders, and some thirty new ones had been added to the several which had preceded the war. And labor had achieved, through Lincoln, at least a measure of government support for its right to strike.

Labor's momentum, moreover, was sustained in immediate postwar years. The war-generated nationwide prosperity continued virtually unabated until 1873 and, aided by its favorable economic conditions (as in earlier business booms), labor's bargaining strength again increased. New members were attracted by announcements of new union gains, but there were now also other reasons for the increased membership totals. The broader organizational foundations which had been laid prior to 1865, particularly in the multiplication of national unions, allowed both more efficient and more varied organizing campaigns. Moreover, the post-Civil War period unleashed formidable threats to the workingman in the form of: (1) accelerated waves of immigrants (increasingly, now, from Southern and Eastern Europe) who were willing to work for low wages; (2) changing technology, with the machine downgrading many skill requirements and allowing the employer to substitute unskilled labor for craftsmen and women for men; and (3) the continued widening of the gap between wages and prices which had begun in the wartime years. Workers thus had more incentive to join in collective bargaining, and acted upon it.

On the other hand, not every union shared in these gains. Particularly unsuccessful, in fact, was the new Molders national union, whose embittered president William Sylvis now turned away from "pure and simple" collective bargaining to espouse cooperative foundries. He seemed totally convinced that the "cause of all (workingmen's) evils is the WAGES SYSTEM," argued that workers "must adopt a system which will divide the *profits* of labor among those who produce them," and was soon instrumental in the establishment of a number of producers' cooperatives.

None of these undertakings proved any more successful than they had in the 1840's, however. By 1870 most of the worker-owned associations had been forced by competitive pressures to cut wages, hire lower-cost labor, and—in general—act very much like the management-run businesses which Sylvis had so lamented.

Sylvis then transferred his energies to a new organization which had been founded in 1866. The National Labor Union, riding the crest of union optimism at the close of the war, constituted the first major attempt at uniting all national unions, city centrals, and locals into a single central federation of American labor since the ill-fated National Trades' Union of 1834. Its first leaders, drawn mainly from the building and printing trades, had unsuccessfully urged legislative enactment of the eight-hour working day. They had also sought, again without tangible success, such further political goals as currency reform and women's suffrage.

Sylvis drew the organization even further from economic action, to such new political objectives as the reservation of public lands for actual settlers only and abolition of the convict labor system, as he declared "Cooperation is the remedy for the ills of labor." But the National Labor Union could not sustain membership enthusiasm with a credo which was so far removed from worker pocketbooks: One by one, its constituent labor organizations deserted it and by 1872 the NLU had passed from the scene.

The failures of the cooperative and political movements were harbingers of more wide-sweeping labor disasters. Business collapsed in 1873, beginning a new period of deep depression which lasted for more than five years. In its wake, most of the local unions (as well as the city centrals) once more disappeared. Many of the nationals fared no better, but the greater financial resources and more diversified memberships of these broader organizations did allow them to offer greater resistance to the slump: Not only did eleven of the nationals, in fact, weather these years but eight new nationals were established during this time. Consequently, for the first time, a depression did not completely stop unionization. Nonetheless, five-sixths of total union membership did erode in the 1873–1878 period: Only 50,000 unionists remained in 1878.

Encouraged by the depression-caused weakening of union bargaining power, employers also turned—in the 1870's—to weapons of their own, in an all-out frontal attack on what was left of organized labor. Acting both singly and through employer associations, they engaged in frequent lockouts, hired spies to ferret out union sympathizers, circulated the names of such sympathizers to fellow employers through so-called "black lists," summarily discharged labor "agitators," and engaged the services of strikebreakers on a widespread scale.

The results of these efforts varied. Most of the labor organizations which were strong enough to withstand the depression could also frustrate the employer onslaughts. But there were at least two notable effects of the management campaign. First, several unions of this period became secret societies to avoid employer reprisal. Such esoteric groups as the Knights of St. Crispin (shoemakers) date from this era. Second, retaliating in kind to the quality of employer opposition (as well as to the widespread unemployment of the times), both unionists and non-unionized workers engaged in actions which for bitterness and violence were unequalled in American history. A secret society of anthracite miners, the Molly Maguires, terrorized the coal fields of Pennsylvania in a series of widely publicized murders and acts of arson. Railroad strikes paralyzed transportation in such major cities as Baltimore, Pittsburgh, and Chicago and, with mob rule typically replacing organized leadership as these ran their course, were most often ended only with federal troops being called out to terminate mass pillaging and bloodshed. Public opinion was almost always hostile to such activities and lacking this support the demonstrations could not succeed. It is probably also true that employers were more easily enabled, by the general resentment directed toward worker groups for these actions, to gain still another weapon in their battle against unions: The labor injunction, first applied by the courts during a railway strike at this time, was to be quite freely granted—as Chapter 3 will bring out—by the judges for more than five decades thereafter.

The Rise and Fall of the Knights of Labor

Prosperity finally returned to the country in 1878 and with it union growth once again resumed. Over the next ten years sixty-two new national unions (or "international" unions, as many of these were now calling themselves, in recognition of their first penetration of the Canadian labor market) were established. Locals and city centrals also resumed their proliferation. Even more significantly, the early 1880's marked American labor's most notable attempt to form a single, huge "general" union, the Noble and Holy Order of the Knights of Labor.

The Knights had actually been established before the depression. In 1869 a group of tailors had founded the organization's first local in Philadelphia. Its avowed goal was "to initiate good men of all callings"—unionists as well as those not already in unions, craftsmen and (unlike virtually all other labor organizations of the day) totally unskilled workers. It particularly desired such a broad base of membership to "eliminate the weakness and evils of isolated effort or association, and useless and crushing competition resulting therefrom." But the Knights' definition of "good men of all callings" was not all-inclusive: The founders specifically wanted "no drones, no lawyers, no bankers, no doctors, no professional politicians."

Surviving the depression as a secret society, the Knights abolished their assortment of rituals and passwords in the late 1870's and thenceforth openly recruited in all directions. Members were enrolled—depending on organizing expediency—in any one of three forms of organization: (1) "trade assemblies," in effect local unions of all workers in a single trade; (2) "industrial assemblies," consisting of all workers, regardless of type of skill, who worked for a single employer; and (3) "mixed assemblies," which served as intermediary coordinating bodies between the local units and the highly centralized national office of the Knights.

Such organizational imagination, combined with what now was the normal increase in union bargaining strength amid general economic prosperity, allowed a slow but steady growth in the Order's membership. There were roughly 9,000 Knights in 1878, and over 70,000 by 1884. Then, following a major 1885 strike victory against the Wabash Railroad, the growth became spectacular: Workers of all conceivable types clamored for membership and by mid-1886 there were 700,000 persons in the wide-sweeping organization.

The aftermath of the Wabash strike was to be the high-water mark for the Knights, however. The leaders of the Order proved wholly unable to cope with the gigantic membership increase, and as the new Knights sought to duplicate the Wabash triumph with one ill-timed and undisciplined strike after another, a steady stream of union defeats ensued. The very diversity of backgrounds among the members also drained the effectiveness of the organization: The old skilled trade unionists found little in common with the shopkeepers, farmers, and self-employed mechanics who shared membership with them, and they rapidly deserted the Order. Nor did the presence of thousands of unskilled and semiskilled industrial workers, often of widely varying first-generation American backgrounds, add anything to group solidarity. Greatly discouraged by the schisms within their organization, many such workers soon followed the path set by the skilled tradesmen and left it.

While each of the above factors was undoubtedly influential in the Knights' rapid decline after 1886—to 100,000 members by 1890 and to virtual extinction by 1900—still another factor was probably even more responsible for the fall of the Order: The system of values held by the Knights' leadership was considerably at variance with the values of most rank-and-file Knights. For all their diversity and essential lack of discipline, the latter could (employers and the self-employed always excepted) at least unite on the desirability of higher wages, shorter hours, and improved working conditions. Under enigmatic Knight president Terrence V. Powderly, however, these goals were significantly minimized in favor of such "social" goals as the establishment of consumer and producer cooperatives, temperance, and land reform. Even the strike weapon, despite its great success against the Wabash management and its popular appeal to Knight members, was viewed with disdain by Powderly to the end: He considered it both expensive and overly militant. The philosophical gap between leadership and followers was thus a wide one, and Powderly was forced to pay the supreme penalty for perpetuating it: Ultimately, he was left with no one to lead.

By the late 1880's a wholly new organization—the American Federation of Labor—had won over the mainstream of the Knights' skilled trade unionists, and the once vast array of other membership types, disillusioned, was again outside the ranks of organized labor. Taft has written an appropriate epitaph:

> The Knights of Labor can best be regarded as a producers', and not specifically as a wage earners', organization. It had no program around which workers in industry could rally for a long campaign. . . . The Knights of Labor expired because it could not fulfill any function. . . .[4]

The Formation of the AFL and Its Pragmatic Master Plan

Almost from its very inception in 1881, the American Federation of Labor was a highly realistic, no-nonsense organization.

Even in that year, the more than one hundred representatives of skilled worker unions who gathered at Pittsburgh to form what was originally entitled the Federation of Organized Trades and Labor Unions

[4]Philip Taft, *Organized Labor in American History* (New York: Harper & Row, Publishers, 1964), p. 120.

included many dissident Knights, disenchanted with Powderly's "one big union" concept and political action emphasis. The rebels were already convinced that the future of their highly skilled constituents lay completely outside the catch-all Knights. They recognized that such craftsmen possessed considerably greater bargaining power than other less-skilled types of Knights members because of their relative indispensability to employers. Consequently, they were anxious to exercise this power *directly* in union-management negotiations. Powderly's idealistic and somewhat hazy legislative goals might be appropriate for workers who could not better their lot in any other way, but they seemed to many FOTLU founders to be a poor substitute for strike threats and other forms of economic action when undertaken by unionists who were not so easily replaceable. Well-versed in American labor history, these early advocates of an exclusive federation of craft unions were also well aware of the fates of earlier organizations which had subordinated economic goals to political ones.

However logical these arguments for a more homogeneous and "pure collective bargaining" federation of skilled craft unions may seem to present-day readers, the FOTLU was not immediately a smashing success. It was initially torn by both personality and philosophical schisms. More importantly, the built-in weaknesses of the Knights had not yet become widely apparent to the large body of American craftsmen: Paradoxically, the craft confederation's ultimate triumph had to await the first real victories—and then the rapid downfall—of the Powderly organization.

Indeed, the basic issue which was to split irrevocably the craft unions from the Knights involved the jurisdiction of the national unions themselves. The dramatic spurt in Knight membership following the 1885 Wabash victory threatened to entirely submerge the craft "trade assemblies," and the parent national craft unions which had thus far retained their separate identities within the Order, in a throng of numerically superior semiskilled and unskilled workers. Nor would Powderly, never the compromiser and now at the pinnacle of his short-lived success, grant any assurances that the Knights would not violate the jurisdictions of the existing national unions. Rubbing salt into the nationals' wounds, the Knights' leadership even went so far now as to organize rival national unions and to try to absorb both these and the established nationals into the "mixed" assembly and district structures of the Order.

The rupture was soon complete. In late 1886, representatives of twenty-five of the strongest national unions met at Columbus, Ohio, transformed the somewhat moribund FOTLU into the American Federation of Labor, unanimously elected Samuel Gompers of the Cigar Makers as the AFL's first president, and thereby ushered in a new era for the American labor movement. Despite their moment of glory, the Knights were soon to begin their rapid decline—with some of the impetus toward their dissolution, to be sure, being directly lent by the secession of the skilled worker nationals. For the next fifty years the basic tenets of the AFL were to remain unchallenged by the mainstream of labor in this country.

Samuel Gompers, the Dutch-Jewish immigrant who was to continue as president of the Federation for all except one of the next thirty-eight years, has frequently been referred to as a supreme pragmatist, a leader convinced that any supposed "truth" was above all to be tested by its practical consequences. Careful consideration of the basic principles upon which he and his lieutenants launched the AFL does nothing to weaken the validity of this description. Essentially, Gompers had five such principles.

In the first place, the national unions were to be autonomous within the new federation: "The American Federation of Labor," Gompers proudly announced, "avoids the fatal rock upon which all previous attempts to effect the unity of the working class have split, by leaving to each body or affiliated organization the complete management of its own affairs, especially its own particular trade affairs."[5] The leader of a highly successful national himself—as were such other AFL founders as Peter McGuire of the Carpenters and P. F. Fitzpatrick of the Molders—Gompers felt particularly strongly that questions of admission, apprenticeship, bargaining policy, and the like should be left strictly to those directly involved with them.

Second, the AFL would charter only one national union in each trade jurisdiction. This concept of "exclusive jurisdiction" stemmed mainly from the unpleasant experiences of the nationals with rival unions chartered by the Knights. It was also, however, due to Gompers' deep concern that such competitive union situations would give the employer undue bargaining advantages by allowing him to pit one warring union against another.

Third, the AFL would at all costs avoid long-run reformist goals and concentrate instead only upon immediate wage-centered gains. As noted above, its founders were determined not to suffer the fates of earlier, reform-centered organizations: "We have no ultimate ends," asserted Gompers' colleague Adolph Strasser on the occasion of his testimony before a Congressional committee at this time, ". . . We are going on from day to day. We are fighting only for immediate objects—objects that can be realized in a few years."

[5]Ibid., p. 117. Quoted from a speech by Gompers to the Web Weavers Amalgamated Association, March 5, 1888.

Fourth, the federation would avoid any permanent alliances with the existing political parties and, instead, "reward labor's friends and defeat labor's enemies." Gompers was willing, however, to accept help for the AFL from any quarter with only one major exception: He had at one time been a Marxian Socialist, but familiarity had bred contempt and long before 1886 he had permanently broken with his old colleagues. At the 1903 AFL convention, he was to announce to the relative handful of Socialists present: "Economically, you are unsound; socially, you are wrong; and industrially, you are an impossibility."[6] To the end, Gompers' philosophy was firmly embedded in the capitalistic system.

Finally, Gompers placed considerable reliance on the strike weapon as a legitimate and effective means of achieving the wages, hours, and conditions sought by his unionists. Shortly before his election to the AFL presidency in May, 1886, he had been one of the leaders of a general strike designed to obtain the eight-hour day. More than 300,000 workers had participated in this action, and almost two-thirds of them had achieved their objective through it. Gompers' own Cigar Makers, too, had rarely hesitated to resort to strikes when bargaining impasses had been reached. And, generally speaking, these latter demonstrations of economic strength had also been successful.

Profiting from the lessons of history, Gompers' federation thus represented a realistic attempt to adjust to an economic system which had become rather deeply embedded in the United States and showed no symptoms of being very amenable to future change. National union autonomy, exclusive jurisdiction, "pure and simple" collective bargaining, the avoidance of political entanglements, and the use of strikes where feasible—these proven sources of union strength were to be the hallmarks of the new unionism. The federation would provide the definition of jurisdictional boundaries for each national, and give help to all such constituent unions in their organizing, bargaining, lobbying, and public relations endeavors. But it would otherwise allow a free hand to its national union members as they pursued their individual goals. And the stress was to be on the needs of skilled workers, not those of "good men of all callings," as the Knights had placed it: Some semiskilled and unskilled workers within a relatively few industries (such as mine workers and electricians, because of the strategic power of their national unions) were encouraged to join, but basically the AFL made no great efforts to organize workers with less than "skilled" callings and was to admit the latter only if they organized themselves and had no jurisdictional disputes with craft unions.

6*AFL Convention Proceedings,* 1903, p. 198.

So successful did this master plan prove to be that, except for slight modifications which will be described later, it was not until the mid-1930's that its logic was in any way seriously questioned.

The Early Years of the AFL and Some Mixed Results

Even in the short run, the policies of the AFL were so attractive to the nationals that within a few years virtually all of them had become members of the new organization. The only notable exceptions were the brotherhoods of railroad operating employees, whose relative unwillingness to strike and emphasis on elaborate accident and health insurance plans had traditionally set them apart from other organizations of craftsmen. Given this reception, the Gompers federation grew steadily, if not spectacularly: It had counted 140,000 members in 1886; by 1898 the figure had risen to 278,000.

It is also noteworthy that the economic depression that swept the country between 1893 and 1896 did not drastically deplete union membership totals, as had been the case in earlier hard times. The new principles of Gompers, reflected at both the federation and national levels, gave labor significant staying-power. Moreover, the now centralized control held by the nationals over their locals both lessened the danger that local monies would be dissipated in ill-advised strikes and provided the locals with what were normally sufficient funds for officially authorized strikes.

On the other hand, organized labor still had a severe problem to contend with in the 1890's: the deep desire of the nation's industrialists, now themselves strongly centralized in this era of trusts and other forms of consolidation, to regain unilateral control of employee affairs. Not since the 1870's had the forces of management been as determined, as formidable, or, particularly in the case of two widely heralded strikes of the time, as successful in opposing unionism.

The first of these two union disasters involved the long-established Amalgamated Association of Iron and Steel Workers and the Homestead, Pennsylvania, plant of the Carnegie Steel Company (predecessor of the United States Steel Corporation). Here, in 1892, the company attempted to reduce wages as part of its renegotiation of an expiring agreement with the union. When the workers refused to agree to the pay cut, the Carnegie management locked them out and imported some 200 Pinkerton detectives to safeguard 2,000 strikebreakers who had been hired to replace the Amalgamated members. In a subsequent pitched battle between detectives and unionists, ten men were killed, several on each side. But the company successfully resumed operations with the strikebreakers, aided by the presence of the state militia, and thus dealt a crushing blow to the once powerful Amalgamated: The latter's morale was badly broken and not for forty-five more years would Carnegie or most of the other fast-growing mills in the Pittsburgh area again operate under a union contract. Adding insult to injury, the Carnegie management also permanently blacklisted many of the defeated strikers and thereby denied them re-employment throughout the industry.

The Pullman Illinois strike of 1894 was unlike Homestead in that it involved the fast-growing American Railway Union, not an AFL affiliate. Otherwise, however, it differed essentially only in degree of violence and exact method of company victory. As in 1892, it was precipitated when the company (here, the Pullman Palace Car Company) attempted unilaterally to cut wages. The workers, not originally ARU members, then walked off their jobs and requested the railway union to intervene in their behalf. The union, welcoming the opportunity for new members, promptly instituted a boycott against all Pullman cars throughout the country. In Chicago, violence ensued when the railroad executives there imported Canadian strikebreakers. Considerable railroad property was destroyed and most train operations were completely halted. When total mob rule then threatened, the United States Department of Justice intervened and obtained a federal court injunction outlawing further union activities. President Grover Cleveland also dispatched federal troops to the scene, despite the objections of the governor of Illinois. Only after a month of further violence, plant destruction, and the killing and wounding of several soldiers and rioters, was the boycott finally ended. But, as at Homestead, the defeat was a crushing one for the union. The railroads refused to reinstate the strikers and, within a few years, the union had permanently vanished from the scene.

Other managers, impressed by the triumphs of the Carnegie and railroad managements, and at times alarmed by what they felt were the overly belligerent stances of the AFL unions, also became more aggressive in their battles with labor. Employers in the metal trades formed a Metal Trades Association to defeat the Machinists in their quest for a nine-hour day, and then adopted a policy of "no outside interference" with their company operations. Builders in Chicago, no less strongly united, completely ousted their workers' union representatives and regained full control of construction activities following a one-year 1899 strike. And the employers in the job foundry industry banded together in the National Founders' Association, which successfully terminated not only long-standing Molders Union work rules but, for all practical purposes, the existence of the union itself. In addition, the general public tended to be no more sympathetic, normally, to the aims of the labor movement: Symbolically, the eminent president of Harvard University,

Charles W. Eliot, reportedly "went so far as to glorify the strikebreaker as an example of the finest type of American citizen whose liberty had to be protected at all costs."[7]

Moreover, magnifying union problems at the turn of the century were the effects of Frederick W. Taylor's influential "Scientific Management" movement. While many of his contemporaries lamented worker inefficiency with no more practical results than they produced when they decried the weather, Taylor was determined to take positive action. He made his life a crusade to eradicate excessive fatigue, wasted time, and lost motion from the workplace by discovering and then implementing what he called "the one best way" of performing a given operation. Two parts of the total Taylor program were particularly assailed by labor leaders: (1) the systematic breakdown of all jobs into elementary task elements and then their recombination into highly standardized "best way" procedures—which often made the new jobs so easily mastered by workers that even skilled factory employees were threatened with becoming as interchangeable and consequently as replaceable as their products; and (2) the stress on incentive methods of wage payment—which threatened to undermine group solidarity by rewarding individual initiative and to make working conditions less palatable by giving companies an excuse for instituting what workers called "speedups." Union fears proved to be justified, as the Taylor movement spread across the factory employer community. Due at least in part to the influence of "Scientific Management," too, any hopes which organized labor might have harbored for enrolling the growing army of American factory workers had to be postponed, essentially for another thirty-five years.

Despite all these adverse factors, union membership growth in this period was unparalleled. From 447,000 unionists in 1897, the figure increased almost fivefold to 2,073,000 in 1904—a rate of expansion which has never been equalled since. The figures reflect the national prosperity of the day and the success of many of the national unions (their problems notwithstanding) in organizing their official jurisdictions along the lines of the AFL principles.

But the labor movement could not indefinitely withstand the continuing employer opposition, now augmented by a series of devastating court injunctions on the one hand and rival union challenges from leftist workingmen's groups on the other. Total union membership dropped to 1,959,000 in 1906, and even its ultimate growth to 3,014,000 by 1917 was quite uneven and—considering the fact that 90 per cent of the country's labor force still remained unorganized—unspectacular.

---

[7]Joseph G. Rayback, *A History of American Labor* (New York: The Macmillan Company, 1959), p. 215.

Intensified employer campaigns for the "open (nonunion) shop," led by the National Association of Manufacturers, resulted in a number of notable union strike losses after 1904 in the meat-packing and shipping industries, among others. Violence often occurred, most drastically at the Colorado Fuel and Iron Company's Ludlow location, when in 1913 eleven children and two women were found burned to death in strikers' tents which the state militia, summoned by the company, had set afire. These were also the peak years of yellow-dog contracts (under which employees promised in writing never to engage in union activities), labor spies, immediate discharge of workers at the slightest evidence of union sympathies, and the use of federal, state, and local troops on a wholesale scale to safeguard company interests in the face of strike actions.

The courts, too, were not particularly restrained in their conduct toward unions. Injunctions banning specific union activities often appeared to unionists to be issued quite indiscriminately. As early as 1906, Gompers had been sufficiently aroused by such court orders to petition the President and Congress for relief from injunctions. His claim that the court orders represented unconstitutional usurpations of legislative power went unheeded, however, and although the AFL leader was enough moved by the rebuff to set up a lobbying agency within the federation, the injunctions continued to be forthcoming. Indeed, the judges now went considerably beyond even their restraining orders in their labor relations decisions: In 1908, the Supreme Court invalidated the pioneering Erdman Act of 1898, which had banned interstate railroads from discriminating against their union member employees, on the grounds that the Act had "unconstitutionally invaded both personal liberty and the rights of property." Nine years later, the Court upheld the validity of the yellow-dog contract.

Still another threat to the established unions, in the years between 1904 and 1917, came from workers themselves. Sometimes impatient with what they considered to be the slow pace of AFL union gains, and sometimes wholly antagonistic toward the very system of capitalism, radical labor groups arose to challenge the Gompers unions for membership and influence. This was the heyday of immigration into the United States—some 14 million newcomers, mainly from Europe, arrived in the first two decades of the twentieth century—and the European political socialism which many of the radical groups espoused found some recruits in this quarter. But the most significant of these radical organizations was essentially a native American one, the colorful Industrial Workers of the World.

The IWW was founded in 1905 by a wide array of dissidents: Western metal miners, loggers, and out-and-out drifters; Socialist Labor Party members; and a few disenchanted AFL union leaders from locals of longshoremen and barbers, among others. Its militant organizers placed no faith in the free-enterprise system and asserted in the very first line of the IWW preamble that "the working class and the employing class have nothing in common." They also: put a premium on inviting all types of workers to join (including, with a hospitality reminiscent of the Knights of Labor, farmers, industrial workers, and intellectuals); were willing to support what they called a "genuine labor party"; and strongly advocated militant direct economic action.

The "Wobblies," as IWW members were termed, achieved several tangible victories. They made major inroads among the miners and lumber workers of the West. Most notably, they assumed leadership of a spontaneous 1912 walkout of Lawrence, Massachusetts, textile workers and led them to victory in the form of wage-cut restorations, despite considerable management opposition and police intervention. But an equally bitter fight, marked by much violence, was lost the following year by the IWW-sponsored silk mill workers in Paterson, New Jersey, and from then on Wobblie membership—never more than perhaps 70,000—rapidly declined. By 1917, strongly opposing United States entrance into World War I, the IWW had lost virtually all public support, and the federal government was in the process of obtaining convictions against its leaders for sedition. Yet, despite its ultimate failure and comparatively small membership, the IWW did demonstrate in its few years of gains that many unskilled and even migratory workers were now beginning to look to collective bargaining to safeguard their interests—indeed, given no alternative by the AFL, that they would support a bargaining agency as removed from their other values as the revolutionary IWW. Gompers' original principles were still quite adequate to meet the needs of the basic labor movement, but the day would come when the concept of skilled worker paramountcy would be more seriously challenged.

For the time being, however, Gompers and the AFL could point with satisfaction to some signal gains. As previously noted these did not lie primarily in the area of over-all organizational growth: In the face of the onslaughts from the employers and the courts, as well as the abortive threats of radical dual unionism, AFL union membership rose only slowly in the pre-World War I years. Rather, the gains rested to a great extent on the outstanding organizing and bargaining successes of a few specific AFL member nationals, particularly in the building trades, the ladies' garment industry, and in coal mining. Ironically, two of these unions (the International Ladies' Garment Workers and the United Mine Workers) owed much of their new strength to membership policies which took in many semiskilled and even unskilled workers, although skilled worker needs were still emphasized (and although both of these unions were definite exceptions to AFL union practice in their actions).

The AFL's further grounds for satisfaction rested on another irony: Despite the continuation of the policy against active involvement in politics, AFL lobbying activities at both the federal and state levels had been instrumental in the enactment of significant progressive labor legislation. Among other such achievements, some thirty states had by 1917 introduced workmen's compensation systems covering industrial accidents, and almost as many had provided for maximum hours of work for women. On the federal level, the 1915 LaFollette Seamen's Act had greatly ameliorated conditions on both American vessels and foreign vessels in American ports and the 1916 Owen-Keating Act had dealt a severe blow to child labor abusers. But Gompers was destined not to be successful in what had appeared at first to be an even greater triumph: Although the Clayton Act of 1914 had seemed to exempt labor from antitrust laws and the penalties of the injunction, in 1921 the Supreme Court was to interpret the Clayton Act in such a way as to render it toothless in labor disputes.

Wartime Gains and Peacetime Losses

From 1917 to 1920, the time of World War I and the months of prosperity following it, the AFL grew rapidly. The 3 million workers in the AFL unions on the eve of hostilities increased to 4.2 million by 1919 and to 5.1 million only one year later.

During the war, military production, the curtailment of immigration, and the draft combined to create tight labor markets and thus gave unions considerable bargaining power and commensurate gains. Real wages for employees in manufacturing and transportation increased by more than 25 per cent during the war.

Even more significantly, labor received for the first time official government support for its collective bargaining activities. The rights to organize and bargain collectively, free of employer discrimination for union activities, were granted AFL leaders by the Wilson administration for the length of the war. In return, Gompers and his colleagues pledged that their unions would not engage in strikes and promised full cooperation with the war effort. Wilson was, of course, not the first chief executive to accept the idea of collective bargaining—Lincoln having done so almost six decades earlier—and the World War I President's actions were undoubtedly based to a great extent on military expediency. But where Lincoln had merely abstained from intervention on the side of the employers, Wilson's program was considerably more positive from the viewpoint of the labor movement. Although it ended with the Armistice, it undoubtedly helped to stimulate the growth of union membership during the war.

But the immediate postwar months were even more conducive to union growth than the war years. The economy's production needs remained high, now to satisfy pent-up consumer demands, and the cost of living hit an all-time high. Company profits also burgeoned, freed of artificial wartime restraints. No longer obliged to honor the no-strike pledges, unions aggressively struck in pursuit of worker wages which were attuned to both profits and cost of living and, with their bargaining power now so high, they generally succeeded. As in earlier times of demonstrated labor triumphs, victory brought further conquest: New recruits flocked into the labor movement to gain their share in prosperity through collective bargaining.

Despite this auspicious entrance into the 1920's, however, the decade was to be one of great failure for unionism. Total union membership rapidly dwindled from the 1920 peak of 5.1 million to 3.8 million three years later and, steadily if less dramatically declining even after this, hit a twelve-year low of 3.4 million at the close of the decade. The drop is even more remarkable given the fact that the economy generally continued to flourish during this period: In every prior era of national prosperity, unions had *gained* considerable ground.

Nonetheless, there were understandable reasons for the poor performance of unionism in the 1920's. A combination of five powerful factors, most of them as unprecedented as organized labor's boom period decline, was now at work.

First, after the beginning of the decade prices remained stable and, with workers generally retaining their relatively high wage gains of the 1917–1920 period, the cries of labor organizers that only union membership could stave off real wage losses fell on deaf ears.

Second, employers throughout the nation not only returned to such measures for thwarting unionization as the yellow-dog contract and the immediate discharge of union "agitators" but now embarked on an antiunion open shop propaganda campaign so extensive that one contemporary observer was moved to remark that never before in its history had

> . . . America seen an open shop drive on a scale so vast as that which characterizes the drive now sweeping the country. Never before has an open shop drive been so heavily financed, so efficiently organized, so skillfully generaled. The present drive flies all of the flags of patriotic wartime propaganda. It advances in the name of democracy, freedom, human rights, Americanism.[8]

[8]Savel Zimand, *The Open Shop Drive* (New York: Bureau of Industrial Research, 1921), p. 5.

The campaign, typically conducted under the slogan of the "American Plan," portrayed unions as alien to the nation's individualistic spirit, restrictive of industrial efficiency, and frequently dominated by radical elements who did not have the best interests of America at heart. Particularly in regard to the last of these charges, the public appeared to be impressed: It was still mindful of the IWW, and now its attention was also called, freely by the newspapers, to the relatively few other significant leftist inroads into labor circles. To many citizens, too, organizations which could even remotely be construed as going against individualism and the free enterprise system in this day of laissez-faire Republicanism were also highly un-American.

Third, but often tied into their "American Plan" participation, many companies introduced what became known as "welfare capitalism." Intending to demonstrate to their employees that unions were unnecessary (as well as dangerous), they established a wide variety of employee benefit programs: elaborate profit-sharing plans, recreational facilities, dispensaries, cafeterias, and health and welfare systems of all kinds. Employee representation plans were also instituted, with workers thus being offered a voice on wages, hours, and conditions—the companies being thereby enabled to satisfy many grievances before they became major morale problems. Although the managements could withdraw the benefits at any time, and although the employee representatives normally had only "advisory" voices, union ills were undeniably compounded by these company moves.

In the fourth place, the courts proved themselves even less hospitable to labor unions than they had been in labor's dark days preceding World War I. Having denied in 1921 that the Clayton Act exempted unions from the antitrust laws and the injunction, the Supreme Court proceeded to invalidate an Arizona anti-injunction law the same year and then struck down state minimum wage laws as violations of liberty of contract in 1923. Encouraged by the implied mandate from Washington, lower court judges now issued injunctions more freely than ever.

Fifth, and finally, some of the union losses were due to unimaginative leadership in the labor movement itself. Gompers died in 1924 and his successor, William Green, lacked the aggressiveness and the imagination of the AFL's first president. Labor's troubles were clearly not to be viewed with equanimity but Green and most of his AFL union leaders were, as Rayback has tersely commented, "content to rest upon past performances, to confine membership to the elite among workingmen, and to remain the junior partner of management in the nation's economic system."[9]

---

[9]Rayback, *op. cit.*, p. 303.

On the eve of the Great Depression in late 1929, then, organized labor remained almost exclusively the province of the highly-skilled-worker minority, apathetic in the face of the loss of one-third of its members in a single decade, militantly opposed by much of the employer community, severely crimped by judicial actions, and often suspected by the general public of possessing traits counter to the spirit of America. It appeared to have a superb future behind it.

The Great Depression and the AFL's Resurgence in Spite of Itself

The stock market collapse of October, 1929, ushered in the most severe business downturn in the nation's history. Between 1929 and the Depression's lowest point in 1933, the gross national product dropped from over $104 billion to around $56 billion, and a staggering 24.9 per cent of the country's civilian labor force was out of work by 1933, compared to an unemployment rate of only 3.2 per cent in 1929.[10]

Figures which specifically relate to organized labor were equally gloomy. Between 1929 and 1933, the average twelve-month membership loss rate for organized labor accelerated to 117,000, and by 1933 union membership stood at 2,973,000—only 200,000 above the 1916 level.[11]

Given this severe loss of dues-payers, plus the necessity of sustaining strikes against the inevitable wage cuts of workers still employed, it is not surprising that many unions soon became as impoverished as their constituents. Symbolically, Ulman reports that "One forlorn strike against a small steel mill had to be called off after the contents of the strikers' soup kitchen had been depleted by a group of hungry children."[12]

It *is* surprising, however, that the mood of the workers themselves seemed to be one of bewildered apathy. The atmosphere was now marked by constant mortgage foreclosures (resulting in thousands moving into shanty-towns on city dumps, which were bitterly called "Hoovervilles" after the incumbent President). It was characterized by the constant fear of starvation on the part of many of those not working, and the fear of sudden unemployment on the part of many of those still employed. Virtually all remnants of welfare capitalism were being abruptly terminated. And, under these conditions, one might have expected a reincarnation of such militant organizations as the IWW, seeking to overthrow the capitalistic system which was now performing so poorly. Some workers did indeed turn to such radical movements

[10]Stanley Lebérgott, *The Measurement and Behavior of Unemployment* (Princeton, N. J.: National Bureau of Economic Research, Inc., 1957), p. 215.
[11]Lloyd Ulman, *op. cit.*, p. 397.
[12]*Ibid.*, pp. 397–8.

as Communism, but in general there was nothing to rival the philo-sophical rebellion of the 1840's, the violent upheaval of the 1870's, or the bitter protests of the 1890's. Instead, the bulk of the nation seemed to have been shocked into inaction.

It is still *more* surprising, even considering its uninspiring perform-ance in meeting the challenge of the 1920's, that the leadership of the AFL did not noticeably change its policies in these dark days. Through 1932, Green and the AFL Executive Council remained opposed to un-employment compensation, old-age pensions, and minimum wage legis-lation as constituting unwarranted state intervention. They asked only for increased public works spending from the government. So far was the AFL from the pulse of general community at this time that although the great bulk of union officials were and had long been Democratic Party supporters it refused, with scrupulous official neutrality, to endorse either candidate in the 1932 presidential election, which swept Democrat Franklin D. Roosevelt into office with what was then the largest margin in American history.

Roosevelt's one-sided victory symbolized the country's (if not the AFL's) willingness to grant the federal government more scope for participation in domestic affairs than it had ever been given before. The business community, upon which the nation had put such a premium during the prosperous years of the 1920's, was now both discredited and demoralized. It had become painfully apparent, too, to the millions who had been steeped in the values of American individualism, that the individual worker was comparatively helpless to influence the con-ditions of his employment environment. In short, the Depression allowed labor unions—which had been so greatly out of favor with their country-men only a few years earlier—a golden opportunity for revival and growth, now with government encouragement.

Even before the election, such a climate had resulted in one notable gain for unions. The Norris–La Guardia Act of 1932 satisfied a demand which Gompers had originally made in his petition to the President and Congress some twenty-six years earlier: The power of judges to issue injunctions in labor disputes on an almost unlimited basis was now re-voked. Severe restrictions were placed on the conditions under which the courts could grant injunctions and such orders could in no case be issued against certain otherwise legal union activities. In addition, the yellow-dog contract was declared unenforceable in federal courts.

The 1932 Act marked a drastic change in public policy. Previously, except for the temporary support which unions received during World War I, collective bargaining had been severely hampered through judi-cial control. Now it was to be strongly *encouraged*, by legislative fiat and —after Roosevelt took office in early 1933—by executive support.

Roosevelt and the first "New Deal" Congress wasted little time in making known their sentiments. The National Industrial Recovery Act of mid-1933, in similar but stronger language than that already existing in the Norris–La Guardia Act, specifically guaranteed employees "the right to organize and bargain collectively through representatives of their own choosing . . . free from the interference, restraint or coercion of employers." Green, in what for him was unusual enthusiasm, immediately praised the Act as giving "millions of workers throughout the nation . . . their charter of industrial freedom" and launched a moderate drive to expand AFL membership among craft workers. More remarkable, however, was the response to the NIRA by rank-and-file workers themselves: Almost overnight, thousands of laborers in such mass-production industries as steel, automobiles, rubber, and electrical manufacturing spontaneously formed their own locals and applied to the AFL for charters. By the end of 1933, the Federation had gained over one million new members.

The largest single gains at this time were registered by those established AFL internationals which had lost the most members during the 1920's and could capitalize upon the new climate in public policy to win back and expand their old clientele. Both the men's and women's clothing unions fell into this category. Most impressive of all, however, was the performance of the United Mine Workers under their aggressive president John L. Lewis. Lewis dispatched dozens of capable organizers throughout the coal fields, had signs proclaiming that "President Roosevelt wants you to join the union" placed at the mine pits, and not only regained virtually all his former membership but organized many traditionally nonunion fields in the Southeast. There were 60,000 Mine Workers at the time of the NIRA's passage: six months later, the figure had grown to over 350,000.

The employers, however, did not long remain docile in the face of this new union resurgence. Terming collective bargaining "collective bludgeoning," many of them responded to the NIRA by restoring or instituting the employee representation plans of the previous decade. Such "company unions," although bitterly assailed by bona fide unionists as circumventing the law's requirements concerning "employer interference," spread rapidly: By the spring of 1934, probably one-quarter of all industrial workers were employed in plants which had them. Many other managements simply refused, the law notwithstanding, to recognize any labor organizations. On many occasions, this latter attitude led to outbreaks of violence, ultimately terminated by the police or National Guard units.

The National Industrial Recovery Act was itself declared unconstitutional by the Supreme Court early in 1935, but Congress quickly replaced it with a law which was even more to labor's liking. The National Labor Relations Act, better known (after its principal draftsman in the Senate) as the Wagner Act, was far more explicit in what it expected of collective bargaining than was the NIRA, in two basic ways. First, it placed specific restrictions on what management could do (or could not do), including an absolute ban on company-dominated unions. And, second, it established the wishes of the employee majority as the basis for selection of a bargaining representative and provided that in cases of doubt as to a union's majority status, a secret-ballot election of the employees would determine whether or not the majority existed. To implement both provisions, it established a National Labor Relations Board, empowered not only to issue cease and desist orders against employers who violated the restrictions, but also to determine appropriate bargaining units and conduct representation elections.

Considerably less than enthusiastic about the Wagner Act, many employers chose to ignore its provisions and hoped that it would suffer the same fate as the NIRA. They were to be disappointed: In 1937 the Supreme Court held that the 1935 Act and its Congressional regulation of labor relations in interstate commerce was fully constitutional.

The CIO's Challenge to the AFL

Meanwhile, however, the AFL itself almost snatched defeat from the jaws of victory. The leaders of the Federation clashed sharply as to the kind of reception which should be accorded the workers in steel, rubber, automobiles, and similar mass-production industries who had spontaneously organized in the wave of enthusiasm following the NIRA's passage. The Federation had given these new locals the temporary status of "federal locals," which meant that they were directly affiliated with the AFL rather than with one of the established national unions. The workers involved, however, wanted to form their own national industrial unions covering all types of workers within their industries, regardless of occupation or skill level. And this, obviously, meant a radical departure from the fifty-year AFL tradition of discouraging nonskilled workers and essentially excluding noncraft unions (the mining and clothing industries, as noted earlier, always excepted because of their particular situations).

John L. Lewis, who had shown such initiative in expanding the ranks of his Mine Workers in the preceding months, led the fight for industrial unionism within the Federation. Allied with Sidney Hillman of the Clothing Workers and David Dubinsky of the Ladies' Garment Workers, he argued that changing times had now made skilled-craft unionism obsolete, that the AFL could no longer speak with any political power so long as it confined itself to what was (with the acceleration of mechanization and the replacement of craftsmen by semiskilled machine operators) a steadily dwindling minority of the labor force, and that, should the Federation fail to assert its leadership over the new unionists, rival federations would arise to fill the vacuum. With perhaps the greatest oratorical powers ever possessed by an American labor leader, Lewis ridiculed the AFL president for not being able to decide the issue: "Alas, poor Green. I knew him well. He wishes me to join him in fluttering procrastination, the while intoning *O tempora, O mores!*" And, in a dramatic speech at the 1935 AFL Atlantic City convention, he warned that should the Federation fail to "heed this cry from Macedonia that comes from the hearts of men" and refuse to allow industrial unionism or to organize the millions still unorganized, "the enemies of labor will be encouraged and high wassail will prevail at the banquet tables of the mighty."

Lewis spoke to no avail. The convention was dominated by inveterate craft-unionists, many of whom possibly believed that Macedonia was somewhere east of Akron and who at any rate were opposed to admitting what Teamster president Daniel Tobin described as "rubbish" mass-production laborers. The demands of industrial unionism were defeated by a convention vote of 18,024 to 10,933. And Lewis, never one to camouflage his emotions for the sake of good fellowship with his AFL colleagues, left Atlantic City only after landing a severe uppercut to the jaw of Carpenter Union president William L. Hutcheson, in a fit of pique.

Within a month, Lewis had formed his own organization of industrial unionists. The Committee for Industrial Organization (known after 1938 as the Congress of Industrial Organizations) originally wanted only to "counsel and advise unorganized and newly organized groups of workers; to bring them under the banner and in affiliation with the American Federation of Labor."[13] But the AFL, having already made its sentiments so clear, was to deny the new organization the latter opportunity: Almost immediately, Green's executive council suspended the CIO leaders for practicing "dual unionism," and ordered them to dissolve their group. When these actions failed to dissuade the CIO, the AFL took its strongest possible action and expelled all thirty-two member national unions.

Lewis and his fellow founders—themselves heads of such nationals, in addition to those in the garment industries, as the Textile Workers, Hatters, and Oil Field Workers—were spectacularly successful in realizing

[13]*Minutes of Committee for Industrial Organization*, Washington, D.C., November 9, 1935.

their objectives. Armed with ample loans from the rebel nationals, aggressive leadership, experienced organizers, and, above all, confidence that mass-production workers enthusiastically *wanted* unionism, the AFL offshoot was able to claim almost 4 million recruits as early as 1937.

By 1941, even more remarkable conquests had been registered. One by one, virtually all the giant corporations had recognized CIO affiliated unions as bargaining agents for their employees: all the major automobile manufacturers, almost all companies of any size in the steel industry, the principal rubber producers, the larger oil companies, the major radio and electrical equipment makers, the important meatpackers of the country, the larger glass-makers, and many others. Smaller companies which had also been unionized in this period could at least take comfort in the fact that they were in good company.

Still, the CIO's organizing campaigns were not welcomed by many of these companies with open arms. United States Steel recognized the CIO's Steel Workers Organizing Committee without a contest in 1937 (ostensibly because it feared labor unrest at a time when business conditions were finally improving). But the other major steel producers unconditionally refused to deal with unionism, the law notwithstanding: In 1941, the National Labor Relations Board ordered these companies to recognize what had by then become the United Steelworkers of America, but four years of company intimidation, espionage, and militia-protected strikebreaking—highlighted by a Memorial Day, 1937 clash between pickets and police which resulted in the deaths of ten workers, injuries to many more, and substantial damage to property—had then elapsed. In other industries, characterized by similar antiunion sentiments, the workers were forced to resort to sit-down strikes—protest stoppages in which the strikers remained at their places of work and were furnished with food by allies outside of the plant. Such stoppages, now illegal as trespasses upon private property, were of considerable influence in gaining representation rights for the unions in the historically nonunion automobile, rubber, and glass industries.

Nor, more significantly, was the AFL itself placid in the face of its new competition. Abandoning its traditional lethargy, it now terminated its "craftsmen only" policy and chartered industrial unions of its own in every direction. AFL meatcutters emerged to challenge CIO packinghouse workers for members of all skill levels within the meat-packing industry. AFL paper mill employees competed against CIO paper workers. AFL electricians tried to recruit the same workers, from all quarters of the electrical industry, as did the CIO electrical union organizers. And the story was much the same in textiles and automobiles. Morever, many of the long-established AFL unions now broadened their jurisdictions: Most notable were the Teamsters, whose president had apparently become oblivious to his former charge that mass-production workers were "rubbish," and who now waged aggressive organizational campaigns among workers in the food and agricultural processing industries. Aided by the same favorable climates of worker opinion and public policy which had originally inspired Lewis, and now also helped by improving economic conditions, the AFL actually surpassed the CIO in membership by 1941. By that time, however, the CIO had paid its parent the supreme compliment: It had modified its framework to include craft unionism as well as industrial unionism and the lines separating the two rival federations had become permanently clouded.

At the time of Pearl Harbor, in December, 1941, total union membership stood at 10.2 million, compared to the less than 3 million members of only nine years earlier. The CIO itself—representing some 4.8 million workers at this time—was destined to achieve little further success, as measured by sheer membership statistics: It would enroll only 6 million employees at its zenith in 1947 and then gradually retreat before the onslaught of a further AFL counterattack. But if Lewis' organization failed to live up to its founder's expectations as the sole repository of future union leadership, neither could it in any meaningful way be described as a failure. When America entered World War II in late 1941, the labor movement was not only a major force to be reckoned with but, for the first time, was to a great extent representative of the full spectrum of American workers. And for this situation, the CIO's challenge to the AFL's fifty years of dominance deserves no small amount of credit.

World War II

As in the case of the First World War, the years after Pearl Harbor saw a further increase in union strength. Although the country's economic conditions had improved considerably in the late 1930's, only after the start of hostilities and the acceleration of the draft did a tight labor market arise to weaken employer resistance to union demands.

Other factors favorable to organized labor were also present. The federal government, sympathetic enough with the goals of unionism for almost a decade, now went even further in its tangible support: In return for a no-strike pledge from both AFL and CIO leaders, labor was granted equal representation with management on the tripartite War Labor Board, the all-powerful institution which adjusted collective bargaining disputes during this period. It was also given an unprecedented form of union security—the still-utilized "maintenance of membership" arrangement, requiring all employees who are either union members when the labor contract is signed or who voluntarily join the union after this date to continue their membership for the length of the contract (subject to a short "escape" period). Finally, unions further profited in the membership area from the fast growth of such wartime industries as aircraft and shipbuilding and the reinvigoration of such now crucial sectors as steel, rubber, the electrical industry, and trucking. By the end of the war in 1945, union ranks had been increased by more than 4 million new workers, or by almost 40 per cent.

By and large, labor honored its no-strike pledge during hostilities. Somewhat less than one-tenth of 1 per cent of total available industrial working time was lost to the war effort through union economic action. But, with the cost of living continually rising, and with the War Labor Board nonetheless attempting to hold direct wages in check (not always successfully, and frequently at the cost of allowing such "nonwage" supplements as vacation, holiday, and lunch period pay), the incidence of strikes did increase steadily after 1942. Particularly galling to the general public were several strikes by Lewis' own Mine Workers, all in direct defiance of President Roosevelt's orders and all given substantial publicity by the mass media.

Managers themselves, regaining much of their lost stature with the stress on war production at this time, could also point to other evidence that labor had become "too powerful." The competition between the AFL and CIO, officially postponed for the duration of the war, in practice continued almost unabated. Such rivalry on occasion temporarily curtailed plant output, as unions within the two federations resorted to "slowdowns" and "quickie strikes" to convince employers of their respective jurisdictional claims. Instances of worker "featherbedding"—the receipt of payment for unperformed work—marked several industries, notably construction. And members of the Communist Party, originally welcomed by some CIO unions because of their demonstrated organizational ability, had now gained substantial influence if not effective control within several of these unions, including both the United Automobile Workers and the Electrical, Radio, and Machine Workers.

The public's attention was also called, by forces unhappy with the labor movement's rapid growth, to union political strength. The AFL had not yet abandoned its traditional policy of bipartisanship, but Lewis had led the CIO actively into political campaigning and had, in fact, resigned his federation presidency (while retaining his Mine Workers leadership) when the CIO rank and file had refused to bow to his wishes and vote for Republican Wendell Willkie in 1940. Under Lewis' successor, Philip Murray, and particularly through the direct efforts of Clothing Worker president Sidney Hillman, the CIO had become even more aggressive and influential—within the *Democratic* Party. It now held considerable power within most northern Democratic state organizations, and such was its influence at the national Democratic level that when a fabricated story swept the country to the effect that Roosevelt had ordered his 1944 Party convention to "clear everything with Sidney" it was widely believed. So effective had Hillman's CIO Political Action Committee become by this time that attacks upon it emanated from the highest of places: The Republican Governor of Ohio claimed that the PAC was "trying to dominate our government with radical and communistic schemes," and the House Un-American Activities Committee (with a membership unfriendly to Roosevelt) called it "a subversive . . . organization."[14]

The American man in the street seemed to be impressed. By the end of the war in 1945, public opinion polls showed more than 67 per cent of the respondents in favor of legislative curbs on union power.

Public Reaction and Private Merger

Organized labor fell even further from public favor in the immediate postwar period. Faced with income declines as overtime and other wartime pay supplements disappeared, with real wage decreases as prices rose in response to the huge pent-up consumer demand, and with layoffs as factories converted to peacetime production, workers struck as they had never done before. While the violence of earlier-day labor unrest did not often recur, the year 1946 saw new highs established in terms of number of stoppages (4,985), number of employees involved (4.6 million), and man-days idle as a percentage of available working time (1.43).[15] The month of January, 1946, alone was marked by almost 2 million workers on strike. And by the end of the year, noteworthy stoppages (many of them simultaneously) had occurred in virtually every sector of the economy, including the railroads, autos, steel, public utilities, and even public education.

Such strikes were not well-received by a frequently inconvenienced public which had already voiced reservations about union strength. The sentiments that the Wagner Act and other public policies of the 1930's had been too "one-sided" in favor of labor grew rapidly, and soon became compelling. In 1947 a newly elected Republican Congress passed, over President Truman's veto, the Taft–Hartley Act.

[14]Rayback, *op. cit.*, p. 386.
[15]*Monthly Labor Review*, 64, No. 5 (May, 1947), 782. Recalling this wave of strikes, one former War Labor Board member has commented that a further major factor was release from controls, "together with the economic uncertainty and even fear of a new depression. Controls were more and more difficult to maintain as time went on. It's hard to say how much longer the lid could have been kept on if the war hadn't ended, but strikes upon gaining freedom were very much to have been expected."

Taft–Hartley drastically amended the Wagner Act to give greater protection to both employers and individual employees. To the list of "unfair" labor practices which already were denied employers were added six "unfair" *union* practices ranging from restraint or coercion of employees to featherbedding. Employees could now hold elections to decertify unions as well as to certify them. Provisions regulating certain internal affairs of unions, explicitly giving employers certain collective bargaining rights (particularly regarding "freedom of expression" concerning union organization), and sanctioning governmental intervention in the case of "national emergency strikes" were also enacted.

While a fuller discussion of Taft–Hartley is reserved for later pages, it might be added here that the 1947 Act was at least as controversial as the Wagner Act had been. Its proponents, consistent with the views of Senator Taft, asserted that it "reinjected an essential measure of justice into collective bargaining." Less friendly observers of Taft–Hartley, including the spokesmen of organized labor, were less happy and hurled such epithets as "slave labor act" at it. That the Act has proven generally satisfactory to the majority of Americans, however, may be inferred from the fact that in the mid-1960's Taft–Hartley, essentially unchanged from its original edition, remained the basic labor law of the land.

Speaking with the self-assurance always allowed one who can draw on hindsight, it is tempting to argue that the AFL–CIO merger of 1955 was inevitable. The issue which led to the birth of the CIO was, as noted, blunted even by the late 1930's when the AFL rapidly chartered its own industrial unions and the CIO began to recognize craft unions as part of its structure. By 1939, indeed, ten of the twenty-nine existing CIO unions were craft organizations, and the AFL encompassed possibly as many noncraft workers as it did craftsmen. But sixteen more years were still to elapse before merger became a reality and significant differences of values, political opinions, and personalities still had to be bridged in this period.

In the first place, the new unions which had been formed, first by the CIO and later by the AFL, were often meeting head-on in their quests for new members and enlarged jurisdiction. Any merged federation would have to resolve not only this kind of overlap but also the membership raiding which was frequently carried on by such rival unions. For a long while, compromise seemed impossible: The AFL tended to regard all jurisdictions as exclusively its own and to insist that the CIO unions be fully absorbed within its framework; on its part, the CIO strongly suggested that its affiliates would participate in a merger only if their existing jurisdictions were given official protection.

Second, the conservative AFL leaders displayed deep hostility toward the Communist-dominated unions within the CIO. Such unions reached a peak in the immediate postwar months when a special report of the Research Institute of America listed eighteen of them in this category. And Taft has gone so far as to assert that for a short while in that period "it was a question whether the anti-Communists in the CIO could muster a majority."[16]

Finally, personalities played a role. Murray, still influenced by his predecessor as CIO president, Lewis, and Green were mutually suspicious leaders. Each was quite unwilling to take the initiative in any merger move which would involve subordination of influence to the other.

By 1955, however, most of these cleavages had been resolved. Murray, his patience with the Communist unions exhausted as the latter became more aggressive and (in particular) strongly opposed the government's Marshall Plan, had taken the lead in expelling most such unions from the CIO in 1949 and 1950.[17] Virtually all other Communist-influenced unions, presumably taking the hint, had voluntarily left the federation shortly thereafter. Murray's move cost the CIO an estimated 1 million members, but new unions were quickly established to assume the old jurisdictions and Murray claimed to have regained most of the lost membership within the next two years.

Further preparing the way for ultimate merger were the 1952 deaths of Murray and Green, both suddenly and only eleven days apart. The two successors—Walter Reuther of the United Auto Workers, for Murray, and AFL Secretary–Treasurer George Meany, for Green—were relatively divorced from the personal bitterness of the earlier presidents.

And beyond these factors were growing sentiments on the part of both AFL and CIO leaders that only a united labor movement could: (1) stave off future laws of the Taft–Hartley variety, (2) avoid the jurisdictional squabbles which were increasingly sapping the treasuries of both federations, and (3) allow organized labor to reach significant new membership totals for the first time since 1947.

In December, 1955, culminating two years of intensive negotiations between representatives of the two organizations, the AFL–CIO became a reality. The new constitution respected the "integrity of each affiliate," including both its "organizing jurisdiction" and its "established collective bargaining relationships." Consolidation of the rival unions was to be encouraged, but was to be on a voluntary basis. And it was agreed that the new giant federation would issue charters "based upon a strict recognition that both craft and industrial unions are equal and necessary as methods of trade union organization." Over a decade later, as will be

---

[16]Taft, *op. cit.*, pp. 623–24.

[17]Support for the 1948 presidential candidacy of Henry A. Wallace by these unions was another leading issue in this split.

seen, complete harmony between the AFL and CIO wings had yet to be achieved, but with the act of merger the open warfare which had first revitalized and then damaged the labor movement passed from the scene.

Organized Labor Since the Merger

Although some observers predicted that the original 15 million membership total (two-thirds of it provided by the AFL) of the AFL–CIO would double within the next decade, the figure had actually declined by 1966, to 13.5 million. The difference can be completely accounted for by the united federation's 1957 expulsion of the 1.5-million-member International Brotherhood of Teamsters, for alleged domination by "corrupt influences." But the fact remains that organized labor has been anything but impressive in terms of membership growth since the merger. The current 18 million figure for all union members (counting those in unions which are at present outside the ranks of the AFL–CIO —Teamsters, Mine Workers, railroad operating employees, and others) is, in fact, almost the same as it was in 1957. And, since this plateau has existed at a time when the nation's total labor force has been rapidly growing, labor has clearly been losing ground on a relative basis: At the time of this writing, as mentioned earlier in this book, unionists made up slightly over 30 per cent of America's total nonagricultural employment, the lowest percentage since 1942.

Several formidable obstacles undoubtedly serve to explain this situation. Paramount among them is, of course, the fact that blue-collar workers, traditionally comprising that sector of the labor force which has been most susceptible to the overtures of the union organizer, have now been substantially organized. And this sector has, it will be recalled, been declining as a source of jobs in recent years. Owing mainly to the onslaughts of automation and to changes in demand, production worker employment in manufacturing (for example) actually fell by somewhat over 5 per cent between 1947 and 1963, despite the over-all growth in national aggregate employment. It remains to be seen whether or not new approaches, fresh leadership, and environmental changes adversely affecting worker morale can gain for organized labor the allegiance of the growing *white*-collar sector. As the statistics in the previous chapter have indicated, however, unions to date have been quite unsuccessful in recruiting this wave of the future.

Beyond this, labor's fall from public favor, which began in the 1940's and led initially to the enactment of Taft–Hartley, had yet to be arrested twenty years later. Congressional disclosures of corruption in the Teamsters and several smaller unions (among them, the Laundry and Bakery Workers) in the late 1950's hardly improved labor's image. The AFL–

CIO quickly expelled the offending unions, but the public seemed to be far more impressed by the disclosures than by the federation's reaction to them, as indeed had been the case following the CIO's expulsion of its Communist-dominated affiliates.

Union resistance to technological change, sometimes taking the form of featherbedding and insistence on the protection of jobs which seemed no longer to be needed (those of diesel firemen and certain airline and maritime employees, for example), also was anything but calculated to regain widespread public support. Nor was it easy to generate sympathy outside the labor movement in behalf of plumbers who threatened to strike for wage rates in excess of $6.50 per hour, electricians demanding a twenty-hour work week, and New York City transit workers seeking a 30 per cent wage increase, a thirty-two-hour work week, and some seventy-five other demands. These few examples are among the extremes: Most unionists showed considerably more concern for the welfare of their industries in the post-merger decade. But such actions as the ones illustrated, being more newsworthy, attracted more attention. It is conceivable that, through this combination of factors ranging from corruption to excessive demands, countless potential union members have been alienated.

The continuing lack of public confidence in unionism has also led, in the recent past, to new legislation restricting labor's freedom of action. In particular, the Landrum–Griffin Act of 1959 stemmed from this climate and, directly, from the union corruption revelations of Congress which were cited above. Among its other provisions, Landrum–Griffin guarantees union members a "Bill of Rights" which their unions cannot violate and requires officers of labor organizations to meet a wide and somewhat cumbersome variety of reporting and disclosure obligations. It also lays out specific ground rules for union elections, rules which have been deemed overly inhibiting (as have most other parts of the Act) by many labor leaders.

It is perhaps also true that labor's conspicuous recent lack of success has stemmed from what Lester views as still four more grounds for union concern: (1) the business leader is no longer the tyrant that he frequently was before the mid-1930's; (2) industrial employees are no longer treated as inferior citizens; (3) unionism's success has decreased its needs; and (4) an affluent society such as ours now is generates moderation and a middle-class outlook which is at odds with the laboring class viewpoint espoused by unions.[18]

But such statements as these last, as thoughtful as they all may be,

[18]Richard A. Lester, "The Changing Nature of the Union," *New York University Thirteenth Annual Conference on Labor* (New York: Mathew Bender and Co., 1960), pp. 19–30.

tend also to be somewhat more conjectural than the earlier offered reasons for the relative decline and absolute plateau of American unionism over the past decade.

At the very least, it was obvious that organized labor could not count the post-merger decade among its golden years and that many of the conditions which could explain unionism's lack of success in these years persisted at the end of this period.

An Analysis of Union History

It is impossible to explain the history of unionism in this country with a single or all-encompassing theory. Economic, structural, and philosophical factors have all been at work, in varying degrees at various times—as has, occasionally, the sheer force of circumstances.

In earlier years, the highly sporadic growth of the American labor movement depended to a great extent on the basic health of the *economy*, and one can rather closely correlate the years of union success and failure with the periods of good and bad times for general business conditions. Union bargaining power and thus the basic attractiveness of union membership was high in the essentially prosperous periods of the years immediately prior to 1819, the 1822–1837 era, and in 1850 to 1873 (with the exception of brief recessions in the late 1850's): In each of these intervals union membership lists significantly rose. By the same token, it was not until the depression of 1873–1878 that the labor movement could even moderately withstand the slumping demand for labor services engendered by periods of economic reversal: The depressions of 1819–1822 and 1837–1850 all but eradicated collective bargaining for their durations.

Nor does such a correlation end with 1878. The record fivefold expansion in union ranks between 1897 and 1904 occurred simultaneously with another economic boom period and the tight labor markets of the two World Wars clearly fostered union growth and labor organization effectiveness. But after the late 1870's there are as many exceptions to this rule of "As the economy goes, so goes unionism" as there are illustrations of its accuracy: Organized labor rode out the drastic 1893–1896 depression without major depletions of either its ranks or its previously acquired bargaining strength; it was forced into an ignominious retreat in the highly prosperous 1920's; and it enjoyed its greatest successes during the most formidable of all American depressions, in the 1930's. It is clear that the analyst of labor history can take the economic conditions factor only so far.

Room must also be reserved for recognition of the pronounced *structural* changes which unionism has been willing to make throughout its existence to accommodate the changing nature of industry. Some of these attempts were premature and consequently abortive—notably the National Trades' Union of 1834, whose ambitious concept had to await the nationalizing of industry in the 1860's. But just as the widening of product markets had given impetus to the growth of local unions at the turn of the nineteenth century, the extension of labor markets following the construction of comprehensive railroad networks ultimately made the coordination of local unionism through the national union structure no less mandatory. Had labor been either unwilling or unable to establish its countervailing power in this fashion, the existence of the movement on any significant scale might have ended with the rise of the large national corporation in the closing decades of the century. It is equally tempting to speculate as to the sanguine effects for labor of the establishment of the AFL's "exclusive jurisdiction" concept: It is a matter of record, however, that the rival unionism of the pre-1886 period had proven highly detrimental to many national unions.

Above all, it is undeniable that labor faced a critical juncture in the midst of the Great Depression, when the continuing wisdom of its craft unionism structure was severely questioned—and that, however begrudgingly the peak federation moved to accommodate the millions of industrial unionist constituents who desired acceptance, an ultimate willingness to adapt to a changing situation was for labor the only logical decision. High wassail did not prevail at the banquet tables of the mighty.

Major *philosophical* decisions, too, have exerted a strong influence on the state and shape of American unionism in the late 1960's. In many ways, Samuel Gompers was not only the father of the modern labor movement but its supreme spiritual symbol. A pronounced strain of pragmatism runs, in fact, through all of labor's history, just as it motivated so many of Gompers' actions. The mainstream of labor, with or without Gompers, has *always* stressed the practical at the expense of the ideal, shunning, as he and his fellow AFL founders did, "objects that cannot be realized in a few years."

Thus such presumed social panaceas as the socialistic agricultural communities, land reform, and producers' cooperatives which were proposed by the zealous reformers of the 1840's had no great appeal to the typical workingman: Their connection with his on-the-job happiness and relevancy to solving the pressing problems of industrialization were too remote to be appreciated. The same can be said of the National Labor Union's advocacy of the termination of the convict labor system, currency reform, and women's suffrage three decades later and of Terrence V. Powderly's campaign for cooperatives and temperance. Nor does the notable failure of the IWW and its revolutionary credo that "the working class and the employing class have nothing in common" detract from this common denominator. Such lofty goals as these and their latter-day reincarnations in the various radical groups which have on many occasions dotted the periphery of the labor movement have been received with total apathy by the average rank-and-file unionist.

What *has* historically concerned the union member has been more in the here and now: more economic benefits, improved working conditions, and above all else a maximum of job security. These great motivators of support for organized labor accounted directly, it will be remembered, for the rise of the first American unions and no labor organization of any lasting influence since 1800 has ever lost sight of such mundane, "bread-and-butter," but also (to the union constituent) vitally important goals.

So greatly does this stamp of "pure and simple", "more and more" unionism permeate labor history that whole schools of academic thought in the labor area have been built around it. Most notable of them is the John R. Commons–Selig Perlman, or "Wisconsin School," theory, which holds that the key to understanding union growth and survival rests primarily on understanding the American worker's "consciousness of scarcity" and of limited opportunity, which in turn fostered a deep desire for improved "property rights" on the job itself. To protect the dignity and security of the individual jobholder, collective bargaining appears to this school to have been accepted by employees as a vital first step.

History seems to support this basic Commons–Perlman thesis as at least a major further explanation of American labor history. It has not been by sheer coincidence that all major periods of union growth, excepting only wartime ones, have been marked by widespread job insecurity: This situation was as true of both 1800–1819 and 1822–1837, when the worker fears stemmed primarily from employer cost-cutting devices necessitated by the new scope of product markets, as it was two decades later, when the menace of interworker competition on a geographic basis due to widened labor markets was the major cause of alarm. It was as much in evidence when the immigrant waves from Europe accelerated in the late 1860's as in the 1897–1904 period, marked by its myriad of "Scientific Management" innovations. And the booming union totals of the 1930's coincided, of course, with the Great Depression. The fact that equally great "consciousness of scarcity" characterized other *less* successful periods for labor (for example, the 1904–1916 period, when European immigration hit its peak) in no way negates the "Wisconsin School" thesis.

But just as some attention must be paid to the economic and structural factors in addition to these "philosophical" ones in understanding the growth of unionism, and just as Maslow's Need Hierarchy can hardly be ignored in dealing at least with *contemporary* unionism, so too must one recognize that some key aspects of labor history defy any theoretical generalizations at all. One can attempt to account for the huge success of AFL and CIO organizational drives in the 1930's, for example, in terms of "willingness to adjust to organizational forms" (structural) or "job-conciousness" (philosophical) —if *not* in terms of the "economic conditions" framework—but in doing so he has only a partial explanation. In retrospect, the evidence is clear that *both* of the above factors *combined* with a *variety* of special economic, public policy, and labor leadership circumstances to foster this great period of union growth, and that in many ways *each* further factor was *unprecedented* in its order of magnitude. Similarly, the adverse technological, public relations, and legal obstacles with which labor has been confronted over the past decade also hinge on unparalleled conditions.

Thus what is past may not necessarily, the declaration of Shakespeare notwithstanding, be prologue. And hopes for a resurgence of union growth which are anchored only to the propositions that labor's growth has "always" been sporadic, that unionism has "always" been able to adapt itself structurally to changing needs, and that worker job-conciousness has "always" guaranteed collective bargaining a firm place in our society are not necessarily justified.

What, then, can one say about labor's future in terms of its past? Even with the high degree of uncertainty which such predictions inevitably involve, and despite all the unprecedented circumstances since the 1930's, at least one factor emerges clearly from a reading of labor history in this country, and it suggests that the current reports of unionism's impending doom may indeed be grossly exaggerated. Organized labor has been surrounded by conditions at least as bleak as those which confront it today at many times in its 165-year history, and on each occasion it has proven equal to the challenge. It has fully recovered not only from the disastrous economic depressions which at various times have wiped out most of its membership, but from the inroads of reformers who temporarily succeeded in divorcing it almost entirely from its collective bargaining functions. It has overcome devastating victories won by employers, and formidable weapons in the hands of the courts. It has incurred deep-rooted public disfavor before, particularly in the 1870's and 1920's, and ultimately surmounted it. And at perhaps the two most critical junctures of all in its still-short history— (1) in the 1880's with the rapid disintegration of the Knights and their "one big union" concept, and (2) on the eve of the Great Depression, when an apathetic AFL remained almost exclusively the province of the highly skilled amid severe membership losses and concerted attacks from without—a Gompers and a

Lewis could emerge to lead unionism to heights previously thought unreachable.

It is entirely possible that labor's remarkable staying-power has been due to the single fact that to many workers, from the early nineteenth century to the present, there has really been no acceptable substitute for collective bargaining as a means of maintaining and improving employment conditions. Whatever its deficiencies, the labor union has offered millions of employees in our profit-minded industrial society sufficient hope that their needs, not only as employees but as individuals, would be considered to warrant their taking out union membership. At the very least, these employees have been satisfied that the only theoretical alternative to collective bargaining—individual bargaining—has for them been no alternative at all from a practical viewpoint.

Thus the strongest of cases can be built, as the earliest pages of this book have indicated, that collective bargaining is here to stay—most probably in the highly pragmatic "bread-and-butter" form from which its successes have always emanated, and quite probably also with future structural modifications (however belated at times these may be in coming) to accommodate future institutional needs—but at least here in some form which is not dramatically different from its present character for the foreseeable future.

From this it necessarily follows that, as Kheel has pointed out, "our objective must be not to find a substitute for bargaining but to discover ways of making it work better."[19] And the latter can be located only after one fully understands not only the labor relations process but the framework in which it operates, toward which understanding such a book as this is, of course, directed.

DISCUSSION QUESTIONS

1. "Without the rise of the merchant-capitalist in this country, there could have been no genuine labor movement." Comment.
2. It has been said that "unions are for capitalism for the same reason that fish are for water." Elaborate upon this statement, drawing from the historical record.
3. Explain the paradox that until relatively recent years skilled workers who enjoyed comparatively high levels of income and status constituted the main source of union membership.
4. "If the Knights of Labor expired because it could not fulfill any function, the American Federation of Labor succeeded because it admirably could fulfill many functions." Elaborate, qualifying this statement if you believe that qualifications are needed.

[19]Theodore W. Kheel, "A Labor Relations Policy for 1964," *Personnel Journal* (April, 1964), p. 181.

5. Richard A. Lester has offered as his opinion that "Even with the New Deal . . . union development experienced, not a marked mutation, but a partial alteration and expansion in leadership, tactics, and jurisdiction. The adjustment in basic union philosophy was neither profound nor completely permanent." Do you agree?

6. If a Gompers and a Lewis could emerge to rescue unionism at critical times in the past, cannot a case be made that there is nothing basically wrong with organized labor today that imaginative leadership could not cure? Discuss fully.

7. Evaluate the argument that, at least in part, unionism has become a victim of its own success.

SELECTED REFERENCES

Commons, John R., and Associates, *History of Labor in the United States*. New York: The Macmillan Company, 1918. 4 vols.

Dulles, Foster Rhea, *Labor in America*, 2nd rev. ed. New York: Thomas Y. Crowell Company, 1960.

Galenson, Walter, *The CIO Challenge to the AFL: A History of the American Labor Movement, 1935–1941*. Cambridge, Mass.: Harvard University Press, 1960.

Goldberg, Arthur J., *AFL-CIO: Labor United*. New York: McGraw-Hill Book Company, 1956.

Harris, Herbert, *American Labor*. New Haven: Yale University Press, 1939.

Perlman, Selig, *History of Trade Unionism in the United States*. New York: The Macmillan Company, 1922.

Rayback, Joseph G., *A History of American Labor*. New York: The Macmillan Company, 1959.

Taft, Philip, *Organized Labor in American History*. New York: Harper & Row, Publishers, 1964.

Ulman, Lloyd, *American Trade Unionism—Past and Present*. Berkeley, California: Institute of Industrial Relations, University of California, 1961.

———, *The Rise of the National Trade Union*. Cambridge, Mass.: Harvard University Press, 1955.

As previous pages have suggested, today's manager is hardly free to deal with the union as he wishes. A growing body of federal and state laws and the judicial and administrative interpretations of these laws now govern the employer at virtually all points at which he comes into contact with organized labor. Legislation today has much to say about management's role in union organizational campaigns and its bargaining procedures in negotiating contracts once a union has gained recognition. It is also outspoken about the acceptable contents of the company's labor agreements and even its actions in administering these agreements. As is also true of the union, whose conduct is at least equally regulated by public policy, the employer can scarcely afford to be poorly informed in the area of the labor law.

If the laws have become extensive, however, they have also become complex and often nebulous. Labor lawyers have been forced to undertake Herculean tasks, not always successfully, in attempting to assess what is "legal" and what is not in the sphere of collective bargaining. And inconsistent interpretations of the labor statutes—stemming from the Na-

3

The legal framework

tional Labor Relations Board, the various state and lower federal judiciaries, and the Supreme Court itself—continue to mark the field. There is, in fact, some justification for those who have termed the last major piece of federal labor legislation, the Landrum–Griffin Act of 1959, the "Lawyers' Full Employment Act."

But if it is impossible to state definitively the exact constraints on union-management relations which the law now imposes, at least what might appropriately be described as "currently useful generalizations" *can* be offered. Moreover, not only such basic principles but also their paths of development *must* be dealt with if the environment in which labor relations operate in the late 1960's is to be fully appreciated. If the lessons of general labor history have greatly influenced the nature of the bargaining process as it exists today, the ever-greater thrust of the laws has had an equally pervasive effect.

The Era of Judicial Control

In view of the present scope of labor legislation, it is somewhat ironic that little more than three decades ago employers were virtually unrestrained by law from dealing with unions as they saw fit. There was, as we have seen, almost no statutory treatment of labor-management relations from the days of the American Revolution until the Great Depression of the 1930's. Instead, individual judges exercised public control over these relations. And the courts' view of union activities was, for the most part, as unsympathetic as was that of most businessmen of the times.

The employers' traditional weapons for fighting labor organizations— such as formal and informal espionage, blacklists, and the very potent practice of discharging "agitators"—were normally left undisturbed by the judges. However, if the members of the judiciary believed that union activities were being conducted either for "illegal purposes" or by "illegal means," they were generous in extracting money damages from the unions and in ordering criminal prosecution of labor leaders.

The qualifications for "illegality" varied to some extent from court to court. In general, however, most aggressive union activities of the day —strikes to obtain agreements whereby the employer would employ only union members (the closed shop), picketing by "strangers" (those not in a direct superior-subordinate relationship with the employer), and the secondary boycott (the exercise of economic pressure against one company to force it to exert pressure on another company which is actually the subject of the union's concern) —were held to be illegal. Many courts went even further: Through the 1920's such remarks as "judicial actions against even peaceful picketing are merely declaratory of what has always been the law and the best practice in equity," flowed freely from the judges. And although it was President Calvin Coolidge who asserted that "The business of the United States is business," the remark could readily have emanated from most members of the judiciary well into the third decade of this century. The courts, viewing their primary role as that of protecting property rights, allied themselves with few exceptions squarely with the employer community to neutralize the economic power of organized labor.

Fully as welcome to employers, too, was the extensive court use of the injunction. This device, a judicial order calling for the cessation of certain actions deemed injurious and for which the other forms of court-provided relief appeared to be unsuitable remedies, was often invoked by the judges following employer requests for such intervention. To unionists, such restraining orders seemed to be issued quite indiscriminately. Even the relatively detached observer of legal history, however, would very likely conclude that it did not seem to take much to convince the judges that union activities should be curbed: The jurists issued their restraining decrees almost as reflex actions; and strikes, boycotts, picketing—virtually any form of union "self-help" activity—thus ran the risk of being abruptly ended if in any way present or imminent damage to the employer's property could be shown as being threatened.

The Norris–La Guardia Act of 1932

Despite its 1932 date, the Norris–La Guardia Act is of considerably more than historical interest. As is true of the later labor laws which will be discussed in this chapter, most of its provisions are still valid and continue today to govern labor relations in interstate commerce.

At the time of its passage, however, the Act was particularly noteworthy. Not only did it constitute the first major federal legislation to be applied to collective bargaining, but—as stated earlier—it marked a significant change in public policy from *repression to strong encouragement of union activity.* Implemented in the final days of the Hoover Administration, it owed its birth mainly to the widespread unemployment of the times and to a general recognition that only through bargaining collectively could many employees exercise any meaningful influence on their working environments. It also stemmed, however, from popular sentiment that justice had not been served by allowing the courts their virtually unlimited authority to issue injunctions in labor disputes.

Accordingly, the Act greatly narrowed the scope of the courts for issuing such injunctions. Peaceful picketing, peaceable assembly, organizational picketing, payment of strike benefits, and a host of other union economic weapons were now made nonenjoinable. Also enacted within the new law were procedural requirements for injunctions issued on other grounds.

Even more symbolic of the major shift in public policy was the Act's assertion that it was now necessary for Congress to guarantee to the individual employee "full freedom of association, self-organization, and designation of representatives of his own choosing, to negotiate the terms and conditions of his employment . . . free from interference, restraint, or coercion of employers." All the federal labor laws passed since 1932 have embodied this same principle.

Nor was the new treatment of unionism destined to be confined only to the federal arena. Within a short period of time, twenty states (including almost all the major industrial ones) had independently created their own "little Norris–La Guardia Acts" to govern labor relations in intrastate commerce.

Norris–La Guardia and its state counterparts did not by themselves, however, greatly stimulate union growth. They clearly expanded union freedoms and placed legal limits on judicial capriciousness, but they did little to restrain employers directly in their conduct toward collective bargaining. Only the previously cited "yellow-dog" contract arrangement, whereby managements had been able to require nonunion membership or activity as a condition of employment, was declared unenforceable by the 1932 Act. Otherwise, employers remained at liberty to fight labor organizations by whatever means they could implement, despite the ambitious language of Norris–La Guardia.

The Wagner Act of 1935

It remained for the National Labor Relations Act of 1935, more commonly known as the Wagner Act, to alter this situation, by putting teeth in the government's pledge to protect employee collective bargaining rights. The Wagner Act, it will be recalled, accomplished this through two basic methods: (1) it specifically banned five types of management action as constituting "unfair labor practices"; and (2) it set forth the principle of majority rule for the selection of employee bargaining representatives and provided that, should the employer express doubt as to the union's majority status, a secret ballot election of the employees would determine if the majority existed. It also created an independent, quasi-judicial agency—the National Labor Relations Board (NLRB)—to provide the machinery for enforcing both of the previous provisions.

Employer unfair labor practices

The five employer unfair labor practices, deemed "statutory wrongs" (although not crimes) by Congress, have been modified to some small extent since 1935, as noted below. They remain, however, a significant part of the law of collective bargaining to this day, and they constitute an impressive quintet of "thou shalt nots" for employers who might otherwise be tempted to resort to the blunt tactics of prior eras in an effort to undermine unionism. The Wagner Act: (1) deemed it "unfair" for managements to "interfere with, restrain, or coerce employees" in exercising their now legally sanctioned right of self-organization; (2) restrained company representatives from dominating or interfering with either the formation or the administration of labor unions; (3) prohibited companies from discriminating "in regard to hire or tenure of employment or any term or condition of employment to encourage or discourage membership in any labor organization"; (4) forbade employers to discharge or otherwise discriminate against employees simply because the latter had filed "unfair labor practice" charges or otherwise offered testimony against company actions under the Act; and (5) made it an unfair labor practice for employers to refuse to bargain collectively with the duly chosen representatives of their employees.

In the more than three decades since 1935, the NLRB and the courts (to which Board decisions can be appealed by either labor relations party) have had ample opportunity to make known their interpretations of all five of these provisions. In dealing with some of them, both public bodies have been quite consistent in their decisions and what the framers of the Wagner Act had in mind is no longer seriously questioned by either management or union representatives. In other cases, however, the Board members and judges have had some difficulty in issuing rulings which have been perceived by the labor relations parties as being compatible with prior rulings on the same subject. But the judges have at least generally proven themselves to be reluctant to reverse the original NLRB decisions when these have been appealed to the courts, and the inconsistencies would in most cases appear to stem more from the changing membership of the five-man Board through the years and from inherent difficulties in the words of the laws themselves than from this "opportunity for appeal" factor.

Relatively clear-cut decisions have been rendered by the NLRB and courts in two of the five areas:

(1) The interpreters of the Wagner Act have consistently held a wide variety of employer practices to be in violation of the "interfere with, restrain or coerce employees" section. Among other management

actions: Bribery of employees, company spy systems, blacklisting of union sympathizers, removal of an existing business to another location for the sole purpose of frustrating union activity, and promises by employers of wage increases or other special concessions to employees should the latter refrain from joining a union have all historically constituted "interference" contrary to the Act. The same can be said of Board and court treatment of employers who have threatened to isolate ("like a rotten apple," in one case) pro-union workers, engaged in individual bargaining with employees represented by a union, or questioned employees concerning their union activities in such a way as to tend to restrain or coerce such employees. When satisfied that any such violations have occurred, the Board has issued "cease and desist" orders against the guilty employer with no hesitation. And when it has found that employees have been discharged unlawfully in the process, the NLRB has most frequently required their reinstatement with full back pay.

Particularly in this area the courts have proven unwilling, by and large, to reverse Board decisions upon appeal, moreover, and the fact that failure to "cease and desist" after the courts have called for this action constitutes contempt of court has at times dissuaded employers from carrying an appeal to the courts in the first place. However, under normal circumstances the employer who both refuses to comply with an adverse Board order and decides not to appeal it (so as not to bring the matter to the court's attention) stands to gain little: The NLRB *itself* can be counted upon to take the initiative and ask the judges for an order calling for employer compliance with the original Board decision.

(2) The Board and courts have also had no apparent difficulty in deciding what constitutes evidence of employer discrimination related to the fourth unfair labor practice. They long ago concluded that such management actions as the layoff of an employee shortly after his testimony before the Board and the discharge of a woman worker immediately after her husband had filed unfair labor practice charges (on other grounds) against the company could be taken as discriminatory, and have consistently ruled in this direction ever since. The Board has further concluded, apparently also without much hesitation, that a company's belief that charges filed by an employee are false in no way justifies its taking punitive action against the employee. On the other hand, considerably fewer cases have had to be decided concerning this fourth unfair practice than any of the others, presumably because employers have themselves recognized that violations here are normally quite obvious to all concerned, and have therefore refrained from taking such action in the first place.

Interpretation seems to have been somewhat more difficult when the issues have involved the three other portions of the employer unfair labor practice section.

(1) The restriction on company discrimination "in regard to hire or tenure of employment or any term or condition of employment to encourage or discourage membership in any labor organization" has clearly made it unlawful for employers to force employees who are union members to accept less desirable job assignments than nonunionists, or to reduce the former type of employee's pay because of the union affiliation. Similarly, it is obvious that companies which demand renunciation of union membership as a condition of continued employment or in order to be promoted within the nonsupervisory ranks do so only at their peril. But the legality of other types of employer conduct has proven to be anything but as clearcut.

Where, for example, there is conclusive evidence that an employee has falsified his employment application and thus failed to reveal a previous criminal record, can he be properly discharged by the company for this offense? Not always, according to at least one NLRB decision covering exactly this situation. Here the Board cited the company's "anti-union bias," its knowledge of the employee's union activities, and its treatment of nonunion employees who had committed comparable offenses, in deciding that the company's official reason for the discharge was only a "pretext" for discriminating against union members.[1] Cases of this kind have proven to be thorny ones for the Board and the courts and have often caused considerable flows of adrenalin on the part of employers.

(2) The proviso restraining company representatives from dominating or interfering with both the formation and the administration of labor unions—included because of the Congress' unhappiness with the widespread creation of employer-influenced company unions in the years preceding 1935—has been the basis of much complex litigation since that date. Falcone has tersely pointed out that "it is generally held that when an employer has control over the union sitting on the other side of the bargaining table, collective bargaining is a farce and a delusion";[2] but determining just when an employer has such control has proven to be no easy matter. Among specific management actions which the Board and courts have looked unfavorably upon as evidence of employer control have been the following: the solicitation of company-union membership by supervisory employees, the company's payment of membership dues for all employees joining the union, and an employer gift to a union of

[1]*Photoswitch*, 99 NLRB. 1366 (1962).
[2]Nicholas S. Falcone, *Labor Law* (New York: John Wiley and Sons, Inc., 1963), p. 213.

$400 and the right to operate a canteen which made a monthly profit of $50 to $100—none of these company moves being especially notable for their subtlety. On the other hand, interpretations have found nothing unlawful in the mere fact that, for example, a labor organization limits its membership to employees of a single employer: The test for unfair practice pivots exclusively upon the question of which party *controls* the organization and in a case such as this only much closer inspection (and the standards for "control" established by the interpreters) can reveal whether or not the employer is in violation of the law.

(3) The fact that the 1935 legislation said little more on the subject of an employer's "refusal to bargain collectively with the representatives of his employees" than can be gleaned from these words perhaps guaranteed that controversies would result from this last section of the Wagner Act's "Rights of Employees" section, and this has indeed been the case. As such new topics for potential bargaining as pensions, health insurance, seniority, and subcontracting have arisen in the years since 1935, the NLRB and courts have been freely called upon to make known their opinions as to what "must" be bargained by employers, and what need not be. The courts have also been asked for a more precise definition of "bargaining" itself than the Act provided. The issue is still far from resolved, and with new possibilities for bargaining constantly emerging it perhaps never fully will be. But the Board and judicial decisions of the past three decades have at least ambitiously attempted to shed light on the scope for employer action in this area, and certain statements can now be made with some authority.

In brief, there are today many "mandatory" subjects of bargaining with which the employer must deal in good faith. Such objects include wages, hours of employment, health insurance, pensions, safety practices, the grievance procedure, procedures for discharge, layoff, recall and discipline, seniority, and subcontracting. Managers are *not* required to make concessions or agree to union proposals on any of these (or various other) subjects. They *are* obligated, however, to meet with the union at reasonable times and with the good-faith intention of reaching an agreement. On "nonmandatory" or "voluntary" subjects—those that are lawful but not easily related to "wages, hours and other conditions of employment"—employers are not so obligated and are free to refuse to bargain about them.

Where there is a duty to bargain, the employer must supply—upon union request—information that is "relevant and necessary" to allow the labor representatives to bargain "intelligently and effectively." The NLRB and courts have ruled, for example, that a union is entitled to information in the employer's possession concerning wage rates and in-increases, on the grounds that the former cannot deal intelligently with the subject without such information. Similarly, if a company claims financial inability to honor the union's demands, it must stand ready to supply the union with authoritative proof of this inability.

The employer's duty to bargain also entails the duty to refrain from taking unilateral action on the "mandatory" subjects. Companies which have announced a wage increase without consulting the employees' designated representatives or have subcontracted work to another employer without allowing their own union a chance to bargain the matter violate this portion of the law.

Yet the apparent finality of such remarks as the above is highly deceptive. Not only is considerable uncertainty left as to what *else* is a "mandatory" subject for bargaining (beyond the specific topics cited and the few others which the NLRB and judges have thus far dealt with affirmatively) and what is "nonmandatory," but the question of what constitutes "the good-faith intention of reaching an agreement" on the employer's part is left an open one.

It remains to be seen what further subjects the Board and courts will ultimately assign to the "mandatory" category. A union demand for moving allowances for workers transferred by the company? A proposal that all production workers be placed on a salaried basis, rather than being paid by the hour? A request by the labor organization that all foreign production of the company's product be terminated? Guarantees by the company that pension funds will be invested in low-cost housing for union employees? Each of these demands has been raised on several occasions in actual bargaining situations in the 1960's: Excepting only the first, company negotiators have been notably reluctant to accommodate any of them, or numerous similarly ambitious union proposals. Yet as Fleming, who raises the possibility of all of them ultimately going before the interpreters of public policy, has pointed out, "in the changing and very real world of bargaining, all [of these, and similar demands] may be close to the felt needs of the parties . . . [and] deciding which of [them] falls into the mandatory category will not be an easy task. Job security and internal union affairs pose extremely delicate issues."[3]

If disposition of such issues as these must thus await future Board and court treatment, it at least appears safe to predict that the books have not yet closed on the list of "mandatory" topics: Most of the subjects with which employers are *now* required to deal in good faith are themselves relative newcomers to such status, and the NLRB and jurists today appear to be more activistic in this regard than ever.

[3]Robben W. Fleming, "The Obligation to Bargain in Good Faith," in Joseph Shister *et al, Public Policy and Collective Bargaining* (New York: Harper & Row, Publishers, 1962), p. 83; see also Guy Farmer, *Management Rights and Union Bargaining Power* (New York: Industrial Relations Counselors, Inc., 1965).

The steadily increasing types of tests adopted by the Board and courts for "good faith"—for example, whether or not employer delaying tactics were used in the bargaining, some evidence of management initiative in making counter-proposals, employer willingness to accommodate completely routine demands (such as the continued availability of plant parking spaces)—have seemingly been attacked more for their naïveté than for the spirit behind them. As the authors of the highly respected Committee for Economic Development's *The Public Interest in National Labor Policy* have asserted:

> The limitations and artificiality of such tests are apparent, and the possibilities of evasion are almost limitless . . . Basically, it is unrealistic to expect that, by legislation, "good faith" can be brought to the bargaining table.[4]

At the very least, however, it is obvious that in being forced to plug the existing gaps in the Wagner Act's "refusal to bargain" interpretations, representatives of public policy have projected themselves more and more into the labor-management arena in the years since 1935, perhaps to an extent which was never contemplated when the Wagner Act was passed.

Employee representation elections

Despite all the interpretative difficulties which have been involved in the employer unfair labor practice provisions, the latter clearly were—and are—wide-sweeping in their implications for collective bargaining. However, they still represent an *indirect* approach to the protection of employee bargaining rights: By themselves, they clearly restrict employer action in the labor relations area, but they say nothing explicit about the key question of initial union *recognition*.

The authors of the Wagner Act were well aware of this gap and proceeded to deal directly with the latter issue in another section of the Act, that pertaining to the secret-ballot election. As noted previously, the NLRB was authorized to conduct such an election should the company express doubt that a majority of its employees had chosen to be represented by any union at all. Prior to this time, a union could gain recognition from an unreceptive employer only through the successful use of such economic weapons as the strike and boycott.

As this part of the Act now stands, the Board can conduct a representation election if requested to do so by a single employee, by a group

4Committee for Economic Development, *The Public Interest in National Labor Policy* (New York: C.E.D., 1961) , p. 82.

of employees, or by a labor organization acting for employees. In any of these three cases the petition must be supported by "a substantial number of employees" who desire collective bargaining representation and it must allege that the employer refuses to recognize such representation. *Employers* may also petition for such an election, presumably with the objective of proving that the employees do *not* desire union representation or for various reasons of scheduling strategy (such as trying to get the Board to hold the election at the time least favorable to the union).

It is also possible for an election to involve two or more unions, each claiming "substantial" employee support. The employees then have the choice of voting for any of the unions on the ballot or for "no union." If none of these choices (including "no union") wins a majority of the votes cast, a runoff election is then conducted among the two choices which have received the highest number of votes.

In administering this portion of the law, the NLRB itself ultimately framed a few further rules designed to foster labor relations stability. Should any union win an NLRB-conducted election and then execute a valid contract with the employer, rival unions may now not seek bargaining rights (through a subsequent election) for a period of three years following the effective date of the contract or for the length of the contract—whichever is the shorter. However, the victorious union is still not guaranteed its bargaining rights for this period of time: If the *employees themselves* have second thoughts about the desirability of retaining the union's services, they can—after one year—petition the NLRB for a decertification election. A majority vote in this latter election rescinds the union's bargaining agency.

From the Wagner Act to Taft–Hartley

As established by the Wagner Act, then, the scope of National Labor Relations Board activities was to be twofold. The Board was charged with investigating employer unfair labor practices and it was given the authority to conduct employee representation elections.

The NLRB's members (appointed by the President, subject to confirmation by the Senate) and its various regional officials outside of Washington even in their earliest years of existence undertook both of these assignments zealously. By 1947, they had processed almost 44,000 unfair labor practice cases, running the gamut in their decisions from dismissing complaints as having no merit to issuing "cease and desist" orders against guilty employers. In the area of representation cases, the Board was even more active. Almost 60,000 such cases were dealt with between 1935 and 1947. In addition to determining whether or not elections should be held and conducting such elections if the answer was in the affirmative, the NLRB often had the further duty of deciding the type of unit appropriate for the particular labor relationship (such as employer, craft, or plant).

Although its activities were necessarily controversial, as was the Act sanctioning these activities, there is general agreement today that in this twelve-year period the Board performed its basic mission of protecting the right of employees to organize and bargain collectively quite creditably. Even at the time, many contemporaries had been impressed: As in the case of Norris–La Guardia, "Little Wagner Acts" were soon enacted in many states to govern labor relations in intrastate commerce.

The modern labor movement in this country can, in fact, justifiably be said to have begun in 1935. Union membership totals boomed after that year, due in no small measure to the Wagner Act and its state counterparts. Other factors were, of course, also responsible: the improving economic climate, the generally liberal sentiments of the times, the keen competition between the American Federation of Labor and the newly born Committee for Industrial Organization, and dynamic union leadership. And it is equally true that prior legislation—not only Norris–La Guardia but also the ill-fated National Industrial Recovery Act of 1933—had paved the way for the new era and had independently led to much spontaneous union organization before 1935. But it is no less a fact that employers could still legally try to counteract unionism by almost any means except the yellow-dog contract and the arbitrary injunction process—up to and including sheer refusal to grant the union recognition under any circumstances—before the passage of the Wagner Act. It is extremely doubtful that organized labor could have grown as it did—from 3.6 million unionized workers in 1935 to more than 14 million by 1947—without the Wagner Act's protection.

Certainly public opinion as registered in Congress did not debate this last point. As the man in the street gradually turned against unionism in the mid-1940's he blamed existing public policy for the union excesses of the times, most notably for the postwar strike waves. As the last chapter has described, his voice ultimately became a compelling one: Congress overrode President Truman's veto and passed the Taft–Hartley Act of 1947, thereby stilling the cries that the Wagner Act had become too "one-sided" in favor of labor.

The Taft–Hartley Act of 1947

With the advent of Taft–Hartley, officially known as the Labor–Management Relations Act, a new period in public policy toward labor unions began: that of *modified encouragement coupled with regulation.*

Much as the Wagner Act was to a great extent designed to correct weaknesses in Norris–La Guardia, which nonetheless was not repealed and remains a part of the legal environment of collective bargaining to this day, Taft–Hartley amended but did not displace the Wagner Act. The Wagner Act, essentially as adjusted by the 1947 legislation, governs the labor relations of the late 1960's.

Indeed, the old unfair employer practices were continued virtually word-for-word by the new legislation. The only significant changes were that the closed shop (and its requirement that all workers be union members at the time of their hiring) was no longer allowed and the freedom of the parties to authorize the *union shop* (which, as noted earlier, allows the employer to hire anyone but provides that all new employees must join the union after a stipulated period of time) was somewhat narrowed. The intention of this amendment related to the third employer unfair labor practice: in its ban on employer hiring and job condition discrimination in order to encourage or discourage union membership, the Wagner Act *had* authorized employers to enter into union and closed shop agreements. The changes clearly symbolized public policy's new attitude toward unions.

Far more indicative of the public's less enthusiastic sentiments toward unions, however, were those portions of Taft–Hartley which dealt with: (1) *union unfair labor practices*, which were now enumerated and prohibited in the same way that the employer practices had been; (2) *the rights of employees as individuals*, as contrasted with those rights which employees now legally enjoyed as *union members*; (3) *the rights of employers*, a subject which the Wagner Act had glossed over in its concentration on employer *duties*; and (4) *national emergency strikes*. To some extent, other major parts of the new law—those relating to internal union affairs, the termination or modification of existing labor contracts, and suits involving unions—also demonstrated a hardening of Congressional attitudes toward labor organizations. We shall consider these various provisions separately.

Union unfair labor practices

Going the framers of the Wagner Act one better, Taft–Hartley enumerated *six* labor practices which unions were prohibited from engaging in. Labor organizations operating in interstate commerce were now officially obliged to refrain from: (1) restraining or coercing employees in the exercise of their guaranteed collective bargaining rights; (2) causing an employer to discriminate in any way against an employee in order to encourage or discourage union membership; (3) refusing to bargain in good faith with their employer about wages, hours, and other employment conditions; (4) certain types of strikes and boycotts; (5)

charging employees covered by union shop agreements initiation fees or dues "in an amount which the Board finds excessive or discriminatory under all the circumstances"; and (6) engaging in "featherbedding," the requirement of payment by the employer for services not performed.

As in the case of the employer unfair labor practices, interpretative difficulties have marked the subsequent treatment of some of these provisions. In addition, the six unfair labor practices directed against unions appear to have varied considerably more widely than in the case of the Wagner Act employer provisions in their effects on labor relations practice.

Two of the six provisions have perhaps had the greatest influence on collective bargaining, and undoubtedly a salutary one, in the two decades since the enactment of Taft–Hartley:

(1) The ban on union restraint or coercion of employees in the exercise of their guaranteed bargaining rights, which also entails a union obligation to avoid coercion of employees who choose to refrain from collective bargaining altogether. What constitutes such restraint or coercion? The myriad of rulings which has been rendered by the NLRB and courts since 1947 has at least indicated that such union actions as the following will always run the risk of being found "unfair": the stating to an antiunion employee that the employee will lose his job should the union gain recognition; the signing of an agreement with an employer which recognizes the union as exclusive bargaining representative when in fact it lacks majority employee support; and the issuing of patently false statements during a representation election campaign. Union picket line violence, threats of reprisal against employees subpoenaed to testify against the union at NLRB hearings, and activities of a similar vein are also unlawful.

This first unfair union practice also extends to the coercion of the employer in the latter's selection of his *own* bargaining representative. Post-1947 rulings have stated, for example, that unions cannot refuse to deal with former union officers who represent employers, or insist on meeting only with the owners of a company rather than with the company's attorney. On the other hand, unions have every right to demand that the employer representative with whom they deal have sufficient authority to make final decisions on behalf of the company: The interpreters of public policy have clearly understood that to have this any other way would be to frustrate the whole process of bargaining.

(2) The Taft–Hartley provision which makes it unfair for a union to cause an employer to discriminate against an employee in order to influence union membership. There is a single exception to this prohibition: Under a valid union shop agreement, the union may lawfully demand the discharge of an employee who fails to pay his initiation fee

and periodic dues. Otherwise, however, unions must exercise complete self-control in this area. They cannot try to force employers to fire or otherwise penalize workers for any other reason, whether these reasons involve worker opposition to union policies, failure to attend union meetings, or refusal to join the union at all. Nor can a union lawfully seek to persuade an employer to grant hiring preference to employees who are "satisfactory" to the union. Subject only to the union shop proviso, Taft–Hartley sought to place nonunion workers on a footing equal to that of union employees.

Occupying more or less middle ground in its degree of influence upon the labor relations process stands the *third* restriction on union practices, pertaining to union refusal to bargain. Here, clearly, Taft–Hartley extended to labor organizations the same obligation that the Wagner Act had already imposed on employers.

To many observers, the law's inclusion of this union bargaining provision has meant very little: Unions can normally be expected to pursue bargaining rather than attempt to avoid it. Nevertheless, the NLRB has used it to some extent in the years since Taft–Hartley to narrow the scope of permissible union action. The Board has, for example, found it unlawful under this section for a union to strike against an employer who has negotiated, and continues to negotiate, on a multi-employer basis, with the goal of forcing him to bargain independently. It has also found a union's refusal to bargain on an employer proposal for a written contract to violate this part of the law. To the employer community, in short, at least some inequities seem to have been corrected by this good-faith bargaining provision.

The *fourth* unfair union practice has given rise to considerable litigation. Indeed, of all six Taft–Hartley union prohibitions the ban on certain types of strikes and boycotts has proven the most difficult to interpret. Even as "clarified" by Congress in 1959, this area remains a particularly murky one for labor lawyers.

Briefly, Section 8 (b) (4) of the 1947 Act prohibits unions from striking or boycotting if such actions have any of the following three objectives: (1) forcing an employer or self-employed person to join any labor or employer organization or to cease dealing with another employer (secondary boycott); (2) compelling recognition as employee bargaining agent from another employer without NLRB certification; (3) forcing an employer to assign particular work to a particular craft.

Particularly in regard to the secondary boycott provision, it does not take much imagination to predict where heated controversy could arise. To constitute a secondary boycott, the union's action must be waged against "another" employer, one who is entirely a neutral in the battle and is merely caught as a pawn in the union's battle with the real object of its concern. But when is the secondary employer really neutral and when is he an "ally" of the primary employer? The Board has sometimes ruled against employers alleging themselves to be "secondary" ones on the grounds of common ownership with that of the "primary" employer and, again, when "struck work" has been turned over by primary employers to secondary ones. But Board and court rulings here have not been entirely consonant.

In its other clauses, too, the Taft–Hartley strike and boycott provision has led to intense legal battles. When is a union, for example, unlawfully seeking recognition without NLRB certification and when is it merely picketing to protest undesirable working conditions (a normally legal action)? It a union ever entitled to try to keep within its bargaining unit work that has traditionally been performed by the unit employees? On some occasions, but not all, the Board has ruled that there is nothing wrong with this. The histories of post-1947 cases on these issues constitute a fascinating study in the making of fine distinctions. At least, however, the large incidence of litigation might indicate that the parties have not been able totally to overlook the new rights and responsibilities bestown upon them by Taft–Hartley (whatever these might exactly be).

Last, and least in the magnitude of their effect, stand the relatively unenforceable provisions relating to (5) union fees and dues, and (6) featherbedding.

The proscription against unions charging workers covered by union shop agreements excessive or discriminatory dues or initiation fees included, it will be recalled, a stipulation that the NLRB could consider "all the circumstances" in determining discrimination or excess. Such circumstances, the wording of the Taft–Hartley Act continues, include "the practices and customs of labor organizations in the particular industry and the wages currently paid to the employees affected." Without further yardsticks and depending almost exclusively on the sentiments of individual employees rather than irate employers for enforcement, this part of the Act has had little practical value. In one of the relatively few such cases to come before it thus far, the Board ruled that increasing the initiation fee from $75 to $250 and thus charging new members the equivalent of about four week's wages when other unions in the area charged only about one-eighth of this amount was unlawful. In another case, it was held that the union's uniform requirement of a reinstatement fee for ex-members that was higher than the initiation fee for new members was *not* discriminatory under the Act.

The *sixth*, and final, unfair labor practice for unions has proven even less influential in governing collective bargaining: Taft–Hartley's prohibition of unions from engaging in "featherbedding." The Board has ruled that this provision does *not* prevent labor organizations from seeking *actual* employment for their members, "even in situations where the employer does not want, does not need, and is not willing to accept such services." And mainly because of this latter interpretation, the antifeatherbedding provision has had little teeth: The union would be quite happy to have the work performed and the question of need is irrelevant. Employer spokesmen for some industries, entertainment and the railroads in particular, have succeeded in convincing the public that their unwanted—but performing—workers are "featherbedding," but under the interpretation of the law as this now exists they are engaging in inaccuracies.

Even these least influential of the six union prohibitions, however, clearly indicate the philosophy in back of Taft–Hartley: in the words of the late Senator Robert A. Taft, "simply to reduce special privileges granted to labor leaders."

The rights of employees as individuals

In other areas, too, the Act attempted to even the scales of collective bargaining and the alleged injustices of the 1935–1947 period.

Taft–Hartley, unlike the Wagner Act, recognized a need to protect the rights of individual employees *against* labor organizations. It explicitly amended the 1935 legislation to give a majority of the employees the right to *refrain* from, as well as engage in, collective bargaining activities. It also dealt more directly with the question of individual freedoms—even beyond its previously mentioned outlawing of the closed shop, union coercion, union-caused employer discrimination against employees, and excessive union fees.

Perhaps most symbolically, Taft–Hartley provided that should any state wish to pass legislation more restrictive of union security than the union shop (or in other words, to outlaw labor contracts which make union membership a condition of retaining employment), the state was free to do so. Many states have proven themselves as so willing: nineteen states, mainly in the South and Southwest, now have so-called *"right-to-work" legislation*. Advocates of such laws, which will be discussed at greater length in Chapter 9, have claimed that compulsory unionism violates the basic American right of freedom of association; opponents of "right-to-work" laws have pointed out, among other arguments, that majority rule is inherent in our democratic procedure. There has thus far, however, been an impressive correlation between stands on this particular question and attitudes toward the values of unionism in general. Individuals opposed to collective bargaining have favored "right-to-work" laws with amazing regularity. Pro-unionists seem to have been equally consistent in their attacks on such legislation. It is still unproven, at any rate, that "right-to-work" laws have had much effect on labor relations in the states where they exist. As Hilgert and Young point out, "The general pattern emerges that existing right-to-work laws have generally been unenforceable and have accomplished little."[5] The laws are, in short, considerably more symbolic than they are of real consequence.

Also designed to strengthen the rights of workers as individuals was a Taft–Hartley provision allowing any *employee* the *right to present grievances directly* to the employer without intervention of the union. The union's representative was to be given a chance to be present at such employer-employee meetings, but the normal grievance procedure (with the union actively participating) would thus be suspended. Few employees have thus far availed themselves of this opportunity: The action clearly can antagonize the union and since the *employer's* action is normally being challenged by the grievance itself the employee may have a formidable task ahead.

Finally, the Act placed a major restriction on the fast-growing *dues checkoff* arrangement. Through this device (which will also be discussed in more detail in Chapter 9) many employers had been deducting union dues from their employees' paychecks and remitting them to the union. Companies were thus spared the constant visits of dues-collecting union representatives at the workplace; unions had also found the checkoff to be an efficient means of collection. Under Taft–Hartley, the checkoff was to remain legal, but now only if the individual employee had given his own authorization in writing. Moreover, such an authorization could not be irrevocable for a period of more than one year. This restriction has hardly hampered the growth of the checkoff: It is today provided for in approximately 80 per cent of all labor contracts, compared to an estimated 40 per cent at the time of Taft–Hartley's passage. The new legal provision has undoubtedly minimized abuse of the checkoff mechanism, however.

The rights of employers

In still a third area, Taft–Hartley circumscribed the union's freedom of action in its quest for industrial relations equity. In this case, it explicitly gave employers certain collective bargaining rights.

For example, although employers were still required to recognize and bargain with properly certified unions, they could now give full freedom of expression to their views concerning union organization, so long as there was "no threat of reprisal or force or promise of benefit." Thus an

[5]Raymond L. Hilgert and Jerry D. Young, "Right-to-Work Legislation—Examination of Related Issues and Effects," *Personnel Journal* (December, 1963), p. 559.

employer may now, when faced with a representation election, tell his employees that in his opinion unions are worthless, dangerous to the economy, and immoral. He may even, generally speaking, hint that the permanent closing of his plant would be the possible aftermath of a union election victory and subsequent high union wage demands. Nor will an election be set aside, for that matter, if he plays upon the racial prejudices of his workers (should these exist) by describing the union's philosophy toward integration, or if he sets forth the union's record in regard to violence and corruption (should this record be vulnerable) and suggests that these characteristics would be logical consequences of the union's victory in his plant—although in recent years the Board has attempted to draw the line here between dispassionate statements on the employer's part and inflammatory or emotional appeals.[6] An imaginative employer can, in fact, now engage in almost any amount of creative speaking (or writing) for his employees' consumption. The only major restraint on his conduct is that he must avoid threats, promises, coercion, and direct interference with the worker-voters in the reaching of their decision. Two lesser restrictions also govern, however: The employer may not hold a meeting with his employees on company time within twenty-four hours of an election; and he may never urge his employees individually at their homes or in his office to vote against the union (the Board has held that he can lawfully do this *only* "at the employees' work area or in places where employees normally gather").

Under this section of Taft–Hartley, employers can also: (1) themselves now call for elections to decide questions of representation (as noted earlier); (2) refuse to bargain with supervisors' unions (the Wagner Act protection was withdrawn for these employees, although they are not prohibited from forming or joining unions *without* the NLRB machinery and other safeguards of public policy); and (3) file their unfair labor practice charges against unions.

Such changes, understandably, were favorably received by the employer community.

National emergency strikes

Of most direct interest to the general public, but of practical meaning only to those employers whose labor relations can be interpreted as affecting the national health and safety, are the *national emergency strike*

[6]See, particularly, the excellent article by Derek C. Bok, "The Regulation of Campaign Tactics in Representation Elections Under the National Labor Relations Act," *Harvard Law Review*, Vol. 78, No. 1 (November, 1964), for a fuller discussion of these and various related organizational campaign legislative matters.

provisions which were enacted in 1947. As in the case of most Taft–Hartley provisions, these remain essentially unchanged to this day.

Sections 206 through 210 of the Act provide for government intervention in the case of such emergencies. If the President of the United States believes that a threatened or actual strike affects "an entire industry or a substantial part thereof" in such a way as to "imperil the national health and safety," he is empowered to take certain carefully delineated action. He may appoint a board of inquiry, to find out and report the facts regarding the dispute. The board is allowed subpoena authority and can thus compel the appearance of witnesses. It cannot, however, make recommendations for a settlement. On receiving the board's preliminary report, the President may apply, through the Attorney General, for a court injunction restraining the strike for sixty days. If no settlement is reached during this time, the injunction can be extended for another twenty days, during which period the employees are to be polled in a secret-ballot election as to their willingness to accept the employer's last offer. The board is then to submit its final report to the President. Should the strike threat still exist after all of these procedures, the President is authorized to submit a full report to Congress, "with such recommendations as he may see fit to make for consideration and appropriate action."

By 1967, the national emergency provisions had been invoked on twenty-five occasions. They had not always been effective in bringing about settlements, however. Rees conveys the majority opinion of detached observers in pointing out that "where the fact-finders have been successful in settling disputes it is often because they have been functioning as high-level mediators, commanding more respect from the parties than the mediators ordinarily furnished by government agencies."[7] There is also evidence that the eighty-day "cooling-off" period has sometimes done no more than delay the strike for that length of time: Only six of these first twenty-four disputes, in fact, were settled within the injunction period. In addition, particularly in recent years, Presidents have tended to avoid using the Taft–Hartley injunction procedures (often because unionists have viewed them as antilabor, as well as because of the more visible reason expressed above, that they have not been especially influential in settling the disputes at hand): Lyndon Johnson exhibited, for example, a notable reluctance to tap Sections 206–210 when basic steel bargaining reached an impasse in the late summer of 1965, and achieved settlement extralegally through personal pressures and recommendations. A once controversial issue regarding the National

[7] Albert Rees, *The Economics of Trade Unions* (Chicago: The University of Chicago Press, 1962), p. 39.

Emergency Strike provisions is no longer debatable, however: the United States Supreme Court, ruling against the Steelworkers union, found the provisions themselves constitutional in 1959.

Other Taft–Hartley provisions

Other provisions of the Act, too, have caused some concern for union leaders.

The 1947 legislation devoted attention to internal union affairs, the first such regulation in American history. Its impetus came not only from the previously cited Communistic taints attached to several unions but also from the fact that, in the case of a few other labor organizations, lack of democratic procedures and financial irregularities (often involving employer wrongdoing as well) had become glaringly evident. Accordingly, the Act set new conditions for unions thenceforth seeking to use the NLRB's services: (1) all union officers were obligated to file annual affidavits with the Board, stating that they were not members of the Communist party; (2) certain financial and constitutional information had to be annually filed by unions with the Secretary of Labor; and (3) unions (as well as corporations) could no longer contribute funds for political purposes in connection with any federal election. The affidavit requirement, judged to be ineffective, was repealed in 1959. The other stipulations were allowed to remain in force until that date, when they were only slightly amended and then substantially enlarged upon (as further discussion will indicate). Essentially, aside from what unionists vocally termed a nuisance value, the provisions are notable for the first recognition of public policy that some internal regulation of the union as an institution was in the public interest—and as a harbinger of more such regulation to come.

Another Taft–Hartley provision which has upset some union leaders involved the *termination or modification of existing labor contracts.* Applicable to both labor organizations and employers, it requires the party seeking to end or change the agreement to give a sixty-day notice to the other party. The law further provides that, during this time period, the existing contract must be maintained without strikes or lockouts. In addition, the Federal Mediation and Conciliation Service and state mediation services are to be notified of the impending dispute thirty days after the serving of the notice. Workers striking in violation of this requirement lose all legal protection as "employees" in collective bargaining, although the law also asserts that "such loss of status for such employee shall terminate if and when he is re-employed" by the employer.

In some instances, leaders of labor organizations have found it both difficult and politically unpopular to restrain their constituents from violating this provision. Unionists have also, on occasion, frankly pointed out that the scheduling prerequisites for striking have deprived their organizations of some economic power, at least insofar as the element of surprise is concerned. Yet many representatives of both parties would undoubtedly agree with Falcone that "these provisions have slowed down the calling of strikes, enabled mediators to intervene before it is too late to help and have generally provided an orderly method for resolving disputes and reaching final settlements."[8] From the point of view of the public interest, it is clearly on this latter basis that the effectiveness of the notice provisions should be judged.

Finally, Section 301 of Taft–Hartley decreed that "*suits for violations of contracts* between an employer and a labor organization representing employees in an industry affecting commerce" could be brought directly by either party in any United States district court. Labor agreements, in short, were to be construed as being legally enforceable, for the first time in American history. Damage suits are not calculated to increase mutual trust or offset misunderstandings between the parties in labor relations, however, and unions and managements have generally recognized this. Consequently, relatively few such suits have come to the courts in the years since this provision was enacted. Many contracts today, in fact, contain agreements *not* to sue, a perfectly legal dodge of Section 301. The remedy of the suit, for employers confronted with union violations of no-strike clauses or for unions faced with management lockouts inconsistent with no-lockout provisions (for example), nonetheless remains an available one for both parties in the absence of any restrictive covenants.

Administrative changes in the law

Taft–Hartley also enlarged the NLRB from three to five members and, in the interests of a faster disposition of cases, authorized the Board to delegate "any or all" of its powers to any group of three or more members. In addition, the office of independent General Counsel was created within the NLRB, to administer the prosecution of all unfair labor practices. This last change was made to satisfy the increasingly bitter charges (particularly from employers) that the same individuals had exercised both executive and judicial roles.

As the NLRB machinery now operates, the Board members and General Counsel delegate most of their work in processing unfair labor

[8]Falcone, *op. cit.*, p. 275.

practice charges and conducting representation elections to twenty-eight regional and two subregional offices scattered throughout the country. Each office deals with these two problems as they arise in its particular geographic area. The General Counsel supervises the work of the offices and the Board members' efforts are thus saved for those issues appealed to it from the regional level. As will be recalled, Board decisions can themselves be appealed to the courts (and ultimately to the Supreme Court), but thus far the judges have supported such decisions fairly consistently.

The Landrum–Griffin Act of 1959

As might have been expected, the Taft–Hartley Act generated considerable controversy. Particularly in the years immediately after its passage, labor leaders bitterly assailed the new law as being—in addition to a "slave labor act"—a punitive one, and invoked such statements in regard to its authors as "the forces of reaction in this country want a showdown with free American labor." Taft–Hartley supporters, on the other hand, have frequently referred to the Act as a "Magna Carta" for both employers and employees, and widely praised its efforts to "equalize bargaining power." Unable to see any appropriateness in these latter remarks, spokesmen for organized labor have in turn responded by pressing for the repeal of the Act—or occasionally, for its drastic amendment—in every session of Congress since 1947. Their complete failure to realize this goal attests to the basic acceptance of Taft–Hartley's provisions in the past two decades by the American public.

The framers of public policy themselves, however, did not long remain satisfied that existing labor legislation was fully adequate to uphold the public interest. And in 1959 the national legislature passed another significant law, the Landrum–Griffin Act (officially, the Labor–Management Reporting and Disclosure Act). This latter Act was the direct outgrowth of the unsatisfactory internal practices of a small but strategically located minority of unions, as revealed by Senate investigations, and it can be said to have marked the beginning of quite *detailed regulation* of internal union affairs, going far beyond the Taft–Hartley treatment of this subject.

Under Landrum–Griffin provisions, as noted earlier, union members are guaranteed a "Bill of Rights" which their unions cannot violate, officers of labor organizations must meet a variety of reporting and disclosure obligations, and the Secretary of Labor is charged with the investigation of relevant union misconduct.

The "Bill of Rights" for union members is an ambitious and wide-sweeping one. It provides for equality of rights concerning the nomination of candidates for union office, voting in elections, attendance at membership meetings, and participation in business transactions—all, however, "subject to reasonable" union rules. It lays down strict standards to ensure that increases in dues and fees are responsive to the desires of the union membership majority. It affirms the right of any member to sue the organization, once "reasonable" hearing procedures within the union have been exhausted. It provides that no member may be fined, suspended, or otherwise disciplined by the union except for nonpayment of dues unless the member has been granted such procedural safeguards as being served with written specific charges, given time to prepare a defense, and afforded a fair hearing. And it obligates union officers to furnish each of their members with a copy of the collective bargaining agreement, as well as full information concerning the Landrum–Griffin Act itself.

Not content to stop here in prescribing internal union conduct, the 1959 legislation laid out specific ground rules for *union elections*. National and international unions must now elect officers at least once every five years, either by secret ballot or at a convention of delegates chosen by secret ballot. Local unions are obligated to elect officers at least once every three years, exclusively by secret ballot. As for the conduct of these elections, they must be administered in full accordance with the union's constitution and bylaws, with all ballots and other relevant records being preserved for a period of one year. Every member in good standing is to be entitled to one vote and all candidates are guaranteed the right to have an observer at the polls and at the ballot-counting.

Lastly, Landrum–Griffin made it more difficult for national and international unions to place their subordinate bodies under *"trusteeships"* for pure political reasons. The trusteeship, or the termination of the member group's autonomy, has traditionally allowed labor organizations to correct constitutional violations or other clearly wrongful acts on the part of their locals. The Senate investigations preceding Landrum–Griffin had found, however, that this device was also being used by some unions as a weapon of the national or international officers to eliminate grass roots opposition *per se*. Accordingly, the Act provided that trusteeships could be imposed only for one of four purposes: (1) to correct corruption or "financial malpractice"; (2) to assure the performance of collective bargaining duties; (3) to restore democratic procedures; and (4) to otherwise carry out "the legitimate objects" of the subordinate body. Moreover, the imposition of a trusteeship, together with the reasons for it, was now to be reported to the Secretary of Labor within thirty days, and every six months thereafter until the trusteeship was terminated.

Landrum-Griffin, however, did not confine itself merely to regulating internal union affairs. It also sought to close loopholes in the *secondary boycott* provisions of Taft-Hartley. Also, as further restriction against secondary boycott activities, it prohibited *"hot cargo"* agreements. Under these agreements the employer could stop doing business with another employer who would (typically) be involved in a labor dispute with the same or a different union and thus be unpopular with the signatory labor organization; agreements in the construction and garment industries were exempted from this provision. The law also limited the opportunity of unions to engage in *recognition and organizational picketing.* It decreed that a union could no longer picket an employer to force him or his employees to recognize it as a bargaining agent if: (1) the employer was lawfully recognizing another union and no representation question could be raised under Taft-Hartley; (2) a valid election had been conducted within the previous twelve months; or (3) no election petition had been filed with the NLRB within a reasonable period (not exceeding thirty days) after the picketing began.

Nor did the Act concentrate solely on actual and potential union misbehavior. The Senate investigations had unearthed rather flagrant instances of *employer wrongdoing* as well: company bribery of union agents and, particularly, situations in which outside agents had been hired by companies to stave off union organizations by illegal means. Such agents, typically self-entitled "labor relations consultants," often acted as intermediaries in "buying off" the threat of unionization or, as • a last resort, in ensuring that the union would at least extract only a minimum of concessions from the company.

Landrum–Griffin made employers responsible for reporting annually to the Secretary of Labor all company expenditures directed at influencing employee collective bargaining behavior. Employer bribery of union officers and other such blunt tactics had constituted federal crimes since the passage of Taft–Hartley, but the new Act expanded the list of *unlawful employer actions.* Payments by companies to their own employees in the exercise of their rights to organize and bargain collectively were now added to the list of crimes. So, too, were many forms of employer payment aimed at procuring information on employee activities related to labor disputes.

Finally, Landrum–Griffin sought to redress a pro-management inequality which had been created by Taft–Hartley. Under the earlier law, *workers* who were out on *"economic" strikes*—those based on disagreements over wages or other economic benefits—were not eligible to vote in NLRB decertification elections. To some employers, this provision had constituted an open invitation for managements to provoke such a strike and then call for the decertification voting. Almost by definition, their course of action (if unfair labor practices were not detected) would lead to the ousting of the union: The only eligible voters were the strikers' replacements plus perhaps those few union members who had gone against the wishes of the majority of unionists by continuing to work. Landrum–Griffin amended the provision and economic strikers were now allowed to vote in NLRB elections held during the year following the start of the strike.

Some Conclusions

It is still too early to evaluate the effects of Landrum–Griffin. Even in the several years since its passage, the NLRB and courts have come to grips with relatively few of its various provisions and even in these instances the interpretations rendered have been, as in so many other cases, far from consistent. It is, in addition, highly debatable whether the Act's cardinal goal of union democracy can ever be legislated into existence: As in the area of civil rights, the solution may very likely have to rest on a stronger foundation than mere Congressional decree. It can be argued as a corollary to this latter remark that the members of any union, local or international, have it within their power to require their organizations to adhere to democratic procedures, that they can accomplish this objective through the existing internal machinery of their unions, and that there is a great deal to be said against a govern-mental policy which requires (for example) union reporting to the membership when the membership is not concerned with the problem.

However, it is *not* premature—almost two centuries after the first court cases involving unions and more than three decades beyond the Wagner Act—to draw some conclusions about public policy and the law of collective bargaining.

First, public policy toward organized labor has changed significantly over the years. As stated previously, it has consecutively valued repres-sion (until 1932), strong encouragement (until 1947), modified en-couragement coupled with regulation (until 1959), and detailed regula-tion (through at least 1966). It seems a safe prediction not only that further shifts in this public policy can be expected but that these changes, as was not always the case in earlier times, will depend for their direction strictly on the acceptability of current union behavior to the American public.

This later point is particularly important to the unionists of today. Especially since 1937, when it held the Wagner Act to be wholly con-stitutional, the Supreme Court has permitted the legislative branch of government the widest latitude to shape public policy. Congress and the state legislatures are judicially free to determine the elements of the framework of labor law. To most citizens, such a situation is only as it should be: Our judiciary is expected to interpret law, but not to make it, and we generally expect actions of the legislative branch to be voided only when the particular statute clearly and unmistakably violates the terms of the Constitution. But since today the polls and not the courts *do* constitute the forum in which our policies toward labor are determined, and since the public *has* in the recent past apparently increased its level of aspiration as to union behavior, labor organizations have been forced to become increasingly conscious of the images which they project. Such a situation accounts to a great extent for the growing union stress on such nontraditional labor concerns as charity work, college scholarships, Boy Scout troops, and Little League teams, which will be discussed in the next chapter. It also accounts for the entire labor movement's uneasiness whenever such newsworthy strikes as the 1966 New York City transit tie-up or such notable black marks as James R. Hoffa's jury-tampering and pension fund defrauding convictions occur. And it undoubtedly has been one major factor in leading to more maturity and self-restraint on the part of some labor leaders at the bargaining table. As Chapter 1 has noted, however, whether this progress will continue sufficiently and in time to satisfy the increasingly high level of public expectation and thereby ward off further laws of the Taft–Hartley and Landrum–Griffin variety remains an unanswered question.

Second, every law since Norris–La Guardia has expanded the scope of government regulation of the labor-management arena. To the curbs on judicial capriciousness enacted in 1932 have been added, in turn, restrictions on employer conduct, limitations on union conduct, and governmental fiats closely regulating internal union affairs. Most of the other parts of the later laws—to cite but two examples, Taft–Hartley's modification of the Wagner Act's closed and union shop provisions and Landrum–Griffin's new conditions regarding the "hot cargo" clauses— represent ever finer qualifications of the freedom of action of both parties. Given both the electorate's impatience with the progress of collective bargaining and Congress' apparently deep-seated reluctance to decrease the scope covered by its laws, future legislation can be expected to move *further* in the direction of governmental intervention. This should hold true whether the future laws are enacted with the implicit goal of "helping" or "hurting" unions.

Individual value judgments clearly determine the advisability of such a trend. But if one believes that stable and sound industrial relations can be achieved only in an environment of free collective bargaining, wherein labor and management—the parties which must "live" with each other on a day-to-day basis—are allowed to find mutually satisfactory answers to their industrial relations problems, there is cause for concern. Government policy which limits this freedom strikes at the very heart of the process.

This is not to say that the more recent labor statutes are entirely barren of provisions which are valuable additions to the law of labor relations. The union unfair labor practices relating to restraint and coercion of employees and to union-caused employer discrimination are clearly a move in the right direction. So, too, are Taft–Hartley's curbs on strikes and boycott activity engaged in at times by some unions for the objective of increasing the power of one union at the expense of other labor organizations, despite all of the litigation which has surrounded these curbs since 1947. Nor does the requirement that unions bargain collectively embarrass any one except the union leader who is uncooperative and recalcitrant.

At the same time, however, the government intervention in regard to such issues as union security, the checkoff, and the enforcement of the collective bargaining agreement (to cite but three) and the decreasing scope for union and management bargaining table latitude in general do raise the question of ultimate governmental control over *all* major industrial relations activities. For one who believes in "free collective bargaining," the increasing reach of the statutes may be steering labor policy in a very dangerous direction.

Third, even if one does conclude that the gains of our present dosage of government regulation outweigh its losses and inherent risks, this hardly proves that the current statutes and their interpretations constitute the most *appropriate* ones to meet each *specific* labor relations topic now being dealt with.

Consider, for as good an example as any in this connection, the current legal treatment of union organizational campaigns and representation elections. In his authoritative article on the subject, Professor Bok offers the following insightful commentary:

> Without an adequate understanding of voting behavior, disputes inevitably arise over the degree of regulation required, for it is difficult to determine how much protection the voters actually need in reaching their decision—or to determine the circumstances in which they are coerced or interfered with, to paraphrase the National Labor Relations Act. Since it would neither be reliable nor feasible to seek answers to these questions from the voters themselves, the law has been built upon inferences of "coercion" or "interference" drawn by officials far removed from the heat of the election campaign. The problems in drawing such inferences are substantial, and they do not disappear with greater familiarity and experience. Indeed, they may even become more difficult, for wider experi-

ence may simply expose the hazards of generalizing in this area. Take the discharge of union sympathizers—surely one of the most obvious and drastic techniques available to the employer. Although this tactic can often frustrate a union drive, any experienced (union) organizer knows that a discriminatory discharge may rally the voters against the employer instead of frightening them into submission. A few organizers have even provoked a discharge deliberately for this reason. Threats and other appeals to fear and emotion may also seem plainly coercive but there is plenty of evidence to suggest that they too can have unintended results, and that they are often less effective in influencing voters than temperate, factual arguments on the same subject. As one moves to the subtler aspects of a campaign—restrictions on distribution, inaccurate statements, interrogation by the employer, and the like—the effects upon the election are much more difficult to gauge.[9]

In short, rather than encouraging rational voting behavior in representation elections (presumably a major legislative intention), public policy may in many instances only be compounding voting *irrationality* by fostering "martyrdom" voter considerations favoring the party which has been the object of "illegal" actions. If so, it is entirely warranted to ask whether or not we have adopted the proper regulatory policy in the first place.

Similarly, one can fully believe that labor relations disputes which imperil the national health and safety should be dealt with aggressively by the federal government even while believing that the present eighty-day "cooling-off" period *augments* the dangers to national welfare by allowing already strained union and management tempers an opportunity to further "heat up."

Uneasy considerations such as these will undoubtedly always be with us, for much speculation incapable of scientific proof is necessarily attached to them. Moreover, one can always find *some* concrete labor relations situations which will accommodate one side or the other of the debate quite amply.

It is entirely possible, however, that in being open to such charges of inappropriateness as public policy in the two illustrative areas (and there are undoubtedly other areas, depending upon how one reads labor law), a certain disrespect for labor law itself has been created. As Archibald Cox has commented: "No small part of the deep dislike which large parts of management and most of organized labor feel for lawyers in the field of labor relations is traceable to their obstructionism and insistence upon following some . . . legal rule, technical and unsuited to the realities of the matter at hand."[10] If this is in fact an accurate description, another unfortunate trend may be developing.

[9]Derek C. Bok, *op. cit.*, pp. 40–41.
[10]*Ibid.*, p. 58.

Finally, and probably also as an inevitable consequence of the increased coverage of public policy, labor laws have become anything but easy to comprehend. The inconsistent NLRB and judicial rulings which have plagued them in recent years may be based to some extent on philosophical and political differences, but they undeniably also stem from the built-in interpretative difficulties in the laws themselves. As Justice Felix Frankfurter could argue in this connection in 1957:

> The judicial function is confined to applying what Congress enacted after ascertaining what it is that Congress enacted. But such ascertainment . . . is nothing like a mechanical endeavor. It could not be accomplished by the subtlest of modern "brain" machines. Because of the infirmities of language and the limited scope of science in legislative drafting, inevitably there enters into the construction of statutes the play of judicial judgment within the limits of the relevant legislative materials. Most relevant, of course, is the very language in which Congress has expressed its policy and from which the Court must extract the meaning most appropriate.[11]

What constitutes "refusal to bargain"? When are companies discriminating in regard to "hire or tenure of employment or any term or condition of employment" to influence union membership? What constitutes unlawful union recognition picketing? It is hard to disagree with the commonly heard lament of unionists and labor relations managers that it has become ever more risky to state definitively what is legal in bargaining relationships and what is not; and the most valuable information available to the management or labor union representative who is concerned with labor law may very possibly be the telephone number of an able labor lawyer. But, given the dimensions of this law today, however unpalatable many of its tenets may be to one or the other party and whatever dangers may be inherent in present trends, the managers and unionists who are *not* concerned with public policy remain so only at their peril.

DISCUSSION QUESTIONS

1. Erect as strong a case as you can for the labor injunction. Then build as strong a case as you can *against* the injunction. Which of the two cases is more persuasive with you, and *why*?
2. "The Norris–La Guardia Act conferred no new rights on workers. It merely adjusted an inherently inequitable situation." Comment.
3. How much truth do you feel lies in the statement that "There was great need for the Wagner Act . . . its sole defect lay in the fact that it was not slightly broadened from time to time to regulate a few union practices of dubious social value"?

[11]Local 1976 *Carpenters Union* v. *NLRB*, 357 U.S. 93–100 (1957).

4. It has been argued that, whatever deficiencies may have accompanied the Taft–Hartley Act, it did "free workers from the tyrannical hold of union bosses." Do you agree?
5. Do you feel that the Wagner Act or the Taft–Hartley Act has been more influential in leading to the current status of organized labor in this country?
6. "In the last analysis, the public must judge the relative merits of the collective bargaining process." Discuss.
7. If all existing national labor legislation could be instantly erased and our statutory regulation could then be completely rewritten, what would you advocate as public policy governing labor relations—and why?
8. Whether or not you agree with the exact scope and specific wording of the present laws, do you consider these laws to be essentially equitable to both management and labor?

SELECTED REFERENCES

Committee for Economic Development, *The Public Interest in National Labor Policy*. New York: Committee for Economic Development, 1961.

Evans, Robert, Jr., *Public Policy Toward Labor*. New York: Harper & Row; Publishers, 1965.

Falcone, Nicholas S., *Labor Law*. New York: John Wiley & Sons, Inc., 1962.

Frankfurter, Felix, and Nathan Greene, *The Labor Injunction*. New York: The Macmillan Company, 1930.

Mueller, Stephen J., and A. Howard Myers, *Labor Law and Legislation*, 3rd ed. Cincinnati: South-Western Publishing Co., 1962.

Northrup, Herbert R., and Gordon F. Bloom, *Government and Labor*. Homewood, Ill.: Richard D. Irwin, Inc., 1963.

Taylor, George W., *Government Regulation of Industrial Relations*. Englewood Cliffs, New Jersey: Prentice-Hall, Inc., 1948.

Wirtz, W. Willard, *Labor and the Public Interest*. New York: Harper & Row, Publishers, 1964.

Witney, Fred, *Government and Collective Bargaining*. Philadelphia: J. B. Lippincott Co., 1951.

To understand the character of any institution, it is necessary to understand its structure, government, and operation. One is entitled to speak with authority about a business, a church, or a college fraternity only if he is fully aware of the relationship of its component parts, the functions of each part, how the institution is governed or managed, and how it conducts its affairs.

This observation fully applies to the American labor movement. To say that the basic philosophy of the labor movement is focused upon improving the conditions under which its members work is not equivalent to understanding its character as an institution. One must further determine how the union movement is *organized* to implement this basic objective. We have stated previously that unions are above all "pragmatic," doing each day what they feel is necessary to improve the lot of the American workingman. But it must also be understood that this pragmatism is expressed within the framework of the union movement as a dynamic and operating institution.

Indeed, unless there *is* a systematic under-

4

Union behavior: structure,

government and operation

standing of the structure of unionism as this has emerged through the years to adapt to changing conditions, and of organized labor's functions, administrative relationships, and methods of operation, the union movement can easily appear incomprehensible and bewildering to the casual observer—for American unionism includes a *variety* of *different* functions, layers of authority, and governing practices.

For example, the AFL–CIO is a federation which contains many different sectors exercising different duties and authority. Most of the 179 national or international unions in existence in the United States belong to the federation, but 47 of them, including such mighty unions as the International Brotherhood of Teamsters and the United Mine Workers operate independently from the AFL–CIO.[1] National unions are themselves, in turn, subdivided into regions or districts for more efficient management and administration. And although the vast majority of the country's 77,400 local unions belong to national unions, several hundred of them do not, and are thus commonly described as "independent" unions.[2] Other union groups include city and state central bodies, trade councils, and joint boards and councils. Finally, some unions are craft in character; others, industrial; and some are both craft and industrial.

Because unions are not similar in terms of heritage, the personalities of their officers, the kinds of workers who are members, their sizes, and their geographic locations, it should be expected that they will differ widely in terms not only of their governments but of their day-to-day operations. Some unions (perhaps most notably the International Typographical Union and the Newspaper Guild) both before and after Landrum–Griffin have operated very democratically, whereas a few (including most but not all segments of the International Brotherhood of Teamsters) have always maintained a highly autocratic system of internal government. Unions are different in terms of the intensity of their political activities, although events of the past two decades have made virtually all labor organizations conscious of a need to become relatively active in political campaigns and thus in influencing the selection of lawmakers. Some unions have engaged in considerably more "social" activities of the type alluded to in the previous chapter than have others. Above all, unions vary in terms of their internal rules, dues and initiation fees, and qualifications for membership. Thus, although in the following pages an effort will be made to present a systematic analysis of union behavior, structure, and government, one should recognize that

[1]From figures furnished by the United States Department of Labor, Bureau of Labor Statistics.

[2]A number of such "independents" nonetheless belong to the AFL–CIO as federal locals.

diversity rather than uniformity characterizes the American labor movement. We must be concerned with common principles and trends, but the student should be fully cognizant that there could be many exceptions.

The AFL–CIO

Relationship to national unions

The decision of the former AFL and CIO to unite forces into a consolidated AFL–CIO in 1955 was made by the *affiliated national unions* of the two federations: The officers of the AFL and the CIO did not themselves have the power to bring about such a consolidation. This observation demonstrates a very important principle of the structure of the American labor movement—the *autonomy* of the national unions. The federation can exist only as long as the national unions which belong in it *agree* to stay in this labor body. Stated somewhat differently, the national unions can exist and operate independently from any kind of federation, but the federation cannot exist without the support of its national union affiliates.

In a sense, the relationship of the national unions to the federation compares closely to the relationship of member nations to the United Nations. No nation *must* belong to the United Nations; any nation *may* withdraw from the international organization at any time and for any reason whatsoever. Nor does the UN have the power to determine the internal government of any of its affiliates, the latter's tax laws, its foreign policy, the size of its military establishment, and similar national specifications. Nations affiliate and remain members of the world body for the advantages that the organization allows in the pursuit of world peace, and for other purposes, but they continue to exercise absolute sovereignty in the conduct of their own affairs.

The same is true of the relationship of the AFL–CIO to its affiliated national unions. A union belongs to the federation because of the various advantages of affiliation, but the national union is autonomous in the conduct of *its* affairs. Each union determines its own collective bargaining program, negotiates its contracts without the aid or intervention of the federation, sets its own level of dues and initiation fees, and may call strikes without any approval from the AFL–CIO (nor, conversely, can the federation prohibit a strike that an affiliated member desires to undertake).

Moreover, the federation cannot force a merger of two of its affiliates which have essentially the same jurisdiction. For example, the International Brotherhood of Electrical Workers of the old AFL and the International Union of Electrical Workers of the old CIO have what strikes the disinterested observer as virtually identical jurisdictions in manufacturing. It may seem logical that these two national unions should merge their forces. Nevertheless, the federation is powerless to compel merger. Indeed, the constitution of the AFL–CIO, to which brief reference was made on an earlier page, states:

> Each such affiliate shall retain and enjoy the same organizing jurisdiction in this Federation which it had and enjoyed by reason of its prior affiliation with either the American Federation of Labor or the Congress of Industrial Organizations. In cases of conflicting and duplicating jurisdictions involving such affiliates the President and the Executive Council of this Federation shall seek to eliminate such conflicts and duplications through the process of voluntary agreement or voluntary merger between the affiliates involved.[3]

We have pointed out that many national unions would not have joined the federation if the merger of parallel jurisdictions *was* a condition of affiliation.

These observations add up to a most fundamental characteristic of the American labor union movement. Labor's structure is *decentralized* in character: Its authority is distributed among all the affiliated unions, rather than concentrated in any single body. The 132 affiliated national unions are masters of their own fates and each of them can pursue its own objectives, conduct its own affairs, and devise what policies and programs it desires to follow without intervention by either the federation or any other national union.

Enforcement of federation rules

The AFL–CIO's constitution does, however, contain certain rules of conduct which a national union must respect if it desires to *remain* a member of the Federation. Each affiliate must pay to the Federation a per capita tax of seven cents per member per month. No union may "raid" the membership of any other affiliate nor may it be officered by Communists, fascists, or members of any other totalitarian group. Among other rules, an affiliate is obligated to conduct its affairs without regard to "race, creed, color, national origin, or ancestry. . . ." Each affiliate is further expected "to protect the labor movement from any and all corrupt influences. . . ."

[3]*Constitution of the American Federation of Labor and Congress of Industrial Organizations,* 1955, Article III, Section 3.

Given the preceding paragraphs, the practical question immediately arises as to what powers the AFL–CIO may exercise when an affiliated national union does not *comply* with these and various other rules of the Federation. If the AFL–CIO had wide-sweeping powers over the national, the Federation officers could swiftly compel the errant national union to correct its improper conduct. The latter could still belong to the Federation, but its violation of the Federation's constitution would be abruptly terminated.

The realities of the situation, however, are such that the Federation is not empowered to correct violations by exercise of such power. It can do no more than to suspend or expel a national union if the national union persists in the violation of the Federation's constitution.

The expulsion weapon has been used in several instances, but never rashly. Before the AFL–CIO expelled the Teamsters Union, for example, that union was put on notice that it stood in flagrant violation of the anticorruption provision of the Federation's constitution. AFL–CIO officials instructed the Teamsters that they would face expulsion unless certain of their national officers were removed, and the corrupt practices eliminated. Only when the Teamsters adamantly refused to comply did the AFL–CIO convert the threat into actuality and take the ultimate step of expelling the union from its ranks.

Moreover, as a practical matter, the Federation is compelled to use even this amount of authority sparingly and with discretion. The expulsion of the Teamsters was prompted by the corrupt practices of union officers who were highly visible to the public. The AFL–CIO could not tolerate such a situation in the light of the existing public clamor against dishonest union leadership and practices: The Federation was fully aware that the retention of the Teamsters would reflect adversely on *every* affiliated union. One would be naïve, however, to believe that all unions scrupulously adhere to the letter and spirit of each rule incorporated in the Federation's constitution. It is, for example, common knowledge that many affiliated unions still discriminate against Negroes, although in recent years progress has been made in eliminating such practices and although certain provisions of the Civil Rights Act of 1964 (which make it unlawful for unions to discriminate because of race, color, or creed) should further help in this regard. Despite all this improvement, however, some unions still prohibit Negroes from joining, fail to represent them fairly and equally in collective bargaining, and otherwise discriminate against them. Such practices, of course, conflict with the AFL–CIO constitutional proscription against racial discrimination, but the Federation is faced with a major dilemma under such circumstances: If it were to expel each union found to be in any way discriminating against Negroes, the size of the Federation would be drastically reduced and its influence as a labor body would be seriously impaired.[4] Indeed, to date *no* union has been expelled from the Federation for racial discrimination; about all that the Federation officers have done has been to use moral suasion to deal with the problem. Such an approach has not yet been particularly effective in many cases, but to do more than this would jeopardize the entire Federation.

Member union autonomy is also evident from the ease with which national unions have *left* the Federation *voluntarily*. The peripatetic United Mine Workers well illustrate this situation. After they were expelled from the AFL for spearheading the formation of the CIO through the efforts of their president John L. Lewis, the Mine Workers became a CIO affiliate when Lewis was elected the latter federation's first president. As part of Lewis' resignation as CIO president following the defeat of Wendell Willkie in 1940, however, the Mine Workers disaffiliated from the CIO and shortly thereafter rejoined the AFL. Yet Lewis *once again* pulled his union out of the AFL, in 1947, after he had attempted to persuade the AFL to pass a resolution to the effect that no union leader should sign the non-Communist affidavit which was then required of union officers by the Taft–Hartley law, and the Mine Workers have continued to be independent to this day.

Nor have the Mine Workers been unique in their actions. Even since 1955, several other affiliates have withdrawn from the AFL–CIO (and, in some cases, returned to it), each time pointing up the fact that the Federation has no power whatsoever to force any of its affiliates to remain in its ranks.

Why, then, *do* most national unions seek to belong to the Federation? Recall that each of the national unions must pay a per capita tax to remain in the Federation. What do they get for their money?

Advantages of affiliation

By far the chief benefit associated with membership is protection against "raiding." One provision of the AFL–CIO constitution states that "each such affiliate shall respect the established collective bargaining relationship of every other affiliate and no affiliate shall raid the established collective bargaining relationship of any other affiliate." This means that once an affiliated union gains bargaining rights in a company, no other union which is affiliated with the Federation may attempt to dislodge the established union and place itself in the plant. Such a

---

[4]See N. F. Davis, *Trade Unions' Practices and the Negro Worker: The Establishment and Implementation of AFL–CIO Anti-Discrimination Policy* (unpublished Ph.D. thesis, Department of Economics, Indiana University, 1960), and Ray Marshall, *The Negro and Organized Labor* (New York: John Wiley & Sons, Inc., 1965).

stricture constitutes a very important advantage of AFL–CIO membership. It frees unions from the task of fighting off raids from sister unions of the Federation. Time and money conserved in this way can either be used to organize the unorganized or devoted to other union programs. Unions which violate the "no-raiding" provision of the constitution may realistically expect to be expelled from the AFL–CIO; and, because mutual self-interest of all members is involved, the amount of raiding has in fact decreased sharply since the formation of the Federation. Though the total membership of the American labor movement has declined since 1958, the decline would very probably have been more pronounced had there been no Federation and no proscription against raiding.

Thus, before a union withdraws voluntarily from the AFL–CIO or engages in conduct which could result in expulsion, the officers of the union must weigh the consequences of operating outside the Federation as these consequences concern proneness to raiding. Such considerations have been particularly influential in maintaining AFL–CIO membership for most smaller and weaker nationals, whom protection against raids benefits to a greater degree than it does larger national unions. But considerations of the money, time, and energy involved in counterattacking raiding attempts have also convinced most *larger* nationals of the wisdom of continued Federation membership.

Federation membership involves still other advantages. With the Federation as the spearhead, the union movement has comparatively more power in the political and legislative affairs of the nation—a particularly influential consideration, given the thrust of the laws today—and labor's impact upon elections and Congressional voting is correspondingly greater than if each national union went its own way. In addition, by *coordinating* political efforts, the Federation can use union funds and such other sources of political persuasion as letter-writing campaigns more effectively. Moreover, the AFL–CIO helps national unions in organizing campaigns, though the nationals are expected to bear the chief responsibility for new organization. And affiliated national unions also receive some help from the Federation in the areas of legal services, educational programs, research, and social activities.

On the other hand, in the best tradition of Samuel Gompers, the Federation does not *negotiate* labor agreements for the affiliated national unions. The Federation is not equipped to render such services; nor do the autonomous national unions desire such intervention. In only one way does a national union directly benefit on the collective bargaining front by its membership in the Federation: A framework is provided whereby unions which bargain in the same industry or with the same company can consolidate their efforts. A large company such as General

Electric, for example, bargains with many different unions, and affiliated unions which deal with General Electric can thus more easily adopt common collective bargaining goals (such as uniform expiration dates of labor agreements and the attainment of similar economic benefits), than would be the case without the availability of Federation coordination: The joint 1966 bargaining endeavors of eleven major unions with General Electric (and subsequently with Westinghouse) were in fact conducted under AFL–CIO auspices, through the coordinating efforts of the Federation's increasingly active Industrial Union Department.

Structure and government of the AFL–CIO

As the accompanying chart indicates, the supreme governing body of the Federation is its *convention*, held once every two years. Each national union, regardless of size, may send one delegate to the convention, and unions with more than 4,000 members can send additional delegates: The Federation's constitution provides a graduated scale whereby up to nine delegates can represent unions with memberships of at least 175,000 members. Each national union delegate casts one vote for every member whom he represents, an arrangement which allows larger unions such as the Automobile Workers and Carpenters more influence in the affairs of the convention.

Financial expenses of the delegates are defrayed by their individual national unions and not by the Federation. Such expenses can at times be quite high and may even dissuade nationals from sending their full quotas of delegates: The convention lasts two weeks, is held in first-rate hotels in a major city, and often involves considerable travel.

The convention reflects any convention of any large group. Federation officers are elected; amendments to the AFL–CIO constitution are proposed and at times adopted; committee reports are rendered; internal policies of the Federation are deliberated and at times changed; and countless resolutions which range from purely trade union affairs to such weighty topics as United States policy in Vietnam are voted upon. There are speakers and more speakers. Delegates must be able to sit for long periods and be capable of absorbing dozens of speeches.

The decisions and policies adopted by the convention are implemented by the AFL–CIO *Executive Council*, composed of the president, secretary-treasurer, and twenty-seven vice-presidents of the Federation. The vice-presidents are elected at the convention and are usually selected from the presidents of the major affiliated national unions, although the 6,000-member Sleeping Car Porters constitutes a notable exception in this regard—primarily because of the personal respect in which its Negro president A. Philip Randolph is held. Only the president of the

STRUCTURAL ORGANIZATION
of the
AMERICAN FEDERATION OF LABOR AND CONGRESS OF INDUSTRIAL ORGANIZATIONS

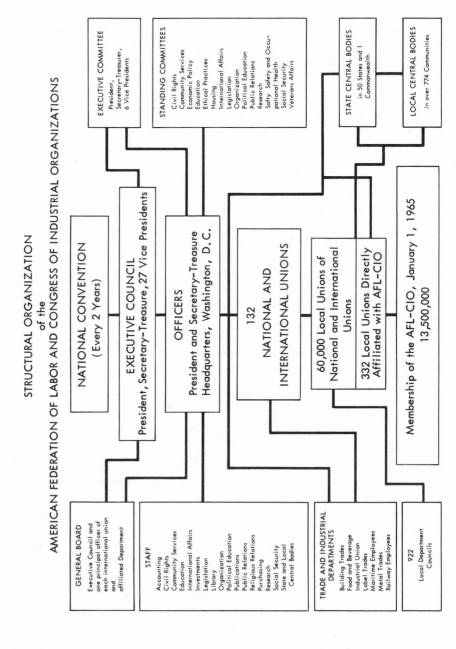

NATIONAL CONVENTION
(Every 2 Years)

EXECUTIVE COUNCIL
President, Secretary-Treasure, 27 Vice Presidents

OFFICERS
President and Secretary-Treasure
Headquarters, Washington, D. C.

132
NATIONAL AND
INTERNATIONAL UNIONS

60,000 Local Unions of
National and International
Unions

332 Local Unions Directly
Affiliated with AFL-CIO

Membership of the AFL-CIO, January 1, 1965
13,500,000

EXECUTIVE COMMITTEE
President,
Secretary-Treasurer,
6 Vice Presidents

STANDING COMMITTEES
Civil Rights
Community Services
Economic Policy
Education
Ethical Practices
Housing
International Affairs
Legislation
Organization
Political Education
Public Relations
Research
Safty Safety and Occu-
pational Health
Social Security
Veterans Affairs

STATE CENTRAL BODIES
in 50 States and 1
Commonwealth

LOCAL CENTRAL BODIES
in over 774 Communities

GENERAL BOARD
Executive Council and
one principal officer of
each international union
and
affiliated Department

STAFF
Accounting
Civil Rights
Community Services
Education
International Affairs
Investments
Legislation
Library
Organization
Political Education
Publications
Public Relations
Religious Relations
Purchasing
Research
Social Security
State and Local
Central Bodies

TRADE AND INDUSTRIAL
DEPARTMENTS
Building Trades
Food and Beverage
Industrial Union
Label Trades
Maritime Employees
Metal Trades
Railway Employees

922
Local Department
Councils

Federation and its secretary-treasurer devote full time to the affairs of the organization, however: The vice-presidents meet with the Executive Council at least three times a year, but remain as presidents of their own national unions.

Among its chief duties, the Executive Council: interprets and applies the Federation constitution; plays a "watchdog" role in legislative matters which affect the interests of workers and unions; assembles, through a full-time staff of legal and economic experts, the data needed for testimony before Congressional committees; keeps in contact with the many federal agencies which have authority in the labor field; and assures that the Federation is kept free from corrupt or communistic influences. If it suspects that a union or its officers *are* in violation of the Federation's constitution, it may investigate the matter, and if it finds that the charges are valid, it may, by a two-thirds majority, vote to suspend the guilty union. It may also recommend the ultimate penalty of expulsion of the union, but only the full convention may actually expel the union from the Federation.

The Executive Council also selects six of its membership, who along with the AFL–CIO president and secretary–treasurer constitute the Federation's *Executive Committee*. This smaller group meets every two months and has the major function of advising and counseling the president and secretary–treasurer on issues involving the Federation and its policies. Only the president and the secretary–treasurer receive a salary for their duties—$45,000 and $43,000 per year, respectively. All other Federation officers serve without salary, although they are compensated for their expenses when attending to Federation business.

A fourth decision-making body within the Federation is the AFL–CIO *General Board*, which consists of all members of the Executive Council and one principal officer of each of the national unions and the affiliated departments (to be described below). Usually, the affiliated national unions designate their chief officer as their representative to serve on the General Board, which must meet at least once a year and may meet more often at the discretion of the Federation's president. Its chief duty is to rule on all questions and issues referred to it by the Executive Council. An important difference exists between the voting procedure of the General Board and the Executive Council, however. General Board members vote as *representatives of their unions*, and each may cast a vote based upon the membership of the union. Members of the Executive Council vote as *individuals*, which means that each member may cast only one vote and that consequently the larger unions have less influence than they do in General Board meetings.

The Federation constitution also requires that the president appoint a number of *standing committees*, and AFL–CIO custom dictates that each committee chairman be president of a national union and that all members be active trade unionists. At present, such committees deal with the following issues and problems: civil rights, community services, economic policy, education, ethical practices, housing, international affairs, legislation, organization, political education, public relations, research, safety and occupational health, social security, and veterans' affairs. The growing scope of interests of the Federation is illustrated by the character of these committees, most of which are relatively new and virtually all of which clearly extend well beyond "strictly trade union" affairs.

The constitution further authorizes the president to supply each committee with an adequate professional staff. These staff members, who need not be trade unionists, are professionals and experts in their fields and work under the direct supervision of the committee chairman. The committees and their staffs keep abreast of all developments in their respective areas, make reports to the Federation president and Executive Council, and, when appropriate, report and make recommendations to the Federation's convention. Frequently, the chairman of the committee and members of the professional staff also testify at Congressional hearings.

Constitutional instructions spell out the specific duties of each committee and much of the day-to-day work of the Federation is actually performed by these committees and their professional staffs. For example, the Committee on Ethical Practices has the responsibility of assisting in keeping the AFL–CIO "free from any taint of corruption or communism." Any initial investigation of alleged corruption of an affiliated union and its officers, as in the case of the Teamsters, is made by the Committee on Ethical Practices. Should the investigation disclose corruption, the committee chairman will make a recommendation to the Executive Council for appropriate action.

Departments of the AFL–CIO

A very important feature of the Federation structure lies in the trade and industrial departments. In a sense, the departments are federations within the AFL–CIO. The constitution establishes seven such departments: Building Trades, Food and Beverage, Industrial Union, Maritime, Metal Trades, Railway Employees, and Union Label; and the posture of the departments in the Federation structure is indicated by the wording of the constitutional provision which broadly defines them: "Each department is to be considered an official method of the Federation for transacting the portion of its business indicated by the name of the department, in consequence of which affiliated and eligible organizations should be part of their respective departments and should comply with the actions and decisions of such departments, subject to appeal therefrom to the Executive Council and the conventions of the Federation."[5] When a national union affiliates with an appropriate department, it is required to pay a per capita tax to the department based upon the number of members whose occupations or jobs fall under the department. These dues are in addition to the dues which the national union pays as a condition of belonging to the AFL–CIO.

In practice, a national union may belong to more than one department. For example, the International Brotherhood of Electrical Workers is composed of members who work in the building trades as well as those who work in factories, and the union is thus eligible for membership in the Building Trades Department and in the Industrial Union Department. The rationale behind the department structure is one of encouraging unions with common interests to work together toward common ends. By establishing an Industrial Union department, for example, the Federation encourages all national unions which have membership in mass-production industries to associate together in their joint endeavors. Thus, all former unions which belonged to the old CIO (as well as industrially oriented national unions, such as the International Association of Machinists, which belonged to the erstwhile AFL) are part of the Industrial Union department.

Each department is concerned with problems of its particular industry. Such problems can involve collective bargaining issues, new organizational drives, legislative matters, or more specialized areas with which the unions of a particular branch of industry are uniquely confronted. Indeed, unlike the AFL–CIO, two of the departments take an active part in collective bargaining: The Railway Employees' Department, which represents the members of the craft unions who work in railroad shops, plays a major role in the collective bargaining with the railroads; and the Metal Trades Department usually engages in the negotiations where large shipbuilding concerns are involved. The Union Label department has as its primary objective the education of the consuming public in the desirability of purchasing union-made goods. It is composed of all AFL–CIO affiliates who stress use of a union label, to show that union members produced the product, in their bargaining demands: To many union members such a label is particularly persuasive before a purchase is made.

As the AFL–CIO, each department holds a biennial convention, in the same city as the AFL–CIO meeting, and immediately before the latter. Each department elects officers, adopts rules of procedure, and

[5]Article XII, Section 5.

passes resolutions. By custom, the president of each department is elected from the ranks of presidents of the national unions affiliated with the department. Some of the departments also issue publications and conduct research of particular concern to their affiliated unions, and for this purpose maintain departmental staffs in the same building in Washington, D. C., which houses the AFL–CIO.

State and city bodies

Though most of the activities of the AFL–CIO are thus centered in Washington, the Federation has also established state and city bodies to deal with problems at the state and municipal level: There are now state bodies in each of the fifty states and one in Puerto Rico, and on the city level the Federation has created city centrals in more than 750 communities.

Note that these state and city central bodies are established *directly* by the AFL–CIO. They are not created by the national unions affiliated with the Federation or by local unions which belong to these national unions. Local unions which belong to national unions affiliated with the AFL–CIO may join a state or a city central body, but the national union must be affiliated with the AFL–CIO; and should a national union be expelled from or withdraw voluntarily from the Federation, its local unions lose membership in the state and city central bodies. Thus, when the Teamsters Union was expelled from the AFL–CIO, the locals of this union were likewise expelled from the state and city bodies.[6] Other points of importance are that national unions do not affiliate with state and city organizations (only their locals may belong to them) and that the Federation does not require that the locals affiliate (although most of the national unions require that their locals affiliate with the state and city bodies).

State federations, also, hold conventions at which they elect officers of the state organization. Delegates to such state conventions are elected by the affiliated local unions. Normally these delegates elect a president, vice-president, and secretary–treasurer who devote full time to the organization's business, and, of course, receive a salary for their work. At times, a state central body will also hire full-time representatives who are concerned with special matters, particularly in the field of legislative lobbying.

Similar to the AFL–CIO, also, the state and city bodies have no ex-

[6]In some cases, however, Teamster locals *were* allowed to keep membership until the national officers of the AFL–CIO forced the issue.

ecutive power over their affiliated unions. They do not engage in collective bargaining, call or forbid strikes, or regulate the internal affairs of their affiliated local unions. Instead, the chief concern of the state and city bodies is political and educational activities. They lobby for or against legislation, offer testimony before state legislative committees, and promote political candidates favored by organized labor. Almost all state organizations now hold schools for representatives of their affiliated unions—the classes being taught by union officials, university instructors, government officials, and on some occasions representatives of the business community. The city bodies, in addition to participating in similar legislative and educational activities, engage in a wide variety of community service work: Promoting the United Fund, Red Cross, and similar community projects, among other endeavors. In many cities and towns, such bodies have even sponsored Boy Scout troops and Little League baseball teams, as well as art institutes, musical events, day-care centers for children of working mothers, and even the purchase of seeing-eye dogs for blind people. Although genuine altruism doubtless motivates many of these good deeds, so, too, does the need for an improved public image which is today so keenly felt by many unionists.

Functions and problems of the federation

For all that the AFL–CIO voluntarily abstains from doing or is restricted by its constitution from attempting, there can be no denying the aggressiveness with which the Federation pursues the activities which it does undertake. In the political arena this is particularly true. As do most other major interest groups in the United States, the Federation now employs a large corps of full-time lobbyists whose mission is to exert pressure upon members of Congress to support legislation favored by the AFL–CIO and to oppose those bills which the Federation regards as undesirable. Its principal officers themselves frequently testify before Congressional committees, and make public declarations of Federation political policies. And, by its very dimensions, the Federation provides a powerful sounding board for all of organized labor. Ostensibly, when the president of the AFL–CIO speaks he represents more than 13,500,000 union members and their families, 132 national unions, 60,000 local unions, 51 state federations and almost 800 city-wide labor bodies. No other labor leader can claim as much attention and exert as much influence as the president of the AFL–CIO. He and other important Federation officials are regularly invited by United States senators, congressmen, and heads of major federal agencies which deal with labor matters to specify labor's position on major issues of the day. And it is doubtful that representatives of any other interest group make as many appearances at the White House as do members of the AFL–CIO high command.

At times of federal and state elections, the role of the Federation is equally important. The Federation has created a Committee on Political Education which coordinates the political action of organized labor during such periods. This political arm of the Federation operates on the national, state, and local levels, where (since the Taft–Hartley law, as we know, forbids unions to contribute union dues to political candidates) it raises money on a voluntary basis from union members. Some of this money is given directly to political candidates who are regarded as friends of organized labor; other money is expended for radio and TV programs of a political nature, the publication of voting records of candidates who have previously served in elective offices, the distribution of campaign literature, and kindred activities. Although it is difficult to assess the political impact of the Federation upon the nation—the AFL–CIO having had both its successes and its failures—the fact that the Federation continues to play an active role in the political affairs of the country would indicate that the victories outweigh the defeats.

The political objectives of organized labor and the Federation are varied in character. The AFL–CIO supports legislation that strengthens the role of organized labor in collective bargaining, organizational drives, the strike, picketing, and boycotting. To these ends, the Federation has, for example, consistently advocated such measures as the repeal of state "right-to-work" legislation, and lobbied for other changes in the federal and state laws which would strengthen the use of such union self-help methods as boycotts and picketing in labor's direct relationship with business. It has also, however, regularly supported such bills as those favoring medicare, low-cost public housing, liberalized minimum wage laws, more comprehensive unemployment compensation statutes, and more effective public education—all of which measures are intended to benefit all the workers of the nation and their families rather than strictly those within the ranks of unionism. The AFL–CIO today fully recognizes that many of these less parochial objectives cannot be achieved through face-to-face union–management collective bargaining and has consequently supported such measures as the ones cited to gain additional leverage in its efforts to improve the status of the American wage-earner.

Beyond the legislative and political function, the Federation carries out a massive research program—the results of which are embodied in its regular publications, such as the monthly *AFL–CIO News* and the *American Federationist*, as well as in special bulletins, briefs for the courts of the nation, and a series of pamphlets, monographs, and books.

Through these varied publications, the Federation tries to keep union members and others abreast of labor developments from the union point of view.

Another important function is that of promoting new organizations. Although the basic responsibility for such new organizations falls upon the national unions, the Federation does organize on its own, and helps affiliated unions in their organizational drives. When the AFL–CIO organizes a union by itself, it charters such a local union directly with the Federation in much the same fashion that the old AFL did in the 1930's. There are about 350 such directly affiliated labor unions now in existence and, through its field officers, the AFL–CIO bargains contracts for these local unions and aids them in time of strikes and other difficulties with management. In return, members of such locals pay dues directly to the AFL–CIO. This collective bargaining function for directly affiliated local unions should not, however, be confused with the principle already established: The AFL–CIO does not bargain collectively for affiliated national unions or for locals which belong to such affiliated national unions. Moreover, most of these directly affiliated local unions are themselves ultimately assigned by the Federation to a national union which has appropriate jurisdiction over the jobs and occupations of its members.

In recent years, the American labor movement has also demonstrated increasing concern with the labor movement in foreign nations. Two major factors lie behind this development. In the first place, the increasing tempo of international trade has threatened the job security and welfare of American workers. The impact in the United States of products produced by foreign labor under conditions of comparatively lower wages and working conditions makes it more difficult for American unions to retain benefits already secured and to obtain improvements in them. American unions understand full well that benefits secured in their contracts are placed in jeopardy because of such competition from low-wage foreign nations. Hence, by strengthening the foreign labor movement, American unions not only improve the status of workers within foreign nations, but at the same time protect the advances which have been gained through collective bargaining in this country.

The second reason concerns the threat of communist domination of foreign labor movements and, through this tactic, the possible seizure of the governments of foreign nations by Communists. Even in the United States, as Chapter 2 has demonstrated, organized labor has been faced with such a threat, although in this country it has been successfully surmounted. The 1949–1950 expulsion from the CIO of the several communist-controlled unions, and the establishment of new unions to take over the membership of such unions, dealt a telling blow to the influence of communism in the American labor movement. The AFL, too, when it was the only federation in the nation, waged a continuous and bitter battle against the left and managed to maintain its basically conservative philosophy and objectives. Happily, there are today only a handful of American labor unions, all of them relatively minor in strategic power (for example, the Mine, Mill, and Smelter Workers and the Furriers Union) which are even remotely believed to be dominated by Communists. But the problem is much more severe in foreign lands: In such nations as Italy and France, communistic elements do have considerable influence in the affairs of the labor movements. And the important officers of American labor movement, well schooled in the potential consequences of communism, believe with considerable justification that should such totalitarianism spread to the governments of these countries the first casualties would be the free labor movement, collective bargaining, and the right to strike. For such reasons, the AFL–CIO works hard to help foreign trade unions remain free from communist domination.

Currently, the AFL–CIO participates in several international labor bodies. It is a particularly active member in both the International Confederation of Free Trade Unions and the International Labor Organization, and through these forums works with the trade unions of other free nations to promote the interests of workers throughout the world. The former organization is composed only of labor movements, while the ILO is tripartite in character and allows representation to each member government, employers, and workers.[7]

Beyond AFL–CIO participation in these labor bodies, the Federation and its affiliates contribute money to aid in the organization of foreign workers, the training of foreign labor leaders, the education of foreign union members, and the promotion of a variety of similar activities. In addition, the AFL–CIO has representation on various committees of the United Nations, hosts many visiting labor delegates from foreign nations who are sent both by their governments and by higher trade union bodies in their respective nations, and even on frequent occasions itself finances the trips of these foreign labor leaders. The AFL–CIO and many of its affiliated national unions have also financed trips of their *own* representatives to foreign lands to see at first hand the problems of other labor movements. Under the AFL–CIO constitution, the Federation's Committee on International Affairs is charged with the responsibility of coordinating and implementing such activities.

---

[7]When the ILO convenes annually, each member nation is allowed four voting delegates, of whom two are representatives of the government, one of the employers, and one of workers. The American delegation is composed of two representatives from the Department of Labor, one selected by employer associations, and one chosen by the AFL–CIO.

Conflict between craft and industrial unions

If the main benefit associated with Federation membership is protection against raiding, one of the most important problems of the AFL–CIO is that of maintaining peace between affiliated unions in their jurisdictional disputes over jobs. Frequently, craft and industrial unions battle each other avidly over such jurisdiction, particularly in establishments where an industrial union holds bargaining rights but where there are jobs which could be carried out in a more efficient fashion by members of a craft union. Such jobs as those involving the routine maintenance of machinery or other equipment, the major overhaul or installation of equipment, and the construction of new facilities often fall into this category.

What could spark a conflict is the desire of members of craft unions whose members are *not* employees of the industrial company to do the work which is being performed by the skilled tradesmen on the payroll of the factory. At times, employers find it cheaper to hire these outside craftsmen to perform the work and therefore seek out contractor–employers who control such skilled employees. Upon other occasions, a skilled trade union, through an employer–contractor, makes overtures to the industrial employer. However, the problem could also arise from the other direction. That is, the industrial employer may have customarily subcontracted out certain maintenance work to outside skilled tradesmen. To secure this work for its own membership, the industrial union which holds bargaining rights in the factory puts pressure upon the employer to cease this practice and to award the work to his own employees who are, of course, members of the industrial union. It is not difficult to understand that when jobs are scarce, the conflict between craft and industrial unions can achieve major dimensions.

Indeed, the problem became so serious in the recession-marked first months of the 1960's that many observers predicted the imminent collapse of the entire Federation through craft–industrial warfare. In the fall of 1961, the *Wall Street Journal* carried this headline: "Craft, Industrial Union Fights Grow, Threaten an End to AFL–CIO; Factions Battle Over Rights to Jobs"; and delegates to the AFL–CIO convention of December, 1961, met under the most ominous of conditions.

Remarkably, however, the important leaders of the craft and industrial unions were able to arrive at a workable solution to the problem at the convention and thereby rescue the Federation from such a collapse. They adopted an "Internal Disputes Plan," often also referred to as the "Live and Let Live" plan, and incorporated it in the constitution of the AFL–CIO. More technically, the constitutional amendment officially preserved the integrity of past practices in work assignments.

Henceforth a union's right to jobs would depend on what relevant customs or practices had been in force where it sought such jobs. If the members of an industrial union had held jurisdiction over new construction in the past, this customary work assignment would be respected by craft unions. If an employer had customarily subcontracted out maintenance work, *this* practice was to be respected by industrial unions, who were not to put pressure upon employers to change the practice.

An elaborate procedure has been adopted to implement this new constitutional provision. In the event that a union charges that another union is violating the terms of the new policy, the AFL–CIO assigns a Federation official to mediate the dispute. If this effort fails, an arbitrator is appointed to make an award. Once the arbitrator hands down his decision, the rival union is expected to abide by the award. However, the losing union has the right to appeal to a three-man sub-committee of the AFL–CIO Executive Council. This subcommittee may disallow the appeal, in which event the decision of the arbitrator is final and there is no other appeal procedure. But if the subcommittee is not fully satisfied with the arbitrator's award, it may refer the case to the entire Executive Council, which will decide the issue by majority vote. The Council may uphold the arbitrator's award, reverse it, or modify it. In any event, however, the decision of the Executive Council is final and binding on the unions involved in the dispute.

If a union fails to comply with the decision rendered through this procedure, the amendment to the constitution provides that the Federation may impose sanctions (described below) on the noncomplying union, and if the violation persists, the union can be expelled from the Federation.

Thus far, the plan has worked successfully and the threat to the Federation no longer exists. In June, 1965, the AFL–CIO announced that from January 1, 1962 through May, 1965, a total of 397 cases had been filed under the Internal Disputes Plan. Of these, the Federation had been successful in settling more than 60 per cent through mediation, averting the need for arbitration. Arbitrators had handed down decisions in 130 other cases, and twelve more were at that time pending before arbitrators. Of the 130 decisions, the arbitrators had determined that there was a violation of the plan in ninety-six cases. There had been, in addition, forty-two appeals to the Executive Council subcommittee from the arbitration decisions—of which thirty-six were denied, one was withdrawn, two were referred to the Executive Council, and three were pending on the date of the report.

With respect to noncompliance with the decisions of the arbitrators, the AFL–CIO reported that in twenty-six instances unions had charged that other unions had not honored the awards: Compliance was ultimately achieved in thirteen of these instances, continuing noncompliance found in eight, four were withdrawn, and one case was pending. No union has been expelled from the Federation for noncompliance, but the Federation has imposed sanctions on six nationals: the Railroad Signalmen of America, the International Typographical Union, the Switchmen's Union, the Journeymen Stonecutters, the National Maritime Union, and the Air Line Pilots Association. When sanctions are imposed upon a union under the terms of the Plan, it may not file charges under the Plan to protest that another union is violating customary job jurisdictions, the Federation will publicly give notice of the union's noncompliance, and the AFL–CIO can deny to such noncomplying union its services and facilities.

With the craft–industrial conflict now having so visibly diminished, it appears that the AFL–CIO will continue to exist as a permanent federation in the United States. At this writing, it is over ten years old and the old antagonisms of the former members and officers of the AFL and CIO have largely subsided. It is safe to conclude that the Federation can overcome future problems, such as the election of new AFL–CIO officers, without falling apart. Moreover, union leaders understand that the collapse of the Federation would seriously impair the future of organized labor in this nation. They understand that they had better "hang together" or they will hang separately. Indeed, the collapse of the Federation would undoubtedly cause incessant raiding and jurisdictional strikes. Very probably, it would also result in some re-emergence of labor violence, a further decline of union membership, a possible resurgence of corruption, and other effects which would adversely affect not only unions and their members, but also employers and the general public. From the point of view of stability in industrial relations, the preservation of the AFL–CIO is a public necessity.

The National Union

Relationship to locals

If the national union is quite autonomous in the conduct of its affairs, the story is quite different when one examines the relationship between the national union and its local unions. Though there are many exceptions, most national unions exercise considerable power over their locals. Before a local union may strike, it must normally obtain the permission of the national union. And, should the local strike in defiance of national union instructions, the national union can withhold strike benefits, refuse to give the local union any other form of aid during the strike, and in extreme cases even take over the local on a trusteeship basis. In addition, consistent with the regulations of many national unions, all local collective bargaining contracts must be reviewed by the national officers before they may be put into force. All national union constitutions today contain provisions which establish standards of conduct and procedures for the internal operation of their constituent locals—usually, the dues which the latter may charge, the method in which local union officers may be elected and their tenures of office, the procedures for the discipline of local union members, the conduct of union meetings, and other rules of this kind.

Violation of these national union standards can result in sanctions placed upon the local union officers, and on the local union itself. Recently, for example, many national unions have been at least as conscious of the problem of racial discrimination within the union movement as has the AFL–CIO, and most national constitutions now contain a non-discriminatory clause, designed to guarantee Negroes equal and fair treatment from the local unions. Several local unions have been seized by their nationals when they have discriminated against Negroes through such mechanisms as providing segregated local union facilities (such as washrooms and drinking facilities), or when they have failed to afford Negroes equal protection in the negotiation of labor agreements or in the grievance procedure.

In addition, within the collective bargaining process the national union is currently exercising considerably greater control and influence over the contracts which locals negotiate. This is particularly true when the members of the locals work for companies which sell their products in national product markets—an ever-increasing number. Nationals desire that companies over whose employees they have jurisdiction and which compete in national product markets operate under common labor-cost standards. They are less likely to exercise control over the unions whose members produce for local markets. This latter situation holds, for example, in the construction industry because the labor costs involved in the construction of a building in one city do not directly compete with those affecting the construction of a building in another.

Service in collective bargaining

The national exercises much of its influence over the local in the direct collective bargaining process through the service which the national union provides its locals in the negotiation of the labor agreements. To understand this national–local relationship, however, one should not regard the negotiation service of the national union as a function which is performed against the will of the local union. On the contrary, local unions not only generally desire and expect the help of the national union when they negotiate labor agreements with the employer, but should the national union either refuse to provide these services or perform them in an ineffective way the local union members and their officers can be counted upon to be sharply critical of the national union. The officers of the national could safely assume, in fact, that such a disgruntled local union would attempt to take political reprisal against the officers of the national in the next election of national officers.

The chief reason for the local union's desire for help from the national union in collective bargaining involves the complexities of the contemporary collective bargaining process. As will be made more evident in future chapters, many of the issues of collective bargaining have become increasingly intricate. Most contemporary collective bargaining contracts focus upon such involved items as adjustment to automation, pension plans, insurance programs, supplementary unemployment benefit plans, job evaluation, production standards, time and motion studies, and complicated wage incentive programs. Beyond the complex character of the contemporary issues, moreover, the modern collective bargaining process is obviously made more difficult because of the character of the law of labor relations. In short, it takes an expert to negotiate under current circumstances.

For effective representation, it is necessary to find people who are knowledgeable, experienced, and have a professional understanding of the collective bargaining process, and few local unions are fortunate enough to include such people in their membership. Each local union elects a negotiating committee, but the members of such committees are typically employed in the plant and work full time on their jobs. They simply do not have the opportunity to keep abreast of current developments in collective bargaining and to make a searching study of the problems involved in the negotiation of the difficult issues. On the company side, moreover, there are normally management representatives who are well trained and equipped to handle the contemporary collective bargaining negotiation. Many of them have received special training in labor relations, and some devote full time to the problems of negotiation and administration of collective bargaining contracts.

Indeed, without the services of the national union there would be a sharp disparity of negotiating talent at the bargaining table. In this light, it is easy to understand why the local union does not regard the intervention of the national union at the bargaining table as an invasion of the rights of the local, but rather views this service as indispensable to the effective negotiation of the labor agreement.

Most national unions have well-qualified people to render this service:

the so-called staff representatives, who devote full time to union affairs. They are hired by the national union, paid salaries and expenses for their work, and expected to provide services to the local unions of the national. All of them are union members, and normally reach their position of staff representative by having demonstrated their ability as union members and local union officers. They are not, however, elected to their jobs, but are hired because of their special talents.

Although the staff representatives perform a variety of duties, such as organizing new plants, engaging in political action work at times of federal and state elections, directing strikes, and representing the union and its members before the federal and state labor agencies, helping the local unions to negotiate labor agreements constitutes one of their primary functions.[8] Staff representatives gain much bargaining experience because they normally service several local unions and in the course of one year they may be called upon to negotiate many different labor agreements, thus gaining on-the-job training which serves as an invaluable asset to them when they confront a specific management at the bargaining table. Many national unions also send their staff representatives to special schools, some of which are held on university campuses and are taught by specialists in the labor education field, for additional training. Moreover, the staff representative is invariably backed up by experts within the national union. Almost every national union has several departments which concentrate on the major issues involved in collective bargaining. For example, the United Automobile Workers has departments which deal respectively with pensions, wage systems, insurance, and other critical areas. The specialists assigned to these national departments may be freely called upon by the staff representatives should their services be needed.

The regional or district office

Staff representatives may work out of the headquarters of the national union, but more frequently they are assigned to a regional or district office. Almost every national union divides the nation into regions or districts, and locals of the national union which are located in the geographical area or the district obtain services from their respective district offices. For example, District 30 of the United Steelworkers of America, headquartered in Indianapolis, covers most of Indiana and Kentucky and is administered by a district director elected by the local unions of the district. About twenty staff representatives are assigned

---

[8] A major exception to all these remarks involves craft unions in local-product market industries: Here local business agents are normally elected to perform such duties.

by the national union to District 30, and work under the immediate supervision of the district director.

Each staff representative services about seven local unions. He attends the local union meetings, works closely with the negotiating committees, hears the problems of the workers in the plant in which the local holds control, and attempts to understand the values and objectives of the members. He is the liaison between the national union and his local union, and in this capacity can do much to influence the local in the acceptance of national union collective bargaining policies. In such a capacity, moreover, the staff representative can serve as a mediator between local unions and the national when differences arise between them.

A good staff representative wins the confidence of local officers and members, and the local union will thus rely heavily upon his counsel in collective bargaining matters. He can exert great influence upon the local to reject or accept the last offer of an employer. Indeed, frequently he can provoke a strike or terminate one by the way in which he reports to the local union and makes recommendations to the members. He is, in short, often in an excellent position to influence the decision-making process in collective bargaining.

Multi-employer bargaining

Although most multi-employer bargaining is in relatively small bargaining units in local-product markets, at times national unions bargain with employers on a multi-employer basis. That is, a group of companies band together and negotiate with the *national* union as a unit. Employers find this structure of collective bargaining valuable because it prevents a given union from "whipsawing" each employer: Usually under a multi-employer bargaining structure, each employer is comparatively small in size and unimpressive in financial resources, and the companies compete fiercely in the product market; in the absence of multi-employer collective bargaining, the union could pick off one employer at a time. Such employer association–national union collective bargaining is found in industries such as clothing, coal, and shipping—all of which contain large measures of the unstabilizing factors noted.

When multi-employer collective bargaining exists and where the product market is not a local one, the national officers themselves typically bargain for the contract and the local unions play a comparatively passive role—a situation which also holds at the other extreme, when unions bargain with the industrial giants of the nation (such as General Motors and United States Steel). The national unions negotiate the agreement in the latter instance since no one local union could possibly measure up to the strength of these companies. Bargaining logic dictates that in both cases the national union rather than the local union play the paramount labor relations role.

Additional national union services

Beyond providing considerable help in the negotiating of labor agreements, the national union renders other valuable services to its local unions. The national usually awards benefits to employees on strike, although the actual amount of money paid in strike benefits is usually very minimal—about $20–$40 per week to each member, on the average. More important, the national union intervenes with the strikers' creditors so that the automobiles, furniture, and other holdings of the union members will not be repossessed. And it ensures that no striking employee or his family goes hungry even if this guarantee involves the actual distribution of food to the strikers. Management should be aware that unions in these days do not lose strikes because of hunger or unpaid bills. If there are insurance premiums to be paid, doctors to see, rent to be paid, or school tuition to be met, the national unions will see to it that the worker does not suffer. This is true despite the obvious fact that the national unions themselves have financial limitations, for virtually all nationals do under normal circumstances have the resources to assure that the minimum physiological needs of their member–workers are met, and many larger unions are quite amply financed: The Automobile Workers, for example, poured out more than $12,000,000 during the six-year 1954–1960 Kohler strike to aid the members of the local engaged in that conflict. In addition, if a national union does run out of money, labor custom dictates that other national unions will lend it money to finance the strike.

The national union also aids the locals in the grievance procedure and in arbitration, both of which subjects will be discussed in detail in Chapter 6. Normally, the staff representative represents the local in the last step of the grievance procedure. Along with the local union grievance committee, he attempts to settle the grievance to the satisfaction of the complaining worker and if the case does ultimately go to arbitration, he usually directly represents the grievant. In general, whether they win or lose their arbitration cases, staff representatives present the union's case very effectively. This fact is often offered by labor leaders as one reason why unions employ lawyers less frequently than do employers when cases go to arbitration. There is no need to incur the expense if the staff representative can do the job as competently as an attorney.

Of course, at times local unions *are* in need of attorneys, as when the local union has a case which requires testimony in the courts. For example, employers may sue a union for breach of contract, or workers may be indicted because of violence in picketing. When attorneys are needed, the local union can normally obtain the services of the national union's legal staff, whose members, although invariably paid less than comparable lawyers who work for corporations, are frequently highly competent and usually quite dedicated to the union movement. Several attorneys, Clarence Darrow and Arthur Goldberg most notably, made their mark by representing labor organizations.

The fact that the local does so readily receive such services from its national constitutes the reason why the vast majority of local unions belong to a national union. Indeed, less than 2 per cent of all locals are not affiliated with a national, and all these "independents" (except for the relative handful of them belonging directly to the AFL–CIO and thus enabled to make use of the Federation's services) must rely upon their own resources, whereas the many local unions which *do* belong to nationals can use the considerable resources of the latter.

Other functions of the national union

Although national union officers and staff representatives devote the major share of their time to providing services to the local unions, the range of the national union's activities includes many other important functions. Today, the major concern of all unions is that of increasing membership in the face of the relative plateau and absolute decline of the past few years. To check the decline, responsible labor union officials understand that the unorganized must be organized, and the chief burden for this also falls to the national union staff representatives. Although the AFL–CIO does do some organizational work, it does not have the staff to perform this function effectively; nor can the responsibility for the organization of new plants be undertaken by local union officers or members. At times, local union people help in organizational drives, but because they are full-time employees, they do not have much opportunity to carry out this function.

Accordingly, the catalyst for new organization falls to the staff representatives of the national unions, upon whom constant pressure is exerted to organize nonunion plants. Indeed, in some national unions not only the advancement but even the continued job tenure of the staff representative is determined by his success in organizing such plants.

The task is hardly an easy one. Most nonunion employers can be counted upon to wage a fierce fight against organization. Many employees who are not members of unions do not want a labor union because management provides them with many of the benefits which they would receive if organized. And the staff representative's organizing mission becomes even more difficult if he attempts to organize in the South or in small communities regardless of sectional location. In any event, the representative must make contacts among the workers, convince them of the value of unions, and dispel notions that unions are corrupt, communistic, or otherwise undesirable institutions. Many workers are ready to believe the worst about organized labor, and staff representatives often admit that these conceptions are difficult to erase.

The staff man is thus forced to use his imagination to the fullest. He may initially attempt to organize "from inside," through the informal leaders in the plant. Then he may visit workers in their homes, distribute leaflets, and arrange organizational meetings (which frequently are poorly attended). Subsequently he must counteract whatever management does to block the organizational attempt: Even in today's more enlightened atmosphere, some employers warn employees of dire consequences should they organize, tell their employees that unions exist only to collect dues for the personal benefit of the union "bosses," and —the organizing tactic laws cited in chapter 3 notwithstanding—on occasion even threaten workers with loss of their jobs if a union is established, as well as promise them benefits if they reject the union.

There are other formidable obstacles for the organizer. If the plant is located in a comparatively small community, there may be a concerted attempt among the leaders of the community to keep the union out. The target employer may have good friends who run the newspaper, the radio and TV station, the Chamber of Commerce, and the local stores, and these power centers may join forces to do what they can to keep the union from gaining a foothold. Indeed, it is not uncommon that the clergy in a town is enlisted in the fight against the union.

The organizational mission of the staff representative is thus a highly challenging one. In recent years, he probably has had more failures than successful ventures. But he is typically persistent and this tenaciousness occasionally reaps its rewards: Illustratively, a large company located in Kokomo, Indiana, was organized in January, 1965, after the Steelworkers' Union, which carried out the organizational campaign, had been defeated in three different NLRB elections over a span of thirteen years!

Another major function of the national union concerns political action, although national unions differ widely in the vigor which they display in this regard. Some, like the Automobile Workers, are constantly engaged in politics; others, like the United Brotherhood of Carpenters, seldom exert much effort to influence elections and the subsequent actions of elected officials. Undoubtedly, however, a larger number of national unions are concerned with political affairs today than were in the past. As has already been noted, their leaders understand that the success of the union depends in large measure upon the fashioning of a favorable legal climate for new organization and for the implementation of traditional trade union weapons when conflicts arise with employers. Moreover, a growing number of national unions share the belief of AFL–CIO leaders that the political programs of organized labor in the areas of social security, medicine, low-cost public housing, full employment, and the like are in the best interests of the nation as a whole.

When the national union officers are politically motivated, they are normally aggressive in exerting pressure upon the local unions and their members to take an active role in political affairs. Their union newspapers (each national union publishes at least one monthly newspaper) are filled with political news, voting records of the candidates, and the union point of view when elections are impending. National unions also arrange political rallies, purchase radio and television time to get the national's story across to the members and the public, and issue a barrage of political leaflets and pamphlets. In some national unions, during the weeks before important elections, the staff representatives are ordered to suspend collective bargaining negotiations, grievance meetings, and arbitrations and devote their full time to political work. Given the fact that each national union employs many staff representatives—in such large unions as the Automobile Workers and Steelworkers, the numbers run into the hundreds—this serves as an important advantage; and if the staff representatives are adroit and hard-working, the favored political candidate can benefit greatly from such support.

Depending upon their sizes and leadership policies, national unions perform other functions. Some arrange educational programs for their staff representatives and local union officers. Most of the courses in these programs deal exclusively with the practical aspects of labor relations— how to bargain labor agreements, the best way to handle grievances, and the like. At times, however, the courses deal with foreign affairs, taxation, economics, government, and other subjects which are not directly related to the bread-and-butter issues of trade unionism. In addition, some national unions administer vacation resorts for their members, award university scholarships to children of members, organize tours to foreign nations, conduct publicity campaigns to acquaint union members and the public in general with the purpose of the union label, and sponsor a variety of social functions which are similar to those maintained by the state and city labor bodies but more tailored to the specific interests and aptitudes of the particular national union members.

Government of the national union

When a national union is formed, a constitution is adopted which spells out the internal government and procedures of the union. Virtually every constitution provides that a convention should be held, and designates this convention as the supreme authority of the union. Under the rules of most national unions, each local union sends delegates to the convention, with the number of delegates permitted to each local being dependent upon the local's paid-up membership totals. Hence, as in the case of the AFL–CIO, the larger locals are more influential than are the smaller units. Within the UAW, for example, the locals range in size from somewhat over 60,000 (the local union representing Ford Motor Company workers at Ford's River Rouge plant) to a literal handful of members in some locals which have contracts with small employers.

Ordinarily, the chief officers of the local unions are elected as delegates, though in the very large locals which have the opportunity to send many delegates rank-and-file members are chosen because the quota cannot be filled by the officers alone. Being sent to a convention represents a plum to the delegates chosen. National conventions, again as the AFL–CIO conventions themselves, are usually held in large and attractive cities; when the delegates lose time in the plant because of their election, the local union normally pays their lost wages; and the convention may last as much as a week or so, allowing a welcome relief from the tedium of working in the plant. Many delegates take their wives and children, so that, along with the business of the convention, selection to the convention may thus become a sort of work-play affair; however, the expenses involved are such that small local unions with limited funds sometimes do not send delegates to the convention even though they are entitled to do so.

Although under the terms of the Landrum–Griffin Act the delegates must be chosen by secret ballot and under an otherwise equitable procedure, the officers of the nationals themselves may be selected in either of two ways. In about three-fourths of the national unions, the constitution requires that the principal officers (president, vice-president, and secretary–treasurer) must be elected by the convention. In the others, the officers are elected by a direct referendum wherein each member of the union may cast a ballot. Some of the largest unions in the nation follow the latter procedure, including the United Steelworkers of America, the Amalgamated Clothing Workers, and the International Association of Machinists, but even among the larger unions most utilize the convention election system.

In addition to the election of chief officers, the convention transacts the business of the national union. Reports and recommendations of the officers are heard, and the delegates have an opportunity to deliberate them and decide whether or not to adopt them. Problems of the various locals are aired, and this provides an excellent opportunity for an exchange of ideas and experiences and for otherwise breaking down the provincialism of the local unions: Delegates from a large local union located in Chicago can learn of the problems of a small local in a small southern community, for example. The convention also permits local union officers to display themselves to their best advantage. Most local union officers would like to rise in the union hierarchy, and the convention offers a testing ground for their talents. A rousing speech by a local union president may attract the attention of the delegates, and the consensus may be "here is a fellow we should watch."

The actual business of the convention may be initiated either by the national officers or by the delegates. Decision making takes the form of resolutions, proposals, and reports on which the delegates vote. As in any large convention, the officers have a distinct advantage in this respect, since the president appoints the committees which bring important issues before the delegates and is in a position to select members for these committees whom he knows are favorable to the national officers' point of view. On the other hand, a determined local union or even individual delegates who feel strongly about their cause can bring to the attention of the convention a resolution, recommendation, or even an amendment to the constitution. There is a limit, in fact, to how far any national president can go in bottling up the resentment of determined delegates. And, particularly if a delegation from a local can enlist the support of delegates from other locals, there is an excellent chance that the entire convention will hear its point of view. For all the authority and control which the nationals exert over the locals, if national officers gain the enmity of a sufficient number of local unions, the delegates of these locals can band together and cause an upheaval at the convention. And, if the issues are of extreme importance, the resentment of these locals could result in a change in national union leadership. Thus, the local unions do have a political check against their national officers. There is a line which the latter can cross only at the risk of losing their jobs.

In short, as long as the national union holds regularly scheduled conventions, the democratic process has an opportunity of working. The convention provides the forum wherein the policies, behavior, and competency of the national union officers can be evaluated, and the key to the democratic operation of a national union therefore lies in the regularity with which conventions are held. More than one-half of the national unions hold conventions either annually or biennially, and most of the rest hold them every three or four years. A small number of national unions, however, simply do not hold conventions at all, and this clearly eliminates almost entirely any practical opportunity for the local unions to participate in the government of their unions. As Seidman has stated, "Since the ultimate authority within the national union is its convention, it is essential that such assemblages be held regularly and frequently, and that they be organized so as to maximize opportunity for democratic control."[9] Nothing in the Landrum–Griffin law, however, requires unions to hold regular and reasonably frequent conventions. The law does require that the union membership be afforded the opportunity to elect its national officers at least every five years, but a union managed by autocrats can legally avoid the holding of conventions indefinitely.

National union officers

The chief of the national union is, of course, its president. He administers the organization with the assistance of such other major officers as the vice-president (or vice-presidents), secretary–treasurer, and members of the executive board. The latter group is composed ordinarily of the district or regional directors (who, in some national unions, are also called vice-presidents), and its members have a variety of official tasks: enforcing the constitution of the national, implementing its policies, filling a national officer's position when vacant, voting on important matters referred to it by the president, placing items on the agenda for deliberation and voting, and a host of related duties. Normally, the executive board of a national union meets regularly and frequently according to the provisions of a constitution, and on occasion also meets at the call of the president to deal with some pressing problem. Since the members of the executive board are from all over the nation and have direct supervision of the locals in their particular districts, the board mechanism provides an excellent way for the national union officers to learn of the problems of all locals throughout the country. Likewise, it provides a channel for communicating policies of the national union to the national union's locals and membership.

In some unions, however, executive boards merely rubber-stamp decisions of the national officers. This is true most often when a president, either by union custom or because of his particular personality, is allowed to exercise autocratic leadership. It is safe to say, however, that in most unions the executive board directs the affairs of the union and establishes the union's basic policies, which the president is then obliged to carry out. In one recent notable exception to this situation, the

[9]M. S. Estey, P. Taft and M. Wagner, eds., *Regulating Union Government*, (New York: Harper & Row, Publishers, 1964), p. 12.

United Steelworkers' executive board, composed of all the district directors of that union, appeared to many members not to have much power in running the affairs of the union in the early 1960's, president David J. McDonald himself retaining it. McDonald was, however, defeated in his 1965 re-election attempt, and the perceived power imbalance has often been cited as one major reason for his ouster. The new Steelworker president, I. W. Abel, has taken pains to alter this image and to encourage the executive board to participate more fully in policy-making decisions.

A responsible, devoted, and active national union president has a difficult job. One day he may be negotiating a contract with a major corporation. The next day he is apt to be speaking at an important meeting of his union, or to the members of some other labor organization. He is also, typically, obligated to: testify before congressional committees, preside over the union's executive board meetings, travel to foreign nations as a participant in international labor organization bodies, take an active role in important national political elections, constantly put pressure upon the staff representatives to organize non-union plants, mollify companies which are disgruntled because of wildcat strikes or other forms of unauthorized union behavior, and perform a variety of other duties which may either be of major importance or strictly routine in character but which also take up his time. Indeed, the management of even a small or medium-sized national union is a difficult one; the job becomes immensely more complicated and difficult the larger the union.

The union president, moreover, is constantly torn between duties of a pressing character. In many cases, he must make the hard decision by himself and hope that the decision is the right one. As any chief executive, he bears the ultimate responsibility for the organization's efficient, honest, and prudent management. Above all, he must satisfy the membership, and at times this is a much more difficult job than dealing with management.

For the discharge of all these duties, national union presidents are moderately paid. In 1963, according to the United States Department of Labor, the average salary of national union presidents was about $25,000 per year, although this amount was normally supplemented by the payment of expenses incurred while on union business. Before the passage of the Landrum–Griffin Act, some national officers, such as Dave Beck of the Teamsters, copiously bought items of a personal nature and charged them to the union. However, the vast number of national officers are scrupulously honest in their expenses, and some, like Walter Reuther, almost to a fault. Reuther refuses to charge his union with telephone calls which are not totally related to union business, and even absorbs such costs as the pressing of his suit and kindred personal items while he is *on* union business. Reuther's salary, as president of the UAW (a union of more than 1,000,000 members, and thousands of locals) amounted to only $24,040 in a recent year, with chargeable expenses totalling an additional $4,439. Clearly, a corporation president managing a business of comparable size would be paid hundreds of thousands of dollars. Indeed, there are even a few college professors who earn $24,000!

Of course, workers pay the national officers' salaries, and the employee who earns $5,000 or less annually may look at the salary of his national president as being exorbitant. Rather than being too high, however, the verdict of the outside observer must be that the typical national union chief executive is underpaid. When measured by the number of members, the number of locals, and his duties, even the $100,000 salary of the Teamsters Union national president (the highest-paid union official in the nation) does not seem unreasonable.

Though modestly paid, the national union president wants to keep his job. He has power, prestige, and plays an important role in our society. Many presidents do indeed remain in office for considerable lengths of time and some of them stay in the chief executive chair for so long that memory does not recall another president. William Hutcheson was president of the Carpenters for 42 years; John L. Lewis of the Mine Workers for 40 years; Daniel Tobin of the Teamsters for 37 years; and James C. Petrillo of the Musicians gave up his job only when he grew so old and feeble that it is doubtful that he had the strength to play his instrument. A trend, however, may be developing to change this situation. With the demands on the national officers becoming ever more formidable, particularly in the field of new organization, some unions are duplicating the practice of business and requiring compulsory retirement at a certain age. In 1964, the UAW constitution was amended to require the retirement of that union's national officers at 65. Rather than work against compulsory retirement, the national officers of the UAW—including president Reuther, who was 57 years old when this amendment was passed—vigorously upheld the measure, as did Emil Mazey, the union's secretary–treasurer, who declared that "some of the board members of some of the unions, when they have a board meeting, they look like a collection of a wax museum."[10] UAW actions have frequently influenced the practices of other unions, and the 65-year compulsory retirement implementation, the first to be effected by a major international, may very well set a pattern which many other unions will follow.

[10] *Wall Street Journal* (March 26, 1964) , p. 8.

There is little doubt that unions need vigorous, young, and dynamic leadership to cope with the problems of modern union affairs. Too many union leaders look with nostalgia at the past, and cherish their previous contributions to the union movement, rather than being concerned with their abilities to make future contributions. The election defeats of several union presidents in the past few years—including James Carey of the International Union of Electrical Workers, as well as McDonald and other leaders—perhaps reflect a growing restlessness among union members and a renewed emphasis on union democracy, and thus the possibility that the period of near-lifetime tenure for many national officers may now be ending.

Still, the problem exists, and the median age and years of service of national union officers remain considerable—about 63 years of age and 25 years of service. It is not difficult to explain why national union officers stay in office for so many years. Once in office, incumbent officials possess sufficient power to minimize centralized opposition and to make it extremely difficult for new candidates to present themselves to the membership in an effective manner. The point has been made that when conventions are not held regularly and frequently, it is difficult for a new face to get much backing. In addition, staff representatives are hired by the national union, and can be removed at the pleasure of the national officers. It would take rare courage for a paid representative to oppose the incumbent president and the tendency is, in fact, understandably in the other direction. In addition, most incumbent presidents get personal mileage out of their union newspapers. The editor of the national union newspaper is also a hired person, and subject to control of the national officers. Any upstart candidate could not expect much favorable publicity, if indeed he received any publicity at all, in the union press.

In short, the incumbent national officers have a political machine which tends to perpetuate them in office. However, it would be incorrect to believe that this is the only reason for long tenure of office. Sophisticated union members understand that frequent changes of national union officers and open displays of factionalism weaken the position of the union against management in collective bargaining. Beyond this, a national union officer may have genuinely earned re-election to office over the years because he has been doing a good job for the membership. A national union president who is devoted, honest, courageous, and competent does not need a political machine to be re-elected. Many national union officers fall within this category and representatives of management should not regard national union officers as incompetent people who hold office only because of political machination.

The Local Union

Where the people are

Although we leave for the last an analysis of the character and functions of the local union, it does not follow that the local union is the least important of the labor bodies in the union movement. On the contrary, it could be argued successfully that for the individual union member the local union is the most important unit of all. In a sense, the federation, the national union and its district organizations, and the other labor bodies discussed previously are administrative and service organizations. Although they are vitally important and carry out a variety of significant activities, as we have seen, no union member really "belongs" to such larger bodies. Unionists are members of these organizations only by reason of their membership in a local union, are geographically close only to the latter organization, and largely condition their loyalty toward an image of the total labor movement by what they perceive to transpire within the confines of the local union. Many union members do not, indeed, even know the names of their national and federation officers, but they do know their local union president, business agent, and stewards. They know the latter officials because they see them in the plant, and because these are the people who handle the union member's day-to-day problems.

Local union officers

Although some locals are formed before the employer is organized, a local union typically comes into existence when there is organization of an employer. After it has organized and secured bargaining rights a local typically applies for and receives a national union charter. This document establishes the local's affiliation with the national union, entitles the local to the services of the latter, and by the same token subjects the local to the rules and discipline of the national union. Depending upon the unit of organization, a local union may be confined to a single plant, several plants of a single company, or may include workers of a single craft, such as electricians who perform their duties in a given geographic area.

Once the local is established, the members, in accordance with their bylaws (which are usually specified in the national union constitution), elect their officers—typically a president, vice-president, secretary-treasurer and several lesser officials. Since such election procedures almost invariably allow direct participation by all union members, the local union officers are elected on a much more democratic basis than are those chosen to lead the national union. Moreover, the union member knows much more from first-hand experience about the local union candidates for office than he does about the national union officers. The vast majority of local union officers, in fact, work in the plant along with the other union members and are under constant and often highly critical observation by the latter. Both democracy and a far higher turnover rate for local officers than for the union's national officials also stem from the fact that the local union officer, unlike the national union president, has little if any patronage to dispense. He does not have a paid staff as does his national counterpart. Nor, generally speaking, can he make use of any other powers of patronage or the purse, since neither exist in any measure.

In general, the local union officers work without pay. In only the large local unions are such officers reimbursed for their work, and even then, their salaries tend to approximate the wages that they would have earned from their companies. And in the relatively infrequent instances when the local union president and secretary-treasurer do receive some small compensation for their duties even when they are full-time employees in the plant, the amount of money is comparatively small when measured against the duties which they perform.[11] For example, in Bloomington, Indiana, one local's secretary-treasurer receives $500 per year for taking care of the books, making financial reports, answering all correspondence, and assuming a volume of other miscellaneous duties. The size of his job is measured by the fact that the local has over 3,000 members, and by the union's requirement that all his duties must be conducted on his own time.

A fair question, then, is why union members desire to acquire and retain local union officer jobs. Despite their nominal or totally nonexistent financial rewards, they must perform a variety of duties and assume considerable responsibility and they are constantly being pressured by the membership under whose direct surveillance they labor. The question is not an easy one to answer, since the motivations are obviously different with different people. A leading reason, however, is that the local union officers acquire prestige and status in the company and in the community. Virtually all people desire recognition once lower needs have been relatively well satisfied, and the attainment of a local officer's job accomplishes this objective for some workers.

Another reason may involve the local union officer's devotion and

---

[11] A few, considerably more notable, exceptions involve the heads of some craft unions operating in local-product markets. Some such officers in Chicago, for example, have salaries which approximate (and in a few instances even exceed) Reuther's, as well as impressive offices and staffs of full-time business agents.

dedication to the union movement. If he really believes in unions, he has the opportunity of making the movement work by carrying out his duties in an honest and effective manner. Still other union members may genuinely court the competitive character which is associated with the office: The local union officers deal with the company on a day-to-day basis, and many of the dealings regularly involve what some workers view as "the struggle" with management. Finally, the reason may be a political one involving the future of the local union officer in his national union. As stated, national union officers are elected officers, and staff representatives are union members who are hired by the national union. Thus, to go up the ladder, the union member must normally start at the local union level: A local union officer's job is commonly the first step in the long and hard pull toward the top. The large majority of all current national union officers and staff representatives have held a local union officer's job at some earlier period of their career.

Functions of the local union: relations with management

The duties of local union officers are dependent, of course, upon the functions of the particular local union, but unless contracts are negotiated on a multi-employer basis or with a very large corporation, local union officers directly negotiate the labor agreement with the employer. If the national union staff representative often aids the local in carrying out this function and usually plays a highly visible role in the process, the fact remains that the local union officers who also are involved in the negotiations are directly responsible to the members of the local union. The staff representative, a hired hand, does not face political defeat if he exercises poor judgment or fails to negotiate a contract that the membership feels is suitable. Should a contract, however, hurt the local union members, it is very likely that in the next election the local union officers will be changed. Because of its local character, factionalism in the local is, in fact, a constant problem. It is comparatively easy for a dynamic, aggressive, and ambitious newcomer to use a poor contract as a weapon to dislodge an incumbent officer.

Another important function of the local is that of negotiating grievances. Indeed, most of the union's time is devoted to this task: The labor agreement is negotiated only periodically, but, through the grievance procedure, it must be administered every day. To this end, each local union has a number of stewards—usually one steward to a department of the company, elected by the union members of that department—who serve as administrative personnel.

In most plants, the members also elect a chief steward, to be chairman of the grievance committee. At the lower steps of the grievance procedure, the worker's complaint is handled by the departmental steward and normally the local union president or chief steward does not enter the picture until the grievance has reached the higher levels. But at the last step of the grievance procedure, the local union president and the union grievance committee (composed of the chief steward and several other stewards) will negotiate the grievance, typically with the staff representative of the national union also being present. Moreover, if a grievance goes to arbitration, the local union president and the union committee will attend the hearing and although at this forum the national staff representative usually presents the union's case, he depends heavily upon the local union officers and the committee for the data which he will present to the arbitrator.

It is difficult to overestimate the vital importance of the effective use of the grievance procedure as a function of the local union. Indeed, to the union member who has a grievance, the handling of his grievance means more to him than what the union secured in the collective bargaining agreement. This is particularly true when the grievant complains against a discharge, or against an alleged company violation of an important working condition.

In this capacity, however, the local union officers are also vulnerable. Take, for example, a grievance which, though important to the employee, does not have merit. If the local union president tells this to the union member, he risks offending a constituent. And if this happens frequently and with many different workers, the union members can demonstrate their resentment in the next election. This appears completely unfair and senseless, but it is what the local union officers have to contend with, and explains why local union officers frequently take up grievances that do not have merit.

At times, too, the local officers are forced to deal with "borderline" grievances, complaints which may or may not have merit but which for a variety of reasons the local union officers cannot persuade the company to grant. Often, the local does not want to risk losing the grievance in arbitration. It therefore refuses to handle the grievance, and the job now is to pacify the employee who may have some justification for being resentful—not an easy mission when the grievance deals with an important issue and has some basis under the labor agreement. Consequently, the local officials may change their minds and *take* such grievances into arbitration, hoping for the best: If the arbitrator denies the grievance, the local union officers can always use the arbitrator as the scapegoat. However, in spite of an effective presentation at the arbitration hearing, the disgruntled union member may still blame his officers. It is said that victory has many fathers, but defeat is an orphan. Fortunately, unions win their share of grievances in the grievance procedure and in arbitration, and in his campaign before the next election, the local union officer can point with pride to his successes and minimize or explain away his defeats.

Judicial procedures

Another function of the local union is that of disciplining union members who are alleged to have violated union rules. As does every organization, unions have standards with which members must comply. These standards are incorporated in the national union's constitution and are duplicated in the local union's bylaws. If a union member violates any of these rules, he may be disciplined by the local union membership in the form of a reprimand, a fine, suspension, and in extreme cases, expulsion from the union.

Commonly proscribed standards of conduct which frequently merit expulsion include the promotion of dual unionism (when a union member seeks to take the local out of one national union and place it in another—true treason in unionism!) ; participating in an unauthorized or "wildcat" strike; misappropriating union funds; strikebreaking; refusing to picket; sending the union membership list to unauthorized persons; circulating false and malicious reports about union officers; and providing secret and confidential information to the employer. Under the official rules of some unions, a member may also be expelled because of membership in a communistic, fascistic, or other totalitarian group. We may quarrel with the justice or fairness of one or more of these rules, but the fact remains that they must be obeyed since they have been adopted by the union at large. From the union point of view, each of them pertains to an important area of conduct.

The procedures which are used at the local level to enforce the rules of the union differ widely, but the following would probably reflect most local union procedures. Any union member may file charges against any other member, including the local union officers. When this occurs, the president has the authority to appoint a so-called "trial committee," composed of union members belonging to the local in question and normally including officers, stewards, and rank-and-file members who take an active role in the affairs of the union. The trial committee has the job of investigating the complaint, holding a hearing if it believes that the charge has substance, and reaching a decision which it will ultimately present to the entire local union body for final determination. To protect against a political situation within the local wherein favorites of the local union officers, or the local union officers themselves, may not be brought to account for a violation, the union members initiating the charge may appeal to the national union. Thus, a "not guilty" verdict, the dismissal of charges by the local union officers, or the pigeonholing of complaints does not necessarily end the disciplinary process.

After its investigation of the charges, the local union's trial committee holds a hearing at which the accused member is present. He may select another union member to act as his spokesman. As in most other private or semiprivate organizations, the union member may not hire a lawyer to defend him while the case is being processed within the union, but witnesses are called, and cross-examination is permitted. And, although no oath is administered for the same reason (since the hearing is not in a court of law), union members who deliberately lie or who grossly misrepresent the facts may themselves be charged with a violation. After the hearing, the trial committee reports its decision and the reasons for the verdict to the local union membership. At this point, the membership may adopt, reject, or modify the committee's decision. At times, the trial is in effect reheld before the local membership, since some members might desire to review the evidence that the trial committee used to arrive at its decision.

If the decision is "not guilty," the member or members who filed the charge may appeal to the executive board of the national union. By the same token, when the decision of the local goes against the charged union member, he may appeal to the national union and, under the provisions of virtually every constitution, the member can also ultimately appeal the decision of the national union officers to the national convention.

On the surface, this judicial procedure appears fair and calculated to protect the accused union member. It would seem that he receives a full and fair hearing, and gains further protection through provisions for the right of appeal. In practice, however, there have been several instances of serious abuses of the local union judicial procedure, although with more than 77,000 locals to consider it is absolutely impossible to make any kind of accurate judgment of the relative extent to which the abuse has existed and any opinion is sheer speculation.

It was because of such union actions, however, that the Landrum–Griffin Act specified that no member could be disciplined, fined, or expelled without having first received a written list of charges, a reasonable time to prepare his defense, and a full and fair hearing. Today, if these legal standards are violated, a union member may bring suit in the federal courts for relief. Under the law, the union member may not go to court before he attempts to get his case settled through union procedures, although to check dilatory union tactics the law also specifies that if the internal procedure consumes longer than four months, the union member need not exhaust the internal remedies of the union before going to court.

In 1957, the United Automobile Workers dealt with the problem of abuse in the disciplinary procedure in a more unique manner. It established a "Public Review Board," composed of seven citizens of respected reputation and impeccable integrity, and having no other relationship with the union. Usually, such men have been members of the clergy, the judiciary, or university faculties, and the Board's membership has in the past included such outstanding names as Clark Kerr, president of the University of California, the late Professor Edwin E. Witte of the University of Wisconsin, the late Rabbi Morris Adler of Detroit, Bishop G. Bromley Oxnam of Washington, D.C., and Msgr. George G. Higgins, Director of the Social Action Department of the National Catholic Welfare Conference. Under the amendment to the UAW constitution which established the plan, the president of the national union selects the Board members, subject to the approval of the national union's executive board and ratification by the national convention. Among other duties, this watchdog committee may reverse the decision of the executive board of the national union which has upheld the discipline of a union member, and experience has shown that the Board has been quite willing to reverse the national union's executive board on the relatively few occasions when it has believed that such a reversal was justified. To date, however, only the Upholsterers International Union has followed the pattern of the UAW. If each national union were to establish such an agency, and if each agency were allowed the same freedom to act which has been granted the UAW Public Review Board, there would clearly be less need for legislation to protect the status of union members.

Political activities

Although the AFL–CIO and national union officers and staff representatives play an effective role in lobbying and in supporting candidates in their campaigns for political office, it can be argued with much justification that the political efficiency of the union movement depends above all upon the vigor of the local. After all, the number of the Federation and national officers and staff representatives is very small in comparison with the number of local union members. And much of the legwork during the national and state elections must necessarily be performed by local union members if it is to be performed at all on any large scale. Indeed, the success of the union movement in "rewarding its friends and punishing its enemies" depends in large measure on the willingness of local union officers and members to engage in politics.

Nonetheless, the degree with which local unions participate in politics often is determined by the basic philosophy of the national union. If the national union officers do not want their union to engage in politics, or merely go through the motions of indicating such a preference, the local unions of the nationals will reflect this kind of leadership. On the other hand, when the national union officers do take an active role in the political affairs of the nation, the local unions typically respond by placing a major emphasis on such political action of their own. However, even when the national unions do cajole their locals into taking this active role in politics, the members themselves may or may not follow the instructions of the national union officers, and the national's efforts must consequently be geared in two directions: toward the local leadership and toward the local membership.

If a constant problem of the national union which is politically inclined is thus to motivate the locals to follow its example, even within the ranks of such unions as the UAW (perhaps the most active national in the political arena) there are many dozens of local unions which either refuse to participate or participate in a lackadaisical way. Locals of less politically conscious nationals often show even greater reluctance. Moreover, just because the AFL–CIO leadership or a national union president supports a candidate for elective office, this does not mean that every union member will vote that way. Some may not vote at all, of course, and postelection analyses of union member districts show that many others vote for the opposite candidate. There is no permanent "labor vote,' as is sometimes claimed by people who view the political participation of the union movement as an evil.

Indeed, as long as we maintain secret elections, even the most homogeneous groups in the nation can never rest assured that their members or followers will vote as the organization urges them to. And if members of the most closely-knit of unions do not lockstep to the polls and vote in accordance with the recommendations of their leadership, members of less cohesive labor groups are often significantly divided in their election choices.

Our society is, moreover, pluralistic in character, and its countless pressure groups have their own favored candidates. Each group has the right and, indeed, the obligation to participate in the election process. This is the hallmark and the dynamics of a democratic society wherein each group seeks the votes of its members and that of the public. And, under such a system of checks and balances, any one group or organization is prevented from dominating the political life of the nation.

A union member may be a good trade unionist and support with vigor his union's collective bargaining policies and its strikes. He may enthusiastically take his place on the picket line. However, when he casts his ballot for the President of the United States, a senator, congressman, governor, and other political candidates, the vote which he casts will reflect his political heritage and his interpretation of the political situation at the time. The union member shares in common with his counterparts in a myriad of other groups the fact that he is not isolated from the multitude of pleas for his vote, arising from countless organizations and sources of political information. The daily press, radio and television, the political candidate, the worker's traditional political affiliation, and many more factors will influence his vote, and his labor organization is only one of many factors that are involved in his political determination at election time.

Nonetheless, a local union which takes an active role in politics can be of great help to a favored candidate and, in a close election, the support can tip the scales in his favor. The local union will encourage each member to register and to cast his ballot at election time. Prior to the election, it will do all in its power to "educate" the union member as to how to vote, through publications, meetings, house-to-house visits, and other forms of active political activity. In addition, the local union may legally make expenditures from union dues for such purposes as the holding of meetings of a political character and the publication and distribution of politically inspired newspapers and leaflets, although (as stated earlier) only money which is raised on a voluntary basis from the membership can be contributed directly to persons running for political office.

Other functions and problems

Beyond the major functions discussed above, local unions at times engage in a variety of social, educational, and community activities. Of late, as in the case of higher labor bodies, the last area has become increasingly important. Union leaders realize that the welfare of their members depends in part on a progressive and well-run community. How the schools are run, for example, is of vital interest to the local unionist who must pay taxes to operate the schools and who may have children attending the schools. As in the case of city labor bodies, representation of local union officials on United Fund Committees, Red Cross drives, and similar endeavors is also increasing in frequency. Moreover, unions recognize that the public image of organized labor, which has beeen tarnished in recent years, tends to improve to the extent that unions engage in such community services. Labor's various forms of participation in community service programs demonstrate that union members are not only collectively a socially oriented group, but also are individually responsible and interested citizens of the community. Likewise, the integration of unions in community work tends to lessen the tensions between management and organized labor. If a union leader can work effectively with the management representatives on the school board or in the Community Chest drive there is a better chance for harmonious labor relations in the plant.

Many local unions also conduct regularly sponsored and generally effective educational programs for the benefit of their local union officers and stewards. As noted previously, the need for these programs arises primarily from the complexity of the contemporary labor-management relationship, but it also stems to a great extent from the brisk turnover of the local union officers and stewards. Some of the programs are sponsored by the national unions, though in many cases the local itself arranges the educational program. Indeed, no union is considered "modern" today unless it has devised a well-planned educational program for its leadership. Such educational programs frequently bring to the surface workers of talent and high native intelligence. Through education, the latter not only are capable of doing a better job for their membership and acting more responsibly and rationally at the bargaining table, but education tends to make them more useful citizens. Of at least as much practical interest to many workers, union members who acquire such measures of education tend to rise more rapidly to important jobs at both the local and national levels.

One of the most important problems of the local is that of interesting the membership in attending regular monthly meetings of the union. Attendance at these meetings is frequently very poor, and the problem is not easy to solve. The vast number of union leaders sincerely want their members to turn out at the meeting. They believe that the union has nothing to hide, and that by regular attendance and discussion at meetings, the members become more active, tend to be more devoted, and in general allow the local to deal with both employers and representatives of the public from a considerably stronger position than would otherwise be the case. The fact remains, however, that union members normally stay away from their meetings in droves; for the regular monthly meetings, only about 5 to 10 per cent of the membership turns out (even a smaller percentage is common enough, especially in large locals) ; and one wonders why there has been so much said about union democracy when the union member himself does not seem sufficiently interested to participate in the affairs of his own union. When unions are poorly managed, when corruption exists, when leadership is second-rate, the fault essentially is that of the union member who does not care enough to attend the regular union meeting.

Thus, although from the days of the earliest unions, labor organizations have undertaken a variety of measures (ranging from more convenient hours to the incorporation of social activities into the meeting schedule) to encourage attendance, in 150 years unions have not found the solution to the problem of worker apathy toward attendance at meetings and there is every likelihood that it will persist in the future. The only notable exception involves meetings at which a strike vote is scheduled to be taken. In general, the union members will turn out at this time because this issue of striking or working is, of course, of crucial importance.

Despite poor attendance at the regular monthly meetings, management should not interpret this situation as meaning that in crisis situations the members will not support their union. In time of a showdown, the typical union member will actively support his union, and consequently a management which makes a decision to chance a strike solely on the grounds of poor attendance at union meetings makes a very unwise choice. The members invariably will rally to the union's cause when there are issues involved which vitally affect their welfare, no matter how little interest they have demonstrated in the day-to-day operation of their local at more peaceful times.

Union Finances

As do all other organizations, the union makes many expenditures and must meet its financial obligations. Chief expenditures of unions include the payment of salaries for their full-time officers and staff representatives, travel expenses, clerical help, office equipment and supplies, telephones, telegrams, postage, arbitration fees, and rent or mortgage payments for office space and the union hall. Beyond this, the strike fund must be built up to pay strike benefits when needed.

At times, people are impressed by the relatively large amounts that unions collect in dues and initiation fees, but forget that the union dispenses formidable amounts of money to meet its bills. Professor Lester estimates that the annual income of American unions from all sources amounts to about two billion dollars,[12] most of this sum being accounted for by the regular monthly dues paid by each member, but with additional sources of income stemming from initiation fees, special assessments, and earnings from investments. To be sure, two billion dollars looks like a lot of money, but when one considers the net worth of unions a more accurate picture is gained. Bloom and Northrup, who have estimated that in 1963 the net worth of all national unions in the

[12]Richard A. Lester, *Economics of Labor* (New York: The Macmillan Company, 1964), p. 175.

United States amounted to $645,431,794, have hastened to point out that "despite the enormous size of union funds, they do not approximate the wealth of corporations. The net assets of the six largest American corporations are in billions, those of the six largest unions in millions. . . ."[13] And however staggering a total the two billion dollars collected as income by unions each year may seem, it should also be remembered that a single corporation in the United States, General Motors, annually earns more than half of this amount in profits after taxes.

In general, the dues paid by union members holding semiskilled and unskilled jobs in manufacturing are less than those paid by members who work in the skilled trades. The obvious reason for this is that electricians, plumbers, carpenters, and kindred skilled employees earn higher wages than do employees whose jobs require lesser skill levels. A substantial majority of union members are probably now paying dues of $4 or $5 per month, although in 1963 Peterson could report that 26 per cent of all locals had at that time dues of less than $3, and nearly 20 per cent had dues of $5 or more. These latter were "almost without exception, . . . relatively small unions composed of highly skilled craftsmen."[14] With respect to initiation fees, about 70 per cent of new members paid in 1963 less than $25 in this form and of this 70 per cent, the majority paid less than $10. Only 8 per cent of union members (primarily in the building trades, airline pilot profession and similarly highly remunerated groupings) were charged more than $100 in initiation fees by their labor organizations.[15]

In the light of all that has been said about the functions of unions, the amount of money which the typical member pays is thus comparatively small. Nonetheless, like everyone else, the union member desires maximum and ever-improving services for the least cost possible. Indeed, union leadership must be very careful when it seeks to raise the monthly dues. Even a modest increase of fifty cents per month could cause an upheaval among the membership. With increasing expenses and frequently declining memberships, unions *must* at times raise dues if they desire to maintain the same level of services to their membership, but this is a step which is normally taken only as an extreme last resort. Illustratively, during one period of declining union membership, the UAW laid off many staff representatives and otherwise tried to curb expenses drastically before requesting a modest dues increase.

13G. F. Bloom and H. R. Northrup, *Economics of Labor Relations* (Homewood, Ill.: Richard D. Irwin, Inc., 1965) , p. 129.

14Florence Peterson, *American Labor Unions*, 2nd rev. ed. (New York: Harper & Row, Publishers, 1963) , p. 96.

15*Ibid.*, p. 95.

A Concluding Word

These pages have demonstrated how the American labor movement is structured and organized to carry out its objectives. They have attempted to outline the functions of the component parts of the movement, and the interrelationships of these functions within the union structure. We have also been concerned with the major duties and problems of union officers and staff representatives, the procedures of internal union government, and the underpinnings of the theory that union members have the ultimate control of their labor organizations—however much in practice union *leadership* has been the catalyst of the policies, programs, and operation of the union.

To be sure, the American labor movement is vast and complicated, but by this time the student should have a firm understanding of the logic of its behavior, structure, and government. Labor's elements fit together in a systematic fashion and provide the framework for the carrying out of the basic functions and objectives of the union movement.

In a day of increasing union dependence upon the sentiments of the general public, particularly as these sentiments are translated into legislative actions, these objectives have increasingly encompassed social and community activities which clearly extend well beyond labor's traditional campaigns for improved "property rights" on the job itself. These more broadly-based endeavors can in no way be expected to diminish in the years ahead, for the advantages for the labor movement which can potentially be derived from them are certain to continue.

Yet this newer emphasis should not obscure either the pronounced strain of "bread-and-butter" unionism which has marked organized labor throughout its history or the internal union political considerations which continue to generate this more basic behavior. If unions are, by and large, not democratic, they are nonetheless highly political in nature. The union leader must above all be conscious of the general wishes of his constituents. And these wishes, particularly at the lower levels of the union structure where the collective bargaining process itself takes place, continue to be closely related to wages, hours, and conditions.

Just as internal political considerations have dictated national union autonomy within the AFL–CIO, so too have such considerations led to the complete responsibility of virtually all national union executives to at least the most pressing desires of local unionists and to such commonly observed phenomena as the high turnover rates of local officers themselves.

It has often been said that a union "is a political animal operating in an economic framework." No one who loses sight of this most fundamental labor relations factor can truly appreciate union behavior.

DISCUSSION QUESTIONS

1. J. B. S. Hardman has described labor organizations as being "part army and part debating society." What considerations on his part might have led to this description?
2. It has been argued in many nonlabor quarters that it is socially undesirable for unions to take the initiative in organizational campaigns and that the public interest is served only when unorganized workers initially seek out the union. Is there anything to be said for this point of view? Against it?
3. "There are both advantages and disadvantages to AFL–CIO affiliation for national unions." Comment.
4. "The increasing sophistication and enlightenment of modern top business executives in dealing with their subordinates has led to a state of affairs wherein managements today are more democratic than unions." Do you agree? Why or not not?
5. "Unions are no less private institutions than country clubs or Masonic lodges and, as such, should be no more subject to government regulation of their *internal* affairs than these other organizations." The present thrust of the laws notwithstanding, is there any validity to this argument?
6. Albert Rees has pointed out that it is "paradoxically true that the presence of strong unions may improve the operation of democratic processes in the general national or state government even if the internal political processes of the nation are undemocratic." Explain this paradox.
7. Daniel Bell, the former labor editor of Fortune magazine, once commented that in taking over certain power from management, "The union also takes over the difficult function of specifying the priorities of demands—and in so doing, it not only relieves management of many political headaches but becomes a buffer between management and rank-and-file resentments." Is there any justification for such a comment?

SELECTED REFERENCES

Barbash, Jack, *Labor's Grass Roots.* New York: Harper & Row, Publishers, 1961.

———, *Labor Unions in Action.* New York: Harper & Row, Publishers, 1948.

Estey, Marten S., Philip Taft, and Martin Wagner, eds., *Regulating Union Government.* New York: Harper & Row, Publishers, 1964.

Ginzberg, Eli, *The Labor Leader.* New York: The Macmillan Company, 1948.

Hoxie, Robert F., *Trade Unionism in the United States.* New York: Appleton-Century-Crofts, 1921.

Lester, Richard A., *As Unions Mature.* Princeton, N. J.: Princeton University Press, 1958.

Perlman, Mark, *Labor Union Theories in America.* Evanston, Ill.: Row, Peterson, 1958.

Peterson, Florence, *American Labor Unions,* 2nd rev. ed. New York: Harper & Row, Publishers, 1963.

Sultan, Paul E., *The Disenchanted Unionist.* New York: Harper & Row, Publishers, 1963.

Taft, Philip, *The Structure and Government of Labor Unions.* Cambridge, Mass.: Harvard University Press, 1954.

part three

COLLECTIVE BARGAINING

However much specific unions may differ in their exact structures, governments, and general operations, virtually all labor organizations share at least the same primary objective. Whatever in the way of concrete demands may be sought from the employer, the union's major goal is to negotiate with him a written agreement covering both employment conditions and the union-management relationship itself on terms which are "acceptable" to the union. But the employer, too, must be able to "live with" these terms, and it is because of this second requirement that bargaining sessions almost unavoidably contain stresses and strains: More for one party—not only in the economic areas of the contract but, as will be seen, in many of the so-called "institutional" and "administrative" areas—all but invariably means less for the other. Moreover, the labor-management tensions are *recurrent* in their nature, since contracts are regularly renegotiated—most commonly today every one, two, or three years. *No* contractual issue can thus ever be said to have been "permanently" resolved.

There is always a certain glamor to any

5

At the bargaining table

interorganizational bargaining situation, particularly when such conflicts as the above can be anticipated. Labor-management negotiations constitute no exception to this rule, and, indeed, the process of arriving at a labor relations agreement has been viewed in a number of rather colorful ways.

Dunlop and Healy,[1] for example, point out that the labor contract negotiation process has been depicted as: (1) a poker game, with the largest pots going to those who combine deception, bluff, and luck or ability to come up with a strong hand on the occasions on which they are challenged or "seen" by the other side; (2) an exercise in power politics, with the relative strengths of the parties being decisive; and (3) a debating society, marked by both rhetoric and name calling. They also note that what men do at the union-management bargaining table has, at other times, been caricatured in a somewhat less dramatic way—as (4) a "rational process," with both sides remaining completely flexible and willing to be persuaded only when all of the facts have been dispassionately presented.

In practice, it is likely that *all* these characteristics have marked most negotiations over a period of time. Occasionally, indeed, one such description seems to be extremely apt. Some bargaining sessions within the automobile industry have had all the attributes of the poker game, except that the "losers" and "winners" have not been quite as easily identifiable. No one present at negotiations between the Teamsters and representatives of the over-the-road trucking companies can fail to be impressed by the influence of the relatively far greater economic strength of the union. There are those who see a parallel between bargaining in the men's clothing industry and debating society activities. And the General Electric Company prides itself on its firm resolution to "let the facts govern," although its major union strongly disagrees that G.E. does in fact adhere to this policy.[2]

---

[1]John T. Dunlop and James J. Healy, *Collective Bargaining*, rev. ed. (Homewood, Ill.: Richard D. Irwin, Inc., 1955), p. 53.

[2]Since the late 1940's, G.E. has religiously pursued a policy of: (1) preparing for negotiations by effecting what company representatives describe as "the steady accumulation of all facts available on matters likely to be discussed"; (2) modifying this information only on the basis of "any additional or different facts" it is made aware of, either by the union or from other sources, during the negotiations (as well as before them); (3) offering, at an "appropriate time" during the bargaining, "what the facts from all sources seem to indicate that we should"; and (4) changing this offer only if confronted "with new facts." A major further part of this policy, known as Boulwarism after former G.E. Vice-President of Public and Employee Relations Lemuel R. Boulware, involves constant company communication to both its employees and the general citizenry of the various General Electric communities, on the progress of the negotiations as these evolve. G.E.'s primary union—the International Union of Electrical Workers—has attacked the policy on legal grounds, and in December, 1964, the NLRB held the company guilty of bad-faith bargaining in its 1960 negotiations with the IUE, but the ultimate legality of Boulwarism must await the results of G.E.'s appeal of this Board decision to the courts.

Nor, since bargaining will *always* by its very nature pit the conflicting interests of the two parties against each other, is there any reason to expect any of these factors to die out. The increasing "maturity" of collective bargaining implies enlargement of the rational process, but it is doubtful that there can ever be such a thing as complete escape from the other elements.

Moreover, a number of *additional* factors, will also, almost inevitably, have a bearing upon the conduct of the negotiations. Items such as the objectives of the parties, the personalities and training of the negotiators, the history of labor relations between the union and management, the size of the bargaining unit, and the economic environment operate to influence the character of collective bargaining negotiations.

Some negotiators try to bluff or outsmart the other side. Other negotiators would never even think of employing such tactics. Some company or union representatives try to dictate a labor contract on a unilateral basis—"take it or else"—but most bargainers recognize that such an approach is ultimately self-defeating. In most instances unions presenting their original proposals will demand much more than they actually intend to get and companies' first counterproposals are usually much lower than the managements are actually prepared to offer. In other situations, however, companies and unions do not engage in these practices to any appreciable extent and original proposals and counterproposals are relatively realistic. Representatives of companies and labor organizations differ in training, preparation, education, experience, personality, concept and standard of equity, and labor relations philosophy.

There are still other sources of variation. In some negotiations, the predominant feature might be union factionalism; in others, disagreement between management officials concerning objectives and policies. The history of labor relations in one situation might reveal that each side has had implicit faith in the other. In other negotiations, because of past experience, the bargaining might be conducted in a climate of mutual distrust, suspicion, and even hatred. Certainly, if the objective of the parties is to find a solution to their mutual problems on the basis of rationality and fairness, the negotiations will be conducted in an atmosphere quite different from one in which the fundamental objective of the union is to "put management in its place," or where the chief objective of the company is to weaken or even destroy the union. All these factors, as well as others, will have a profound influence upon the conduct of collective bargaining negotiations.

Two other preliminary remarks are in order. First, because so many variables do have a bearing upon the negotiations, a portion of the following discussion highlights some procedural practices that might help to reduce friction between companies and unions, to minimize the possibility of strikes, and to promote better labor relations. Nonetheless, *if* labor relations in a company have been harmonious in the past, and if collective bargaining negotiations have been conducted with a minimum of discord, there is little reason to change procedures. "Let sleeping dogs lie" is a sound principle of collective bargaining negotiations. These observations should be kept in mind throughout the following discussion.

Secondly, there has been a marked change in the general atmosphere of negotiations in relatively recent years. Perhaps twenty-five years ago the typical collective bargaining session involved a tussle between table-pounding, uninformed, and generally ill-equipped people. Possibly the side that came out better was the one whose representatives shouted the louder or could use overt power threats more effectively. And conceivably the typical negotiation was a matter of each side's taking the adamant position of "take it or else."

At present, however, collective bargaining is most commonly an orderly process in which employee, employer, and union problems are discussed relatively rationally and settled more or less on the basis of facts. There is less and less place in modern collective bargaining sessions for emotionalism, name calling, table pounding, and the like. Not many negotiators use trickery; distortion, misrepresentation, and deceit are not dominant characteristics of the modern bargaining session. Advantages gained through such devices are temporary, and the side which sinks to such low levels of behavior can expect the same from the other party. Such tactics will merely serve to produce bad labor relations and to encourage the possibility of industrial strife. Certainly, one objective of collective bargaining sessions should be the promotion of rational and harmonious relations between employers and unions. To achieve this state of affairs, persons to whom negotiations are entrusted should have the traits of patience, trustworthiness, friendliness, integrity, and fairness. If each party recognizes the possibility that it may be mistaken and the other side right, a long stride will be taken in the achievement of successful collective bargaining relations.

Preparation for Negotiations

By far the major prerequisite for modern collective bargaining sessions is preparation for the negotiations. Both sides normally start to prepare for the bargaining table long before the current contract is scheduled to expire, and in recent years the time allotted to such planning has steadily lengthened. Six months or even a year for this purpose has become increasingly observable in both union and management quarters.

The now general recognition of the need for greater preparation time rests on the previously cited fact that the contents of the "typical" labor agreement have undergone a major transformation in the comparatively recent past. In recognizing and attempting to accommodate new goals of the parties, contracts have become steadily more complex in the issues which they treat.

Take, for example, wage clauses—which have appeared in almost all contracts since the days of the earliest unions. Today they make anything but easy reading. Where once such clauses noted the schedule of wages (generally the same for all workers within extremely broad occupational categories) and the hours to be worked for these wages, and usually said little more than this, over the past relatively few years they have become both far lengthier and considerably more complicated. Today subsections relating to labor-grade job classifications, rate ranges, pay steps within labor grades, differentials for undesirable types of work, pay guarantees for employees who are asked to report to work when no work is available for them, and a host of other subjects are commonplace in contracts. Moreover, most of these subsections spell out their methods of operation in detail.

Nor can the question of hours any longer be cavalierly disposed of. The extension of premium pay for work on undesirable shifts, holidays, Saturdays, and Sundays has increased the room for further bargaining In addition, the contract must resolve the question of remuneration for hours worked in excess of a "standard" day or week: All nonexempted workers in interstate commerce today by law receive time and one-half pay after forty hours in a single week, but an increasing number of contracts have more liberal arrangements from the worker's viewpoint. And having opened *these* issues to the bargaining process, the parties must now anticipate a whole Pandora's box of further but related issues. Do workers qualify for the Sunday premium when they have not previously worked the full weekly schedule? Where employees are normally required for continuous operations or are otherwise regularly needed for weekend work (firemen, maintenance men, and watchmen in certain operations, for example) can they collect overtime for work beyond the standard week? The bargainers on both the labor and management side must prepare their answers, and their defenses of these answers, to such questions and many similar ones: all may reasonably be expected to arise during the actual bargaining. And this necessity for anticipation is no less true merely because a *previous* contract has dealt with these matters, for each party can count on the other's lodging requests for *modifications* of the old terms in the negotiations.

The same can be said concerning the wide range of employee benefits, from paid vacations to pension plans, which have increased dramatically over the past two decades. This benefit list promises to become even lengthier. Job insecurity in an age of automation should lead to increased income security devices. Collectively bargained profit-sharing and allied gain-sharing plans have received some impetus from recent single-company developments at American Motors and Kaiser Steel, respectively —and may now, after years of achieving only a foothold in industry, realistically be expected to spread. But it is even more likely that the continuous liberalization in the existing benefits and the attendant costs and administrative complexities involved in all of them which have marked the histories of each since its original negotiation will continue. No one is better aware of this fact than the experienced labor relations negotiator.

Finally, increasingly thorny problems have arisen at the bargaining table regarding the so-called "administrative clauses" of the contract. These provisions deal with such issues as seniority rights, discipline, rest periods, work crew and work load sizes, and a host of similar subjects which vary in importance with the specific industry. All these topics involve, directly or indirectly, employment opportunities. As such, treatment of them has become ever more complicated in a competitive industrial world which pits a management drive for greater efficiency and flexibility against a commensurately accelerated union search for increased job security.

Fuller discussion of all these areas is reserved for Chapters 7 through 10. Even the cursory treatment offered here, however, offers ample evidence that bargaining the "typical" contract necessitates far more sophistication than in an earlier, less technical age. Labor agreements can no longer be reduced to the backs of envelopes, and ever more specialized subjects confront labor negotiators. Accordingly, the need for thorough and professional preparation well in advance of the bargaining is no longer seriously questioned by any alert union or management.

In today's increasingly data-conscious society, much general information can aid the parties in their advance planning. The United States Bureau of Labor Statistics is a prolific issuer of information relating to wage, employee benefit, and administrative clause practices—and not only on a national basis, but for many specific regions, industries, and cities. Many employer groups stand ready to furnish managers with current and past labor contracts involving the same union with which the latter will be bargaining, as well as other relevant knowledge. International unions perform the same kind of function for their local unions and other subsidiary units, where the bargaining will be on a subinternational basis. And, for both parties, there is also no shortage of facts emanating from such other sources as the Federal Reserve Board, the United States Department of Commerce, private research groups, and various state and local public agencies.

Each bargaining party may also find it advisable to procure and analyze information which is more *specifically* tailored to its needs in the forthcoming negotiations. Most larger unions and almost all major corporations today enlist their own research departments in the cause of such special data-gathering as the making of community wage surveys. On occasion, *outside* experts may also be recruited to make special studies for one of the parties: Much of the bargaining stance taken by the Maintenance of Way Employees in the late 1950's, for example, rested on a painstaking analysis of employment trends in that sector of railroading conducted at union expense by a highly respected University of Michigan professor. Many managements have also made major use of the research services of academicians and other outsiders on an *ad hoc* basis. In multi-employer bargaining situations, whether or not an official employers' association actually handles the negotiations, the same premium on authoritative investigation has become increasingly visible.

The list of uses to which such research can be put is literally endless. Depending upon its accuracy and stamp of authority, it can be used to support any stand from a company's avowal that certain pension concessions would make it "noncompetitive" to a union's demand for increased cost-of-living adjustments. The management may find support for a desired subcontracting clause in the revelation that the union has been willing to grant the same clause to other employers. The union may gain points in its argument for a larger wage increase by mustering the bright outlook for the industry which has been forecast by the Commerce Department. On the other hand, where poker, power, or debating traits mark the bargaining, and the "rational process" of appeal to facts counts for little, the whole effort may seem a fruitless one. Most frequently, however, negotiators who approach the bargaining table without sufficient factual ammunition to handle the growing complexities of labor relations operate at a distinct disadvantage: The burden of proof invariably lies with the party seeking contractual changes and, in the absence of facts, "proof" is hard to come by.

As painstaking a task as the fact accumulation process may seem to be, farsighted managements and labor leaders recognize that considerably *more* must be done to adequately prepare for bargaining.

Increasingly, the top echelons within both union and company circles have come to appreciate the necessity of carefully consulting with lower-level members of their respective operating organizations before framing specific bargaining table approaches. Superintendents, foremen, industrial engineers, union business agents, union stewards, and various other people may never become directly involved in the official negotiation sessions;[3] and the distance separating them from the top of the manage-

---

[3]This depends upon the scope of the negotiations, however. Where the bargaining is on the local level (as opposed to area wide, industrywide or nationwide bargaining), the business agent (for example) will very likely be an active union participant in the formal sessions. The same can be said for many management superintendents.

ment or union hierarchy is usually a great one. But the growing maturity of labor relations has brought with it a stronger recognition by the higher levels of both organizations that the success or failure of whatever agreement is finally bargained will always rest considerably upon the *acceptance* of the contract by such people. In addition, unless the official negotiators are well informed on *actual operating conditions* in advance of the bargaining, there is every chance that highly desirable modifications in the expiring agreement will be completely overlooked.

On the management side, since the daily routines of the operating subordinates require their close contact with the union, such men are in a position to provide the bargainers with several kinds of valuable information. They can be expected to have knowledgeable opinions as to what areas of the expiring contract have been most troublesome: They can, for example, provide an analysis not only of grievance statistics within their departments but of employee morale problems which may lie behind the official grievances which have been lodged. They presumably have some awareness as to existing pressures on the union leadership, and their knowledge of these political problems can help management to anticipate some of the forthcoming union demands. They may be able to assess how the union membership would react to various portions of the contemplated *management* demands.

Not to be dismissed lightly, either, is the fact that this process of consultation allows lower managers genuine grounds for feeling some sense of participation in at least establishing the framework for bargaining. The company thus stands to gain in terms of morale, as well as in information.

For the *union*, the need for thorough internal communication may be even more vital. The trend to centralization of bargaining in the hands of international unions has in no way lessened the need of the union officialdom to be responsive to rank-and-file sentiments. It has, however, made the job of *discovering* these sentiments, and incorporating them into a cohesive bargaining strategy, considerably harder; and "middlemen" within the union hierarchy must be relied upon to perform this assignment. Thus business agents, grievance committeemen, and other lower union officials can play a key role even where the negotiations themselves have passed upward to a higher union body, for only they are in a position to take the pulse of the rank and file.

The long list of widely varying and frequently inconsistent rank-and-file demands cannot, however, be passed upward to the international level without some adjustment. Most internationals screen these workers' proposals—inevitably giving more weight to those of important political leaders at the lower levels than to those stemming from totally uninfluential constituents—through committees composed of the subordinate officials at successively higher levels within the union hierarchy. Ultimately, a "final" union contract proposal may be placed before the memberships of each local or at least before representatives of these locals, for their official stamps of approval. And here again the support of lower union officialdom is vitally needed by the union negotiators— to rally rank-and-file support behind the finalized union demands, and to gain membership willingness to strike, if need be, in support of these demands. Aside from the fact that the local unionists may be as well equipped to help the negotiators plan their strategy as are their management counterparts, local leaders who have been bypassed in the consultation process do not typically make loyal supporters of the union's membership-rallying effort.

Finally, both legal and (on many occasions) public relations considerations now clearly demand a major place in preparation for bargaining. Specialists in both of these areas must be engaged and utilized by both sides to ensure that bargaining demands will be compatible with the labor statutes, and that public support (or, at the very least, public neutrality) will be forthcoming, if this is needed. The legal ramifications of present-day trucking contract negotiations, for example, have necessitated for the union the employment of a 400-man corps of lawyers who have become collectively known as the "Teamsters' Bar Association" and through whose high levels of remuneration Teamster president Hoffa could claim to have "doubled the average standard of living for all lawyers in the past few years," although the personal legal problems of Hoffa himself undoubtedly account for some of the high statistics. And for the importance of public relations to both parties in the railroad industry one need look no farther than to the myriad of full-page newspaper advertisements placed separately throughout the early 1960's by the railroad unions and managements to state their respective labor relations cases to the general citizenry in advance of the bargaining.

For both management and union, bargaining preparation also involves more mundane matters. Meeting places must be agreed upon and the times and lengths of the meetings must be decided. Ground rules regarding transcripts of the sessions, publicity releases, and even "personal demeanor" (a designation which in labor relations can deal with a spectrum extending from the use of profanity to appropriate attire for the negotiators) are sometimes drawn up. Payment of union representatives at the bargaining table who must take time off from work as paid employees of the company must also be resolved. Only on rare occasions have the parties reached a major prebargaining impasse on such issues as these, but where relations are already strained between union and management such joint decision-making can be a time-consuming and even an emotion-packed process.

The Bargaining Process: Early Stages

No manager who is prone to both ulcers and accepting verbal statements at face value belongs at the labor relations bargaining table. Negotiations often begin with the union representatives presenting a long list of demands in both the economic and noneconomic (for example, administrative clause) areas. To naïve managements many of these avowed labor goals seem, at best, unjustified and, at worst, to show a complete union disregard for the continued solvency of the employer. Although extreme demands such the appointment of union officers to the company's Board of Directors and free transportation in company cars to and from work for all employees are rarely taken seriously, the company negotiators may be asked for economic concessions which are well beyond those granted by competitors and noneconomic ones which exhibit a greater use of vivid imagination than that shown by the late William Faulkner.

The *experienced* management bargainer, however, takes considerable comfort in the fact that the union is, above all, the *political* animal which the previous chapter has depicted: There is no sense in the union leaders alienating constituents by throwing out untenable but "pet" demands of the rank and file (beyond what the various screening committees have been able to dislodge) when the company representatives stand fully ready to do this themselves and thus to accept the blame. This is particularly true when the pet union demands originate from influential constituents or key locals within the international: Alienation of such sources is a job for which the company representatives, not being subject to the election procedure, are better suited.

There are other logical explanations for the union's apparent unreasonableness. Excess demands allow leverage for trading some of them off in return for management concessions. In addition, the union can camouflage its true objectives in the maze of requests and thereby conceal its real position until the proper time—vital for any successful bargaining.

Beyond this, labor leaders have frequently sought novel demands with the knowledge that these will be totally unacceptable to managements in a given bargaining year, but with the goal of providing an opening wedge in a long-range campaign to win management over to the union's point of view. Only in this light can, for example, Walter P. Reuther's demand for supplementary unemployment benefits in the early 1950's be understood. Dunlop and Healy furnish further insight on the psychological ramifications involved, and also emphasize the increasing importance of the prebargaining research which was commented upon earlier in this chapter:

> . . . Neither side can ordinarily be expected to concede a new demand the first time it is presented. A new idea may initially produce only opposition from the other party. The demand will be less novel and appear less outrageous a year later. The other side may have had occasion to think it through and to consider administrative problems which need mutual exploration. Thus, a pension or a health and welfare proposal introduced by the union for the first time will ordinarily receive a cool reception. Management may need several years to consider types of plans, to gather data on the age distribution and health distribution of its work force, and to get used to considering this range of issues. New contract demands ordinarily require a period of gestation, and some demands are on the list to be seasoned.[4]

Finally, since contract negotiations frequently extend over a period of weeks (and, on occasion, months), the union can gain a buffer against economic and other environmental changes which may occur in the interval. Technically, either party can introduce new demands at any time prior to total agreement on a contract, but the large initial demand obviates this necessity.

There is thus a method in the union's apparent madness. Demands which seem to managements to be totally unjustified and even disdainful of the company's continued existence may, on occasion, be genuinely intended as union demands. Far more often, however, they are meant only as ploys in a logical bargaining strategy. They are to be listened to carefully, but not taken literally.

In fact, if imitation is the sincerest form of flattery, there is ample evidence that some managements have increasingly come to appreciate the strategic value of the large demand. Many company bargainers have, in recent years, engaged in such "blue-skying" in their counterproposals, and for many of the same reasons as the union (although other companies have adamantly refused to engage in this process and even at least partially accepted a G.E.-type approach).

As a result of the premium placed on exaggerated demands and equally unrealistic conterproposals, however, the positions of the parties throughout the early negotiation sessions are likely to remain far apart.

Standing in the way of early agreement, too, is the fact that these initial meetings are often attended by a wide variety of "invited guests," from the ranks of each organization. Given a large and interested

4John T. Dunlop and James J. Healy, *op. cit.*, p. 56.

audience of rank-and-file unionists, or a union negotiating committee which is so large as to be totally unable (and unexpected) to perform the bargaining function but is nonetheless highly advisable from a political point of view, the actual union bargainers sometimes find it hard to refrain from using creative but wholly extraneous showmanship. Management representatives, too, frequently succumb to a temptation to impress their visiting colleagues as to their negotiating "toughness." And when lawyers or other consultants are engaged by either party to participate in the bargaining sessions, the amount of acting is often also significantly expanded.

Even amid the theatrics and exaggerated stances of these early meetings, however, there is often a considerable amount of educational value for the bargainers. The excessive factors still do not preclude each party from evaluating at least the general position of the other side and from establishing weaknesses in the opposing position or arguments. Frequently, indeed, if negotiators are patient and observing at this point, they will be able to evaluate the other side's proposals along fairly precise qualitative lines. Thus, during the first few sessions when each side should be expected to state its position, it often can be discerned which demands or proposals are being made seriously and which, if any, are merely injected for bargaining position. Such information will be of great help later on in the negotiations.

Actually, the principle of timing in negotiations is very important. There are times for listening, speaking, standing firm, and conceding; there are times for making counterproposals, compromising, suggesting. At some points "horse-trading" is possible; at others, taking a final position is called for. There is a time for an illustration, a point, or a funny story to break ominous tension, and there is likewise a time for being deadly serious. Through experience and through awareness of the tactics of the other side, negotiators can make use of the time principle most effectively.

The Bargaining Process: Later Stages

After the initial sessions are terminated, each side should have a fairly good idea of the over-all climate of the negotiations. The company should now be in a position to determine what the union fundamentally is seeking, and the union should be able to recognize some basic objectives of management. In addition, by this time, each side should have fairly well in mind how far it will be prepared to go in the negotiations. Each party to the negotiations in secret internal sessions should establish with some degree of certainty the maximum concessions that it will be prepared to make, and the minimum levels that it will be willing to accept. Negotiators will be in a better position to bargain intelligently if certain objectives are formulated before the negotiations enter into the "give-and-take" stage. However, even at this time in the negotiations, it is not wise to take extreme positions, and to appear inflexible in the approach to the problems under discussion. Skilled negotiators who are striving to avoid a strike—and this is the attitude of the typical company and union—will remain flexible right down to the wire. It is not a good idea to climb too far out on a limb since at times it may be difficult, or at least embarrasing, to crawl back to avoid a work stoppage.

Indeed, after the original positions of the parties are stated and explained, skilled negotiators seldom take a rigid position. Rather than take a definite stand on a particular issue, experienced negotiators (often, where negotiation units are large, through the use of subcommittees to focus upon the major bargaining issues individually before these are dealt with at the main bargaining table) "throw something on the table for discussion and consideration." The process of attempting to create a pattern of agreement is then begun. In this process, areas of clear disagreement are narrowed whenever they can be, mutual concessions are offered and tentative agreements are effected. Counterproposals of companies and unions are frequently offered as something "to think about" rather than as the final words of the negotiators. In this manner, the parties are in a better position to feel one another out as to ultimate goals. By noting the reaction to a proposal thrown on the table for discussion, by evaluating the arguments and the attitudes in connection with it, a fairly accurate assessment can be made of the maximum and minimum levels of both sides.

Actually, flexibility is a sound principle to follow in negotiations because the ultimate settlement between companies and unions is frequently in the terms of "packages." Thus, through the process of counterproposals, compromise, and the like, the parties usually terminate the negotiations by agreeing to one package selected from a series of alternative possibilities of settlement. The package selected will represent most closely the maximum and minimum levels acceptable to each of the parties. The content of the various packages will be somewhat different because neither side in collective bargaining gets everything it wants out of a particular negotiation. By remaining flexible throughout the negotiation, certain patterns of settlement tend to be established over which the parties can deliberate.

The package approach to bargaining is particularly important in reference to economic issues. Once the parties obtain an agreement on a total cost-per-hour figure, it becomes a relatively uncomplicated task to allocate that figure in terms of basic wage rates, supplements to wages, wage inequities, and the like. The more difficult problem, of course, is to arrive at a total cost-per-hour figure. If, for example, through the process of bargaining, the parties established $.15 per hour as the level of agreement, the parties might finalize the money agreement in terms of a $.09-per-hour basic wage increase, $.02 per hour to correct any wage inequities, $.01 per hour to improve the insurance program and $.03 per hour to increase pensions. Other subdivisions of the $.15 would be possible depending upon the attitudes of the parties and their objectives in the negotiations.

Trading points and counterproposals

In establishing the content of the alternative packages, experienced negotiators employ a variety of bargaining techniques. Two of the most important are trading points and counterproposals. These procedures are best explained by illustrations.

Let us assume that management employs the *trading point* procedure. The first prerequisite in the use of this technique is to evaluate the demands of the union. Evaluation is necessary not only along quantitative lines, but also along the line of the "intensity factor," which requires an assessment of the union demands to determine which demands the union is most anxious to secure. Management representatives should make mental notes of these strongly demanded issues as the negotiations proceed. For example, after a few sessions it may become apparent that the union feels very strongly about securing the union shop. At the same time the labor organization also demands a $.10-per-hour wage increase and seven paid holidays. The use of the trading point technique in this situation may be as follows: Management agrees to the union shop but insists that in return for this concession the union accept a $.07-per-hour increase and six paid holidays.

Labor organizations also employ the trading point technique, as illustrated by the following example. Assume that, during the course of the negotiations, the union representatives sense that management will not concede to the union demand for a reduction of the basic work week from forty hours to thirty-six. Assume further that the union feels that the issue is not worth a strike. Under these circumstances the union may be able to employ the hours issue as a trading point. Let us say that, along with the hours demand, the union has insisted upon also securing a union shop and a $.10-per-hour increase in pay. After the union presses the hours issue vigorously for some time (the union as part of the strategy may, of course, threaten a strike over the issue), the union negotiators agree to withdraw the hours demand in return for obtaining the union shop and the wage increase.

Counterproposals are somewhat different from trading points. Counterproposals involve the compromise that takes place during the bargaining sessions. As a matter of fact, the use of counterproposals is one element which the National Labor Relations Board will consider to determine whether management and labor unions bargain in good faith. However, under the established rules of the Board, employers and unions do not have to make *concessions* to satisfy the legal requirement of bargaining in good faith: The implementers of public policy are more interested in whether or not there have been *compromises*. The union may request three weeks' vacation with pay for all employees. Management might counter by agreeing to two weeks' vacation with pay for employees with ten years of service and one week for the remainder. A union may demand a $.12-per-hour increase, and management may agree to an $.08 per hour increase. At times three or four counterproposals may be made before a final agreement is reached on an issue of collective bargaining.

The Bargaining Process: Final Stages

There is almost no limit to the ingenuity which skilled negotiators use in attempting to create an agreement pattern. At more sophisticated bargaining tables, even highly subtle modes of communication may do the trick, while at the same time allowing the party making a concession to suffer no prejudice for having "given in." Stevens, for example, points out that

> In some situations, silence may convey a concession. This may be the case, for example, if a negotiator who has frequently and firmly rejected a proposal simply maintains silence the next time the proposal is made. The degree of emphasis with which the negotiator expresses himself on various issues may be an important indication. The suggestion that the parties pass over a given item for the present, on the grounds that it probably will not be an important obstacle to eventual settlement, may be a covert way of setting up a trade on this item for some other. . . . The parties may quote statistics (fictitious if need be) as a . . . way of suggesting a position, or they may convey a position by discussing a settlement in an unrelated industry.[5]

Yet, however much the gap between the parties may be narrowed by such methods, even the most adroit bargainers frequently reach the late stages of negotiations with the complete contract far from being resolved. Given the potential thorniness of many of the individual issues involved, this should not be surprising: More than both bargaining sophistication and flexibility is still generally required to bring about agreement on

[5]Carl M. Stevens, *Strategy and Collective Bargaining Negotiation* (New York: McGraw-Hill Book Company, 1963), pp. 105–106.

such delicate substantive topics as management rights, union security, the role of seniority, and economic benefits. And the fact that the bargainers seek an acceptable package which in some way deals with *all* these issues clearly makes the assignment a much more complicated one than it would otherwise be.

It is the *strike deadline* which is the great motivator of labor relations agreement. As the hands of the clock roll around, signalling the imminent termination of the old contract, each side is now forced to re-examine its "final" position and to balance its "rock-bottom" demands against the consequences of a cessation of work. And with the time element now so important, each party can now be counted upon to view its previous bargaining position in a somewhat different light.

For example, paid holiday demands—which once seemed of paramount importance to the union—may now appear less vital when pursuing them is likely to lead to the complete *loss* of paid holidays through a strike. The labor leaders may also now conclude that although the union membership has authorized the strike should this prove necessary, a stoppage of any duration would be difficult to sustain—through either lack of membership *esprit de corps* or union resources which are insufficient to match those of management.

On its part, the company may also prove more willing to compromise as the strike deadline approaches. Up until now, it has sought to increase its net income by improving its labor cost position. Now the outlook is for a *cessation* of income as operations stop.

These threats, in short, bring each party face-to-face with reality and can normally be expected to cause a marked reassessment of positions. The immediacy of such uncertainty generates a willingness to bridge differences which has not been in evidence at the bargaining table before.

The final hours before time runs out are, therefore, commonly marked by new developments. Frequent caucuses are held by each party, followed by the announcement of a caucus representative that his side is willing to offer a new and more generous "final" proposal. Leaders from each side frequently meet with their counterparts from the other side in informal sessions that are both more private and have fewer participants than the official sessions themselves. These are also likely to result in new agreements. And issues which are still totally insoluble may be passed on to a newly established long-range joint study committee, with the hope that their resolution can be achieved at some later and less pressure-laden date.

Thus, Stevens, in attempting to develop a systematic conceptual apparatus for the analysis of collective bargaining negotiation, examines the implications of the deadline in the following terms:

The approach of the deadline revises upward each party's estimate of the probability that a strike or lockout will be consequent upon adherence to his own position . . . an approaching deadline does much more than simply squeeze elements of bluff and deception out of the negotiation process. It brings pressures to bear which actually change the least favorable terms upon which each party is willing to settle. Thus it operates as a force tending to bring about conditions necessary for agreement.[6]

Paradoxically, the imminency of the deadline can also foster positive *attitudes*, as well as positive actions, between the parties: Its approach dramatically brings home to both groups that each will pay major costs, and thus emphasizes the existence of a common denominator. Walton and McKersie, illustratively, report an event occurring during the negotiations of a New Hampshire shoe company:

. . . The atmosphere was tense, and bargaining was definitely an adversary affair until the lights went out. Their common fate was dramatized by this incident, and the parties quickly reached settlement.[7]

Strikes do, however, occur. Sometimes the impasse leading to a work stoppage stems from a genuine inability of the parties to agree on economic or other terms: the maximum that the company feels that it is able to offer in terms of dollars and cents, for example, is below the minimum that the union believes it must gain in order to retain the loyalty of its members. Or, where rank-and-file ratification is required to put the contract in effect, the negotiators may *misjudge* membership sentiments, bargain a contract which they feel will be fully acceptable to the membership, and then see their efforts overturned by the latter's refusal to approve what they have negotiated.

On other occasions, inexperienced or incompetent negotiators fail to evaluate the importance of a specific concession to the other side, and refuse to grant such a concession where they would gladly have exchanged it for a strike situation. At times, pride or overeagerness causes bargainers to adhere to initial positions long after these become completely untenable. And, in rare instances, one or even both of the parties may actually *desire* a strike—to work off excessive inventories, to allow pent-up emotions a chance for an outlet, or for various other reasons.

The strike incidence has been almost steadily declining in the United States since the beginning of the 1960's and strikes today, as noted earlier, idle less than 0.18 per cent of total available working time. As

---

[6]*Ibid*, p. 100.
[7]Richard E. Walton and Robert B. McKersie, *A Behavioral Theory of Labor Negotiations* (New York: McGraw-Hill Book Company, 1965) , p. 232.

long as workers are free to strike, however, it is realistic to expect that they occasionally will do this.

Crisis Situations

It would be strange, as a matter of fact, if there were not *some* crisis items involved in *any* particular negotiation. In the typical situation some issues will be extremely troublesome, and they will tax severely the intelligence, resourcefulness, imagination, and good faith of the negotiators. Actually, if both sides sincerely desire to settle without a strike, a peaceful solution of any problem in labor relations can usually be worked out. As previously implied, the possibility of a work stoppage is increased when both sides are not sincere in their desire to avoid industrial warfare or when one of the parties to the negotiation is not greatly concerned about a strike. If negotiators bargain on a rational basis, keep open minds, recognize facts and sound arguments, and understand the problems of the other side, crisis situations can be avoided or overcome without any interruption to production or any impairment of good labor relations.

One way to avoid a state of affairs wherein negotiations break down because of a few difficult issues is to bypass these issues in the early stages of the bargaining sessions. It is a good idea to settle the easy problems and delay consideration of the tough ones until later in the negotiations. In this way, the negotiation keeps moving, progress is made, and the area of disagreement tends to be isolated and diminished. Thus, at the early stages, the parties might agree to disagree on some of the items. If only a few items are standing in the way of a peaceful settlement toward the close of the negotiations, there is an excellent chance for full agreement on the contract. Moreover, what might appear to be a big issue at the beginning stages of the negotiations might, of course, appear comparatively insignificant when most of the contract has been agreed upon and when time is running out.

At times, crisis situations are created not as a result of the merits of certain issues, but because some negotiators make mistakes in human relations. For example, it is good practice to personalize the things that are constructive, inherently sound, and defensible, and depersonalize the items which are bad, destructive, or downright silly. Under the former situation, the union or the company, as the case may be, commends the other party, by saying "That is a good point," or "The committee certainly has an argument," or "Bill certainly has his facts straight." In the latter situation, it is sound policy to deal with the merits of a situation. Thus, in face of a destructive or totally unrealistic proposal, the reaction of the other side might be something like this:

"Let's see how this proposal will work out in practice if we put it into the labor agreement." It is elementary psychology that people like to be commended and dislike to be criticized. If this is recognized, rough spots and danger areas in the negotiations may be avoided.

Another way to avoid crisis situations is to be prepared in advance of negotiations to propose or accept alternative solutions to a problem. For example, suppose that the union desires to incorporate an arrangement in the labor agreement making membership in the union a condition of employment. In mapping its over-all strategy for the negotiation, the union committee might decide first to propose a straight union shop, but be prepared, in the face of strong management resistance, to propose a lesser form of union security. Suppose, for another illustration, that the company wants to eliminate all restrictions on the assignment of overtime. It plans first to suggest that the management should have the full authority to designate any workers for overtime without any limitation. At the same time, the company is prepared to suggest some alternative solution to the problem in the event that this proposal appears to create strong resistance. For example, it may propose that seniority be the basis for the rotation of overtime insofar as employees have the capacity to do the work in question. If both sides are prepared in advance to offer or to accept alternative solutions to particular problems, there will be less possibility for the negotiations to bog down. Instead the negotiations will tend to keep moving to a peaceful climax. The momentum of progress is an important factor in reaching the deadline in full agreement on a new contract.

One additional procedure is available to minimize the chances of negotiation breakdowns. It has already been pointed out that many of the issues of contemporary collective bargaining are complicated and difficult. Issues such as working rules, pension plans, insurance systems, and production standards require study and sometimes are not suitable for determination in the normal collective bargaining process. As contract termination deadlines approach, a strike may result simply because not enough time has been allowed for *jointly* attacking these particularly complicated matters in a rational, sound, workable, and equitable manner. All the *unilateral* preparation in the world still does not dispose of this problem. The parties are, however, at liberty to consider such issues by the use of a *joint study group* composed of management and union representatives *during the existing contractual period*. At times, the management and union may see fit to invite disinterested and qualified third parties to aid them in such a project. The joint study group does not engage in collective bargaining as such; its function, rather, is to identify and consider alternative solutions. But, by definition being freed from the pressure of contractual deadlines, such a group can gain sufficient time to study these necessarily difficult issues in a rational manner.

To work effectively, the joint study group should be established soon after a contract is negotiated; it should be composed of people who have the ability to carry out meaningful research and the necessary qualities to consider objectively and dispassionately the tough issues confronting labor and management. These are no small prerequisites, but such a procedure has worked successfully in industries such as basic steel, and modified versions of it are also currently being used with beneficial results in the basic automobile, glass, rubber, and aluminum industries. There is no reason to believe that other collective bargaining parties, including those bargaining on an individual plant basis, could not also profit from it in avoiding crisis situations.

Some companies and unions have found the mediation process helpful when crisis situations *are* reached in negotiations. The Federal Mediation and Conciliation Service of the United States Government and state conciliation services make mediators available to unions and companies. The Federal Service maintains regional offices in New York, Philadelphia, Atlanta, Cleveland, Chicago, St. Louis, and San Francisco, as well as field offices and field stations in many other large industrial centers. It employs several hundred mediators whose services are available without charge to the participants in the collective bargaining process.

Mediation is based upon the principle of voluntary acceptance. Suggestions or recommendations made by the mediator may be accepted or rejected by both or either of the parties to a dispute. Unlike an arbitrator, the mediator has no conclusive powers in a dispute. The chief value of the mediator is his capacity to review the dispute from an objective basis, to throw fresh ideas into the negotiations, to suggest areas of settlement, and at times to serve to extricate the parties from difficult and untenable positions. Some time ago the then General Counsel of the Federal Mediation and Conciliation Service, George E. Strong, succinctly stated some of the outstanding features of mediation and the advantages of the use of a mediator in labor disputes as follows:

A friend in whom the parties have confidence can emphasize the mutuality of their interests. Such a mediator can assist in deflating extreme ideas and positions and sow seeds of understanding of human as well as institutional rights, duties, needs, and objectives. Of course, the climate of industrial relations created by the parties as well as by the community and the mediator can and does promote the sprouting of these seeds. However, I do not mean to imply that mediation should be utilized in every or even in a majority of negotiations, nor do I suggest that it is always a quick and certain method of avoiding strikes, lockouts, or other coercion. If the parties can settle their disputes without mediation, they should do so but they should not wait until the situation is frozen before utilizing mediation. Furthermore, if their desire is to destroy each other they should not seek mediation. If on the other hand, the parties are willing to be reasonable and seek a fair, just, and peaceful solution of their problems they will be benefited and assisted by mediation. Fortunately, enlightened self-interest usually suggests that the parties are interdependent. They know that a mutually acceptable agreement is preferable to embittered strife which injures both parties as well as the overriding interests of the noncombatant public.[8]

Testing and Proofreading

When all issues under consideration have been resolved, the contract should then be drafted in a formal document. Many unions and managements permit lawyers to draft the formal contract. No objection is raised against this practice provided that the lawyer writes the document so that it can be understood by all concerned. A lawyer does not perform this function effectively if he includes in the contract a preponderance of legal phraseology. Such a contract will serve to confuse the people affected by its terms.

Regardless of who writes the final document, the author or authors should draft the agreement in the simplest possible terms. No contract is adequately written until the simplest, clearest, and most concise way is found to express the agreement reached at the bargaining table. Whoever drafts the agreement should recognize the basic fact that unfamiliar words and lengthy sentences will cause confusion once the document is put into force, and may lead to unnecessary grievances and arbitration. Hence, it is sound practice to use a word which has special meaning in the plant or in the industry. Some contracts wisely include illustrations to make clear a particular point in the agreement. And it is of particular value to explain in detail the various steps of the grievance procedure. The contract is designed to stabilize labor relations for a given period. It is not drawn up for the purpose of creating confusion and uncertainty in the area of employer–employee relations.

Before signatures are affixed to the documents, the negotiators should have the contract test-read for meaning. No person who was associated with the negotiations should be used; his interpretation will be colored by his participation in the negotiations. A better practice is to select some individual who had no part in the conference. For this purpose the union may utilize a shop steward or even a rank-and-file member. An office employee, such as a secretary, or a foreman can serve the same

[8]From a lecture delivered at Indiana University on October 23, 1956.

purpose for management. If the people who are to administer the contract were not parties to the negotiation, such individuals should also be used for testing purposes. This is an excellent opportunity for these people to determine whether they understand the provisions before they attempt to administer the document. If the testing indicates confusion as to meaning, the author must rewrite the faulty clause or clauses until the provision is drafted in a manner that eliminates vagueness.

The final step before signing is the proofreading of the document by each negotiator. Particular attention should be given to figures. Misplacing a decimal point, for example, can change a sum from 1 per cent to one-tenth of 1 per cent. Human errors and typographical mistakes are inevitable, and the proofreading of the contract should have as its objective the elimination of any such errors.

The signing of the contract is an important occasion. Newspapers may be notified of the event. Pictures may be taken to be inserted in union and company papers. The tensions of the negotiation terminated, the parties to the conference may well celebrate. They have concluded a job which will affect the welfare of many employees, the position of the labor union, the operation of the company, and, indeed, sometimes the functioning of the entire economy. They have discharged an important responsibility. Let us hope that they did it well!

Reciprocal Character of Collective Bargaining

The fact that collective bargaining is a two-way street is clearly evidenced in negotiation sessions. Some people hold the view that the collective bargaining process involves only the union's demanding and the company's giving. On the contrary, as earlier portions of the chapter have noted, the company frequently will resist and refuse to concede to some issues. And when the company believes that the stakes are extremely important, it will take a strike rather than concede to a particular union demand. Thus, one function of management in collective bargaining is to review union demands in terms of the functions that management must perform in the operation of the plant. It will frequently resist when it believes that the union demands could impair the ability of the company to operate on a dynamic and efficient basis. In addition, most companies play a positive role in the negotiations by making demands on the union. Skilled negotiators on both sides of the table recognize that companies do and should get something out of the negotiations.

Management demands, of course, will be dictated by the character of a particular collective bargaining relationship. In some cases, for example, management will have reason to demand that the labor agreement be negotiated for a longer period than every twelve months; that the union be more responsible for the elimination of wildcat strikes; that the company have more freedom in the assignment of workers to jobs; that skilled employees get a larger proportionate increase in wages than unskilled and semiskilled employees; that certain provisions of the labor contract which have served to interfere unnecessarily with the efficient operation of the plant or which have established "feather-bedding" practices, be eliminated; or that job descriptions be revised in the light of changing plant technology. Collective bargaining sessions are normally as productive in terms of protecting the basic interests of management as they are in protecting the legitimate job rights of employees. This result, however, cannot be accomplished when management remains constantly on the defensive.

Management demands need not be simulated. Over the course of a contractual period events will arise that will provide the basis for legitimate management demands. Experienced union negotiators recognize their responsibility to agree to company demands which are sound and fair, just as they expect such behavior on the part of the company representatives in reference to union demands. To the extent that companies and unions recognize in good faith that collective bargaining is a reciprocal process, the negotiation sessions and the ensuing labor agreement will be conducive to serving the interests of all concerned. In this manner, the labor contract will not be a dictated peace treaty, but a document which will establish a rational relationship between the employees, the union, and the employer.

Some Further Complexities

Generalizations such as those offered above cannot, of course, do justice in accounting for a *specific* contract settlement or strike. To appreciate adequately the complexities and variations involved in the negotiation process, one must turn to the interdependent variables which are apt to be influential in determining bargaining outcomes.

The current healths of both the economy and industry, for example, have been of major effect in determining the relative settlements of the United Automobile Workers and major car manufacturers in several recent years. In 1955, a boom year, management resistance to union demands was weak and the UAW gains were consequently significant ones. The strike threat meant relatively little to the companies in 1958, a recession year, and the union could improve the 1955 contract only slightly and after considerable frustration. Economic conditions were somewhat better than they had been in 1958 in 1961 and the union demands of the latter year fared correspondingly better. And in 1964, when automobile company production and profitability set new all-time records, the management quest for uninterrupted production led the companies to grant Walter Reuther terms which dwarfed even those of 1955.

On the other hand, the shoe industry has been plagued by consistently poor economic conditions for many of its specific employers for years and, in the face of this variable and its persuasive logic, the Shoe Workers have shown considerable bargaining self-restraint for well over a decade.

Technological innovations—running a wide gamut from turbojet aircraft to computerized newspaper typesetting—have been the primary cause of many major recent bargaining stalemates and subsequent strikes, as even the cursory follower of current events is well aware. In turn, job insecurity resulting partly from *improved technology in such competitive industries* as trucking and the airlines has made railroad workers a particularly touchy group to deal with in the past several years.

The influence of other major variables, all of them noted earlier in this book, can be illustrated. It took years for Swift and Company and the Amalgamated Meat Cutters to establish a *cooperative labor relationship*, but this had been generally effected at the time of this writing and the most recent negotiations between those two parties had been marked by a statesmanlike joint approach to difficult problems. By contrast, mutual trust is not the case at Armour, and resolutions of Meat Cutter–company differences there have sometimes strained the imagination of both parties with no noticeable success. The *relative strengths of the two sides* can be decisive in particular negotiations, as in those between the aforementioned over-the-road truckers and the Teamsters Union, and in almost all recent negotiations involving the International Ladies Garment Workers Union and any of its many highly competitive and marginal employers. Some negotiations have not been easily resolved because of *political problems within the union*: The 1963 International Longshoremen's Association–East and Gulf Coast Shipping Operators bargaining was followed by a lengthy strike, due in large measure to a three-way scramble for leadership within the union and the accompanying jockeying for position of the contenders. Nor have these political problems been confined to top-level unionists. In recent years, the rank and file of an increasing number of unions—among them the previously cited UAW and Steelworkers—have supported the charges of their local leaders that the bargainers were ignoring local problems by temporarily refusing to ratify their negotiated settlements. On occasion, they have engaged in protest work stoppages as well.

The *personalities* of labor and management representatives often have a major bearing on the outcome. Despite the greater bargaining power of his union, former Teamster president Dave Beck's avowed philosophy that "for every friend I lose in the ranks of labor, I make two friends in the Chamber of Commerce" won him the wholehearted approval of many of his employers. It also made many Teamster negotiations under his presidency extremely amicable affairs. More commendably, the proven willingness of the late Pacific Maritime Association president J. Paul St. Sure and West Coast Longshoreman leader Harry Bridges to subordinate their personal goals to the welfare of their industry resulted, in the early 1960's, in a Mechanization and Modernization Agreement that represents a high level of statesmanship for both parties.

For negotiators whose bargaining can be in any way construed to affect "an entire industry or a substantial part thereof" in such a manner as to "imperil the national health or safety," there may be at least one further possible determinant. Under the Taft–Hartley Act of 1947, as Chapter 3 has explained, the President of the United States has the authority to postpone a strike consistent with the above specifications for eighty days.[9] Other forms of *government intervention* may also be present in such cases: suggestions to uncooperative bargainers that restrictive legislation might be enacted should a strike take place, statements by public officials aimed at throwing the weight of public opinion to one side or the other, mediation by high-level personnel of the above-mentioned Federal Mediation and Conciliation Service or respected private citizens, and a variety of other devices. The possibility that any of these forms of intervention may be used can influence the actions of the negotiators at the bargaining table. Steelworker Union settlements in the early 1960's, for example, were both peacefully arrived at and relatively mild in their economic increases (that is, "noninflationary"). Many observers have explained this situation, somewhat ironic in view of the turbulence accompanying steel negotiations as recently as 1959, by asserting that the government would have it no other way.[10]

And the railroad operating unions, as a second illustration in this

---

[9]The railroads and airlines have their own forms of government intervention, under the Railway Labor Act of 1926 and its amendments. The parties in these industries are free to strike only after procedures of the Act's National Mediation Board have been exhausted.

[10]Other analysts, however, dispute this point as it pertains to 1962–63. One such source doubts, in fact, "that the government played much of a role on the amount of settlement" in those years and suggests that, if anything, public intervention "may have increased the package somewhat in 1962."

area, were widely accused of being unwilling to compromise in their long-standing work rules dispute of the 1960–65 period with the railroads. This was said to be due to their feeling that government intervenors would ultimately decide these rules anyhow—and, hopefully, on better terms than the unions could extract from their employers.

The preceding examples are only a few of the many that could have been chosen to illustrate each category of variable. In any given contract negotiation, one factor might be of major importance—or of no significance at all. The degree of importance of each also, of course, changes over time. And, clearly, many (or none) of these variables can be at play at one time on the bargainers. Contract negotiation is, in short, no more susceptible to sweeping statements than are the unions and managements which participate in the process.

The foregoing *has* indicated, however, that the negotiation of the labor contract in the contemporary economy is a complex and difficult job. The negotiators are required to possess a working knowledge of trade union principles, plant organization and operations, economics, psychology, statistics, and labor law. They must have the research ability to gather the data necessary for effective negotiations. Negotiators must be shrewd judges of human nature. Often, effective speaking ability is an additional prerequisite. Indeed, the position of the negotiator of the modern contract demands the best efforts of individuals possessing superior ability. Modern collective bargaining sessions have no place for the uninformed, the inept, or the unskilled.

DISCUSSION QUESTIONS

1. Assume that a large, nationwide company is negotiating a contract at the present time. What economic, political, legal, and social factors might be likely to exert some influence upon these negotiations?
2. It has been argued by a union research director that "a fact is as welcome at a collective bargaining table as a skunk at a cocktail party." Do you agree?
3. Evaluate the statement that "in the absence of a strike deadline, there can be no true collective bargaining."
4. What might explain the frequently heard management observation that "highly democratic unions are extremely difficult to negotiate with."?
5. How do you account for the fact that the joint study approach still remains confined to a relative handful of industries?
6. From the viewpoint of *society* is there anything to be said in favor of strikes?
7. Of all of the personal attributes which this chapter has indicated are important for labor relations negotiators to have, which single one do you consider to be the *most* important, and why?
8. "Successful labor contract bargaining should no longer be viewed as an 'art.' It is far more appropriate today to refer to it as a 'science.'" Discuss.

SELECTED REFERENCES

Dunlop, John T., *Industrial Relations Systems*. New York: Holt, Rinehart & Winston, Inc., 1958.

Henderson, James A., *et al.*, *Creative Collective Bargaining*. Englewood Cliffs, N. J.: Prentice-Hall Inc., 1965.

Hill, L. H., and C. R. Hook, *Management at the Bargaining Table*. New York: McGraw-Hill Book Company, 1945.

Kornhauser, Arthur, Robert Dubin, and Arthur M. Ross, eds., *Industrial Conflict*. New York: McGraw-Hill Book Company, 1954.

Peters, Edward, *Strategy and Tactics in Labor Negotiations*. New London, Conn.: National Foremen's Institute, 1955.

Schelling T. C., *The Strategy of Conflict*. Cambridge, Mass.: Harvard University Press, 1960.

Siegel, Sidney, and L. E. Fouraker, *Bargaining and Group Decision Making*. New York: McGraw-Hill Book Company, 1960.

Sloane, Arthur A., "Collective Bargaining in Trucking: Prelude to a National Contract," *Industrial and Labor Relations Review* (October, 1965).

Stevens, Carl M., *Strategy and Collective Bargaining Negotiation*. New York: McGraw-Hill Book Company, 1963.

Walton, Richard E., and Robert B. McKersie, *A Behavioral Theory of Labor Negotiations*. New York: McGraw-Hill Book Company, 1965.

When agreement *is* finally reached in contract negotiations, the bargainers frequently
call in news reporters and photographers,
smilingly slap each other on the back (as the
cameras snap) and announce their satisfaction with the new contract. The exact performance, of course, varies from situation to
situation. In general, however, such enthusiastic phrases as "great new era" and "going
forward together for our mutual benefit" are
often heard.

There is a minimum of sham in these
actions. Public relations are, as has been
stressed at several earlier stages in this book,
important to both sides; and both management–stockholder and union leader–union
member relationships are also not overlooked
by the company and union participants, respectively, as they register their happiness
with their joint handiwork. But typically the
negotiators are genuinely optimistic about
what they have negotiated: Compromise and
statesmanship have once again triumphed.

It will be some time, however, before one
can tell whether this optimism is justified.
The formal signing of the collective bargain-

6

Administration of the agreement

ing agreement does not mean that union–management relations are terminated until the next negotiation over contract terms. After the new labor agreement goes into effect, management and union representatives have the job of making the contract *work*. The labor agreement establishes the general framework of labor relations in the plant. It spells out in broad language the rights and benefits of employees, the obligations and rights of management, and the protection and the responsibilities of the union. But during the course of the contractual period, many problems will arise involving the *application* and the *interpretation* of the various clauses in the labor agreement.

The application of the contract is, in fact, a daily problem. Representatives of management and the union normally devote a considerably larger share of their time to the administration of the labor agreement than to its negotiation. Moreover, the climate of labor relations in the plant will be determined to a large extent by the manner in which management and union representatives discharge their obligations in the day-by-day application of the labor contract. Whether there will be good or bad labor relations depends to a significant degree on the character of the administration of the labor agreement. For these reasons, it is vital that the parties to a collective bargaining relationship understand thoroughly the problems and the responsibilities which grow out of the application of a contract.

The source for many administrative problems is in the language of the labor agreement. Owing to the conditions under which bargaining takes place, many contractual clauses are themselves written in rather broad terms. The day-to-day job in labor relations is to apply the *principles* of the labor agreement.

Many problems can arise under a single clause of the labor agreement. For example, a contract may limit the right of management to discharge for "just cause." An employee is discharged for speaking back to his foreman in harsh terms. Is this "just cause" within the meaning of the agreement? In another case, a seniority arrangement may provide that the employee with the longer service in the plant will get the better job, provided that he has ability to perform the job equal to that of any other employee who desires the position. Whether or not the employee with longer service *is* awarded the job is an administrative problem. Or, the parties may have agreed that employees will be expected to perform jobs falling within their job description. An emergency arises in the plant, and the company directs some employees to work outside their job description. Did the company violate the agreement? Or, as a final example, the labor agreement provides that wage rates of new jobs created in the plant are to be established in a manner which is equitable in terms of comparable jobs. Does a rate established for such a job in fact compare fairly with that for kindred jobs?

These illustrations suggest the multitude of problems that can arise in connection with the operation of a labor agreement on a day-by-day basis. Practically every provision in a collective bargaining contract can be the basis for problems that must be resolved.

Grievance Procedure

Problems such as those posed above are handled and settled through the grievance procedure of the labor contract. The grievance procedure provides a system whereby representatives of the company and the union can settle problems arising under a contract in a speedy and peaceful manner.[1] The machinery makes it absolutely unnecessary for the parties to resort to such weapons of industrial conflict as the strike as the method for determining the solutions for the problems which arise under the terms of a labor agreement.

In the typical situation, a problem is referred to the grievance procedure after a decision is made under some provision of the contract. For example, as above, the company discharges an employee for some reason which it believes to be fair and proper under a contract which provides that the employer may discharge only for "just cause." The discharged employee and the union believe that the reason for which the discharge was made was *not* proper within the meaning of the labor agreement. Under these circumstances the union files what is known as a "grievance."

[1]Depending upon the attitudes of the company and the union, the grievance procedure can be used for functions other than the settlement of complaints arising under the labor agreement. In this connection, the National Planning Association reports that in its studies *Causes of Industrial Peace Under Collective Bargaining* many of the companies and unions used the grievance machinery to *prevent grievances from arising* as well as to dispose of employee, union, and employer complaints. Thus, it reports that "in most of our studies, the parties used the grievance machinery . . . as a fire prevention as well as a firefighting device. Important grievances are viewed as symptoms of underlying problems, and the parties attempted to work out satisfactory solutions for such problems in order to prevent the future occurrences of similar grievances." Some of the studies revealed, moreover, that the grievance procedure was viewed in even a broader light. For example, in one company the machinery was used to study and discuss a variety of mutual problems. "The parties disposed of formal grievances as rapidly as possible at the beginning of joint meetings, and then the parties customarily used the grievance meetings to feel each other out on all kinds of issues, many of them lying far beyond the scope of customary collective bargaining—such things as the economic position of the company, proposed new machinery and processes, issues in the forthcoming contract negotiations, and other matters not related to grievances. This meant, in effect, broadening the grievance machinery into a semiformal negotiation of two-way management–union communications." *Causes of Industrial Peace Under Collective Bargaining, A Final Report*, Case Study No. 14 (Washington, D.C.: National Planning Association, 1953), pp. 86–87.

In labor relations terminology, a "grievance" is, in short, an allegation that a provision or provisions of a labor agreement have been violated. The union and/or employees may file grievances alleging that the company violated the terms of the labor agreement. Likewise the company may file grievances alleging that the union or a particular employee violated the collective bargaining contract.

In actual practice, the union files many more complaints against the company than the company files against the union or employees. The major reason for this state of affairs is that management makes the initial decision relative to the administration of the labor agreement. After representatives of the company make such a decision, the union, if it desires, may allege that a violation has taken place. However, from time to time employers do file complaints against unions and employees. For example, a company may file grievances alleging that particular employees have been disregarding safety regulations; that the union has disregarded its obligations under a no-strike clause; that the union officers have misrepresented the position of management to the members of the labor organization; or that the union and employees are slowing down on work to achieve an objective.

Characteristics of the grievance procedure

A chief characteristic of the grievance procedure is that it provides for several stages of settlement. Most agreements provide for three and four steps, exclusive of arbitration, and at each step the grievance will be discussed by different but specified representatives of the union and the company.

A typical four-step procedure might be one in which the foreman of the department in which the grievance arises and the employee in question, with or without a union steward, handle the problem at the first step; if a settlement is not reached at this stage, the second step might involve discussions by the general foreman and the chairman of the union grievance committee; should there be no agreement at the second step, the grievance would then go to the third stage of the grievance procedure, where there could be deliberations by the local union president and the superintendent of the plant, perhaps together with other designated union and company representatives; and then, if no settlement is reached at the third step, the final bilateral step of the grievance procedure is invoked. At this terminal step of the procedure, the grievance might be handled by the Director of Industrial Relations of the company with other key management representatives, and a representative of the international union and key representatives of the local union. This is only one illustration and clearly it is not meant to be universal in character. Depending on the size of the plant, the customs of the union–management relationship, and the history of labor relations in the company, labor contracts will vary as to the number of steps in the grievance procedure and the personnel participating at each step.

The purpose of a multistep grievance procedure is to permit different personnel of the company and the union to take a fresh look at the problems of each of the preceding stages. Equally important, it provides the parties to the labor agreement every opportunity to gather all the relevant facts and to review past practices that may bear upon the grievance. In this manner, there is an excellent chance for the grievance to be settled by the parties without resorting to arbitration, and in a manner which is in keeping with the terms of the collective bargaining contract. Sometimes, however, companies and unions do not take full advantage of the opportunity of a multistep grievance procedure. Instead, grievances are resolved in the first place by the highest authorities in the company and the union. When this is done, the final position of the company and the union is merely rubber-stamped at each succeeding stage of the procedure. Under these circumstances the grievance procedure might just as well provide for only one step before arbitration.

Under many labor agreements or the customs of a particular plant, a worker complaint is first discussed orally by the worker and the foreman. At times the employee's union steward or grievance committeeman will participate in the discussion. Only if settlement is not reached on an oral basis is the grievance formally written. A vast number of workers' complaints are settled on an oral basis to the satisfaction of all concerned.

The great majority of grievance procedures specify definite time limits for each stage of the grievance procedure. For example, a contract may stipulate that a grievance must be filed within a certain number of days after the alleged violation of the contract takes place. Companies are required to give their answers within a certain number of days at each stage of the procedure. In addition, the union must appeal to the next stage of the procedure within a certain time limit if it is not satisfied with the answer of the company at any particular stage of the procedure. Failure to comply with specified time limits may result in the forfeiture of the grievance by the union or the granting of it by the company. However, many companies and unions will grant extensions of the time limits upon request.

By providing for time limits, the contract requires the company and the union to give speedy attention to the problem. In this manner, the grievance can be settled promptly, reducing or eliminating friction in the plant. The chief problem involved in the establishment of specified time limits is that of striking a balance between prompt and orderly progress of the grievance through the various steps of the grievance procedure and provision for a sufficient amount of time at each of the stages for the accumulation of all relevant facts so that the grievance can be discussed and settled in an intelligent manner. To accomplish this objective many contracts provide a three-to-five working-day interval between the various steps of the grievance procedure, and some a somewhat longer interval. (Case No. 1 at the end of this chapter, the first of ten illustrative cases contained in the remaining chapters of this book, deals with some of the ramifications of time limits.)

Since most grievances are presented, investigated, and processed during working hours and since the union representatives are usually regular workers in the plant, the question of payment for union officials who leave their jobs for grievance work arises. Under most labor contracts, the company pays union officials for the time which they devote to grievance duties. However, a number of limitations are provided in connection with this. Under some contracts, the time that union officials devote to grievance matters is specifically limited or the amount of pay that they can receive for such duties is specified. Likewise, union officers who desire to leave their regular jobs in order to participate in grievance duties must first obtain permission from their respective foremen. In addition, many contracts clearly establish the principle that payment for grievance work relates only to that time which is spent in sessions directly with management representatives on a vis-a-vis basis, and not for time spent for investigation or other preparatory duties.

Grievance procedure and harmonious labor relations

As suggested above, the grievance procedure provides the parties to the labor contract with an excellent opportunity to improve labor relations; to increase plant efficiency; and to promote a better understanding of management, employee, and union problems. It serves as a device whereby complaints of workers, employers, and unions can be aired and discussed. In this manner, the grievance procedure may be regarded as the "psychotherapy" of industrial relations. Small problems can be discussed and settled promptly before they become major and troublesome issues in the plant. Serious problems can be analyzed in a rational manner and resolved speedily, peacefully, and in keeping with the terms of the collective bargaining contract. The rights of employees, employers, and unions guaranteed in the labor contract can be protected and implemented in a prompt and orderly fashion. Not only does the grievance procedure serve as a means for the enforcement of the labor agreement but it also provides the parties with the opportunity of establishing the reasons for complaints and problems, and in this way it acts to facilitate the adoption of policies which would tend to prevent grievances from arising.

In the last analysis, the grievance procedure should not be regarded as a device whereby companies or unions can "win" a grievance. Rather, it should be viewed as a means for obtaining a better climate of labor relations in a company than as the machinery whereby the company or the union can exercise authority over each other. This does not mean that rights guaranteed in the labor contract should be waived or compromised, but that in discharging obligations under the grievance procedure the parties should understand the broader implications involved in the processing of complaints. Company and union representatives who regard the grievance procedure in this light gear their behavior, arguments, and general approach toward the objective of the improvement of labor relations. In short, the grievance procedure should not be regarded as an end in itself. It should be viewed as a channel of reciprocal communication between the company, the union, and the employees for the promotion of mutual understanding and for the improvement of the labor relations environment.

These objectives are not realized when representatives of management look upon their obligations under the grievance procedure as burdensome chores, as wastes of time, or as necessary evils. Likewise these objectives are not attainable to the extent that unions stuff the grievance procedure with complaints that have no merit whatsoever under the collective bargaining contract.[2] They cannot be achieved when the parties regard the grievance procedure as a method to embarrass the other side or to demonstrate authority or power. In addition, the opportunities for more harmonious labor relations through the use of the grievance procedure cannot be realized to the extent that the system is used to resolve internal political conflicts within unions or the management. If the grievance procedure does not contribute to a better labor relations climate, the fault lies not with the system, but with the representatives of unions and management who either misunderstand or distort the function that the grievance procedure plays in the industrial relations complex.

Arbitration

The vast majority of problems that arise as the result of the interpretation and application of collective bargaining contracts are resolved bilaterally by the representatives of management and the labor orgnization. Through the process of negotiation, the parties to a contract manage to

[2]Many unions specifically instruct their stewards and grievance committeemen not to process grievances that have no merit under a labor agreement. Thus, in one union manual the labor organization instructs its stewards as follows: "After you have thoroughly investigated the case, if you decide that no grievance exists, it is your duty to the worker and the union to state this, and to take time to explain why."

find a solution to grievances at some step in the grievance procedure. Such a record testifies to the utility of the grievance procedure as a device for the speedy, fair, and peaceful solution of disputes growing out of the application of the collective bargaining contract. It also shows rather clearly that the great majority of company and union representatives understand fully the purpose of the grievance procedure and discharge their responsibilities on the basis of good faith.

Indeed, in healthy union–management relationships, the great bulk of grievances is disposed of at the lower levels of the procedure. This is as it should be: Were most such complaints merely bucked up the union and management hierarchical ladders, the time and efforts of the more broadly based officials would be hopelessly drained. Lower-step settlement also helps maintain the status of lower supervision and assures that the grievance is allowed treatment by the people who are apt to be most familiar with the circumstances under which it arose.

Under even the most enviable of labor relationships, however, there undoubtedly will be some grievances that prove themselves completely incapable of being solved by *any* level within the bilateral grievance procedure. Each party genuinely believes that its interpretation of the contract is the right one, or the company and union remain in disagreement as to the facts of the case.

There may also, on occasion, be less commendable reasons for a stalemate. The union leadership may feel that it cannot afford to "give in" on an untenable grievance because of the political ramifications of doing so. Management may at times prove quite unwilling to admit that the original company action giving rise to the grievance was in violation of the contract, even though in its heart it realizes that the union's allegation is right. The union may, the remarks previously offered in this connection notwithstanding, seek to "flood" the grievance procedure with a pot-pourri of unsettled grievances, with the hope of using the situation to gain extracontractual concessions from the company. The company may, in turn, seek to embarrass the union leadership by making it fight to the limit for any favorable settlement. And grievances involving such thorny issues as discipline, work assignment, and management rights are sometimes accompanied by emotional undercurrents that make them all the more difficult to resolve by the joint conference method of the grievance procedure.

In short, the amount of challenge which management can expect through the grievance procedure can vary widely because of the existence of such complex variables as: (1) the wisdom and extent of development of the legislated policy which is embodied in the labor agreement itself (and, no less important, the degree of operating policy development which the company has effected to supplement the labor agreement);

(2) the political environment and militancy of the local union; (3) the calibre of the company's personnel administration and supervision; (4) the nature of the existing union–management relationship; and (5) economic and related variables affecting employment and working conditions.

Given all these variables, it is, in fact, a tribute to the maturity of labor–management relations that the great majority of all grievances *are* settled by the joint process.

Nonetheless, some contractual provision must be made by the parties to handle the relatively few issues for which the grievance procedure proves unsuccessful: those occasions upon which the parties to the labor contract are still in disagreement over a problem arising under the contractual terms after all bilateral steps in the grievance procedure have been exhausted.

To break such deadlocks, the parties have the opportunity to resort to the arbitration process. An impartial outsider is selected by the parties to decide the controversy. His decision is invariably stipulated in the contract as being "final and binding upon both parties."

Through the arbitrator, the dispute is resolved in a peaceful manner. In the absence of arbitration, the parties might use the strike or lockout to settle such problems, a process which is not only costly to the company, the union, and the employees, but which would tend to foster embittered labor relations. In the light of these observations, it should elicit no surprise that at present some 95 per cent of all United States labor agreements provide for arbitration as the final step in the grievance procedure. This national percentage is significantly greater than it was in the early 1930's, when fewer than 8 to 10 per cent of all agreements contained such a clause. And even by 1944, arbitration provisions had been included in only 73 per cent of all contracts.[3]

Not surprisingly, either, the recent statistics involving arbitration case loads have been of no small order of magnitude. In 1962, for example, neutrals were called upon to make awards in no less than 15,000 labor–management disputes and wrote an estimated million words in support of their opinions.[4] In an era of uncertainty as to the future growth of union membership totals, moreover, there is no collective job insecurity in the profession: According to the American Arbitration Association, the case load of arbitrators keeps increasing at the rate of roughly 10 per cent annually.[5] Much of the most recent impetus for growth was

[3]"Arbitration Provisions in Collective Agreements, 1952," *Monthly Labor Review* (March, 1953), pp. 261–66.
[4]Lawrence Stessin, "A New Look at Arbitration," *The New York Times Magazine* (November 17, 1963), p. 26.
[5]*Ibid.*

provided by a major judicial decision of the late 1950's: In June, 1957, the United States Supreme Court held that the federal courts may apply the Taft–Hartley law to enforce arbitration clauses. Under this ruling, an employer may not refuse to arbitrate unresolved grievance disputes when the labor agreement contains an arbitration provision.[6]

The "Trilogy" cases

On June 20, 1960, the United States Supreme Court handed down three other decisions which provide even greater integrity to the arbitration process.[7] These decisions are commonly referred to as the "Trilogy" cases. Each of them involved the United Steelworkers of America and each demonstrates that the system of private arbitration in the United States has now received the full support of the highest court in the land.

In the *Warrior and Gulf Navigation* case, the court held that in the absence of an express agreement excluding arbitration, the court would direct the parties to arbitrate a grievance. To put this in other terms, the court would not find a case to be nonarbitrable unless the parties specifically excluded a subject from the arbitration process. The court stated that a legal order to arbitrate would thenceforth not be denied "unless it may be said with positive assurance that the arbitration clause is not susceptible to an interpretation that covers the asserted dispute. Doubts should be resolved in favor of coverage."

More precisely, the courts will not decide that a dispute is *not* arbitrable unless the parties have taken care to *expressly remove* an area of labor relations from the arbitration process. This could be accomplished by providing, for example, that "disputes involving determination of the qualifications of employees for promotion will be determined exclusively

---

[6]*Textile Workers* v. *Lincoln Mills* (1957), 77 Sup. Ct. 54. However, in 1962 the United States Supreme Court refused to enjoin a strike engaged in by a union during a contractual period, despite the fact that the labor agreement contained no-strike and arbitration clauses. (*Sinclair Refining Company* v. *Atkinson*, (1962) 82 S. Ct. 1328.) The union could have submitted the grievances which caused the strike to arbitration instead of striking. In its decision, the Court reasoned that it could not issue an injunction to stamp out the strike on the grounds that it was forbidden to do so under the Norris La Guardia Act. As such, current law would appear to discriminate against employers, since they must arbitrate unresolved grievances. In contrast, a union may by-pass arbitration and strike free from the fear the courts will issue an injunction to stop the strike. However, it is extremely doubtful that many unions would strike over grievances rather than using the arbitration process, for the reasons previously indicated.

[7]*United Steelworkers of America* v. *American Manufacturing Co.*, 363 U.S. 564 (1960); *United Steelworkers of America* v. *Warrior and Gulf Navigation Co.*, 363 U.S. 574 (1960); *United Steelworkers of America* v. *Enterprise Wheel and Car Corp.*, 363 U.S. 593 (1960).

by the company and such decision will not be subject to arbitration."[8] But, needless to say, not many unions would agree to such a clause since management would then have the unilateral right to make determinations on this vital phase of the promotion process.

In so ruling, the *Warrior and Gulf Navigation* decision eliminated a course of action that some companies had followed. When faced with a demand by a union for arbitration, some employers had frequently gone to court and asked the judge to decide that the issue involved in the case was not arbitrable. On many occasions, the courts had agreed with the company, with the effect of sustaining the company position in the grievance, and denying the union an opportunity to get a decision based on the merits of the case.

In the instant case, the Warrior and Gulf Navigation Company employed forty-two men at its dock terminal for maintenance and repair work. After the company had subcontracted out some of the work, the number was reduced to twenty-three. The union argued in the grievance procedure that this action of the company violated certain areas of the labor agreement—the integrity of the bargaining unit, seniority rights, and other clauses of the contract which provided benefits to workers. On its part, the company claimed that the issue of subcontracting was strictly a management function and relied on the management rights clause in the contract which stated that "matters which are strictly a function of management should not be subject to arbitration." When the Supreme Court handled the case, it ordered arbitration because the contract did not *specifically* exclude such activity from the arbitration process. It stated:

> A specific collective bargaining agreement may exclude contracting-out from the grievance procedure. Or a written collateral agreement may make clear that contracting-out was not a matter for arbitration. In such a case a grievance based solely on contracting-out would not be arbitrable. Here, however, there is no such provision. Nor is there any showing that the parties designed the phrase "strictly as a function of management" to encompass any and all forms of contracting-out. In the absence of any express provision excluding a particular grievance from arbitration, we think only the most forceful evidence of a purpose to exclude the claim from arbitration can prevail, particularly where, as here, the exclusion clause is vague and the arbitration clause quite broad.

One additional important point must be made relative to the significance of this court decision. It does not mean that private arbitrators do not have the authority to dismiss a grievance on the basis of its non-

[8]For other examples of such limiting language, see *To Protect Management Rights* (Washington, D.C.: Chamber of Commerce of the United States, 1961), pp. 7–22.

arbitrability under a contract. Arbitrators before and after the decision have frequently held that a grievance is not arbitrable under the contract. Indeed, the authors at times after the *Warrior and Gulf Navigation* decision have upheld the arguments of companies that grievances were not arbitrable under the labor agreement. The major importance of the *Warrior and Gulf Navigation* doctrine is in its ruling that courts may not hold that grievances are not arbitrable *unless* specific and clear-cut language excludes the matter from the arbitration process. The private arbitrator is still fully empowered to dismiss a grievance on the basis of nonarbitrability. (The problem of the arbitrability of grievances is raised in Case No. 2 at the end of this chapter.)

In the second case, *American Manufacturing*, the issue of arbitrability was also involved, but in a somewhat different way from that of *Warrior and Gulf Navigation*. The American Manufacturing Company argued before a lower federal court that an issue was not arbitrable because it did not believe that the grievance had merit. Involved was a dispute involving the reinstatement of an employee on his job after it was determined that the employee was 25 per cent disabled and was drawing workmen's compensation. The lower federal court sustained the employer's position and characterized the employee's grievance as "a frivolous, patently baseless one, not subject to arbitration." When the United States Supreme Court reversed the lower federal court, it held that the federal courts are limited in determining whether the dispute is covered by the labor agreement and that they have no power to evaluate the merits of a dispute. It stated:

> The function of the court is very limited when the parties have agreed to submit all questions of contract interpretation to the arbitrator. It is then confined to ascertaining whether the party seeking arbitration is making a claim which on its face is governed by the contract. Whether the moving party is right or wrong is a question of contract construction for the arbitrator. In these circumstances the moving party should not be deprived of the arbitrator's judgment, when it was his judgment and all that it connotes that was bargained for.

Essentially, this means that the courts may not hold a grievance to be nonarbitrable even if a judge believes that a grievance is completely worthless. It is up to the private arbitrator to make the decision on the merits of a case. He may dismiss the grievance as being without merit, but this duty rests exclusively with him, and not with the courts.

In the third case, *Enterprise Wheel and Car Corporation*, a lower federal court reversed the decision of an arbitrator on the grounds that the judge did not believe that his decision was sound under the labor agreement. The arbitrator's award directed the employer to reinstate certain discharged workers and to pay them back wages for periods both before and after the expiration of the collective bargaining contract. The company refused to comply with the award, and the union petitioned for the enforcement of the award. The lower court held that the arbitrator's award was unenforceable because the contract had expired. The United States Supreme Court reversed the lower court and ordered full enforcement. In upholding the arbitrator's award, the court stated:

> Interpretation of the collective bargaining agreement is a question for the arbitrator. It is the arbitrator's construction which was bargained for; and so far as the arbitration decision concerns construction of the contract, the courts have no business overruling him because their interpretation of the contract is different from his.

The significance of this last decision should be perfectly clear. It shows that a union or a company may not use the courts to set aside an arbitrator's award. The decision, of course, cuts both ways: it applies to both employers and labor organizations. Whereas the other two decisions definitely favor labor organizations, this one merely serves to preserve the integrity of the arbitrator's award. Thus, even if a judge believes that an arbitrator's award is unfair, unwise, and not even consistent with the contract, he has no alternative except to enforce the award.

Thus, the Trilogy cases demonstrate that the private arbitration system has been strengthened by the judiciary. They establish the full integrity of the arbitration process. As a result of these decisions, companies and unions must be more careful in the selection of arbitrators. This is one reason why they have increasingly voiced a desire to use seasoned and experienced arbitrators.

For the arbitrator, the decisions are equally meaningful. Private arbitrators bear an even greater degree of responsibility as they decide their cases. Not only is the post one of honor in which the parties have confidence in the arbitrator's professional competency and integrity, but the arbitrator must recognize that for all intents and purposes his decision is completely "final and binding" upon the parties. Indeed, if the system of private arbitration is to remain a permanent feature of the American system of industrial relations, arbitrators must measure up to their responsibilities. Should they fail in this respect, companies and unions would simply delete the arbitration clause from the contract and resolve their disputes by strikes or by going directly to the courts. These are not pleasant alternatives, but the parties may choose these routes if they believe that arbitrators are not discharging their responsibilities in an honorable, judicious, and professional manner. Arbitrators should not feel so smug as to believe that their services are indispensable to labor unions and companies. They are as expendable as last year's calendar.

Limitations to arbitration

If employers and unions support the arbitration process as an accepted method of disposing of disagreements relating to problems arising under the terms of a labor contract already in existence, there is almost *no* approval on the part of industry and organized labor for using arbitration as the means of breaking deadlocks in the negotiations of *new* agreements. Most employers and unions would rather have a work stoppage than refer to arbitration such latter disputes. Though many reasons are advanced in support of this position, the chief consideration lies in the parties' extreme aversion to having an outsider determine the conditions of employment, the rights and obligations of management, and the responsibilities and rights of the union. Employers and unions almost invariably believe that since the labor agreement will establish their fundamental relationship, they should have the full authority to negotiate its terms. For these reasons, the use of arbitration during the negotiation stage of a labor contract is rare. In only a very few industries do the parties surrender their rights to negotiate new contracts and establish arbitration as the method to break deadlocks.

It is also important to note that in the United States the system is one of *private and voluntary arbitration*. That is, the government does not force the parties to include arbitration clauses in their labor agreements. They do so voluntarily as they negotiate the latter. Either party can refuse to incorporate any arbitration provisions at all, as has been the case in the building construction industry, where the duration of the job is deemed too brief to make use of a neutral feasible, and in the trucking industry, where the Teamster hierarchy has traditionally insisted that neutrals "attempt to please both sides and actually please nobody."

Equally significant is the fact that arbitrators are private and not government officials. Most of them are lawyers and college professors. In some nations, such as Spain, arbitration is imposed by government fiat, *must* be used to resolve contractual interpretation disputes, and the arbitrators are government officials or appointees. Let us hope that the American system never takes this route. To follow the pattern of Spain and other totalitarian labor relations systems would mean the demise of the free collective bargaining system.

Characteristics of arbitration hearings

Since the decision of the arbitrator *is* final and binding, arbitration is quite different from mediation, a process wherein the parties are completely free to accept or reject the recommendations or suggestions of the mediator. Whether or not the arbitrator rules for or against a party to the arbitration, his decision must be accepted. This is true even when the losing side believes that the decision is not warranted by the labor agreement, by the evidence submitted in the hearing, or on the basis of fairness or justice. Frequently an arbitrator's decision will establish an important precedent in the plant that must be followed by the company, the union, and the employees. At times the party which suffers an adverse ruling in an arbitration case will attempt to change those sections of the labor agreement which proved to be the basis of the decision during the next labor contract negotiations. Obviously the side which is benefited by the decision will be reluctant to alter those features of the labor agreement which were interpreted and applied by the arbitrator.

These considerations tend to show the seriousness of arbitration as a tool of labor relations. When the decision to arbitrate is made, the company and union representatives are undertaking a deep responsibility. To discharge this responsibility in a competent and intelligent manner, it is necessary to put the arbitrator in such a position that he can make his decision in the light of evidence and of the relevant contractual clauses. Consequently, the parties have the obligation of preparing fully before coming to the hearing. This means the accumulation of all evidence, facts, documents, and arguments that may have a bearing on the dispute. Careful preparation also means the selection of witnesses who can give relevant testimony in the case.[9] Company and union representatives should leave no stone unturned in preparing for the arbitration.

At the arbitration hearing each side will have full opportunity to present the fruits of its preparation. Normally, though arbitration hearings are much more formal than grievance procedure negotiations, they are considerably less formal than court proceedings. In addition, the rules of evidence which pertain in the courts of the land do not bind the conduct of the arbitration.[10] This means that the hearing can be conducted not only more informally but much faster than a case in court. However, the parties should not be deluded into believing that the arbitrator's decision will not be based upon evidence and facts. Even though the arbitration proceedings might be regarded as semiformal, the fact remains that

---

[9]A competent elaboration of this topic is contained in Elkouri, Frank and Edna, *How Arbitration Works* (Washington, D.C.: Bureau of National Affairs, Inc., 1960).

[10]Thus, the rules of the American Arbitration Association provide as follows: "The parties may offer such evidence as they desire and shall produce such additional evidence as the Arbitrator may deem necessary to an understanding and determination of the dispute. . . . The Arbitrator shall be the judge of the relevancy and materiality of the evidence offered and conformity to legal rules of evidence shall not be necessary." *Voluntary Labor Arbitration Rules* (New York: American Arbitration Association, 1960), pp. 5–6.

the arbitrator's decision will most likely be based *strictly* on facts, evidence, arguments, and the contractual clauses that are involved in the proceedings. Arbitration cases are not won on the basis of emotional appeals, theatrical gestures, or speechmaking. The arbitrator is interested in the facts, the evidence, and the parties' arguments as they apply to the issues of the dispute. Such material should be developed in the hearing through careful questioning of witnesses and the presentation of relevant documents.

The parties cannot, moreover, take too much care to make sure that they have presented *all* evidence that might support their case. Representatives of unions and companies who have dealt with a problem in the grievance procedure and who therefore are fully aware of all the facets of a case at times will not fully present their case because they believe that the arbitrator is likewise familiar with the facts and issues. Unless prehearing briefs are filed by the parties, it should be recognized that the arbitrator knows absolutely nothing about the case at the time of the hearing. It is the responsibility of the parties to educate him about the issues, the facts, the evidence, the arguments, and the relevant contractual clauses. Clearly, if the arbitration process is to have a significant positive value in the area of labor relations, the parties to the arbitration must discharge their obligations fully and conscientiously. Company and union representatives must be indefatigable in their efforts to prepare for the arbitration and must be absolutely thorough in the presentation of their case to the arbitrator.

Responsibilities of the arbitrator

The arbitrator, of course, is the key man in the arbitration process. His is the cold responsibility for the decision in the case. He decides, for example, whether a discharged employee remains discharged or returns to work, which of two workers gets the better job, whether the company placed a correct rate on a new job, whether an employee worked outside of his classification, whether the company rotated overtime correctly, or whether an employee forfeited his seniority under the contract. Indeed, one of the most important jobs that a person can receive is the assignment by a company and a union to an arbitration case.

In discharging his responsibilities, the arbitrator is expected to adhere to a strict code of ethics. His decision must be based squarely on the evidence and the facts presented to him. He must give full faith and credit to the language of the labor contract at the time of the case. It should be recognized by all concerned that the language of the labor agreement binds the company, the union, the employees, *and the arbitrator.* It is not within the scope of the arbitrator's authority to decide whether or not a particular contractual clause is wise or unwise, desirable or undesirable. His job is to apply the language of a labor contract as he finds it in a particular case. For an arbitrator to follow any other course of action would not only be a breach of faith to the parties but would create mischief with the labor agreement. The arbitrator must regard the collective bargaining contract as a final authority and give it full respect. If a case goes against a party because of the language of the contract, the responsibility for this state of affairs lies not with the arbitrator but with the parties who negotiated the agreement.

Much has been said and written about the necessity of the arbitrator's being "fair" in his decision. A decision is fair *only* when it is based upon the evidence of a case and the accurate assessment of the relevant provisions of the labor agreement. Furthermore, fairness does not mean charity, compromise, or an attempt to please both sides. At times a company and union arbitrate a number of different grievances in one hearing. An arbitrator is not worthy of the confidence of the parties if he deliberately sets his mind to compromise or "split" the grievances. An arbitrator who is a "splitter" not only violates the ethics of his office, but causes untold confusion and damage to the parties. What companies and unions desire in arbitration is a clear-cut decision on each grievance based upon the merits of each dispute; they do not want splitting. Compromise or "horse-trading" of grievances may be accomplished in the grievance procedure. However, once grievances are referred to arbitration, each and every one of them must be decided on its own merits. Clearly, a "split-the-difference" approach to arbitration can do irreparable harm to the parties, the collective bargaining contract, and the arbitration process. Companies and unions would quickly lose confidence in arbitration if cases were decided not upon their merits but upon the determination of the arbitrator to "even up" his awards.

In fact, before hearing a case, each arbitrator normally takes a solemn oath of office that he will decide the dispute on the evidence, free from any bias. Any arbitrator who transgresses this oath by striving to decide a case on a split-the-difference formula has absolutely no business serving as an arbitrator. A famous and respected baseball umpire once said he called them as he saw them. Though umpiring a baseball game is quite different from arbitrating a labor dispute, and though the qualifications for baseball umpires are quite different from those for arbitrators in labor relations, the homely statement "call them as you see them" has real significance for arbitration of any kind of dispute.

Additional responsibilities and personal qualities are required in the person serving as an arbitrator. Not only must he be incorruptible, free from any bias, and aware of the principles of arbitration, but he must also have a deep and well-rounded understanding of labor relations. It takes more than honesty and integrity to serve effectively as an arbitrator. Arbitrators who are not trained in labor relations matters, though they be paragons of virtue, at times can cause irreparable damage to the parties by decisions which do violence to the collective bargaining contract.

At the hearing the arbitrator should treat both sides with the dignity and the respect that is characteristic of the judicial process. He should be patient, sympathetic, and understanding. Experienced arbitrators do not take advantage of their office by being arrogant or domineering. Arbitrators who have a tendency to exaggerate their own importance should be aware of the fact that arbitration, though important, plays a distinctly minor role in the over-all union–management relationship. The arbitrator should permit each side to the dispute the fullest opportunity to present all the evidence, witnesses, documents, and arguments that it desires. Experienced arbitrators frequently will lean over backwards to permit the introduction of evidence which may or may not be relevant to the dispute. This procedure is better than a policy which could result in the suppression of vital information.

The arbitrator also has the responsibility of keeping the hearing moving. When the arbitrator notes deliberate or unconscious waste of time by either or both of the parties, he is obligated to take remedial action. This does not mean that the arbitrator should not permit recesses, coffee breaks, or the occasional telling of a humorous story; what it means is that the arbitrator earns part of his fee by conducting a fair, orderly, thorough, and speedy hearing. To this end, the arbitrator, though at all times demonstrating the qualities of patience and understanding, must remain in full *control* of the hearing. Individuals who unwittingly or by design attempt to take over the hearing must be dealt with courteously but firmly by the arbitrator. Of course, if the arbitrator is not experienced, is unsure of himself, or for some reason cannot or will not make definite decisions, the hearing can get out of hand.

The arbitrator also has an obligation to the witnesses called upon to give testimony in the hearing. Though witnesses should be subject to searching examination, the arbitrator should make sure that they are treated in a courteous manner by the examining party, or by the arbitrator himself if he asks questions of witnesses to clarify a point. He should not permit witnesses to be "badgered" or insulted. Even in cross-examination, where the examining party has more leeway with witnesses than it does in direct examination, witnesses should be treated with decorum.

Finally, the arbitrator has a responsibility to the parties relative to the award. Since one of the great advantages of arbitration is the comparatively fast disposition of disputes which it allows, the arbitrator has an obligation to get his decision into the hands of the parties rather quickly after the termination of the hearing. Unless unusual conditions are involved, such decisions should be forwarded to the parties in not less than thirty days after the termination of the hearing.[11] In discharge cases, the interests of the parties and the grievant may be best served by a decision rendered in about fifteen days. Of course, when the parties elect to file post-hearing briefs, the thirty-day limit starts from the date of the receipt of such briefs.

The award should be clear and to the point. There should be no question in the minds of the parties as to the exact character of the decision in the case. If the grievance is denied, the award should simply state that fact. Under these circumstances, some arbitrators in the decision also mention the contract provision or provisions that the company did not violate. For example, in a work-assignment case, the award might read as follows:

> The grievance of Mr. Tom Jones, Grievance No. 594, is denied on the basis that the company, under job description for Tool- and Die-makers, Class A, Code 286, and for Maintenance Men, Class A, Code 263, and without violating Article XVI of the Labor Agreement, may properly assign either category of employees to repair the classes of machinery in question in this case.

When a case is decided in favor of the union, the award should clearly and specifically direct the company to take action to bring it into compliance with the contract. In addition, to avoid any misunderstanding, the decision should require the action within a certain number of working days after the receipt of the award. For example, in a "bumping" case, the award might read as follows:

> Within three working days after the receipt of this award, the Company is directed to place the grievant, Betty Smith, into the job of Spray Painter, Class "B," Labor Grade No. 7, and to make her whole for any financial loss that she suffered because of the refusal of the Company to permit her to roll into the aforementioned job on the grounds that the Company violated Article IX, Section 7, Paragraph A and B of the Labor Agreement.

In addition to the incorporation of a clear award, the arbitrator is charged with the responsibility of writing an opinion to support his decision. Although technically opinions are not required to explain a decision, the fact is that arbitrators almost universally write an opinion.

---

[11]Thus, the Federal Mediation and Conciliation Service expects arbitrators appointed under its jurisdiction to make their awards ". . . thirty (30) days from the date of the closing of the hearing, or the receipt of a transcript and any post-hearing briefs . . . unless otherwise agreed upon by the parties or specified by law."

What is more important in this connection, companies and unions *expect* their arbitrators to write them, and agencies such as the Federal Mediation and Conciliation Service and the American Arbitration Association, which submit to companies and unions the names of arbitrators, likewise tacitly expect the arbitrator to write an opinion.

In the opinion the arbitrator sets forth the basic issues of the case, the facts, the position and arguments of the parties, and the reasons for his decision. He deals with the evidence presented in the case as it relates to his decision. Arbitrators frequently are extraordinarily careful to deal in an exhaustive manner with each major argument and piece of evidence offered by the losing side. Patently, the arbitrator has an obligation to tell the losing side just why it lost the case. Since normally the losing side will be very disappointed with the decision, the arbitrator should at least indicate in a careful manner the reasons for the adverse ruling. This probably will not make the losing side feel any better, but at least an opinion which is carefully written and which covers thoroughly the major arguments and areas of evidence will demonstrate that the character of an arbitration opinion is a guide to the amount of time, energy, and thought that the arbitrator puts into the case.

Selection of the arbitrator

After the parties decide to arbitrate a dispute, the problem of the selection of the arbitrator arises. To solve this problem, most labor agreements provide that the parties will select the arbitrator from a panel of names submitted by the above-mentioned Federal Mediation and Conciliation Service or the American Arbitration Association. When called upon by the parties to an arbitration, these agencies will supply the company and the union with a list of names. After the receipt of the panel, the parties, in accordance with a mutually acceptable formula, will select the arbitrator from the list of names. Under some labor agreements the Federal Mediation and Conciliation Service and the American Arbitration Association have the authority to select the arbitrator on a direct-appointment basis in the event that none of the names in the panel is acceptable.

The Federal Mediation and Conciliation Service is administered independently of the Department of Labor under a director appointed by the President of the United States. It maintains a steadily growing roster of experienced professional arbitrators, totalling approximately 850 names in 1965. Consistent with the significant growth in arbitration volume in recent years, its requests for approved panels of arbitrators have increased greatly over the past decade: Where in fiscal 1955, for example, the Service received 1,240 such requests, in fiscal 1964 the parties to agreements sought panels on 4,791 occasions.[12] Upon the selection of the arbitrator, the Service withdraws from active participation in the case and the relationship thereafter is strictly between the parties and the arbitrator.

Unlike the FMCS, the American Arbitration Association is a private organization. In its formative years, it devoted itself almost exclusively to the promotion of commercial arbitration, but since 1937 its Industrial Arbitration Tribunal has become increasingly active in labor disputes and currently has an annual load of about 4000 cases. In addition to furnishing the parties with arbitrator selection aid similar to that of the Mediation Service, it administers arbitration hearings in accordance with a number of formalized rules. Under AAA provisions, for example, either party intending to use a lawyer must give notice to this effect prior to the hearing date; and the expenses of witnesses for either side are to be paid directly by the party producing such witnesses. The Association's panel of available arbitrators totalled 1,400 names in 1965.

Other methods are utilized to select arbitrators. Some parties directly contact one of the more than three hundred arbitrators listed in the membership directory of the highly prestigeous National Academy of Arbitrators, the major society of the profession and an organization to whose ranks only the most experienced of neutrals are admitted.[13] In some contracts, a person of unimpeachable integrity is designated to select an arbitrator. Under such arrangements the parties have confidence that the person so designated will select a qualified arbitrator. Thus, under some labor agreements, a federal district judge, the president of a university, or a high-ranking public official will be called upon to appoint the arbitrator.

Regardless of the method, the vast majority of labor contracts provide some definite procedure for the appointment of the arbitrator. At times, companies and unions find that in practice they cannot agree on any arbitrator when the contract merely states that an arbitrator "mutually acceptable" to the parties will decide the dispute. It is sound procedure to incorporate some method for the selection of the arbitrators by an outside agency, when the parties are unable or unwilling to agree on an arbitrator on a mutual-acceptance basis.

Some companies and unions solve the problem of selecting the arbitrator by appointing a permanent arbitrator under the terms of a labor agreement. Under this arrangement, a single person will decide each dispute that is arbitrated. However, companies and unions are not in agreement on the use of a permanent arbitrator as against the *ad hoc* method of selection in which a different arbitrator may be chosen for each case.

12Federal Mediation and Conciliation Service, *Seventeenth Annual Report* (Washington, D.C.: U.S. Government Printing Office, 1965), p. 55.

13Most of the Academy's members are also registered with the Mediation Service and AAA, and can be engaged by the parties on this basis as well.

Some companies and unions as a matter of policy will use a different arbitrator for each dispute. Other companies and unions find it a better practice to use the same arbitrator. The permanent arbitrator is used most frequently when a company has a number of different plants. Such a procedure makes for uniformity of labor policy within the different operating units of the enterprise. Though the permanent arbitrator is not used as frequently in single-plant situations, there is now also a growing tendency for single-plant companies and their unions to use this system.

On the other hand, the parties should never install a permanent arbitrator unless they anticipate a sufficient number of cases to justify his appointment. One of the authors was some time ago selected as a permanent arbitrator for a six-year period: In this entire length of time, he arbitrated only five grievances!

Actually, there are advantages and disadvantages to each method. Perhaps the chief argument in favor of the *ad hoc* method is that the parties will not be "stuck" with an arbitrator that they do not want. The parties can simply dispense with him if he proves incompetent or otherwise unqualified, though it appears unlikely that a company and a union would have selected such a person to arbitrate on a permanent basis in the first place. Balancing the chief advantage of the *ad hoc* system are several disadvantages. The time and effort required to select an arbitrator for each case delays the rapid disposition of the grievance, sometimes to the detriment of plant morale. At times, out of desperation, a person who has little or no experience or real qualifications is selected to serve as an arbitrator. Such a choice may be made because he is the only person available who has not handed down an award somewhere at some time that the company and the union do not like. Moreover, because each new arbitrator must be educated to the local conditions, a comparatively long period may sometimes be required to conduct the hearing. The arbitrator's fees and expenses, which are typically shared equally by the management and union, must also be considered. A 1965 American Arbitration Association study, covering 370 arbitrators, found that the vast majority of these neutrals charged per diem fees ranging from $100 to $150[14] On this basis, it might conceivably be cheaper for the parties to adopt a permanent arrangement (such extreme cases as the personal experience cited above always excepted) and pay an annual retainer for an arbitrator's services.

[14]These amounts constituted a fairly large increase since 1954. On the other hand, the AAA's executive vice-president, in announcing the study's results, appears to have been justified in stating that "the increase has certainly not exceeded the increase in the cost of living since (1954), and in fact the per diem charges of arbitrators appeared to be conservatively related to the necessary training and competence required of similar professions." See Robert Coulson, "Spring Checkup on Labor Arbitration Procedure," *Labor Law Journal* (May, 1965), p. 264.

Perhaps the chief disadvantage of *ad hoc* arbitration, however, is the fact that this method does not assure consistency in decisions or the application of uniform principles to contract construction. No arbitrator is bound by any other arbitrator's decisions or principles of contractual construction. Consequently, disputes involving fundamentally the same issues could be resolved in as many different ways as there were abitrators chosen to decide cases. Thus, there is no assurance that a particular decision will bring stability to labor relations. It may have precedent value only until the next time the issues involved in the case are tested before another arbitrator.

The latter consideration indicates the greatest advantage of the *permanent* method of selection of arbitrators. The parties have the assurance of consistency and uniformity of decisions and consistent contractual interpretation. As a result, precedent will be established, the parties will know what to expect, and cases dealing with essentially the same issues as contained in a grievance which has previously been decided in arbitration can be settled in the earlier stages of the grievance procedure. In addition, the permanent arbitrator becomes familiar with the labor agreement, the technology of the plant, and the "shop language." This means that cases can frequently be expedited much more effectively than under circumstances of *ad hoc* arbitration.

Perhaps the chief *disadvantage* of the permanent selection method is that the parties involved may tend to arbitrate more disputes than are absolutely necessary, rather than first exhausting the possibilities of settling disputes in the grievance procedure. This is particularly true when the arbitrator is paid a set fee for a year and has the obligation to arbitrate any and all cases submitted to him.

This possibility, of course, is a serious charge against the permanent method of selection. As stated before, arbitration should be employed only after the parties have honestly exhausted every possibility of settling disputes in the grievance procedure. One method that might be effective in obtaining the advantages of the permanent method without incurring the possible disadvantages of excessive arbitration would be to compensate the *permanent* arbitrator on a *per-diem* or a *per-case basis* rather than on an annual-fee basis. In the last analysis, however, the amount of arbitration needed by a company and a union depends upon the attitudes of the parties rather than on the method of selection or the procedure of payment.

DISCUSSION QUESTIONS

1. Barbash has offered his opinion that the "handling of workers' grievances on the job is perhaps the single most important function of modern unionism." What considerations might have led to such a statement?

2. It is generally agreed that a low grievance rate does not necessarily prove the existence of good union–management relations, and that a high grievance rate does not necessarily prove the existence of poor relations between the parties. Why might the grievance statistics be misleading as a guide to the quality of the relationship?
3. From the company's viewpoint, what advantages and disadvantages might there be in reducing a grievance to writing?
4. Harold W. Davey has argued that "a genuine grievance requires an airing, even if it is not strictly in order under the existing contract." What considerations, again from the company's point of view, might justify this opinion?
5. Why might (a) a company or (b) a union prefer *not* to have an arbitration provision in the contract?
6. Dunlop and Healy have pointed out that although it is often said that "arbitration is an extension of collective bargaining," it is also frequently held that "arbitration is a judicial process." What are your own feelings regarding these two apparently inconsistent descriptions?
7. Given the fact that arbitrators have no compulsion to follow any other arbitrator's award or line of reasoning, how do you account for the fact that there are available at least three widely distributed publications which feature arbitration awards from all over the country? On the surface, would it not appear that such publications are a waste of time and money, since each arbitrator is in effect a "law unto himself"?
8. How could the present system of labor contract administration, as described in general terms in this chapter, be improved?

SELECTED REFERENCES

Cox, Archibald, "Rights Under a Labor Agreement," *Harvard Law Review,* LXIX (February, 1956), 601–57.

Davey, Harold W., *Contemporary Collective Bargaining,* 2nd. ed. Englewood Cliffs, N. J.: Prentice-Hall, Inc., 1959, pp. 117–56.

Elkouri, Frank, and Edna Elkouri, *How Arbitration Works.* Washington, D.C.: Bureau of National Affairs, Inc., 1960.

Roberts, Harold S., *Essentials of Labor Arbitration.* Honolulu: University of Hawaii, 1956.

Slichter, Sumner H., James J. Healy, and E. Robert Livernash, *The Impact of Collective Bargaining on Management.* Washington, D.C.: The Brookings Institution, 1960, pp. 692–806.

Smith, Russell A., "The Question of 'Arbitrability'—The Roles of the Arbitrator, the Court, and the Parties," *Southwestern Law Journal,* XVI (April, 1962), 1–42.

Stessin, Lawrence, "A New Look At Arbitration," *The New York Times Magazine* (November 17, 1963).

Stone, Morris, *Labor Grievances and Decisions.* New York: Harper & Row, Publishers, 1965.

———, *Labor-Management Contracts at Work.* New York: Harper & Row, Publishers, 1961.

Witte, Edwin E., *Historical Survey of Labor Arbitration.* Philadelphia: University of Pennsylvania Press, 1952.

As in the eight other cases which follow in subsequent chapters, the two arbitration reports below are drawn from the authors' own experiences. They are intended to shed further light on specific problems which can arise under collective bargaining and not to indicate the "appropriate" award for the specific controversy: Other arbitrators would, perhaps, have ruled differently in many of these cases. To preserve anonymity, the names of companies, unions, grievants, and witnesses have been concealed, but each case otherwise is based completely on an actual situation.

CASE NO. 1

Time Limits Under Grievance Procedure

(The facts of the following case show that the grievant took a leave of absence to attend to union affairs. When his work with the union was completed, he applied to the company to return to his job. The company refused him re-employment. The arbitration case deals with the problem of whether or not the union submitted his grievance to arbitration within the time limits established by the labor agreement.

It should be noted that the arbitrator does not deal with the case's *merits*, limiting himself instead to the question of time limits. If he were to find that the demand for arbitration *was* timely, he would in *another* hearing deal with the merits of the grievance.)

On January 25, 1962, C filed the following grievance:

Employee C on December 28, 1961, applied for re-employment with A Company. In a letter to Employee C dated January 11, 1962, the Company refused re-employment to C and advised him that his services with the Company were terminated.

The Union contends that the Company in its refusal violated Article V, Section 2, specifically, and other pertinent sections of the Working Agreement.

The Union and Employee C request that he C be re-employed consistent with the provisions of Article V, Section 2. It is further requested that Employee C be made whole for all benefits of employment with A Company, retroactive to date of application for re-employment.

Relevant Provisions of Contract

ARTICLE XIII, Section 3, Step 4

In the event the Company and the Union are not able to adjust a grievance concerning a question of fact in dispute under the procedure above provided for, during the term of this Working Agreement, and that dispute is not settled by the Grievance Procedure, the grievance of dispute shall, on the written demand of either party, be submitted to arbitration within twenty (20) days from the date of the disposition referred to in Step 3. For the purpose of such arbitration, there shall be established for the particular grievance or dispute an Arbitration Board consisting of one (1) person selected by the Company, one (1) person selected by the

Union, these two to be selected within five (5) days of receipt of demand for arbitration, and a third person to be impartial chairman of this Board, to be selected by these two. In the event the appointees of the Company and the Union are unable to agree within five (5) days upon such third and impartial member of the Board, such third member shall be appointed by the following procedure.

The Background

This dispute is concerned with the timeliness of the Union's demand to submit the grievance to arbitration. No inquiry is made relevant to the merits of the case. The Arbitrator is not authorized to determine whether under the circumstances of the case the Company violated Article V, Section 2, of the Labor Agreement as charged in the complaint. In fact, the Arbitrator did not hear any of the evidence dealing with the merits of the case. Testimony and documents adduced in the arbitration dealt solely with the timeliness issue. However, the parties agreed that the instant Arbitrator will hear the grievance on its merits if he finds in this proceeding that the Union's request for arbitration is timely.

As demonstrated in the chronology of the grievance, the complaint was filed originally on January 25, 1962. The parties waived the first step of the Grievance Procedure. On January 29, the Company denied the grievance in Step 2 of the Grievance Procedure. Subsequently, the Company and Union held a meeting in accordance with the Step 3 requirement of the Grievance Procedure. In this meeting, held on February 1, 1962, the parties discussed several grievances and problems, including the one involving the instant grievant. The minutes of the meeting were introduced as Union Exhibit No. 1. Relevant to the instant complaint, these minutes state as follows:

Grievance: Union Leave—C

The Union contends a violation of Article V, Section 2, paragraph D of the Working Agreement when C was denied re-employment. The Union stated that at the time C was granted his leave he was placed on loan from the International Union and to the knowledge of the local Union C is still in the employ of the Union and entitled to re-employment. If the Company denies his request the Union will submit the grievance to arbitration.

On February 5, 1962, the Company denied the instant grievance. This action constituted a denial in Step 3 of the Grievance Procedure. Subsequently, the Union wrote a letter to the Company and demanded to arbitrate the employee's grievance. Such letter was dated February 26, 1962, and provides in part as follows: "Local 4–467 would like to arbitrate their disputes with the Company in the following cases; (1) the Employee Relation grievance involving C . . ." This letter, accepted in evidence as Company Exhibit No. 1, was handed by an officer of the Union to Mr. J, Manager of the Company's Employee Relations Division, on February 27, 1962.

On March 1, 1962, the Company wrote a letter to the Union, accepted in evidence as Company Exhibit No. 2, to the effect that the Company "is not required nor will it agree to submitting (this grievance) to arbitration" because of "the untimeliness of the Union's request to arbitrate (this grievance) ."

Basic Question

The basic question in this case is framed as follows: Under the circumstances of this case, did the Union comply with the provisions of the Labor Agreement establishing the time limits for arbitration?

Position of the Parties

It is the Union's contention that the grievance should be regarded as timely for purposes of arbitration. In this respect it argues that the Union demonstrated its clear intent to arbitrate the grievance and refers in this connection to Union Exhibit No. 1. Thus, it states: "We say that on February 1, 1962, as in the Company minutes of the meeting, this intent was made evident. The inclusion of Paragraph 7 shows clearly this intent. We feel that by this inclusion it was the intent of the Union to submit the issue to arbitration and any other indication of the Union to the Company does not waive the right of the Union to arbitration. If the Union renotified the Company of its intent, it merely restated its original intent." The Union also contends that it made clear its intent to arbitrate the C grievance upon other occasions.

Another argument of the Union involves the fact that February 24 was a Saturday, and February 25 was a Sunday. On this point the Union claims that on Saturdays and Sundays there are no representatives of the Company's Labor Relations staff available, and, therefore, "there would have been no point in bringing the letter (Company Exhibit No. 1) to the Labor Relations Department on Saturday or Sunday."

Further, the Union claims that: "The written demand for arbitration was made evident by the Union's intent to arbitrate—this in itself lives up to the written demand request of the contract"; the Company itself upon occasions in the past did not meet the time limits which the contract imposes on it, and the Company despite such untimely conduct did not forfeit grievances; and the Grievance Procedure is "an amicable means to an end."

On these grounds the Union claims that the request for arbitration should be regarded as timely within the meaning of the aforementioned provisions of the Labor Agreement.

The Company claims that the request for arbitration was not timely, and, therefore, the grievance should be dismissed. Thus, it states: "It is apparent that from the dates involved that the request was not timely." Further, the Company argues that its representatives never waived its right to invoke the time limit of the contract; the Union oral declaration of its intent to arbitrate does not nullify the relevant contractual provisions; that the contract requires written notice to arbitrate and that the Union did not comply wih this mandate within the 20-day standard established in Article XIII, Section 3, Step 4. On this basis the Company requests the dismissal of the grievance.

Discussion of the Evidence

Union intent to arbitrate

There is no question that the Union demonstrated its intent to arbitrate the *C* case. This intention is made apparent not only by the declaration which it made in the meeting of February 1, 1962, but by other discussions with Company representatives. For example, even before the February 1, 1962, meeting, a Union officer testified that "I told the Company that this case would have to go to arbitration." On another occasion, a Union officer testified that the Union was willing "to waive all the intermediary steps in the Grievance Procedure and proceed directly to arbitration." Indeed, the Company itself was aware that the Union would undoubtedly arbitrate the *C* complaint. *J* testified in this respect that "the Company recognized that this case would probably be arbitrated." Also, *H*, Employee Relations Assistant, testified that "he believed that they would arbitrate the grievance."

Accordingly, the question is whether this clear intent of the Union to arbitrate supersedes the undeniable fact that the Union failed to comply with the time limit established in the Labor Agreement. As stated, the Company denied the grievance in the third step of the Grievance Procedure on February 5, 1962. Under the provisions of Article XIII, Section 3, Step 4, the Union had 20 days to file a written demand for arbitration. Therefore, the time limit expired on February 25. However, the letter demanding arbitration which the Union filed with the Company is dated February 26, and the document was not received by the Company until February 27. On the basis of these circumstances, there is no dispute that the Union did not meet the time requirements agreed to by the parties in negotiations and solemnized in the Labor Agreement.

Written demand within 20 days required

In considering the Union's position that its demonstrated intent to arbitrate the grievance amounts to making its demand for arbitration timely, it is necessary to make reference to the language of Step 4 of the Grievance Procedure. Here we find a simple, understandable, and reasonable standard of obligation written in unambiguous and unequivocal language, to which both parties agreed: The Union has 20 days to file a written demand for arbitration after a grievance is denied in Step 3. It says nothing about the intent to arbitrate. Rather, the parties voluntarily agreed in collective bargaining negotiations that a *written demand* must be made within 20 days after the Company denies a grievance in Step 3. If the parties had desired to waive this 20-day period when the Union shows its intent to arbitrate, they would, of course, have adopted appropriate language to provide for this state of affairs.

In the last analysis, what the Union requests is that the arbitrator shut his eyes to most clear-cut contractual language. It wants him to forget about the 20-day limitation to which the Union itself agreed, and find its request to arbitrate as timely because the Union had announced its intent to arbitrate. For the Arbitrator to follow this procedure would result in his rewriting of the Labor Agreement. Certainly, these parties, skilled and knowledgeable in labor relations, must recognize that no arbitrator is authorized to rewrite contractual language. In this case the Union in effect states: Forget about clear-cut contractual language and find our request timely because we demonstrated our intention to arbitrate. Under other circumstances, would the Union be content with a decision in which this Arbitrator would deny an absolutely valid grievance based upon clear-cut contractual language because the Company did not "intend" to violate the Labor Agreement? The answer to this question should be obvious to all concerned. These considerations also demonstrate the evils that can result in labor relations and to the rights of employees, employers, and labor organizations when an arbitrator simply ignores clear-cut and unambiguous contractual language.

This Arbitrator does not treat contractual language which secures rights or imposes obligations in a cavalier manner. He does not believe that such language ought to be adhered to in some cases but disregarded in others. He does not believe that plain contract language should be ignored, twisted, distorted, or amended depending upon the circumstances and the expediencies of a particular case. In short, either the parties have a contract that must be honored *under all circumstances*, or else they do not have a collective bargaining contract.

Surely, this agreement between the parties must be honored in this proceeding. If the parties did not intend that the Union forfeit its right to arbitrate when it does not comply with the time limit in question, they would not have incorporated an unambiguous time limit in their Labor Agreement. Why put a precise time limit in the contract if the Union may implement the arbitration process after the time limit has expired?

Oral declaration of intent does not comply with contractual standard

These considerations make wholly unacceptable the Union's argument herein considered. *Oral* declaration of the intent to arbitrate simply does not constitute a *written demand* for arbitration as established by the literal language of Step 4. Announcement of the intent to arbitrate is not sufficient. It is clear beyond any reasonable doubt that Step 4 requires a *written* demand for arbitration. Such a demand to be timely under Step 4 must be served on the Company *within 20 days* after the Company denies a grievance in Step 3 of the Grievance Procedure.

Of course, the Union argues that the minutes of the February 1, 1962, meeting amount to a written demand to the Company within the meaning of Step 4. Beyond the fact that as of February 1, the Company did not yet dispose of the grievance in Step 3, this position is rejected because these minutes merely reflect the Union's oral declaration of intention to arbitrate. The minutes do not constitute a written demand made by the Union on the Company to arbitrate. This Union argument would be more convincing to this Arbitrator if it demonstrated that in the past the Union demanded arbitration in this fashion. Undoubtedly, the practice has been that the Union files a *written demand* on the Company to arbitrate, and this written demand is in the form of a letter and not in the form of the minutes of grievance meetings.

Beyond these considerations is the conduct of the Union itself subsequent to February 1, 1962, and subsequent to other occasions on which it orally announced its intention to arbitrate. If the Union really believed that these oral declarations satisfied the requirements of Step 4, how does one account for the fact that the Union on February 26 did write a letter to demand arbitration? Why write the letter if oral declaration of intent is sufficient? Surely, the Union recognized that such oral declaration was not sufficient, because it wrote the letter of February 26.

In this respect the Union explains away the letter of February 26 by stating that it was a mere renotification of the Union's demand to arbitrate, which, it argues, was timely made under the contract on February 1, 1962. Frankly, this is not a convincing argument because why need there be renotification if the February 1, 1962, declaration of intention was timely and in the form required by Step 4? Further, the Union explanation ignores the heart of the problem herein considered. What did the letter of February 26 renotify? It did not renotify a *written demand* for arbitration because the declaration of the Union in the February 1, 1962 meeting merely expressed an oral intention to arbitrate. And it has already been established that oral declaration of the intent to arbitrate does not measure up to the *written* obligation required in Step 4. Therefore, if the letter of February 26 "renotified" anything, *it renotified the oral intention* of the Union to arbitrate which in itself did not measure up to the standards of Step 4.

In short, the letter of February 26 was the Union's first attempt to demand arbitration in the form spelled out in Step 4. Previous declarations of intent, including those of February 1, 1962, which were reproduced as part of the minutes of the grievance meeting, do not fulfill the standards established in the Labor Agreement.

"Saturday–Sunday" argument rejected

The Union now argues an entirely different position in the effort to gain a favorable award in this proceeding. Thus, in effect, it instructs the Arbitrator as follows: If you do not find that oral declaration of intent to arbitrate is sufficient to comply with the requirement of Step 4, and if you do not find the minutes of February 1 as constituting a written demand under Step 4, the Union advises the Arbitrator that February 24 was a Saturday and February 25 was a Sunday. Therefore, you should find the demand for arbitration as contained in the letter of February 26 as timely on this basis.

The Arbitrator does not find this argument as an adequate excuse to explain why the Union was late in filing its written demand for arbitration. Though it is, of course, true that February 24 and 25 were, respectively, a Saturday and a Sunday, and that members of the Company's labor relations staff were not available on these two days, how does one account for the fact that the Union did not avail itself of the opportunity to demand arbitration from February 5 until February 25? *Here were 20 full calendar days wherein the Union could have complied with the simple task of filing a written demand for arbitration.* Still, during this entire period the Union did not take advantage of its right to demand arbitration.

Furthermore, this "Saturday–Sunday" argument of the Union is not convincing to the Arbitrator because the parties fully intended that Saturdays, Sundays, and holidays are to be counted in computing the 20 days in which arbitration can be demanded after the Company denies a complaint in Step 3. This is true because the parties expressly *excluded* Saturdays, Sundays, and holidays from the calculation of the time period in which a grievance may be filed in the *first* step of the Grievance Procedure. Surely, if the parties had intended to exclude Saturdays and Sundays in the calculation of the

20 days under Step 4 they would have adopted language similar to that found in Step 1 of the Grievance Procedure. Since they did not do so, the clear intent of the parties is that the 20-day period constitutes calendar days which, of necessity, include Saturdays, Sundays, and holidays. Such omission cannot possibly be regarded as an oversight on their part when they specifically excluded these days from the calculation of time limits in the first step of the Grievance Procedure.

Company did not waive time limits

If the Company had expressly or tacitly waived the 20-day time limit in question, the case could be decided upon its merits. But the record is clear that the Company did no such thing. In fact, a Union official testified that "*J* did not say that he agreed to arbitrate"; and another Union official testified that "I don't say that the Company said that it would waive the written agreement."

Apparently the Union does suggest that the Company did waive the time limits under the circumstances of this case. This argument proceeds from the fact that the parties agreed to waive Step 1 of the Grievance Procedure. However, the Company's willingness to waive Step 1 cannot possibly be construed to mean that it thereby waived all other requirements of the Grievance Procedure. This is so obvious that there is no further need of comment.

Also, the Union suggests that the Company waived the time limits because it was aware that the Union intended to arbitrate the case, but that the Company insisted that the parties go through the "formalities" of the Grievance Procedure. Thus, a Union official testified: "*J* said 'we understand that you will have to arbitrate this case, but let's go through the formalities of the Grievance Procedure.' " Though this may be perfectly true, the Arbitrator still does not see how this condition resulted in the Company's waiver of the time limits. To repeat, it was the testimony of Union officials that the Company did not say at any time during the negotiations that "it would waive the written agreement."

Finally, the record is perfectly clear that after the Union failed to meet the contractual time limits, the Company refused to arbitrate the case on its merits. Its letter to the Union on March 1, 1962 (Company Exhibit No. 2), and its subsequent action demonstrates without question that the Company did not explicitly or implicitly waive the 20-day time limit wherein the Union had the opportunity to demand arbitration.

Past practice: evidence not adequate

To buttress its case the Union argues that there were other instances wherein the Company and Union filed untimely grievances which nevertheless were decided on their merits. Thus, a Union official testified:

> I recall instances in the past when other untimely acts were committed by the Union and Company. There have been times when the Company has not met the time limits of the contract. I remember once when the Company was considerably late in their answer and this Union wrote a letter to the Company about this. Since the Company was not timely, we asked whether the Company believed that the lateness meant that the Company considered the grievance granted. But the Company stated it made an honest mistake, and it was not going to grant the grievance on this basis.

Herein the Union admittedly raises a significant point, and if the evidence were adequate it could have had an important bearing upon this case. But it is quite clear that the aforementioned statement does not amount to the kind of evidence which is convincing in arbitration. Specific instances are not mentioned wherein acts of untimeliness were committed. The grievances are not cited; the circumstances are not mentioned; and the dates are not spelled out.

Instead, the statement constitutes a vague generalization. Indeed, the Company could not have defended itself against such ambiguous generalizations since the particulars are not spelled out. If the Union desired to make a convincing point of such alleged past practice, it had the obligation to cite the particulars and the exact circumstances. In short, it would be entirely improper to base a decision on the kind of evidence which the Union offers in this respect. After all, arbitration is a judicial process, and requires evidence which is concrete, precise, and definite. These standards are obviously not met, and, therefore, the Arbitrator cannot possibly use such vague and ambiguous testimony as the basis for his decision.

Union failed to comply with time limit

No matter how one regards the circumstances of this case, it simply is not possible to find the Union's demand for arbitration to be timely under the Labor Agreement. The only way that this can be done would be for the Arbitrator to shut his eyes to the words "20 days" and "written demand" spelled out in Step 4 of the Grievance Procedure. Such conduct on his part would be wholly indefensible and would amount to a breach of the obligations of his office.

Of course, the Arbitrator understands that the Union in this case probably made an innocent error—an error, however, which cannot be overlooked in arbitration. The Union had a clear obligation to demand arbitration in *writing* and *within 20 days*. The hard and cold fact is that it did not meet this obligation, and regardless of the valiant attempt which the Union made in this proceeding, this failure on its part cannot be ignored or explained away. Rather, the failure of the Union to comply with the contractually stated time limits must stand as the determining feature in this proceeding.

Precedents

The issue involved in this case is not a novel one in arbitration. Many cases have been decided wherein the question of timeliness of the filing of grievances and demands for arbitration have been involved. In this respect, professional and seasoned arbitrators have normally denied grievances wherein unions have failed to meet clearly defined time limits. Thus, as stated in a standard volume on arbitration: "If the agreement does contain clear time limits for filing and prosecuting grievances, failure to observe them generally will result in a dismissal of the grievance if the failure is protested."[15] Many arbitration decisions underscore this principle in arbitration:

> *International Harvester,* 10 LA 525 (1948) [16]
> *Northeast Airlines,* 37 LA 741 (1961)
> *Valley Dolomite,* 11 LA 98 (1948)
> *Barbet Mills,* 19 LA 677 (1952)
> *Phillips Petroleum,* 7 LA 595 (1947)
> *Jones & Laughlin Steel Corp.,* 17 LA 277 (1951)
> *Tim Processing Corp.,* 26 LA 732 (1956)
> *Bethlehem Steel Co.,* 6 LA 397 (1947)
> *Standard-Coosa-Thatcher Co.,* 4 LA 79 (1946)
> *Southeastern Greyhound Lines,* 4 LA 459 (1946)
> *Kaiser Aluminum & Chemical Co.,* 32 LA 704 (1959)
> *Kroger Co.,* 36 LA 270 (1960)
> *Olin Mathieson Chemical Corp.,* 37 LA 588 (1961)
> *West Penn Power Co.,* 31 LA 297 (1958)
> *Square D Company,* 25 LA 225 (1955)
> *Truit Manufacturing Co.,* 27 LA 157 (1956)
> *Walker County Hosiery Mills,* 13 LA 387 (1949)
> *Bauer Bros.,* 15 LA 318 (1950)
> *Walter Kiddie & Co.,* 16 LA 369 (1951)

A review of these precedents demonstrates that many of them were decided by respected and seasoned arbitrators, including Ralph Seward, Peter Kelliher, and Whitley McCoy; several of them in-

15Elkouri, *How Arbitration Works* (Washington, D.C.: Bureau of National Affairs, 1960), p. 105.

16Bureau of National Affairs, ed., *Labor Arbitration Reports,* Vol. 10 (Washington, D.C.: Bureau of National Affairs, Inc., 1948), 525.

volved cases wherein employees were terminated from their jobs; and in some cases the union failure to comply with time limits amounted to a very short period of time. Thus, in *Olin Mathieson Chemical Corp.*, 37 LA 588 (1961) which involved the discharge of an employee, the arbitrator in that case dismissed the grievance because the labor organization was two days late in complying with grievance procedure time limits.

These precedents are cited to show that the arbitrator's decision in this case is in keeping with an accepted principle of labor arbitration. He understands, of course, that these precedents are not binding upon him, but still it is very significant that arbitrators have established the principle that failure of unions to comply with clear-cut time limits results in forfeiture of the right to arbitrate grievances on their merits.

To be sure, there have been some instances wherein arbitrators have found grievances to be timely submitted over the protest of the company. In these cases, however, there were involved extenuating or special circumstances which prompted the arbitrators to hold the grievances to be timely. For example, in *Levinson Steel*, 23 LA 135, the arbitrator held that the United States Post Office was responsible for the union's failure to meet the time limits; in *Lapham-Hickey*, 3 LA 327, the arbitrator found that the company waived time limits by its action of discussing the case on its merits *after* time limits had run out, and did not mention time limits during these negotiations; and in *United States Pipe and Foundry*, 28 LA 777, the issue was found to be arbitrable because time limits in the contract were ambiguous. Clearly, the circumstances of the instant proceeding are distinguishable from these cases.

Conclusions and Award

The Arbitrator is fully aware of the significance of his decision. What it means is that *C* cannot get his job back, and he cannot even have the benefit of an arbitration hearing wherein the merits of his case can be determined. Unless the Company, despite this decision, elects to arbitrate the *C* case on its merits, the employee's job is terminated. Naturally, the Arbitrator is sympathetic to the grievant. After all, it wasn't the grievant who caused his complaint to be dismissed without even so much as a hearing to examine its merits.

The Arbitrator is frank enough to state that he reaches his decision with real and deep regret. He would have preferred to hear the case on its merits, since here we have an employee terminated, not because of the substance of his claim, but because of a procedural issue.

Further, the Arbitrator passes no judgment on the wisdom of the Company's insistence that the grievance be dismissed because of the failure of the Union to comply with contractual time limits.

As the Union states, the Grievance Procedure is designed to promote the "amicable" disposition of disputes arising between the parties. What the Union really is saying is that the dismissal of this grievance on the basis of time limits does not resolve the actual problem which gave rise to the dispute in the first place, and, further, it suggests that the real purpose of the Grievance Procedure is not effectuated by the Company's stand in this proceeding.

Still the fact remains that the Arbitrator cannot find in the evidence that the Union's demand for arbitration was timely within the meaning of the Labor Agreement. Since it was not timely, the Union forfeited the right of the grievant to have his case heard on its merits. The Arbitrator is bound by the written Labor Agreement which the parties negotiated. Part of this agreement is the requirement that the Union demand arbitration *in writing within 20 days* after a grievance is denied in Step 3 of the Grievance Procedure. Regardless of how one looks at the evidence in this case, the cold and hard fact is that the Union did not comply with this precise and clear-cut statement. Since it did not comply, this Arbitrator has no choice except to deny the grievance. The alternative would be for the Arbitrator to blatantly disregard a clear-cut contractual standard, voluntarily agreed to by the Union and the Company. Such conduct on his part would amount to the forfeiture of the trust and faith reposed in him by the parties and to a repudiation of the best and accepted standards of arbitration.

After carefully considering the evidence, including the relevant provisions of the Labor Agreement, and in his best judgment, the Arbitrator makes the following Award:

The grievance of *C*, dated January 25, 1962, is denied on the grounds that the Union's demand for arbitration was not timely within the meaning of Article XIII, Section 3, Step 4 of the Labor Agreement.

QUESTIONS

1. How would *you* have decided the case? Justify your decision with cogent arguments.
2. Would the integrity of the time limits included in the labor agreement be jeopardized if the decision went for the Union?
3. Should a discharged employee be denied a hearing on the merits of his case because someone in a union does not comply with time limits established in a contract?

CASE NO. 2

Arbitrability of Grievance

(In this case the grievants contend that the Company involved violated the labor agreement because they were not credited for 20 minutes' "downtime." When employees are paid under an incentive wage system, the question arises as to the payment for the time that their machine is not in operation, or where the machine is "down." A machine may not be in production for a variety of reasons, such as mechanical breakdown, the need to await materials, maintenance, and the like. Under the contract involved in this case, when the Company approves "downtime," such situation will not detract from the earnings of the employee. In the situation which gave rise to the grievance, the Company *refused* to approve the downtime, and the union carried the dispute into arbitration, contending that the Company *should have* approved the downtime and that, by its refusal to do so, the grievants' earnings were adversely affected.)

On March 7, 1963 *C* and *B* filed Grievance Number 1884, which states:

The foreman wouldn't accept 20 minutes downtime from 2 employees *B* and *C* for having to wait on Inspector before unloading rack out of oven.

Involved in this dispute are the following provisions of the Labor Agreement:

Paragraph 08:15
The arbitrator shall have no power to add to, or subtract from or modify any of the terms of this Agreement or any Agreement made supplementary hereto, such as, establishing or changing any wage, or passing on any matters arising under wages, or passing on matters having to do with production standards, or concerning new jobs.

Paragraph 22:05
When it is necessary to transfer an incentive worker to down-time, due to tool trouble, lack of material, etc., such employee will remain on his regular incentive group and be paid at the earned weekly efficiency for all hours worked; however, such hours of regular rates work will be credited to his incentive group at 100% of his regular hourly base rate. It will be the responsibility of any employee requesting loss time, down time, etc., to contact his supervisor immediately upon starting such claim, secure authorization for the starting and ending of such time. Time not approved will not be credited to the group.

Paragraphs 24 and 25
(These paragraphs establish the basic wage structure of the plant. In Paragraph 25, there is recited each classification in the plant, together with the wage rates to be paid each of the classifications upon the employee being hired into the classification, and the rates to be paid after 8 and 16 weeks within the classification. There is no need to reproduce these paragraphs in this Opinion, since they are established on pages 44 and 45 in the Labor Agreement, Joint Exhibit No. 1.)

Basic Question

The basic question in this dispute is whether Grievance Number 1884 is a proper subject for arbitration.

Background

As the grievance indicates, the grievants charge that the Company improperly refused to accept 20 minutes' downtime while they allegedly waited for an inspector to check their work before unloading certain material from the oven. In the plant a group incentive system is in effect which permits employees to make 125 per cent of efficiency working at normal pace. Under Paragraph 22:05, approved downtime of an employee, for whatever cause, will be credited to his incentive group at 100 per cent of his regular hourly base rate. In short, approved downtime will not detract from the earning capacity of an incentive group. On the other hand, downtime which is not accepted by the Company tends to reduce the earnings of an incentive group. In the instant case the grievants believe that the improper rejection of downtime by the Company adversely affected the earnings of the incentive group in which they were working.

Position of the Parties

The central question in this dispute is whether grievances concerning downtime are arbitrable under the Labor Agreement. The Company claims that such disputes are beyond the proper jurisdiction of the Arbitrator under the terms of Paragraph 08:15 of the Labor Agreement. Specifically, it claims that downtime is a feature of production standards, and, therefore, any controversy involving downtime is beyond this Arbitrator's authority. Thus, it states: "It is quite clear that any grievance pertaining to 'Production Standards' is not arbitrable. In no place in the contract is downtime referred to except in Article XXII, 'Production Standards.' Therefore, it must follow that downtime is associated only with Production Standards." Further, the Company charges that the Union is seeking an objective in arbitration which is unsuccessfully sought in contract negotiations. It points out that in the last negotiation, the Union attempted to make any grievance subject to arbitration. In this attempt the Union was unsuccessful, the Company argues, despite the fact that it was "one of the Union's most serious requests." Thus, the Company believes that it would be entirely improper for the Arbitrator to hold that downtime grievances may be a proper subject for arbitration.

The Union holds that downtime grievances are arbitrable and that Paragraph 08:15 does not prevent the Arbitrator from determining the merits of the grievance. It claims that the downtime cited in the instant grievance was justifiable, and, because it was not accepted by the Company, there was created "a loss of wages for all the employees in a particular group." With reference to

Paragraph 08:15, the Union contends that it "has no bearing on the case whatsoever. We (the Union) have charged the Company with violation of Articles 24 and 25. We maintain that the rate structure was agreed on by both parties and therefore, is final and binding." Thereupon the Union attempts to buttress its case with an example: Thus, "if of three employees working in an incentive group, two were earning their 125 per cent and the third one was down for four hours with a machine breakdown, should the Company refuse to pay the appropriate rate for this four hours' downtime, the employees themselves, instead of the Company, would be paying for the four hours." In short, improper denial on the part of the Company for downtime not only adversely affects the earning capacity of incentive groups, but likewise violates the wage rate structure of Paragraphs 24 and 25, the Union contends.

Discussion of the Evidence

Production standards and downtime

The key to the determination of this dispute is the fact that there is in effect a wage incentive system based upon production standards. Under a straight time method of wage payment, production standards normally are not established. Regardless of output, employees receive the same hourly rate of pay. Earnings are not tied to the rate of output. As against the straight hour system, employees working under an incentive system can earn more than their guaranteed hourly rate of pay depending upon their capacity to exceed standard levels of production.

At times, employees being paid under a wage incentive system based upon production standards must wait because of machine breakdown, tool trouble, material shortages, etc. Under these circumstances, the capacity of the employee to meet or exceed production standards is adversely affected. By the same token, his earning capacity could be reduced because of waiting or downtime. Therefore, any incentive wage system must provide some method of adjusting downtime as it relates to the capacity of employees to achieve production goals. In short, as long as employees' earnings are based upon production standards, the downtime issue must be handled in some way. No such problem exists under a straight hourly system, because the employees' wages remain the same regardless of output.

In the light of these observations, it should be apparent that the problem of downtime is an integral feature of wage incentive systems based upon production standards. In fact, downtime is a chief problem under any production-oriented pay system. In recognition of this fact, the Company and Union deal with the downtime problem only under that area of the Labor Agreement which treats with production standards. This, of course, is perfectly logical and understandable, because downtime affects the capacity of employees to achieve production goals or standards.

"Matters arising under wages"

Actually, this Opinion could be terminated at this point, because the Arbitrator has no jurisdiction over the establishment or the administration of production standards. Such power is specifically denied to him by the express and unequivocal language of Paragraph 08:15. As developed above, the problem of downtime is an integral part of the administration of production standards and the language of Paragraph 22:05 specifically recognizes it as such. Still, the Arbitrator would make additional comments on the issues involved in this dispute. The Union charges the Company with a violation of Paragraphs 24 and 25 of the Labor Agreement. Its reasoning in this respect has already been expressed in that section of this Opinion which deals with the Union's position in this case. The Arbitrator, of course, understands that if an employee in an incentive group is unfairly denied credit for downtime, the earnings of the entire group are adversely affected. On this basis, it could be argued that in a sense the affected employees "pay" for the uncredited downtime in the sense that their earnings would be higher if the employee received credit for the downtime.

Now, even if the allegation is regarded as true, and even if it is assumed that this tends to affect the wage structure as outlined in Paragraphs 24 and 25 of the Labor Agreement, the fact remains that the Arbitrator still does not have jurisdiction over this dispute. The reason for this finding is again based upon the explicit language of Paragraph 08:15. Note that this provision denies the Arbitrator the authority to pass on "any matters arising under wages." Therefore, even if this position of the Union is regarded as perfectly valid, the Arbitrator is still forbidden to deal with the issue contained in the grievance. Certainly, the grievance poses a "matter" relating to wages, an area of controversy which is held as not arbitrable under the unequivocal language of Paragraph 08:15.

Conclusions

In short, the Union requests the Arbitrator to exercise authority in an area which is specifically denied him under the Labor Agreement. To hold that the instant dispute is arbitrable would be a raw abuse of the powers which the contract confers upon him. It may be true that downtime grievances should be arbitrable. Perhaps, also, the Company has unfairly refused to credit employees with downtime. On these matters, the Arbitrator passes no judgment. However, whether or not such problem should be arbitrable is a decision which the parties themselves must make in contract negotiations. Whether or not it would be wise or unwise, desirable or undesirable, fair or unfair, are issues which the Company and the Union themselves must resolve. Unless the Arbitrator completely ignores the plain language of the instant contract, he simply must find and conclude that downtime grievances are beyond the proper scope of his authority.

QUESTIONS

1. Assuming that you are familiar with the United States Supreme Court decisions in the "Trilogy" cases, do you believe that a federal court would have held the dispute to be nonarbitrable?
2. What reasoning would you use if you disagreed with the arbitrator and held the dispute to be arbitrable on the merits?
3. Do you believe that the arbitrator's decision will complicate the negotiations of the next labor agreement?

Almost all contract negotiations pivot upon, and most grievances and arbitration procedures thus ultimately deal with, four major areas: (1) wages, and issues which can be directly related to wages; (2) employee benefits, or economic "fringe" supplements to the basic wage rate; (3) "institutional" issues, dealing with the rights and duties of employers and unions; and (4) what might be most appropriately described as "administrative" clauses, treating such subjects as work rules and job tenure. In this chapter and the three which follow it, each of these areas will be discussed in turn. As in the previous chapter, arbitration cases also will be used, where appropriate, to illustrate particular problems.

Probably no issues under collective bargaining continue to give rise to more difficult problems than do wages and wage-related subjects. When negotiations reach a stalemate, they frequently do so because company and union representatives are not able to find a formula to resolve wage disputes. And wage controversies are, for that matter, by far the leading overt cause of strikes: In 1964, for example, they accounted for almost 40 per

7

Wage issues under

collective bargaining

cent of all strikes and were responsible for approximately 41 per cent of all time lost in production because of work stoppages.[1]

This record highlights the vital character of wage negotiations in collective bargaining, and also suggests that in the area of wages much can be done to decrease management–labor conflict substantially. In any area of human relations, ignorance breeds suspicion, distruct, and conflict; this principle of human behavior is fully applicable to wage negotiations under collective bargaining. To the extent that understanding is substituted for ignorance there will be a greater opportunity for peaceful settlement of wage controversies, even if conflict of interest in such matters will never disappear.

It is not difficult to understand why wages do play such an important and controversial role in labor relations. For workers, wages are normally the only source of income, and the standard of living of the employee and his family is determined almost exclusively by this source. For workers' families, the weekly paycheck establishes the character and quality of their dwelling, food, clothing, education, recreation, and of all other items which are included in the concept of "standard of living."

But if from the point of view of the worker, wages are income which establishes a standard of living, from the viewpoint of the *company*, wages are a cost of production. And here is the heart of the wage controversy. On one hand, employees press for higher and higher wages with the objective of raising their standard of living. On the other hand, employers are confronted with increasing pressures on the cost of production. When wages are a significant element of cost of production, when wage increases are not offset by such economic phenomena as increased efficiency, and when the union has been unable (or unwilling) to extract equal wage concessions from all competitive firms, wage increases tend to place the firm in an undesirable economic position. A company so placed might not be able to survive for long in the competitive struggle. Under such a state of affairs, union wage policy, instead of advancing the standard of living of its members, could plunge them into economic oblivion.

As a result of the difficult and controversial nature of wage problems, it is crucial that they be dealt with in an intelligent and sound manner. Perhaps as no other area of collective bargaining, wage problems test the skill, understanding, and attitudes of negotiators. The latter are, as we know, now confronted with a *legion* of wage issues, including the establishment of the basic wage rate, wage differentials, overtime rates, and wage adjustments during contractual periods, as well as with the thorny problems involved in the negotiation of the so-called "fringe" or supple-

---

[1] "A Review of Work Stoppages During 1964," *Monthly Labor Review*, LXXXVIII, No. 6 (June, 1965), 665.

mental wage payments which will be discussed in the next chapter. It is hoped that the following discussion of some of the principles, practices, and trends concerning these several wage and wage-related areas will contribute to better understanding of them.

Determination of the Basic Wage Rate

If union and management representatives are exhibiting an ever greater willingness to deal with factual information at the bargaining table, there is still no single standard for wage rate determination which has anything approaching a "scientific" base. Both of the bargaining parties, indeed, commonly utilize at least *three different* such standards, each of which has definite advantages from the viewpoint of achieving an "equitable" settlement but also significant limitations: the "comparative-norm," ability to pay, and standard of living criteria.

Comparative-norm principle

To a great extent, company and union negotiators make use of the "comparative-norm principle" in wage negotiations. The basic idea behind this concept is the presumption that the economics of a particular collective bargaining relationship should neither fall substantially behind nor be greatly superior to that of other employer–union relationships, that—in short—it is generally a good practice to keep up with the crowd, but not necessarily to lead it.

The outside observer would very likely agree with this principle, at least on the surface. When a firm is operating with a highly competitive product or in highly competitive labor markets, there is safety for employee relations in keeping labor costs and wage rates consistent with the local and industrial pattern, but not necessarily any need to exceed this pattern. Unions tend to maintain harmony and contentment among the rank and file as long as wage conditions are uniform; on the other hand, it is at times quite difficult and embarrassing for union leaders to explain to the membership why their economic terms of employment are *not* at least equivalent to those of other unionists (particularly where one local of an international union falls substantially behind another local of the same international). In short, the comparative-norm principle is often valid for economic, sociological, and psychological reasons.

Thus companies and unions frequently make a careful and comprehensive study of the community and industry wage structure before negotiations begin and then compare these rates to the rates in existence in the plant involved in the negotiations. The strategic implications of such comparisons, already cited in Chapter 5, are quite obvious. If the plant rates are below the community or industry pattern, the union can be expected to argue for a wage increase on this basis. When the plant rates are in excess of the community or industry pattern, the company has an argument *against* a wage increase.

Notwithstanding these considerations, there are limitations to this approach to the bargaining process. All firms do not have the same capacity to meet economic demands. This is the case not only for firms in different industries but also for companies operating within the same industry. Though economic forces are at work which tend to place firms operating within the same industrial grouping on the same economic footing, many other factors—such as imperfections in the product market, technological differences, location, stage of economic development, and financial resources—*may*, at any one time, place such firms on different economic levels. From this it follows that at any one time firms may be quite different in their individual capacities to meet economic demands and that the optimum wage level for one firm of a particular industry could be quite low (or quite high) in comparison with that of the industry in general.

Negotiations in the steel industry serve to illustrate this point. Most of the basic steel manufacturers, whether large or small, are organized by the United Steelworkers of America. So, too, are most steel fabrication firms, which purchase their steel from the basic steel companies, fabricate it, and then sell the resultant steel products directly to other industrial plants or to private consumers. The membership of the union is, in fact, divided about equally between employees who work in these two sectors of the steel industry.

In negotiations with the basic steel companies, the union's highest national officers deal directly with a small employer committee agreed upon by the larger of these companies (United States Steel, Bethlehem, Republic, Jones & Laughlin, and similar large producers). From this key negotiation, a "pattern," or comparative norm is established. The union then officially tries to gain about the same wage settlement individually from the smaller basic steel plants and the steel fabrication firms. Clearly, however, the financial and market circumstances of the large basic steel producers are quite different from those confronting the other types of managements—and the inevitable result is a wide variety of different degrees of pattern following and pattern deviation in what is nonetheless still referred to as the "steel industry".

Many other examples could be used to demonstrate the same principle. Within the rubber industry, the economic conditions, and thus the wage-paying abilities, of the large firms oriented toward the rubber-tire market are quite different from those of the smaller footwear manufacturers. And highly competitive rubber-heel plants, for example, normally settle with the Rubber Workers for considerably less than the rubber-tire pattern established with Firestone, Goodrich, and similar rubber-tire titans, even though many of the latter firms also manufacture footwear. Large meatpackers (such as Swift and Armour) are generally in better positions to allow higher wage levels than are their smaller competitors. In the automobile industry, there are obviously significant economic differences between General Motors and American Motors. These considerations must be recognized before one accepts the proposition that the comparative-norm principle of wage determination should be used as the exclusive, or the most desirable, standard for wage settlements in collective bargaining.[2]

There are at least four other factors to be considered in regard to the comparative-norm principle. First, not only do firms within a given industry at any given time have unequal capabilities to meet economic demands, but frequently it is quite difficult to *classify* a firm in a particular industrial grouping for wage comparison purposes. Some firms may logically be classified in two or more industries because of the products they manufacture or the services they provide. Likewise, even if a firm is classified within a particular industry, there are frequently highly meaningful subgroupings in each major industrial classification. Within the oil industry, for example, there are large, medium, and small producers of oil, and producers can be classified considerably further in terms of exact product and nature of operations. Such complicating circumstances illustrate the difficulty of classifying a particular firm in a particular industry or in a segment of an industry for purposes of wage determination.

A second limitation involved in the use of the comparative-norm wage principle for collective bargaining is the fact that it is at times misleading to compare employees within a particular job classification, because the content of jobs may be substantially different among plants within the same labor market. The duties of an employee classified as a "subassembler, B" in one plant may be quite different from those carried out by an employee classified identically in another plant. The fact is that job classifications within industry have not been standardized. As long

---

[2] Recognition of the differences between firms and industries should also be taken into account when the *nonmoney* items of collective bargaining are negotiated. A seniority system, for example, which is suitable for one employer–union relationship, may not fit the needs of the employer and employees of another plant. Union security formulas, checkoff arrangements, managerial prerogative systems, grievance procedures, discharge and disciplinary arrangements, and the character of union obligations should be geared fundamentally to the particular collective bargaining relationship. Company and union representatives are at times astonished to learn of the contractual arrangement of another employer–union relationship. The fact is, however, that such a formula frequently can be explained logically in terms of the environment of that firm.

as this situation exists, and there is reason to believe that it will continue to exist, the usefulness of the comparative-norm wage principle is proportionately reduced.

This wage criterion is limited in its applicability by still a third complication. It is difficult to use the principle when comparing workers who are within the same job classification but who are paid by different systems of wage payments. Some workers are paid on a straight hourly-rate basis, others under an individual incentive system, and still others on a group incentive plan. The kind of wage system in operation can in itself have a significant impact upon wage rates.

Briefly described, incentive wages constitute a method of wage payment by which earnings are geared more or less directly to actual output instead of to time spent on the job. Employees are thus granted a relatively clear-cut financial motivation to increase their outputs, essentially by increasing the effort on which such outputs depend.

On the other hand, determination of the actual rate of pay for each "piece" or unit of output is, of course, open to union–management controversy: the company's conception of an appropriate rate is typically somewhat less liberal than is the union's. And the problem is compounded when the original job on which the rate has been set is in any way "modified" (as virtually all jobs ultimately are, because of a host of factors ranging from worker-implemented short cuts to management job re-engineering) and each party seeks a new rate which is beneficial to its own interests.

Some unions have historically opposed such plans from their inception, through fear of management rate-cutting (for example, artificial reconstruction of the job in order to pay it a lower rate) and because of a deeply harbored suspicion that there is nothing "scientific" to *any* established rates. But managements which have yielded too *readily* to union requests for higher rates have *also* suffered, in inequities between earnings and effort, and in consequent problems involving not only finances but also employee morale. Increased automation of industry to the point where many workers cannot control their output rates has caused some further de-emphasis of incentive plans in recent years. However, 26 per cent of all production-plant workers in the United States continue to be paid under such plans, and it is obvious that the presence of such workers can make the comparative-norm principle severely misleading.

Fourth, and finally, consideration must be given to the existence of the wide variety of fringe benefits previously cited. These benefits are not distributed equally throughout industry. Thus it could be wrong to conclude that workers in different plants are not equal in terms of net economic advantage where one group earns a lower basic wage rate but surpasses another group in terms of paid holidays and vacations, retirement, social insurance, and the like.

These considerations do not mean that the comparative-norm principle is of no value in collective bargaining. Its utility is demonstrated by its widespread use. But bargainers who utilize this avenue of wage comparisons without recognition of the several problems and limitations involved in its implementation do so only at their peril.

Ability to pay

A second leading criterion involved in wage determination under collective bargaining is the ability of the firm or industry to pay a wage increase. Frequently the outcome of wage negotiations will be shaped by this factor, and many strikes do occur where there is disagreement between company and union negotiators relative to the wage-paying capacity of the enterprise. Careful consideration and better understanding of this factor of wage determination is no less imperative for reducing the area of disagreement between industry and organized labor than is familiarity with the comparative-norm factor.

The level of profits is one indicator of the wage-paying ability of the firm involved in the negotiations. If a firm is earning a "high" rate of profit, union representatives will frequently claim that the company can afford all or most of the union wage demand. If the firm is earning a "low" rate of profit, management negotiators will frequently argue that the firm does not have the financial capacity to meet the union's wage demands. But the heart of this controversy is, clearly, the determination of what constitutes a rate of profits sufficient to meet a given union wage demand. Unfortunately, there is no economic formula which can answer this question with precision and exactness.

As in the case of the previous criterion, the problem is complicated by further considerations. In the first place, it is not certain whether a given rate of profits earned by a company over a given time in the past will hold for the future. Future profits may fall or rise depending upon the behavior of a number of economic variables, which are themselves uncertain: Changes in sales, output, productivity, price, managerial efficiency, and even the state of international relations will all bear upon the future profit experience of a particular firm or industry. Thus a wage rate negotiated in the light of a given historical profit experience may not be appropriate in the future. Moreover, if profits are to be used as an indicator of the firm's ability to meet a given wage demand, consideration must be given to anticipated government tax structures. The wage-paying ability of the firm may be quite different before and after the payment of the federal income tax, as many business administrators can testify. There are additional elements of the never-static national and state tax programs which tend to have an impact on the wage-paying ability of industry.

Secondly, the use to which a company intends to put its profits also has a vital bearing upon this problem. Since profits frequently are used to promote plant growth and improvement, the future plans of the enterprise itself must receive consideration by the negotiators. The problem of whether profits should be used for plant growth and improvement, for lower commodity price, or for higher wages is one of the most troublesome issues in industrial relations. The complexities of the problem involve such highly controversial matters as business-cycle theory, the orderly and sound growth of the economy, adequate purchasing power to buy the goods that industry produces, the varying expansion needs of different firms and industries, the justice or the injustice of plant expansion instead of wage increases, the specific amount of the profits which should be used for wages, and alternative methods of financing growth and plant improvement other than the use of profits. These are only some of the secondary problems involved in the use of profits as an indicator of the ability of a company or industry to meet union wage demands. Clearly, the multitude of problems and questions that come to light in this connection demonstrates the difficulty of the utilization of this determinant of wages.

Third, though the level of profits is an important factor in the determination of a firm's ability to pay wages, it is not the only factor. Other considerations which have an important bearing on the problem are: the ratio of labor costs to total costs, the amount of money expended for the financing of fringe benefits, the character of the product market in which the firm operates, the degree of elasticity of demand for the firm's product, and the ability of the company to increase productivity.

The ratio of labor costs to total costs particularly conditions the ability of a firm to afford increased wage rates. An employer is in a better position to grant higher wages when the firm's labor costs represent a comparatively small part of the total costs. For example, a 10 per cent increase in wage rates will result in a 1 per cent increase in total costs when wage costs are 10 per cent of total costs (as they are, for example, in portions of the petroleum industry). Where, however, wage costs are 50 per cent of total costs, (as in segments of the leather industry), a 10 per cent increase in wage rates will result in a 5 per cent increase in total costs. This illustration, of course, is based upon the assumption that there is no increase or decrease in labor productivity after the wage rates are negotiated. If output increases faster than the wage rise, labor cost per unit of production tends to decrease. The reverse would be true where labor productivity does not increase with higher wages.

Moreover, the ratio of labor cost to total cost cannot by itself be taken as conclusive evidence of the wage-paying ability of a particular firm. Firms with a low labor cost do not necessarily have the capacity to pay higher wages. By the same token, it would not be accurate to conclude that firms with a high labor cost can never afford wage increases. All that can be said with some degree of accuracy is that if all economic variables were held constant, a firm with a low labor-cost ratio could afford to pay higher wages more easily than a firm with a high labor-cost ratio.

As in the case of the comparative-norm principle, it should also be re-emphasized that an employer's total wage bill includes not only direct wage costs but costs incurred in providing employees with so-called "fringe" benefits. Though basic wages constitute the major labor cost, industry each year pays a considerable amount of money in financing supplements to the basic wage bill. Into this category fall such items as sickness, accident, hospital, and dental insurance, pensions, severance pay, and paid holidays and vacations.

Industry's payments for such benefits have been rising rapidly. In a comprehensive survey conducted by the United States Chamber of Commerce for 86 identical companies, for example, it was estimated that these benefits rose from an equivalent of 15.5 per cent of payroll in 1947 to 28 per cent in 1963, an increase of 81 per cent. Even more impressive were the *absolute* gains revealed by the Chamber: Fringe benefits increased from 21.7 cents per payroll hour in 1947 to 84 cents in 1963 (for an increase of 287 per cent) and from $439 per employee in 1947 to $1,704 in 1963 (for more than a 300 per cent increase) ![3]

The ease with which a company can pass on the costs of a wage increase in the form of higher prices to other firms or to the consuming public is still another determinant of its wage-paying ability. Some firms (in the brewing and cigarette industries, for example) operate in a highly competitive selling market. Under these circumstances it is very difficult, if not impossible, for an employer to shift the burden of a wage increase to the consumer. Even a slight increase in price could result in a significant decrease in sales, since consumers would simply buy from other sellers. To the degree that a firm sells its products in a highly competitive market, it will find strong consumer resistance to price increases. In contrast, some companies (for example, newspaper publishers in single-newspaper cities) operate in monopolistic markets. Under these circumstances, companies have a greater degree of freedom to raise prices without experiencing sharp decrease in sales. This would be particularly true where the product in question is sold under conditions of inelastic demand. Such a demand characteristic would apply to goods which are

[3]Economic Research Department, U. S. Chamber of Commerce, *Fringe Benefits*, 1963 (Washington, D.C.: U. S. Chamber of Commerce, 1964) .

necessities or to those for which there are few satisfactory substitutes. Thus, if a company is operating in a monopolistic market and selling a product for which the demand is relatively inelastic, it has an excellent opportunity to shift the costs of wage increases to other firms or to the general public in the form of higher prices.

Negotiators at times take advantage of such an economic environment. Wage increases are agreed upon and the result is higher prices. From the public point of view it would be much more desirable if unions and employers could work out an arrangement whereby wages could be increased without price increases. Certainly, a wage agreement which increases the prices of basic economic commodities and thereby generates a general inflation of the price level cannot be regarded as socially sound.

In recent years, the federal government has made its feelings on this latter point abundantly clear. Since January, 1962, the President's Council of Economic Advisers has argued that labor cost increases should be limited to the nationwide annual rise in worker productivity (as measured by output per man-hour). Over the past few years, according to CEA statistics, this annual productivity increase for the economy has averaged 3.2 per cent, and the Council consequently has urged that contract settlement, through "voluntary restraint" by the bargaining parties, remain below this figure, or at a level which would presumably negate the need for price increases. Consistent with the sentiments of former CEA chairman Walter W. Heller that "the public interest today, more than ever, requires that the stability of our costs and prices be protected,"[4] the Council guideposts (or "guidelines," as they have also been called) have been viewed by government officials as a mechanism for advancing national prosperity, aiding the nation in its balance of payments problems, and generally protecting the broader public interest.

Neither managements nor labor organizations, generally speaking, have, however, given much endorsement to these wage-price guideposts. Managers have tended to view them as a not-very-subtle form of government intervention, and even as a harbinger of ultimate price controls. Company spokesmen have also argued that the CEA's recommendations would stifle business initiative and that, in addition, the current levels of unemployment, unused plant capacity and domestic and foreign competition are sufficient in themselves to ward off inflation. Symbolically, one steel executive has commented that the guidelines are "based on the economics of the Potomac, not the economics of the steel industry."

To many unionists, the guideposts have appeared to ignore "special situations," such as that existing in the automobile industry prior to the 1964 negotiations there: With auto profits at record highs in that year,

4T. R. Brooks, "A Look Ahead to the Auto Negotiations," *The Reporter* (May 21, 1964), p. 27.

UAW president Reuther could argue that the industry could pay considerably more than 3.2 per cent to its workers and still cut prices, thereby making a settlement noninflationary. Labor spokesmen have also attacked the guideposts as inequitably "freezing" worker shares in the income distribution pie at their pre-1962 levels, in the absence of a convincing reason why such wage income shares should not be *increased*. And, as have their counterparts on the management side, they have also viewed with some alarm the increased government intervention implicit in the guideposts. It has, symbolically, been commented by one leading unionist that the 3.2 per cent guideposts are "as welcome to organized labor as 3.2 beer."

Indeed, in February, 1966, the AFL–CIO Executive Council officially condemned the guidelines. At that time, Federation president George Meany, in characteristically blunt language, stated that:

> Labor does not, cannot, and will not accept the guidelines. We see no way it can be applied equitably in an economy such as we have. We just don't like the guidelines. It destroys our collective bargaining. It works only one way—against us.[5]

Given this wave of opposition, the guideposts had, by early 1966, not proven particularly effective in many situations. Settlements reached in 1965 in the can, aluminum, rubber, textile, oil, and construction industries—among others—all breeched the 3.2 figure in varying degrees. And Reuther's own 1964 settlement with the automobile manufacturers was most commonly estimated as running between 4.7 and 5.0 per cent.

On the other hand, some parties had exercised *greater* restraint. Many unions did appear to have been more conservative in their wage demands than they might otherwise have been and some companies clearly had absorbed at least a portion of an increased wage bill from profits. Whether primarily because of these guidepost-oriented actions, or mainly because of such economic phenomena as unused plant capacity and unemployment, the rises in the over-all level of prices between 1962 and early 1966 were not pronounced ones (although the exigencies of the war in South Vietnam, at the time of this writing, hardly guaranteed that this situation would continue).

Much more can be done by the parties, however. If management and workers strive for greater productivity and efficiency, it is possible that some of the costs of an increased wage bill can be offset by increased output and by the reduction of nonlabor costs. Many companies and unions have not fully examined the possibilities of joint cooperation in eliminating waste and scrap, decreasing absenteeism and tardiness, and

[5]*Christian Science Monitor* (February 26, 1966), p. 4.

reducing industrial accidents. Management may be able to increase its efforts to purchase raw materials at cheaper prices, modernize machine technology, decrease material-handling costs, improve plant layout, or otherwise innovate for greater efficiency. Unions might examine their policies with the view of eliminating those which retard production, interfere with the efficient operation of the plant, or otherwise operate to curtail output. Indeed, at times unions can do much to improve the capacity of a company to produce without jeopardizing the health and safety of their members or impairing the members' legitimate job rights.

The preceding analysis indicates that many factors condition the ability of a firm to pay additional wages. This wage determinant cannot be applied automatically or in a whimsical manner. Its importance to intelligent and peaceful wage negotiations is counterpoised by its complexity and difficulty in application. All the factors bearing upon the wage-paying ability of a company must be weighed accurately and fairly. In this manner wage negotiations can be conducted on a factual basis with minimized controversy and industrial strife.

In April, 1956, the United States Supreme Court handed down an important and still applicable decision dealing with the legal obligation of employers who argue that they cannot afford wage increases.[6] At times a company which is confronted with a wage request by a union will claim that it lacks the financial capacity to meet such a demand. When an employer takes this position, labor organizations will ordinarily request that the company furnish them with information bearing upon the company's wage-paying ability. In the Truitt Manufacturing Company case, the Supreme Court held that when the employer argues that he lacks the economic ability to meet a particular wage demand, he must make financial information available to the union. In justifying this policy, the high court stated:

> Good faith bargaining necessarily requires that claims made by either bargainer should be honest claims. This is true about an asserted inability to pay an increase in wages. If such an argument is important enough to present in the give and take of bargaining, it is important enough to require some sort of proof of its accuracy.

The Truitt decision, of course, does not mean that company must capitulate to union wage demands. In fact, the company can refuse to meet the union request even if the information induced by the union shows conclusively that it *has* the ability to pay the wages demanded by the union. In addition, the Supreme Court did not specify that the employer must automatically produce proof in every instance where he

[6]*N.L.R.B.* v. *Truitt Manufacturing Co.* (1956), 351, U.S. 149.

pleads inability to pay. The Court held that each case must turn upon its own merits. Thus, in this connection it declared:

> We do not hold . . . that in every case in which economic inability is raised as an argument against increased wages it automatically follows that the employees are entitled to substantiating evidence. Each case must turn upon its particular facts. The inquiry must always be whether or not under the circumstances of the particular case the statutory obligation to bargain in good faith has been met.

Finally, the Truitt decision did not establish a hard and fast rule as to the character of evidence that the employer must show when he pleads lack of ability. As is apparent from the general tone of the Court's decision, this determination would also be made on a case-by-case basis, as indeed has been the case in the decade since Truitt was decided. These considerations, however, do not detract from the important principle established in the Truitt decision. The fact is that employers who argue economic inability to meet union wage demands must now generally be prepared either to produce relevant evidence to substantiate this position or to face charges of unfair labor practice.

Standard of living

Orientation of the plant wage structure to community and industry levels and ability to pay are not the only criteria utilized for wage determination in contemporary industry. Many management and particularly labor representatives are concerned with the problem of the *adequacy* of wages to guarantee workers "a decent standard of living." Disagreements arise, however, as to what constitutes such a standard.

The problem is most often resolved by personal judgment and opinions of the negotiators. More objective information is, however, at the disposal of the parties, and it has frequently been used to support demands and counterdemands at the bargaining table.

At the present time, the most widely publicized source of standard-of-living information is that published by the United States Department of Labor's Bureau of Labor Statistics. First developed in 1946–1947 at the request of Congress, and revised periodically since that time, the BLS's "City Worker's Family Budget" attempts to describe and measure a "modest but adequate standard of living." It is necessarily selective, restricting itself to a measurement of the income needed by a family of four (a 38-year-old employed husband, a wife not employed outside the home, and two children of school age—a 13-year-old boy and an 8-year-old girl) living in a rented dwelling in a large city or its suburbs. By studying the prices of a "representative list of goods and services" presumably purchased by such families, for twenty major cities (weighted according to their populations), the BLS endeavors to show the cost of "a level of adequate living standards prevailing in large cities of the United States in recent years."

Although the income required by the City Worker's Budget varies widely from one city to another—ranging in 1965 from $5,577 annually in Houston to $6,900 in Seattle—the over-all weighted average of $6,418 at the time of this writing was sufficiently beyond that earned by most workers to make the budget an attractive bargaining weapon for union negotiators. Labor spokesmen had not been hesitant about arguing the "need" for substantial wage increases to reach the budgeted levels, while also pointing out (as the official AFL–CIO monthly magazine did) that the $6,418 "is required to meet the necessities of life, pay taxes, and enjoy a few of the amenities of life—but with no allowance for luxuries or savings."[7]

Employers, equally logically, had taken bitter exception to this most recent City Worker's Budget. They had argued that the items used in computing the Budget were far too generous to warrant the description "modest but adequate": Frequently cited in this regard were the Budget's $132 annual allowance for gifts and contributions, and certain of its provisions for furniture, appliances, automobiles, and recreation. In addition, they pointed out that wage earners do not have uniform responsibilities in terms of dependents (with many, of course, having no dependents) and that many families have more than one wage earner.

The arguments and counterarguments can be expected to continue indefinitely, without mutual agreement as to their validity: The line of demarcation between "luxury" and "necessity" has never been susceptible to exact location and the concept of "decency" allows much room for emotion. Moreover, despite the increasingly frequent use of the standard-of-living criterion at the bargaining table, it does not carry as much weight as the other wage factors analyzed in the previous sections of this chapter. After all, an employer who truthfully cannot pay wages which will realize the "modest but adequate standard of living" may be entirely sympathetic to his workers' needs, but the cold realism of economic life will not persuade him to grant the additional wages. Likewise, a union will not stop at the level of wages required of the budget if it can get more from the employer because of the operation of the other wage criteria; indeed, under these circumstances, the union will probably argue that the items of the budget are too meager.

But use of such standard-of-living information as that provided by the BLS—and by such other sources as the Census Bureau, Federal Reserve

[7]"The Income Needs of the City Worker's Family," *The American Federationist* (May, 1965), p. 16.

Board, Department of Commerce, and independent studies of the parties themselves—is still to be preferred to *total* recourse to personal opinion on the subject. The data may not be accepted, but even in rejecting it the recalcitrant party is forced to deal with information which is more objective than mere individual sentiment. (NOTE: Case No. 3, found at the end of this chapter, focuses upon wage determination and is intended to shed further light on the various criteria for wage determination discussed on these pages, as these criteria are applied to a specific company.)

Cost of Living: Escalator and Wage-Reopener Arrangements

In addition to the comparative-norm, ability-to-pay, and standard-of-living principles, experienced negotiators pay close attention in wage negotiations to the status of the *cost* of living. This economic phenomenon is important because trends in the cost of living have an important bearing upon the real income of workers. Increases in the cost of living at a given level of earnings result in decreased capacity of workers to buy goods and services. By the same token, real income tends to increase with decreases in the cost of living at a given wage level. Real income for a particular group of workers also increases for a time when money wages increase faster than the cost of living.

It is beyond the scope of this volume to analyze the multitude of factors which influence the cost of living in the American economy. This cost is affected by a variety of forces, including the general climate of business activity, productivity, financial and monetary policies followed by financial institutions, the rate of new investment, and the propensity of consumers to spend money, as well as by the wage policies which are followed under collective bargaining itself. Government policies relating to interest rates, tariffs, the lending capacity of national banks, taxation, and agriculture also have an impact upon the cost of living.

The uncertain character of the forces which determine the cost of living makes it very difficult to predict with certainty its future trends. The difficulty inherent in using the cost of living as a determinant in wage negotiations is simply this: Wages are negotiated for a future period, whereas cost-of-living data are *historical* in character. It is a comparatively simple task to adjust wages for historical trends in the cost of living if this is the desire of the negotiators. The criterion is of limited usefulness, however, in the attempt to orient wage rates to *future* trends in the consumer price index. The capricious character of the index makes forecasting extremely hazardous. In any event, for intelligent utilization of this wage determinant it becomes necessary not only to have accurate information of historical trends, but also to make an assessment of the future trends of the factors which determine the consumer price index.[8] It cannot be emphasized too much that such predictions are fraught with difficulties and uncertainties.

Some companies and unions have, however, adopted one or both of two procedures—escalator clauses and wage reopeners—which take into account the capriciousness of the cost of living and likewise recognize the importance of trends in the consumer price index as they relate to the real income of employees and to the financial position of companies.

Escalator clauses

The philosophy behind the incorporation of so-called "escalator clauses" in labor agreements is that wages of workers should rise and fall automatically with fluctuations in the cost of living. The escalator arrangement first attained national prominence in the 1950 General Motors–United Automobile Workers collective bargaining agreement. As a result of the anticipated price inflation growing out of the Korean War, many other companies and unions soon negotiated similar arrangements and by 1952 such arrangements covered about 3.5 million workers —concentrated mainly in the automobile, railroad, textile, aircraft, agricultural implement, and flat-glass industries. They also appeared in a wide variety of other manufacturing and nonmanufacturing industries.

To date, however, the spread of escalator arrangements has not been impressive. Since 1952 use of the wage escalator clause appears to have depended to a great extent on the upward movement of the cost-of-living index. By 1955, for example, three years of comparatively steady prices had elapsed and the number of workers covered by such escalator clauses had dropped considerably, to about 1.7 million.[9] In 1956, on the other hand, the Consumer Price Index moved strongly forward, and a study which was conducted late in that year estimated that approximately 3.5 million workers were once again covered by escalator arrangements.[10] The incorporation of an escalator formula in the 1956 basic steel contract—covering 600,000 workers—alone accounted for almost one third of this increase. But, with relatively modest annual price movements since that time, through 1965, interest in the escalator appeared once more to have at least temporarily waned. By 1965, the railroads, electrical industry, and (ironically) basic steel had completely abandoned the device, and only about 2 million workers—concentrated mainly in automobiles

[8]The price index that is almost universally utilized in collective bargaining by employers and unions is the one prepared and published by the Bureau of Labor Statistics. It is called the "Consumer Price Index" (CPI) and appears each month in the Bureau's *Monthly Labor Review.*

[9]"Wage Escalation—Recent Developments," *Monthly Labor Review,* LXXVII (March, 1955), 315.

[10]Bureau of National Affairs, ed., "What's New in Collective Bargaining Negotiations and Contracts," No. 300 (November 30, 1956), p. 4.

and automobile parts, farm and construction equipment, trucking, and meatpacking—were covered by escalator clauses in the latter year.[11]

If most unions have not pushed hard for the escalator in the face of the limited price advances, moreover, this arrangement has also at times encountered intense *management* opposition. Employers have voiced fears that prices could not be commensurately raised without undesirable effects on profits. They have also argued what they view as the inequities of a system which allows workers to benefit without effort of any kind on their part: One recent increase in the cost-of-living index, for example, was attributed by government spokesmen primarily to increases in sugar and cigarette prices—a situation which even the most sugar-consuming and chain-smoking work force could not noticeably influence. Still other managers have stressed the potential inflationary ramifications of the escalator in opposing its use. Above all, however, employers have attacked the constant "freezing" of cost-of-living allowances into basic wage rates: Most labor contracts ultimately make such allowances a permanent part of rates when the agreements are renegotiated and to many workers the allowances are, consequently, really additional wage increases temporarily couched in other terms.

Managements could, understandably, be expected to generate greater enthusiasm for the escalator in the event of a prolonged national period of markedly *downward* prices, but this appears an unlikely possibility for the foreseeable future. And it seems apparent that a new major union push for the device must await strong upward price movements comparable to those of the early Korean War period and 1956 (not, at the time of this writing, completely improbable). But, even in the continuing absence of either of these situations, it is possible that *some* impetus will be provided for the escalator in the general gradual lengthening of the terms of labor contracts.

The evidence that contracts are becoming longer is persuasive. Where in 1948 about 75 per cent of collective bargaining agreements were for one year or less,[12] by 1963 the proportion of contracts running for longer than one year had increased sharply—to as much as 86 per cent, by some estimates.[13] Longer-term contracts lend greater stability to labor relationships, and by definition they reduce the problems of negotiation and

[11]"Deferred Increases Due in 1965 and Wage Escalation," *Monthly Labor Review*, Vol. LXXXVII, No. 12 (December, 1964), 1384. Some employees in chemicals, retail trade, and public transit also remain covered by escalator clauses.

[12]"The Trend to Longer-Term Union Contracts," *Management Record*, XVIII (June, 1956), 206.

[13]See, for example, "Agreement Duration, Renewal, and General Wage Adjustments," published jointly by the School of Business of Indiana University and the Indiana State Chamber of Commerce (Bloomington, Ind., 1963). *Labor Relations Reporter* (June 29, 1959) pp. 198–225 found that even by 1959 only 24 per cent of all contracts were for one year or less.

the traumas of frequent strike threats. However, as contracts are negotiated for longer periods of time, negotiators must recognize the necessity of providing some method for the adjustment of wages during the contractual period. Some authorities believe that increasing awareness of this situation, together with the *continuation* of the trend to contracts of longer duration will lend greater allure to the escalator formula, even in the absence of the price movements cited above and despite the unconvincing escalator statistics of the moment.

Although there are a wide variety of escalator arrangements, all contain a number of common principles. The most significant characteristic of the escalator formula is its automaticity. For the duration of the labor agreement, wage changes as related to cost of living are precisely determined by the behavior of a statistical index—almost always the Bureau of Labor Statistics' "Consumer Price Index." Wages are increased or decreased in accordance with comparatively small changes in this index. For example, the 1964–1967 labor agreements between the UAW and the "Big Three" automobile manufacturers provide for a $.01-per-hour adjustment of wages for every 0.4-point change in the CPI.

Escalators frequently work on a quarterly basis. Under this arrangement, used by the farm equipment industry (among others), the cost-of-living index is reviewed every three months and wages are changed in accordance with the escalator formula. On the other hand, the over-the-road trucking industry currently provides for essentially annual determination, and several other sectors which use the escalator operate it on a semiannual basis. In addition, the escalator arrangement often specifies the floor to which wages can fall in response to changes in the cost-of-living index: Under the auto contracts, for example, wages will not be decreased if the CPI falls lower than 106.5 (1957–1959 = 100). However, the escalator formula does not usually contain a *ceiling* on wage increases occasioned by increases in the CPI.

Finally, the escalator principle of wage adjustment is often accompanied by a definite and guaranteed increase in wages on an annual basis. This feature of the wage contract is popularly referred to as the "annual improvement factor." Under the 1964–1967 auto contracts, for example, wages were to be increased in 1965 by 2½ per cent or $.06 per hour (whichever was the greater), continuing the same formula for these three-year contracts that had been applied to each year except 1964 (when the formula was suspended to allow increased fringe benefits) of the 1958–1961 and 1961–1964 automobile contracts.[14] Workers were guaranteed this increase regardless of fluctuations of the CPI during the contractual period.

---

[14] In 1966, however, there was to be a change: The annual increases would be advanced to 2.8 per cent, with a minimum of 7 cents.

Wage reopeners

A second method for wage adjustments during the life of a labor agreement involves a provision which permits either the company or the union to *reopen* labor agreements *for wage issues* at stated intervals. Where such a procedure is employed, labor agreements normally provide that contracts that are negotiated for one year may be reopened for wage issues after six months. Contracts that are written for two-year periods or longer customarily are open for wage negotiations once each year.

Two major characteristics of the wage-reopening clause arrangement distinguish it from the escalator principle as a method of wage adjustment. The most important involves the fact that whereas the escalator arrangement provides for an *automatic* change in wages based upon a definite formula, the parties must *negotiate* wage changes under wage reopeners. This could be an advantage or a disadvantage, depending upon the particular circumstances of a given collective bargaining relationship. In addition, the wage-reopener arrangement can be utilized to take into account determinants of wages other than the cost of living. The fact that both the escalator and the reopener arrangements are frequently found together in industry indicates that *both* procedures apparently fill the needs of employers, employees, and unions. What may be suitable for one collective bargaining relationship, however, clearly might be unsuitable for another company and union.

To invoke a wage-reopening clause, collective bargaining contracts require that the party which desires to change wages give a written notice to the other party within a specified period. Under the terms of the Taft–Hartley law, as we know, a party to a collective bargaining agreement desiring to modify or terminate the agreement must give 60 days' notice of its intention to do so. Following such notice, the law declares that there may be no lockout or strike "for a period of sixty days . . . or until the expiration date of such contract, whichever occurs later." Employees who engage in a strike during this period lose their status as employees under Taft–Hartley and have no legal right to be reinstated.

These provisions of the Taft–Hartley law are important in connection with this discussion because wage-reopening arrangements invariably provide that a union may call a strike over wage issues if a settlement is not reached during the negotiation period. Such a strike takes place after the negotiation period as provided for in the wage-reopening clause but before the termination date of the entire labor contract. The question therefore arises as to whether or not a strike under these circumstances is lawful under the Taft–Hartley law. It is stressed that the law provides that no strike may take place during the 60-day notice period or until the date the contract expires, "*whichever occurs later.*"

In 1954, the United States Supreme Court sustained a decision of a circuit court of appeals which held that a strike is unlawful under the Taft–Hartley law when it takes place after the 60-day period but before the expiration date of the labor contract.[15] In this case, however, the issue of whether or not a strike called *pursuant to a wage-reopening clause* is lawful under national labor law was not squarely put to the courts.

When the National Labor Relations Board itself dealt with this question, it held that such a strike is lawful even though it occurs before the terminal date of the entire labor contract, provided that the 60-day notice requirement of the Taft–Hartley law is met.[16] In reaching this decision, the Board was compelled to interpret that portion of Taft–Hartley which forbids a strike during the 60-day notice period or until the date of expiration of a contract, "whichever occurs later." It held in this connection that for purposes of the law the term "expiration date" refers not only to the terminal date of the entire collective bargaining contract but also to the date agreed upon in the contract when the parties can effect changes in its provisions. On this point, the Board declared,

> The term "expiration date" as used in Section 8 (d) (4) thus has a twofold meaning: It connotes not only the terminal date of a bargaining contract, but also an agreed date in the course of its existence when the parties can effect changes in its provisions.

Upon a review, a circuit court of appeals, however, rejected the meaning attributed by the Board to the term "expiration date." In this court's view, the term must be held to mean "termination" date, and all strikes for modification before the contract's actual termination are unlawful. Concluding that the labor agreement had not been "terminated" within the meaning of the Taft–Hartley Act at the time of the strike, the court ruled that the employees in the strike lost their status as employees for purposes of the law and that they could be discharged by the company. Because of the obvious importance of the issues involved in the controversy between the National Labor Relations Board and the circuit court, the Board appealed to the Supreme Court for a review of the case. In January, 1957, the Supreme Court sustained the position of the Board and held that the Taft–Hartley law permits a strike, after a 60-day notice, during the life of collective bargaining contracts that contain wage-reopening clauses. To the date of this writing, labor relations continued to be governed by such a principle.

[15]*United Packinghouse Workers of America* v. *Wilson & Co., Inc.* (1954), 210 Fed. Rept. 2d ser., 325 (C.C.A., 8th cir.). Certiorari denied (1954), 348 U.S. 822.
[16]*Lion Oil Co.* (1954), 109 NLRB 680.

Wage Differentials

Under certain circumstances collective bargaining contracts provide for different rates of wages for different employees performing the same kind of work and holding down the same type of jobs. Such differentials are completely lawful, except when used by the parties to discriminate on the basis of race, color, religion, sex, or national origin; as of July 2, 1965, the latter practices were forbidden under the terms of Title VII of the Civil Rights Act of 1964.[17] To many employers (as well as to unions), moreover, utilization of the "nondiscriminatory" differentials appears mandatory to ensure an adequate supply of willing employees for work under arduous or otherwise unpleasant conditions.

The most common of these differentials involves premium payment for work on relatively undesirable shifts—in the late afternoon, evening, night, and early morning hours. Within industry as a whole 98 per cent of workers in plants running such late shifts now receive extra pay for this work.[18]

In addition, under most contracts there is now a graduated increase in compensation for working the second and third shifts. In 1965 all but 2.9 per cent of workers in establishments where there was a third, or "graveyard," work schedule received a rate for it which was higher than that received by second-shift workers. But second-shift workers themselves have received relatively significant premiums for their acceptance of these working hours: Premium rates for second-shift work are now most commonly at least five cents per hour, and often as high as 10 per cent above first-shift rates. Premiums of at least 10 cents per hour, and often up to 10 per cent of second-shift rates, are the general rewards for the graveyard-shift workers.[19]

The rationale for the shift differential is quite easy to understand. When an employee works a less common shift, there is obvious interference with his family life and with his full participation in the affairs of society. In Western society the school system, recreational activities, cultural pursuits, and the like assume that employees work during the day. Since working the odd hours tends to interfere with the employee's family and societal affairs, the premium is designed to compensate him for this sacrifice. And although it is a fact of industrial life that some

[17]Title VII did, however, grant exemptions for one year to employers with less than 100 employees, for two years to those having fewer than 75 employees, and for three years to employers with fewer than 50 employees. In addition, its provisions are not applicable at all to work forces of less than 25 persons.

[18]Bureau of National Affairs, ed., *"Facts for Bargaining,"* II (Washington, D.C.: Bureau of National Affairs, Inc., June 4, 1965), 522.

[19]*Ibid.*

employees because of certain conditions may actually *prefer* to work the afternoon or midnight tour (under these circumstances, the employee reaps a net benefit for the shift differential premium), because the overwhelming number of employees prefers the day shift, the shift differential will undoubtedly always be a common feature in the collectively bargained wage package.

Under many collective bargaining contracts, special premiums are also provided for workers who handle: certain supervisory or instructional duties; especially demanding tasks; or particularly hazardous, dirty, or undesirable work. For these jobs, extra pay is again granted as a premium to the basic wage rate of the worker concerned. For example, under one 1966–1969 Midwestern agreement a $.50-per-hour premium is paid to employees who are engaged in "dirty work." Such work is spelled out in the labor agreement and includes, among other possibilities for premium-rate reimbursement, "work in oil tanks where not cleaned out." Another labor agreement provides for the regular overtime rate for employees engaged in hazardous work. This provision covers employees working at elevations "where there is danger of a fall of fifty feet or more."

In addition to these *premium* rate practices, many collective bargaining contracts allow *lower* differentials for other situations. A number of agreements provide lower rates for workers who are handicapped, superannuated, temporary, or learners. Such differentials are rooted in the belief that these qualities make workers comparatively less productive and even the federal government, recognizing the persuasive economic logic involved, has gone along with this employer argument to the extent of exempting such workers from the minimum wage laws. Abuses have occasionally been in evidence, however: Some "temporary" employees turn out, upon closer inspection, to be deserving of twenty-five-year pins; and some "handicapped" employees appear to have nothing more than color-blindness. Such situations notwithstanding, employer good faith in regard to these workers is far more the rule than the exception and the differential can be defended on the grounds that the alternative to a lower rate of remuneration for such employees is, most often, unemployment.

Until the passage and implementation of the Civil Rights Act, some contracts also contained lower wage rates for women than for men and for Negroes than for white employees. For women, the practice was traditionally defended on such presumed grounds as a lesser productivity of women than men, a female inability to do all the tasks performed by men in accomplishing a job, and the argument that the employment of women at times involves extra costs not incurred when men are employed. Racial discrimination *per se* appears to have motivated the Negro differential, although some of the lower-productivity claims used to defend lower women's wages were also heard. Since mid-1965, neither type of differential is, understandably, promulgated by labor contracts which are governed by the Act, although whether or not the *practices* involved will continue is subject to employer and union compliance which goes well beyond the official wording of their agreements. At least for women, one convenient and perfectly legal dodge has been available to recalcitrant managers: the *alteration* of certain jobs—often by removing some minor portion of the original job sequence—and then rewarding such work to qualified women applicants as "female work."

Overtime Rates of Pay

Collective bargaining agreements invariably establish a standard number of hours per day and per week during which employees are paid their regular rate of pay. For hours worked in excess of the standard, however, employers are required to pay employees overtime rates. By far the most common standards found in labor agreements are eight hours per day and 40 hours per week, with only a fraction of labor agreements establishing standards differing from this formula. In the wearing apparel, printing, and publishing industries a number of agreements do provide for a basic 7- to 7½-hour day and 35-hour work week, and in the food-processing, retail, and service industries some contracts establish a standard 44-hour week, but these remain the exceptions.

The fact that the Fair Labor Standards Act provides a basic 40-hour week undoubtedly has caused the adoption of a 40-hour standard work week under collective bargaining. Labor agreements which provide for a basic work week in excess of 40 hours without premium overtime pay presumably do not fall within the scope of this legislation, or within the reach of the several state wage and hour laws which regulate this activity within certain states for their intrastate commerce. On the other hand, nothing in the federal wage and hour law prohibits employers and unions from negotiating a work week of *less* than 40 hours and (although thus far with more potential than actuality) the shorter work week as a partial answer to the unemployment threats of automation loomed as a new labor relations issue in the late 1960's, after years of relative quiescence. In addition, the Fair Labor Standards Act places no restriction on employers who desire their employees to work *more* than 40 hours in a work week, other than that the employees who work more than 40 hours must be paid at least one and one-half times their regular rate of pay for all hours in excess of 40.

The vast majority of labor agreements provide overtime rates of exactly one and one-half times the regular rate of pay for employees who work in excess of 40 hours per week, thus offering a not surprising conformity to the minimum provisions of the Fair Labor Standards Act, but a relatively small number of labor agreements do call for overtime rates of greater than time-and-one-half pay, most frequently double-time. With respect to hours worked in excess of the *daily* standard, most labor agreements also provide for time-and-one-half, although some labor agreements provide for double-time after a certain number of hours are worked or after a stipulated hour of the day or night. For example, some employers and unions have agreed that double-time rates should be paid if employees work more than four hours' overtime on any one workday. In this connection it should be noted that—since the Fair Labor Standards Act does not establish a basic work*day*—if employees are to be paid for working hours in excess of a certain number per day, the parties to the collective bargaining contract must negotiate this objective.

In addition to establishing standard workdays and work weeks and providing the rate for hours worked in excess of these standards, collective bargaining contracts deal with other phases of the hours and overtime problem. Most labor agreements prohibit the "pyramiding" of overtime. This means that weekly overtime premiums are not required for hours for which daily overtime premiums have already been paid; moreover, many contracts provide that only one type of overtime premium can be paid for any one day. And in many collective bargaining relationships the company also has the unlimited authority for *ordering* overtime.

As in the case of the shorter work week, this latter issue of overtime scheduling authority also promised to become a major collective bargaining issue at the time of this writing. Because of the economy's large unemployment totals since 1950—rarely, on a monthly basis, less than 4.8 per cent of the labor force and never under 3.7 per cent—and because of the constant menace of even greater displacement through automation, some unions were pressing for a flat prohibition against overtime in an attempt to preserve job opportunities. Few unions had thus far succeeded in this goal, although several bargaining units in the wearing apparel industry did enjoy such a situation, but under some other agreements employees did have the right to *refuse* overtime without any penalty. Potentially more successful, however, was a by-product of this union campaign: a 1964 proposal of the Johnson administration that minimum overtime pay rates in selected industries be increased to double-time, with the goal of discouraging employers from working present employees at overtime at all and consequently lessening the national unemployment rate by encouraging new hiring.

Still only a cloud on the horizon to the business community by mid-1966, the proposal had nonetheless incurred heated opposition from employers. Chase Manhattan Bank president David Rockefeller had typified the general management reaction in declaring that:

The claims made for the Administration's proposal are unjustified, the economics unsound, and the penalties unreasonable. . . . The Administration's plan . . . would penalize employer, employee, and consumer, and would not create any substantial number of new jobs. It aims at creating jobs not by making it more attractive to hire additional workers, but by making it less attractive to assign overtime. . . . The plain fact is that unemployment can be reduced only through the achievement of an economic growth rate high enough to sustain full employment with a "full" work week.[20]

In rebuttal, such Administration spokesmen as Secretary of Labor W. Willard Wirtz had argued that:

The evidence at hand is persuasive that a significant increase in employment could be obtained by distributing to other employees work which is presently performed on an overtime basis, and that this could be done without impairment of operating efficiency.[21]

Given the continuing hold of the time-and-one-half overtime-pay arrangement in collective bargaining agreements, it was at least obvious that any government regulation adopting double-time as the minimum standard would be widesweeping in its effects, and that in many cases it would render the employer's typical authority to order overtime an essentially valueless prerogative.

Even without government limitations, moreover, the employer's overtime authority has rarely been an unrestricted one. About one half of all collective bargaining contracts provide that overtime work must be shared equally within given classifications of employees, or that at least this obligation of the employer is binding to the extent that overtime is to be rotated equally "as far as is practicable." Some agreements limit overtime to regular employees as against seasonal, temporary, part-time, or probationary employees. A number of labor contracts require that the employer give some advance notice of overtime work, the time period of this notice varying from early in the workday in question to early in the work week during which the overtime is to be done; failure to provide such notice normally relieves the employee of the obligation to work overtime (or at least assures him of special meal pay).

By the same token, however, under many collective bargaining agreements, penalties may be assessed against employees who refuse to work overtime. Such penalties range from discharge to ineligibility to work overtime at the next opportunity. For all that has been said regarding union pressures for overtime discouragement, the premium earnings even of overtime at time-and-one-half remain sufficiently attractive to indi-

[20]*Wall Street Journal* (February 18, 1964), p. 3.
[21]*Ibid.*

vidual employees on most occasions to make the ineligibility penalty a meaningful one.

Indeed, a prolific source of grievances and even arbitration is the employee complaint that the employer has improperly, under the labor agreement, failed to offer him the opportunity to work overtime. Where the grievance is found to have merit, the employer typically has the obligation of paying the employee the amount of money which he would have earned on the overtime tour of duty.

The employee, of course, has nothing to lose by filing such grievances, even if he would have refused the assignment had he been *offered* the opportunity to work overtime. If the opportunity has *not* been offered him, he can file his grievance and possibly get paid for work which he never intended to do in the first place. For these reasons, employer representatives are very careful to assure that eligible employees are afforded the opportunity to work the overtime. Where a foreman, for example, makes an error in this regard, the company may be faced with the situation of paying for the same work twice and at *premium rates*. To say the least, the company controller would take a dim view of this state of affairs! (NOTE: Case No. 4 at the end of this chapter deals with the problem of rotation of overtime.)

Job Evaluation and Job Comparison

Thus far we have been dealing with general changes in the level of wages under collective bargaining. The comparative-norm, ability-to-pay, standard-of-living and cost-of-living principles—as well as the principles relating to wage differentials and overtime rates—rather than affecting any *particular* jobs, apply either to all jobs within the plant or to all jobs which fall within certain widely delineated areas (for example, night work, "dirty work," and overtime work).

Another important problem, however, involves the establishment of *relative* wage rates (or rate ranges) for each particular job so that wage differentials are rationalized (jobs of greater "worth" to the company are rewarded by greater pay) and the over-all wage structure is stabilized on a relatively permanent basis.

Essentially, companies adopt one of two methods to achieve the above goal: (1) job evaluation; and (2) what, for lack of a universally accepted descriptive designation, might be best described as "job comparison."

Job evaluation in its broadest sense is actually used by all companies. As French argues,

> [it] is a universal phenomenon in organizations which pay wages. For example, if the owner of an insurance brokerage decides that the recep-

tionist should be paid more than the typists, job evaluation has occurred. Thus, job evaluation occurs whenever decisions are made about relative worth of jobs and it is therefore an inescapable factor in organizational life.[22]

In the more technical sense in which it is used here, however, job evaluation requires a more *systematic* approach than that presumably adopted in French's brokerage example. Briefly, job evaluation—through the use of thorough job descriptions and equally detailed analyses of these descriptions—attempts to rank jobs in terms of their (1) skill, (2) effort, (3) responsibility, and (4) working requirement demands on the jobholder. *Each job* is awarded a certain number of points, according to the degree to which each of these four factors (or refinements of them) is present in it, and the total number of points consequently assigned to each job (usually on a weighted-average basis, depending on the importance of each factor) determines the place at which the particular job falls in the job hierarchy of the plant. Wage rates or ranges are then established for all jobs falling within a single total point spread (usually called a "labor grade") of this hierarchy. All jobs awarded between 250 and 275 points, for example, might constitute Labor Grade 4 and be paid whatever wages are called for by this Labor Grade.

Many managements have found the appeal of such a system to be irresistible. In addition to simplifying the wage structure through the substitution of a relatively few labor grades for individual job listings, it allows the company a basis for defending particular wage rates to the union and provides a rational means for determining rates for new and changed jobs (through using the same process for *these* jobs, and then slotting their point totals into the hierarchy of labor grades). At least three quarters of all American managements probably make use of such a system today.[23]

This growth of job evaluation, at least for unionized companies, has nonetheless been accomplished only in the face of rather adamant union opposition. Only a few unions—most notably the Steelworkers—have done anything but strongly attack the system. Virtually all others have voiced deep suspicion of the technique itself and have decried the reduced possibilities for union bargaining on individual wage rates allowed by job evaluation.

---

[22]Wendell French, *The Personnel Management Process* (Boston: Houghton Mifflin Company, 1964), p. 240.

[23]No reliable current figures are available, but even as far back as 1957—according to W. R. Spriegel, J. R. Bushline, and A. G. Dale, *Personnel Practices in Industry* (Austin, Tex.: University of Texas, 1958), p. 47—72 per cent of a large sample of firms used job evaluation and this mechanism is widely believed to have won even greater popularity since then.

Why, then, has this method of evaluation spread so pervasively to industry? Livernash conveys an authoritative opinion:

> In part, unions have been bought off. Objection was not strong enough to turn down evaluation if an increase in the rate structure was also involved. . . . In part, unions became willing to accept less bargaining over individual job rates. . . . Unions found that job evaluation did not freeze them out of a reasonable voice in influencing the wage structure and continuous wage grievances became a union problem. Particularly when accompanied by formal or informal joint participation in the evaluation process, the technique became acceptable.[24]

Thus as the same observer concludes,

> Clearly union practice indicates a far higher degree of acceptance of and tolerance for evaluation than do official [union] pronouncements.[25]

Job comparison is, in many cases, the manager's answer to intransigent union opposition to job evaluation where this *remains* a force. It also has been utilized by many companies whose job structures do not appear complex enough to warrant job evaluation, or (in some cases) where the management itself is divided on the efficacy of the evaluation technique. Although it has certain refinements, it most frequently involves (1) the establishment of an appropriate number of labor grades with accompanying wage rates or ranges, and (2) the classification of each job into a particular labor grade by deciding which already classified jobs the particular job most closely resembles. The systematic approach of the evaluation method is, in short, dispensed with—and so are the many subsidiary advantages of such an approach. By the same token, however, whatever deficiencies the management or unions see in evaluation are also by-passed. The procedure, a not-too-satisfactory compromise between evaluations and individual rates for each job, is not now common in industry and, for the reasons indicated in the discussion of evaluation, can probably be expected to become increasingly less so in the years ahead.

A Final Word

As this chapter has demonstrated, wage rates and allied wage issues pose highly difficult collective bargaining problems. But if the resultant complications do make wage controversies the leading overt cause of strikes, the fact remains that such strikes take place in only a compara-

---

[24]Sumner H. Slichter, James J. Healy, and E. Robert Livernash, *The Impact of Collective Bargaining on Management* (Washington, D.C.: The Brookings Institution, 1960), pp. 563–64.
[25]*Ibid.*, p. 564.

tively few instances. Although the stakes can be very high and the problems formidable, employers and unions in the vast majority of cases ultimately find a peaceful solution in the wage area as in other areas of bargaining.

Some of the settlements, admittedly, may not be the kind which would be advocated by economists, and some clearly fail to adjust the issues in a way which reflects equity and fairness. But the parties, most often, do resolve their wage disputes in a manner which proves generally satisfactory to all concerned.

It should be remembered that these wage problems are not resolved in an antiseptic economic laboratory where wage models may be constructed. If the settlements do, at times, offend the economic purist, it must be appreciated that these issues are dealt with in the practical day-to-day world, wherein pressures, motives, and attitudes cannot be isolated from the negotiations. Given such realities, it is to the credit of both parties that mutual accommodation has become increasingly visible.

DISCUSSION QUESTIONS

1. Both industry *A* and industry *B* are extensively organized by militant and honestly run labor unions. Still, since 1947, the wages within industry *A* have risen at about three times the rate of those in industry *B*. How might you account for the difference in the wage situation between these two industries?
2. "Though the actual wage rate which will be negotiated in a particular negotiation is not determinable, it is certain that the set of arguments which union and management representatives will use to support their respective positions will not change from negotiation to negotiation." To what extent, if any, do you agree with this statement?
3. "The wage-price guideposts of the Council of Economic Advisers represent the greatest threat to free collective bargaining that this country has ever known." Discuss.
4. Compare the methods available for the adjustment of wages during the effective period of a labor agreement and defend what you would judge to be the most desirable arrangement.
5. "From the employer's point of view, it is inherently inequitable to require the payment of equal wages to women and to men for performing the same job." Construct the strongest case that you can in support of this statement and then balance your case with the most convincing *opposing* arguments that you can muster.

SELECTED REFERENCES

Dunlop, John T., *Wage Determination Under Trade Unions*. New York: The Macmillan Company, 1944.

Lester, Richard A., *Economics of Labor*. New York: The Macmillan Company, 1964.

Phelps-Brown, E. H., *The Economics of Labor*. New Haven: Yale University Press, 1962.

Rees, Albert, *The Economics of Trade Unions*. Chicago: University of Chicago Press, 1962.

Ross, Arthur M., *Trade Union Wage Policies*. Berkeley, Calif.: University of California Press, 1948.

Taylor, George W., and Frank C. Pierson, *New Concepts in Wage Determination*. New York: McGraw-Hill Book Company, 1957.

Whittaker, Edmund, *A History of Economic Ideas*. New York: Longmans, Green & Company, 1940.

CASE NO. 3

Wage Determination

(As is true of all other cases found at the end of the chapters in this volume, the decision in the dispute was established in arbitration. It should be re-emphasized, however, that arbitration is only infrequently used to determine wages under collective bargaining relationships, and, for that matter, that the process is seldom used to establish *any* terms of collective bargaining contracts; in the United States, the parties do not desire to have an outsider establish such terms. The situation treated below has been included, despite its relative infrequency of occurrence, because of its many illustrations of the wage criteria points made earlier in this chapter.)

This case involves the *K* Division, which is a subsidiary of the *V* Company, and the Local Union, hereinafter styled the Company and the Union.

The *K* Division produces a variety of illuminated and nonilluminated signs which mark such establishments as gasoline service stations, beer companies, retail paint stores, and airlines. *K* provides its customers with "a complete service, ranging from assistance with original art work and layout, through engineering, selection and processing of materials, assembly, and often field erection of the completed sign or display." As such, the Company falls within the electrical sign industry. Actually, the industry is divided into two major branches. One manufactures and assembles the signs, and the other is concerned with the installation, service, and maintenance of the signs. Some of the individual companies fall within both categories, and some fall exclusively in either the manufacturing sector or the installation, service, and maintenance sector. *K* falls mainly in the manufacturing branch of the industry, though it apparently from time to time performs services in the other branch of the industry.

Basic Issue and Contractual Language

The basic issue in this case involves the determination of wage rates for the bargaining unit employees which will be effective as of March 1, 1965. The Labor Agreement under which this case arises was put into force on March 1, 1963. It expires on March 1, 1966. When it was signed, the parties agreed that for the first year of the contract period the employees would receive no increase in wages. For the second year the contract provided a two cent per hour wage increase for all classifications. Such wage increase was made effective as of March 1, 1964. For the third year of the Labor Agreement the parties stipulated that wages would be subject to negotiation between the parties. Thus, Article I of the Labor Agreement provides that "it is agreed that the contract will be reopened for wage negotiations only on March 1, 1965." However, Section 4 of Article I provides that "there shall be no stoppage of work either by strike or lockout because of any dispute arising under the terms of, or any proposed changes or amendment to this agreement. All such matters must be handled through the Grievance Procedure."

In accordance with the wage-reopening clause, the parties attempted to negotiate a wage agreement for the third year of the contractual period; that is, wage rates which would be effective as of March 1, 1965. However, the parties failed to reach such an agreement, and in accordance with the terms of the Labor Agreement, this arbitration has been instituted to determine finally the wage structure of the Company for the third year of the contractual period. In Article IV, Section 3, the parties agreed that "the arbitrator's decision shall be rendered in writing within thirty (30) days after presentation of the dispute and shall be final and binding on all parties."

Thus, the Arbitrator has the responsibility to determine the wages which the bargaining unit employees shall receive for the final year of the contemporary contractual period. Should the Arbitrator grant a wage increase, the employees shall have the benefits of the wage increase retroactively to March 1, 1965. Should he deny a wage increase, the same wage rates in effect as of March 1, 1964 shall remain in force until the termination of the current Labor Agreement.

Arguments of the Parties

On its part the Union recommends that the wage scale to be effective as of March 1, 1965, be a ten cent general wage increase for all classifications. To support this position, the Union offers a variety of data and arguments. It claims that other companies in this area pay higher wages than K and that the wage rate increase which the city's employees working for other companies received in 1964 and 1965 is higher than the one proposed by the Company during the negotiations; that other companies within the sign industry paid a higher wage rate increase than that offered by K; that one plant of the V Company, located in another city, paid a higher wage rate increase than that offered by the K Division; and that the cost of living is high in the city in which K is located. Also, it argues that the Union "updated government statistics to show that an hourly wage of $3.07 is needed for adequate support of a family of four and that inspection of the K wage schedule will establish the need for a substantial increase in wages."

On these grounds, the Union requests an award which will raise the general wage level in the plant by ten cents per hour.

The Company argues that the Arbitrator should direct that there be no wage increase during the final year of the contract period. During the wage negotiations, the Company apparently offered the Union and the employees a three and one-half cent per hour wage increase. However, at the arbitration hearing the Company withdrew any such offer, stating that "we can't stand a wage increase this time."

Major items of the Company's argument that no wage increase should be granted include its claims that: the Company has generally been losing money in recent years; its competitors are paying lower basic wages than it is; its markets are national in character and it faces stiff market competition from firms which pay lower wages than K; it is not proper to compare the Company's wage scale with industries located in the city, such as basic auto, steel, and power and light; direct labor costs as a percentage of sales is 20 per cent; and the Company in 1963 paid the group insurance costs, and, hence, it claims that though no wage increase was granted for 1963, the Company did incur additional labor costs.

On these grounds, the Company requests that the Arbitrator direct no wage increase for the period under consideration.

Analysis of the Evidence

To arrive at wage criteria which are meaningful for purposes of this case, the Arbitrator will reject at the outset a number of wage standards which he believes are improper guides upon which to base a sound decision. To be sure, these rejected standards are not intrinsically without merit. Under other circumstances, they could be used wholly or in part to determine wage rates in an arbitration hearing. However, after due reflection, the Arbitrator finds that it would be improper to use them as the criteria upon which to arrive at the wage rate under the circumstances of this case.

In the first place, it would be improper to use comparative rates existing in the city within the basic auto, steel, and public service industries as a wage criteria. As the Union data show, the wage rates within these companies are much higher than those being paid by the instant Company. One would be surprised if this were not the case in the light of the sharply different economic circumstances surrounding these industries and the sign industry. In terms of competition, financial resources, capital investment, and the ratio of labor costs to total costs, it is no wonder that companies which are much larger in size than K pay much higher wages. There is no need to belabor this point—the standard which the Union herein urges simply cannot be used as a realistic guide to determine this dispute. The kind of economic world in which K finds itself is totally different in almost every respect from the kind of world in which these large corporations operate. To use their rates as a standard in this case would be wholly unrealistic and inequitable.

The Union states that the instant Company's wage structure should not fall behind the rates in force within these industrial giants which operate in the K area. It claims that unless the wages of K keep pace, the Company will have difficulty in attracting and keeping an adequate labor force. New workers, attracted by the higher wages in the other plants, will not be willing to work for K. Also, employees on the payroll would leave K and seek work in other companies. This is a sound economic analysis and reflects the operation of the labor market. However, this is the problem of the management of the Company. It is not the concern of the Union, since it is up to the management to maintain an adequate labor force.

Also, the Arbitrator rejects as without merit the Union argument that the K employees must pay the same price within the city for food, lodging, clothing, and the like as do the higher-paid employees. Of course, this is true in the same sense as that an employee working in the lower-paid retail trades must pay the same prices for consumer goods as the comparatively higher-paid K employees. Wage rates within our economy and society are not determined on what it costs employees working in different industries to buy consumer goods within a given locality but upon a host of economic and industrial factors. If this argument of the Union were pushed to its logical conclusion, everybody within a given community should receive the same rate of pay. Clearly, organized labor would be the first to protest against such a wage policy.

The Union argues that the "cost of living in this area is high." Increases in the cost of living are, of course, a recognized standard for wage determination. When the cost of living increases, as measured by the Bureau of Labor Statistics' Consumer Price Index, and wages do not match the escalation of the index, workers suffer a decrease in real income. Hence, unions and employers generally give consideration to the trend of the CPI in wage negotiations, and this criterion is quite acceptable as evidence in the arbitration of a wage dispute.

Despite these considerations, this Arbitrator does not believe that he can base his decision on this standard in this particular case. In the first place, the Union offers no evidence of the concrete trend of the CPI or any other price index in the area. It argues that within this community the cost of living is "high." This may be perfectly true, but the record is barren of evidence showing precisely the trend in the cost of living. In the second place, the financial position of the Company and other economic factors must be placed in juxtaposition to any increase in the cost of living.

For purposes of this particular case, the Arbitrator also believes that the BLS "City Worker's Family Budget", of which he is well aware, cannot be regarded as controlling. The union presents a document issued by the AFL–CIO in May, 1965 which updates the BLS study. The AFL–CIO study states that for the typical family of four, a worker would require an income of $123 per week, or $3.07 per hour to obtain the income needed by a worker to buy the goods and services specified in the BLS budget.

True, the wages of the average employee in K fall below this figure. In rough figures, the median wage in K is calculated at about $2.36 per hour. It is not that income needs of employees to achieve the BLS standard for a modest but adequate level is not a proper wage criterion in collective bargaining. Nevertheless, it cannot be used as a controlling factor in this case because other considerations outweigh this standard in comparative importance.

Comparative wage rates within the sign industry

In contrast with the wage standards reviewed above, the comparative wage rates within the sign industry are squarely relevant in this proceeding. Both parties offer data in this respect, and such evidence is carefully considered by this Arbitrator. The Union presents data which shows that the average wage rate increase enjoyed by employees in recent years, including 1965, of companies which fall within the industry in which K operates range from three cents to twelve cents per hour. Close inspection of the data indicates that the median wage rate increase is about eight cents per hour. Thus, the Union presents the following compilation of its research:

Company	1965 Increase
A	7 to 10¢
B	3 to 12¢
C	10¢
D	Data Not Available
E	9¢
F	8¢

Also, the Union offers evidence that a V subsidiary located in another city granted a wage increase of eight cents in 1962; ten cents in 1963; and seven cents in 1964.

Here exists a comparison which is quite relevant to the dispute at hand. Comparative wage rates of companies in the same industry are a common and accepted wage standard in collective bargaining. If this standard were used exclusively, it would follow that the Arbitrator should direct a wage rate increase of about eight cents per hour. However, there are two considerations which would make the direction of such a wage increase improper.

Comparative basic wage rates

In the first place, the basic wage structure in force within some of the companies cited by the Union is lower than that of K. The minimum wage rate in X city of a V plant is $1.50 per hour, whereas the lowest rate in K is $2.01 per hour. In the case of F company, the starting rate as of April 1, 1964, was $1.92, nine cents below the current lowest rate currently in force at K. D pays a starting rate of $1.87 per hour, fourteen cents below that of K. Also, the record shows that the wage structures of A and B are not fully comparable with that of the instant Company. Employees at B Company are paid under a wage incentive system, and A subcontracts "at least a majority" of its metal work, presumably to plants which pay lower rates than A, and this tends to explain in part the higher rates of this company as compared to K, which presumably does not take advantage of subcontracting as a means of achieving lower labor costs. E presumably does pay higher rates than K. The "helper" classification of E receives, for example, a higher rate than the "general labor" classification at K Division. The record does not demonstrate the basic wage structure currently in force at C company.

Since K and the companies cited by the Union operate in a national competitive product market, it follows that the basic wage structure has much to do with the competitive position of K. The president of K company testifies that upon occasion the Company has lost orders because of the lower prices quoted by competitive companies, and it is reasonable to believe that one factor in the price differential was lower wages.

Clearly, on the basis of elementary economics, and as a matter of common sense, K faces a tough situation in the competitive struggle to acquire orders when the competing companies pay generally lower wages. Undoubtedly, the Union is striving to equalize the wage structure within the sign industry so that competition in the product market is not based upon wages. However, the record plainly shows that important wage differentials exist between the companies cited by the Union and other companies which compete with K in the product market.

Without refutation, the president testifies that beyond the companies cited by the Union, K faces stiff competition from other companies within the sign industry. The record shows that each of these companies pays generally lower wages than K. True, the studies put out by the Union compare the wage structure of the companies within the sign industry in terms of certain job classifications which may not be strictly accurate in describing the actual work performed by the employees. As is well known, workers who hold a similar classification but who work in different companies may perform different duties. Nevertheless, the conclusion is inescapable that these companies which compete with K in the product market pay lower wages and that in some instances the differentials are quite significant.

Thus, it would not be proper to direct a wage increase in this case based strictly on the wage increase which employees in competing companies have recently received. Attention must be devoted to the comparison of the basic wage structure of these companies with that of K. To do otherwise would be not only inequitable, but also economically unsound. The Arbitrator does not, of course, dismiss the wage increase pattern as unimportant. All that he says at this point is that if attention is paid to wage rate increase pattern in the sign industry, some consideration should also be devoted to the differential of the basic wage structure.

Financial structure of company

In the second place, some consideration should be given to the financial structure of the Company. Considerable controversy develops as to whether the Arbitrator should accept the financial records of the Company into evidence, and as to whether he should give such data, if accepted, any weight. The reason for this conflict is that the Union contends that the Company refused to provide it with such financial data while the parties were negotiating the dispute. On its part, the Company argues that it offered the Union a synopsis of its financial position. The Arbitrator would remind the Company that under the Truitt doctrine (*NLRB* v. *Truitt*, 351 U.S. 149, 1956) the United States Supreme Court has held that a company does not bargain in good faith under national labor law if it refuses to provide a labor organization with relevant economic data when the Company argues that it does not have the ability to pay the wages demanded. In any event, after reflection, the Arbitrator decides to consider the financial data presented by the Company. There is merit in the Union's position, but the Arbitrator fears that if he closes his eyes to the financial data offered by the Company his decision would not be sound and might result in a wage structure which could imperil the capacity of the Company to operate in the competitive product market.

The financial records of the Company reveal that it lost $106,838 in 1964, $24,869 in 1962, and $25,915 in 1961. Within the last few years the Company showed a profit for only one year, 1963; this profit was $18,228. The Arbitrator, of course, being an economist, understands that the poor profit position of the Company within the last several years is not solely attributable to the Company's wage structure. Other factors could be involved. Indeed, the financial data of the Company show that its gross sales stand at $2,351,297 for 1962, $2,587,307 for 1963, and $3,160,239 for 1964. Thus, its sales picture is healthy, but still the Company is losing money. Undoubtedly, factors other than labor costs tend to explain the deteriorating financial picture of the Company.

Also, the Arbitrator does not accept the proposition that the Company's workers should shoulder the burden for its poor profit posture. Indeed, the Union and the employees accepted the current contract without *any* wage increase for 1963 and received only a two cent increase in 1964, in an effort to permit the Company an opportunity to get its house in order and improve its financial structure. Clearly, this gesture of the employees was most cooperative, and must be considered in the ultimate disposition of the case. No company should be permitted to shift to its employees the burden for a deteriorating financial posture which could be within the control of the employer. After all, it is the management and not the workers or the labor union which must adopt the necessary methods, policies, and procedures to result in a profitable venture. Nevertheless, the Arbitrator must give some weight to the financial structure of the Company in the disposition of the instant case.

Tube benders

Whatever the wage increase, if any, that may ultimately be directed in this award will not apply to the Tube Bender classification because when the parties negotiated the current Labor Agreement, they agreed upon the wages for this classification for each year of the contractual period. Employees received $3.40 per hour, effective March 1, 1963; $3.45 per hour, effective March 1, 1964; and, most important of all, the wage schedule shows that the parties agreed that they receive a five cent per hour wage increase, effective March 1, 1965. As such, the wages for this classification are not open for negotiation for the final year of the contractual period. The Arbitrator therefore has no jurisdiction in the case over the wages of this classification.

Conclusion and award

The foregoing has demonstrated that the Arbitrator has carefully considered every major aspect of this dispute. He is now prepared to render his decision based upon the evaluation of the evidence. As everyone understands, this is a vital and important dispute. At stake are the wages of the workers, the economic position of the Company, and in a sense the prestige of the Union, and it is recognized further that his decision will have a bearing upon future wage negotiations in this Company. Whatever the decision, it will have an important impact upon all these elements, and the Arbitrator is aware of his responsibility to all concerned. He does not assume these responsibilities lightly and without full knowledge of his important role in this case.

After careful evaluation of the entire record, and after long and sustained thought, he directs that the wages for all classifications, except that of Tube Bender, be increased by five and one-half cents per hour. He believes that this decision is equitable and under the circumstances of this case is economically sound.

QUESTIONS

1. Are you as sure as the Arbitrator appears to be that his wage award is equitable and economically sound? If not, what decision would you make in the case?
2. What wage criteria other than "comparative norm" did the parties use in support of their positions?
3. Which wage criteria did the Arbitrator reject as not important and which did he believe were significant? Would you have regarded these criteria differently if you were the Arbitrator?

CASE NO. 4

Rotation of Overtime

(The labor agreement involved here, reflecting a common collective bargaining practice, requires the company to rotate overtime on a seniority basis within a job classification. As is also customary, it permits the company to depart from the rotation system under certain conditions. The issue in this case is whether on the basis of the evidence the company was authorized to depart from the rotation system.)

Nature of the Grievance: Position of the Parties

This case involves the grievance of *M*. He charges that the Company violated the overtime provisions of the Labor Agreement and that he is entitled to four hours' overtime pay for January 26, 1956, at the rate of time and one-half. As will be developed more fully below, the Company on this date assigned overtime work to *H*. The grievant alleges that this action on the part of the Company violates the collective bargaining contract. The basic question involved is whether the Company violated Article IX, Section 5 (A), of the Agreement when it assigned *H* to the overtime work on January 26, 1956. Under this article of the Labor Agreement, the Company is obligated to rotate overtime work among employees of a particular job classification within a specified department in the order of seniority. The Company is relieved from this obligation only under the conditions spelled out under the subsections of Article IX, Section 5 (A). This provision reads as follows:

> Overtime is normally not worked unless there is extreme urgency in getting out a job, or in doing certain kinds of maintenance work. The Company shall, within shifts, rotate overtime work within the job classifications within departments in the order of seniority, subject to the provisions of the balance of this section.

Thus, unless a departure from the standards of assignment of overtime work is authorized by a subsection of Section 5 (A), the Company has the obligation to rotate overtime assignments on the basis of seniority within job classifications of a particular department.

The position of the Union is that the Company transgressed Section 5 (A) when it assigned *H* to the overtime work in question. It alleges that the Company did not rotate overtime work within a given job classification as required by the Labor Agreement. It charges that the obligation of the Company to rotate overtime under the circumstances of this case is not eliminated or diminished by any subsection of Article IX, Section 5 (A). It contends further that the nature of the overtime work performed by *H* on January 26 could have been carried out by any other worker within the job classification involved in this case in essentially the same manner and with about the same rapidity as accomplished by *H*. (Union Post-Hearing Brief, p. 1.) Accordingly, the Union requests that the grievance be granted.

If these allegations of the Union are true, the grievance would of course have to be granted. The facts show that the job classification involved in this case is Storekeeper, Code 602, Labor Grade 6. The evidence likewise reveals that *H* is classified as a storekeeper and that he receives the same rate of pay as all other storekeepers. It also is true that *M*, the grievant, and other storekeepers of the department in question are covered by the same job descriptions as *H*. This means that *H* as well as the other storekeepers is expected to perform all duties spelled out or reasonably inferred from the language of Code 602. On these grounds there would be no basis for the Company to depart from the standards of Article IX, Section 5 (A), in the assignment of overtime work within the storekeeper classification in the department in question. *H* and every other storekeeper in the department would obtain overtime work on a strict rotation basis in the order of seniority.

The Company's position rests fundamentally upon the application of Article IX, Section 5 (A) (1), to the circumstances and facts of this case. This provision relieves the Company of the obligation to rotate overtime on a seniority basis when the job carried out by an employee during regular working hours is of the character that another employee could not perform it without a serious loss of time. Its exact language reads as follows:

In the case of jobs where the work performed by the employee on such job during the regular shift is such that a second employee would not perform the overtime work required without a serious loss of time, the obligation to rotate overtime shall not apply.

The position of the Company raises a central question of the case: Is the work performed by *H* during the regular shift of the character that another storekeeper could not perform his job on overtime without serious loss of time within the meaning of Article IX, Section 5 (A) (1)?

Record Keeping in Storeroom of Building "O"

In December, 1955, the Company instituted a new system of record keeping in the storeroom of Building "O" of Plant No. 3. For purposes of this case the significant feature of the new system is the concentration of record-keeping duties in the hands of one of the storekeepers. Under the new system the storekeeper selected for the record-keeping job performs three major duties as they relate to record keeping. (1) As parts are sent to the storeroom from the production departments of the plant, this storekeeper would cause to be designated upon the "Traveler Form" the location at which the parts are to be stored. Apparently it is the normal practice for him to tell another storekeeper the location for storing of such parts and for the latter individual to physically designate such a location on the Traveler. The second storekeeper, acting upon the instructions of the storekeeper designated for the record-keeping job, would then physically locate the parts in the place designated on the Traveler. (2) The record-keeping storekeeper has the additional responsibility to make entries on Stock Cards relative to the receipt of such parts. In this connection he designates on them the date of receipt, the order number under which the parts are received, the amount received, and the location of the parts so obtained. Evidence indicates that there are some 4200 such Stock Cards in the storeroom files of Building "O". (3) The storekeeper designated for the record-keeping job has the additional duty to indicate the location of parts on Order Forms requested by the production departments of the plant. In this connection the department requesting parts forwards to the storeroom an Order Form. The Order Form has on it the parts needed by the operating department. Apparently each Order Form contains requests for many parts. For example, on the Order Form introduced as evidence in this case, there appears a request for about 20 different parts. When the aforementioned individual receives such Order Forms, he designates the exact location for each part adjacent to the name of each part. He obtains this information from the files containing the Stock Cards. After so designating the location for each of the parts he gives the Order Form to another storekeeper. The latter individual then secures the parts in accordance with the locations spelled out on the Order Forms by the record-keeping storekeeper.

Although there are some additional duties performed by the record-keeping storekeeper in Building "O," the crucial considerations, for purposes of this case, involve the duties in connection with record keeping. According to the testimony of *H*, the storekeeper who obtained the job in question, he devotes about 65 per cent of his total time to record keeping. He stated that when the record-keeping system was first introduced he devoted a larger share of his time to record-keeping duties.

In its post-hearing brief, the Union states that "since this (record-keeping) phase of the job is covered by the Job Description of Storekeeper, Code 602, we can see no reason for making it an exclusive job of its own as far as overtime or for that matter, anytime." (Union Post-Hearing Brief, p. 2.) Paragraph 1 of Code 602 establishes the general character of the duties of Storekeeper as follows: "Place stores material in proper location and fill requisitions for same. Keep inventory on material in storerooms and records on control-numbered parts." It should be noted that this job description holds for all storekeepers in the Company regardless of the storeroom or building in which they work. Likewise, as stated, all storekeepers receive the same rate of pay, being classified in Labor Grade 6.

These considerations, however, do not establish the validity of the aforementioned Union argument. The nature of a job description is not such that it requires the Company to make sure that every worker so covered by a job description performs the same duties. Within the framework of a job description the Company may, if it desires, assign particular or specialized duties to specified workers. As long as the limits of a job description are not transgressed, the Company retains the right of job assignment. There is no provision of the Labor Agreement and there is nothing in the language of job descriptions negotiated as a consequence of the Labor Agreement which guarantees to a worker the right that the Company will assure him of the opportunity to perform each and every duty spelled out in a job description on an equal basis with every other worker covered by such a job description. Likewise there are no restrictions on the authority of the Company to concentrate certain duties in a particular worker as long as such action is consistent with a particular job description and exercised on a nondiscriminatory basis.

These considerations apply to the authority of the Company to vary procedures or methods from department to department even though the same classification of workers is used. For example, the fact that record-keeping duties are handled a certain way in the storeroom of Building "AA" does not mean that the Company must use the same system in Building "O" even though storekeepers are used to accomplish these duties in both cases. Management has the right to innovate relative to methods, procedures, or technology as long as such action does not violate the terms of the Labor Agreement or instruments which flow from the collective bargaining contract. In this manner the Company is in a better position to respond to the requirements of a dynamic, competitive economy with the objective of improving efficiency, productivity, and quality of product for the benefit of all concerned.

In this case there is no evidence that the Company assigned *H* to the job in question on a discriminatory or on an otherwise unfair basis. He apparently obtained the job in accordance with the terms of the Labor Agreement. Moreover, there is no evidence that the Company established the new system of record keeping in the storeroom in Building "O" with the objective of impairing job rights secured to workers under the collective bargaining contract. The Arbitrator finds no evidence of foul play on the part of the Company relative to the establishment of the new record-keeping system in the storeroom of Building "O" or in the selection of *H* for the job.

Character of Duties on January 26

Discussion can now return to the application of Article IX, Section 5 (A) (1), to the circumstances of this case. Does this provision of the Labor Agreement relieve the Company from rotating overtime within the job classification of storekeepers in the storeroom of Building "O" to the extent that the overtime work relates to record keeping? Would the assignment of another storekeeper (presumably the grievant) instead of *H* to the overtime work on January 26, 1956, have resulted in a serious loss of time within the meaning of the Labor Agreement?

To answer these questions it becomes necessary to deal with the actual overtime work that *H* accomplished on January 26, 1956. The evidence shows that he was requested to work at that time to record locations on Order Forms. *H* testified that he completed about 25 to 30 of these Order Forms on the day in question. *W*, foreman of the storeroom in Building "O," testified that *H* filled out 15 to 20 Order Forms. *W* also testified that if *H* had not performed the overtime work in question there would have been no work for the other storekeepers assigned to the storeroom of Building "O" the next day.

When asked how many Order Forms could have been filled by another storekeeper during the overtime period in which H worked, W replied about five or six. Such testimony was not refuted by the Union, and even if the lapse of time between January 26 and the date of hearing is taken into consideration, it appears reasonable to believe that H filled a substantially greater number of Order Forms than could have been accomplished by the grievant even though the precise number cannot be established.

This conclusion tends to be supported by viewing H's job as a whole. It is not that the job in question is unduly complicated or unusually difficult to master. In this connection W testified with candor that any of his storekeepers could learn H's job. He claimed that the job could be learned in about two weeks and that presumably within that time any of his storekeepers could achieve the level of proficiency of H. These considerations, however, do not alter the fact that on January 26 H was in the position to fill a substantially greater number of Order Forms than any of the other storekeepers because of previous training and experience. H came by this knowledge and experience through the performance of his regular duties carried on during normal working hours.

It would be very significant to the outcome of this case if the evidence had shown that the grievant or some other storekeeper entitled to work overtime on January 26 on the basis of seniority could have been able to fill about the same number of Order Forms on January 26 as did H. The fact, however, is that the testimony proferred in the hearing and the careful consideration of the development and the operation of H's job do not support this point of view. In this connection the record shows that the Union adduced evidence that all storekeepers in the storeroom in question had "access" to the files kept by H; that supervision did not tell such storekeepers not to use these files whenever necessary; and that from time to time storekeepers other than H actually used those files and to that extent duplicated H's duties. Such evidence, though entirely relevant to the case, does not, however, sweep away the fact that H on January 26 was able to perform the overtime job in question in a more efficient and rapid manner than the grievant. Clearly, there is no basis to conclude that the grievant could have accomplished about the same number of Order Forms on the date in question.

Serious Loss of Time

As stated above, Section 5 (A) of Article IX which established the formula for the rotation of overtime does not apply when the work performed by an employee during his regular shift is of a character that a second employee could not perform the overtime work required without a "serious loss of time." Since the Labor

Agreement does not provide standards dealing with the construction of "serious loss of time," the concept of necessity must be interpreted and applied in the light of the circumstances of a particular case. Actually it would be extremely difficult to establish a set of hard and fast rules that could be applied intelligently to each instance.

In this case, the facts show that the employment of the grievant on the overtime tour of duty in question would have resulted in a substantially fewer number of Order Forms being filled. The Union did not produce competent evidence to refute the testimony of W that such a situation would have resulted in the layoff of storekeepers in Building "O" on the next regular shift because of lack of work. Such a layoff would probably have had an adverse impact upon the producing departments which depend upon the sufficient and orderly flow of parts from the storeroom for continued and efficient operation. It is, of course, impossible to establish exactly to what extent there would be layoffs in the storeroom or curtailment or interference of production in the operating departments if H did not work the overtime tour of duty in question. However, from the evidence there is reason to conclude that there would have been a layoff and an adverse impact upon production. Such circumstances in the judgment of the Arbitrator would have resulted in a "serious loss of time" within the meaning of Article IX, Section 5 (A) (1).

The Award

After considering all the evidence adduced in this proceeding, after giving due attention to the relevant provisions of the Labor Agreement, and in the best judgment of the Arbitrator, the following award is made: The grievance of M, Grievance No. 709, is denied on the basis that under the circumstances of this case the Company was relieved from the obligation of rotating overtime within the job description of storekeepers in Building "O" on January 26 in the order of seniority under the authority of Article IX, Section 5 (A) (1).

QUESTIONS

1. What evidence did the Arbitrator use to support his finding that the assignment of the grievant to the overtime work would have resulted in a "serious loss of time" within the meaning of Article IX, Section 5 (A) (1) of the Labor Agreement?
2. Why did the Arbitrator refuse to base his decision on the job description for storekeepers which stated that record keeping is part of their duties?
3. Under what conditions would the arbitrator have granted the grievance?

We have indicated that the incorporation of employee supplementary economic benefits—from paid vacations to pension plans—in collective bargaining contracts is widespread throughout American industry. Such benefits have increased dramatically since World War II, in both their value to the employee and their variety. And, since these supplements to the basic wage rate are now commonly equivalent to as much as 28 per cent of payroll, it is understandable that some managers express hostility when the once accepted designation "*fringe* benefits" is used to describe this area.

Many of these benefits are not new to personnel administration and, indeed, some of them were introduced by employers on a unilateral basis before the advent of unionism. However, such benefits now play a much more important part in labor relations than was ever the case in the past. By the end of World War II, many unions had succeeded in bargaining vacations and holidays for their members; the federal government's regulation of wages during 1942–1945 had proven influential in guiding the labor negotiators in this direction. And in the two decades since the

8

Economic supplements under

collective bargaining

War, many other benefits have found their way into labor documents with increasing regularity and employer largesse: pension plans; various health insurance arrangements, including life insurance and hospital and other medical benefits; accidental death and dismemberment payments; and dismissal and reporting pay, among many others. Supplementary unemployment benefit plans, a comparatively recent major collective bargaining issue, also may properly be regarded as a supplement to the basic wage rate.

Pension Plans

Pension plans became a significant issue in labor relations and collective bargaining in the period immediately following World War II. Many factors operated to make them a major feature of the bargaining process, particularly the 1949 ruling of the United States Supreme Court which held that employers and unions have the obligation to bargain over this issue.[1] The Court rejected the point of view that pensions were not covered as a bargaining issue under national labor law. But other factors, particularly in more recent years, have also contributed to the growth of pension plans: the modest character of the benefits provided under the federal social security program; the fact that employees are increasingly expected to live considerably longer and to have more years of retirement after the termination of their industrial lives than in the past; the spread of union-sponsored seniority and related provisions (to be discussed in Chapter 10), making it all but impossible to terminate employment for older employees *except* by pension; and a growing managerial awareness of a company *obligation* to employees after their retirement. On the last point even in 1949 one public commission could comment that:

> . . . pensions should be considered a part of normal business costs to take care of . . . permanent depreciation in the "human machine" in much the same way as provision is made for depreciation and insurance of plant and machinery. This obligation should be among the first charges of revenues.[2]

From a modest beginning in 1946, pension plans in American industry have grown phenomenally. Negotiated pension plans are today found in

[1]*Inland Steel Co.* v. *United Steelworkers of America* (1949), 336, U.S. 960.

[2]These conclusions were incorporated in the report of the Steel Fact-Finding Board appointed by President Truman in July, 1949, to inquire into the facts of and to make recommendations in the dispute which was then taking place relative to pensions between the United Steelworkers of America and the steel corporations.

about 68 per cent of all labor agreements.[3] Even this total, moreover, understates the degree of growth: The coverage of pension plans doubled during the period 1950–1960, and is expected to double again by 1980.[4]

As might be expected, there is a wide variety of plans in existence, but a number of common characteristics are found in almost all of them. Whereas the earliest bargained pensions integrated their benefits with payments received from the operation of the federal social security program—and thus, in the late 1940's and early 1950's, enabled employers to realize considerable savings as the benefits of the Social Security Act were liberalized, there has been a distinct trend away from this practice in recent years. One method of thus passing the statutory increases directly along to the worker has been the establishment of a flat monthly payment per year of service, regardless of the amount the retired worker receives from the federal government. Thus under the automobile settlement of 1964, for example, employees were to be credited with $4.25 per month for each year of service upon normal retirement and anything obtained from the operation of the public system would be in addition to this amount. Automobile workers fared considerably better than most other workers covered by negotiated pensions, however: The amount of private plan benefits now ranges from $10 a month to more than $150 (depending on not only the generosity of the plan but also, of course, the length of service of the worker) but, on the average, monthly payments to employees with thirty years' service are between $75 and $85 per month, exclusive of social security.

Under most plans, the mandatory retirement age is set at 65, and although many companies still permit workers upon mutual annual agreement to stay on their jobs until they are 70 years of age, there has been some move away from this flexibility in recent years. Many manufacturing employee unions (in steel and rubber, for example), influenced by the size of the unemployment figures in their sectors of the economy, have generally not opposed this increasing trend toward compulsory retirement at 65. In fact, labor organizations have increasingly sought to open up further job opportunities in the face of automation and changing market demands by a new emphasis on early retirement *before* age 65, and some provision for this benefit is now made under the pension stipulation of many contracts.

By and large, voluntary early retirement (as opposed to retirement necessitated by permanent disability) carries with it reduced benefits for

[3]Bureau of National Affairs, ed., "Pension, Deferred Profit-Sharing, and Savings Plans" *Labor Policy and Practice* (Washington, D.C.: Bureau of National Affairs, Inc., 1963), 227: 1.

[4]"Characteristics of the Private Pension Structure," *Monthly Labor Review*, LXXXVII, No. 7 (July, 1964), 774.

the employee. This typically amounts to a reduction of more than one third in monthly benefits for a worker retiring at age 60 and of more than 20 per cent for an employee who chooses to retire at age 62. Under a few agreements in which the negotiating parties have actively sought to encourage early retirement, however, the employee can gain considerably more income than these modal figures would indicate. As of 1965, for example, Chrysler workers of age 60 with 30 years of service and a wage of $3 per hour could receive $110.54 in basic pensions (actuarially reduced from the age 65 level) plus a supplement of $253.46, for a $364 monthly total; the basic pension is a lifetime one, but the supplement is ended when the retired employee reaches age 65, to be replaced by Social Security payments at a lower figure. Four months after these and similar Chrysler provisions went into effect in early 1965, the plan had already succeeded in realizing its goal of creating new job opportunities for other workers: In these four months, almost as many Chrysler workers retired as in all 1964. Nor was it necessarily inevitable that *any* income decrease would be suffered by early retirement: under contracts in the clothing, maritime, and mining industries, to name only three of a fast-growing number, the benefits are identical for all retired workers—regardless of age—subject only to their meeting minimum service requirements. In general, however, the service requirements remain rigid: No employee is eligible for a full annuity until he has served with a company for at least 20, and most often 30, years.

Under plans which provide for pension benefits to workers who have been permanently disabled and who have not reached the normal retirement age, it is also usually required that such workers have a specified number of years of service with the company to be eligible for such benefits. Under many of these contracts, 10 to 15 years of service is required before an employee may expect to draw pension benefits because of permanent disability.

The question of who is to finance the pension plans—the employer alone or the employer and the employee jointly—has been an important issue ever since collectively bargained pensions attained prominence, and it continues to pose problems at the bargaining table. At the present time, employers finance the entire cost of retirement benefits (and the plans involved are therefore called "noncontributory," in recognition of the lack of expense to the employee) in about three out of four plans, with the remainder being financed jointly (and thus on a "contributory" basis).[5] Jointly financed plans remain common in some manufacturing industries (notably textiles, petroleum, and chemicals) as well as in the nonmanufacturing area (finance, for example).

[5] *Ibid.*, p. 778.

In favor of *noncontributory* plans, the usual arguments are that: (1) the average employee cannot afford to contribute; (2) the employee is already contributing toward part of his retirement under the social security program; (3) (consistent with the previously cited statement of the public commission in 1949) costs of pensions should be borne exclusively by the employer on the ground that this expense is no less important than depreciation expenses for machinery and plant; (4) the return to the employer from the plan in terms of lower labor turnover rates and increased efficiency justifies the cost; and (5) although employers can charge contributions to pension plans against taxes, employees cannot. Proponents of *contributory* pension plans, on the other hand, claim that: (1) since there is a definite limit to the economic obligations that employers can assume at any given time, employee contributions assure better pensions; (2) requiring employees to pay for a share of their pensions tends to educate employees in the knowledge that retirement programs must be paid for by someone; (3) employees will take a far greater interest in plans to which they contribute and hence will advocate better administration, sounder funding, and less waste; and (4) when employees contribute, they have a stronger claim to their pension as a matter of right.

Regardless of whether pension programs are financed on a contributory or noncontributory basis, however, the program must be financed and funded in a manner which positively guarantees employees the benefits provided for by the plans upon their retirement. There is no need to dwell upon the catastrophe that would befall a worker who upon retirement finds that the pension he expected is not available. Funded plans —those in which pensions are paid from separated funds, isolated from the general assets of the firm—ensure that such benefits are in fact guaranteed, whereas unfunded plans must necessarily depend upon employer ability and willingness to comply with the pension provisions of the labor agreement. In addition, employers may currently minimize their federal income taxes by obtaining tax credits as they make fund contributions, rather than waiting until the pensions are actually paid, and the earnings of the pension trust fund are also exempted from income taxes. Because of these considerations, there is an unmistakable preference among employers and unions for a fully funded and actuarially sound plan: Only 7 per cent of all workers covered by private pension arrangements belonged to unfunded plans as early as 1960,[6] and the figure is probably even smaller today.

Finally, recent contract renegotiations have seen a marked increase in

[6]"Unfunded Private Pension Plans," *Monthly Labor Review*, LXXXVI, No. 12, (December, 1963), 1414.

"vesting" allowances for workers covered by pensions—giving, with more or less qualifications concerning years of service and sometimes age, the employee the right to take his credited pension entitlement with him should his employment terminate before he reaches the stipulated retirement age. Only 25 per cent of plans studied by the Bureau of Labor Statistics in 1952 allowed vesting, but 67 per cent of those examined in 1963 did so, however much the vesting privilege remained qualified.[7] Considerations of equity, worker morale, and the displacement threats in many industries have given unions the incentive to push hard for the expansion and liberalization of this benefit over the past decade. So, too, has an equally cogent argument for meaningful vesting rights: In the absence of such rights, the individual worker's ever-increasing stake in pension plan entitlement may stifle desirable labor mobility and thus result in the underutilization of manpower. Workers who *can* take their pension privileges with them are afforded maximum opportunity for employer-to-employer and industry-to-industry movement, a situation which is presumably a desirable one from the viewpoint of our not only efficiency minded but democratically oriented society.

Vacations With Pay

Vacations with pay for production workers constitute, as was noted earlier, a comparatively new development in American industry. Prior to World War II only a fraction of workers covered by collective bargaining contracts received pay during vacation periods and, at that time, other employees were permitted time off only if they were willing to sacrifice pay. At present, vacations with pay are a standard practice in practically every collective bargaining contract and this has been true for some time. As far back as 1957, in fact, a Department of Labor Study of 1,813 agreements, each covering more than 1,000 workers, found that only 8 per cent of these contracts did not provide some form of paid vacation;[8] and the employer not furnishing this type of pay for time not worked *today* is a true individualist.

In addition to the influence of the National War Labor Board's wage controls in spearheading the spread of paid vacations, a growing recognition on the part of employers, employees, and unions of the benefits of such a policy (in terms of worker health, personal development, and productivity) has contributed to the growth.

Paid vacations have also undergone steady *liberalization* as a worker

---

[7]"Vesting Provisions in Private Plans," *Monthly Labor Review*, LXXXVII, No. 9 (September, 1964), 1014.

[8]U.S. Bureau of Labor Statistics, *Paid Vacation Provisions in Major Union Contracts, 1957*, Bulletin No. 1233 (June, 1958).

benefit. An annual five-week vacation (normally requiring 20 years of service or more) is currently found in 2 per cent of all contracts, after being essentially nonexistent until now. And four-week vacations (usually after exactly 20 years) are today included in 50 per cent of all agreements, or more than half again the 1960 frequency. Of more significance to shorter-term workers is the three-week vacation, provided for in 84 per cent of contracts (as against 78 per cent in 1960) and most frequently requiring 10 years of service (where 15 years was the modal prerequisite a very few years ago). Virtually all employees, moreover, can count on a two-week vacation after building up five years of seniority, and contracts increasingly allow this length of time off after only two or three years of service. The only stagnation which has occurred, is, in fact, in the one-week vacation area: One year of service has entitled most employees to a single week of vacation with pay for well over a decade now, and the next frontier relating to the one-week vacation will probably be its total abolition in favor of the two-week vacation after one year—an arrangement which is even now granted by 10 per cent of all agreements.[9]

An innovation which thus far has not spread beyond the scope of influence of the United Steelworkers of America is considerably more imaginative than the mere liberalization denoted by the above statistics. In 1962, the Steelworkers and metal can manufacturers negotiated a "sabbatical" paid vacation of thirteen weeks' duration, allowed all employees with fifteen or more years of service *every five years*, and the basic steel industry incorporated essentially the same agreement for the senior half of *its* work force the following year. The rationale behind this device is a twofold one: greater leisure time for employees (with, at least in theory, greater attendant benefits to worker health, personal development, and productivity than under less liberal vacation allowances) *and* the creation of new jobs through the major immediate need for additional employees brought about by the sabbatical. After three years, the plan had received mixed evaluations: It was particularly hard to isolate the effects of the plan from such other employment-increasing factors as a strengthened market demand for the products involved in those years; and the fact that many eligible employees had exercised an option of accepting extra pay in lieu of some of the leave time had also to be reckoned with. It was at least apparent that, if the "sabbatical" was to achieve either of its objectives, employees would be obliged to actually take their vacations—and also to abstain from taking other paid work during the vacation period. It also seemed clear that bargainers in

[9] All statistics cited in this paragraph are based upon: Bureau of National Affairs, ed., "Length of Vacations," *Labor Policy and Practice* (Washington, D.C.: Bureau of National Affairs, Inc., 1963), 223: 13–14.

other industries were awaiting more conclusive proof of the benefits of the plan before pushing for its incorporation in their contracts.

In qualifying for vacations, most labor agreements require that an employee must have worked a certain number of hours, days, or months prior to the vacation period, and failure of the employee to comply with such stipulations results in the forfeiture of the vacation benefits. The rate of pay to which the employee is entitled during his vacation is ordinarily computed on the basis of his regular hourly rate, although (in a comparatively small number of agreements) vacation benefits are calculated on the basis of average hourly earnings over a certain period of time preceding the vacation and, in some agreements, vacation pay is calculated as a specified percentage of annual earnings; usually this latter figure amounts to between 2.0 and 2.5 per cent of the annual earnings.

A problem arises involving the payment of workers who work during their vacation periods. In some contracts—as in the case of the steel and can provisions alluded to previously—the employee has the option of taking the vacation to which he is entitled or of working during this period. Other labor agreements allow the company the option of giving pay *instead of* vacations if production requirements make it necessary to schedule the worker during his vacation period. No less than in the case of the sabbaticals, when employees work during their vacation periods either upon their own or the company's option the principles upon which paid vacations are based (health, productivity, etc.) are, of course, violated. In any event, the question arises as to how to compensate employees for their vacation time when they work during this period. In most labor agreements, employees under these circumstances are given their vacation pay plus the regular wages which they earn in the plant. In a few cases, particularly when the employer schedules work during a vacation period, the wage earned by the employee working on his job during his vacation period is calculated at either time-and-one-half or double the regular rate. Such earnings are in addition to the employee's vacation pay.

In a majority of contracts, management has the ultimate authority to schedule the vacation period. Under an increasingly large number of agreements, however, the company is required to take into consideration seniority and employee desires. A fairly sizeable number of labor agreements permit management to schedule vacations during plant shutdowns.

An additional vacation problem involves the status of employees who are separated from a company before their vacation period. In some collective bargaining agreements, these employees are entitled to accumulated vacation benefits when they leave the employment of companies under certain specified circumstances, such as permanent layoff, resignation, and military duty. In a comparatively small number of contracts, workers discharged for cause may also claim vacation benefits.

Holidays With Pay

Similar to paid vacations, paid holidays for production workers was not a common practice before World War II. When a plant shut down for a legal holiday, the workers simply lost a day of work. And, also as in the case of vacations with pay, the National War Labor Board permitted employers and unions to negotiate labor agreements providing for paid holidays under its wartime wage regulations. As a result paid holidays became a common feature in collective bargaining contracts during World War II and the practice continued after hostilities terminated. By 1948 about 70 per cent of all labor agreements provided for paid holidays, and at present nearly 100 per cent of all labor agreements incorporate some formula for paid holidays.

The median number of such holidays granted in 1965 was 7.4, with 14 per cent of contracts allowing 6 or 6½, 39 per cent sanctioning 7 or 7½, 31 per cent granting 8 or 8½, 14 per cent 9 or more and only 2 per cent listing fewer than 6. There is almost universal agreement among the contracts on at least 4 of these specific holidays: More than 98 per cent allow paid time off for Independence Day, Labor Day, Thanksgiving, and Christmas. And well over 92 per cent of all contracts pay for holidays on New Year's Day and Memorial Day. Wider variation takes place where more than 6 holidays are sanctioned, but half days before Thanksgiving, Christmas, and New Year's Day are frequently specified, and in an increasing number of cases a seventh (or eighth) holiday is oriented on an individual basis—such as the employee's birthday. Under this latter arrangement, the company by definition is not penalized with whatever inefficiencies may result from a plant shutdown. Six per cent of all agreements also recognize any of a variety of state and local holidays, ranging from Patriot's Day in Massachusetts to Mardi Gras in parts of the South. Company—and even union—picnics are declared occasions for paid holidays in a somewhat smaller number of contracts.[10]

Most labor agreements place certain obligations upon employees who desire to qualify for paid holidays, with the common objective in this respect being that of minimizing absenteeism. The most frequently mentioned such requirement is that an employee must work the last scheduled day before and the first scheduled day after a holiday. The obligation is waived when the employee does not work on the day before or after the holiday because of illness, authorized leave of absence, jury

---

[10]Bureau of National Affairs, ed., "Pay for Unworked Holidays," *Labor Policy and Practice* (Washington, D.C.: Bureau of National Affairs, Inc., 1965) , 223: 502.

duty, or death in the family. Under some collective bargaining relationships, illness must be proved by a doctor's certificate, by nurse visitation, or by some other device. (NOTE: Case No. 5 concerns itself with this issue of eligibility for holiday pay.)

Production requirements and emergency situations at times require that employees work on holidays, and such circumstances raise the problem of rates of pay for work on these days. About three quarters of all labor agreements provide for double-time for work on holidays, and a small number of contracts now call for triple-time. In the continuous-operation industries such as the hotel, restaurant, and transportation sectors, labor agreements frequently substitute another full day off with pay for a holiday on which an employee worked.

An additional problem involves payment for holiday time when the holiday falls on a day on which the employee would not ordinarily work. For example, if a plant does not normally work on Saturdays, and if in a particular year July 4 (a paid holiday under the collective bargaining agreement) falls on Saturday, the question arises as to whether employees are entitled to holiday pay. Another aspect of the same general problem involves a paid holiday falling during an employee's vacation period. Some unions claim that pay for holidays constitutes a kind of vested benefit to employees, regardless of the day of the calendar week on which the holiday occurs. Thus, if the holiday falls on a regular nonworkday, some unions ask that another day be designated as the holiday or that the employee be given a day's wages; or if the holiday falls during an employee's vacation period, that he receive another day's paid vacation or wages for the holiday. The opposing view holds that payment for holidays falling on a day on which employees do not regularly work violates the basic principle underlying paid holidays, which is protection of employees from loss of wages. Many labor agreements reflect the thinking of labor unions on this issue and designate, for example, another day off with pay if a holiday falls on a nonworkday, but a large number of labor agreements do not treat the problem one way or the other, and frequently because of the nature of the language establishing holidays with pay, controversies in this respect are settled in arbitration.

Negotiated Health Insurance Plans

Health insurance plans are now a common feature of collective bargaining contracts. These plans provide for one or more of the following: life insurance or death benefits; accidental death and dismemberment benefits; accident and sickness benefits; and cash or services covering hospital, surgical, maternity, and medical care. Recently the boundaries of the package have been extended to such areas as major medical insurance (often defraying all such expenses up to 80 per cent of their total), dental insurance, and psychiatric treatment benefits. By 1966 the vast majority of workers under collective bargaining contracts were covered, although in considerably varying degrees, by some or all parts of this over-all insurance mechanism.

A number of factors provide the basis for the spread of insurance plans under collective bargaining. Insurance programs were also a major fringe issue in the period of wage control during World War II, although to a far smaller extent than were vacations and holidays. Many employers and unions have, moreover, increasingly recognized that industrial workers—particularly with health costs rising rapidly in recent years—are not prepared to meet the risks covered by such plans. The Internal Revenue Service has also given incentive to the spread of such insurance, by permitting employers who contribute to these programs to deduct payments as a business expense, for tax purposes, where such plans conform to the standards of law for tax relief. In addition, group insurance permits purchasing economies not available to individuals. Finally, the fact that the federal social security program has not provided protection for most risks covered by these insurance plans has made the private insurance system a widely sought one.

Today's typical bargained health and welfare package is of no small dimensions. There is a strong likelihood that it includes: group life insurance for an amount which approximates 85 per cent of the employee's annual salary; disability and sickness benefits of $50 to $65 weekly for twenty-six weeks; semiprivate hospital room and hospital board for as long as seventy days—together with such extras as drugs and medicines, X-ray examinations, and operating room expenses (under either Blue Cross or a private insurance company plan); surgical expenses up to a $225 to $350 maximum for contingencies not covered by workmen's compensation legislation; and coverage for the employee's dependents as well as himself for all or most of the above benefits.[11] And, as in the cases of pensions, vacations, and holidays, these emoluments are continuing their own process of liberalization, with discernable trends in recent years involving: an increase in the amount and duration of the benefits; the extension of the benefits to retired workers, as well as to those dependents not yet covered; and the added protection for catastrophic illnesses and accidents and addition of dental and mental health benefits which were cited previously. (NOTE: Case No. 6 deals with one part of this package in some depth, focusing upon a grievance involving disability and sickness pay under a group insurance policy.)

11Gordon F. Bloom and Herbert R. Northrup, *Economics of Labor Relations*, 5th ed. (Homewood, Ill.: Richard D. Irwin, Inc., 1965) pp. 715–16.

There has been a commensurately strong trend toward exclusive employer financing of the health benefit package: Twenty-one per cent of all unionized employers paid the full cost in 1949; roughly 40 per cent did so in 1956;[12] and it is very likely that as many as 50 per cent currently pay all expenses for the greatly enlarged package of the late 1960's. With the continuing union emphasis on health expense defrayal, no reversal of this trend seems to lie on the horizon.

Dismissal Pay

Unlike all the wage supplements discussed above, dismissal, or "severance," pay is still not a common product of collective bargaining. A contemporary study of 1,773 major (1,000 workers or more) and thus presumably more liberal agreements found only 30 per cent of these contracts providing such a benefit.[13] And on an industrywide basis the practice remains largely confined to contracts negotiated by the Steelworkers, Auto Workers, Communications Workers, Ladies' Garment workers, and Electrical Workers—although many sectors of the newspaper and railroad industries also have such plans.

Dismissal pay provisions normally limit payments to workers displaced because of technological change, plant merger, permanent curtailment of the company's operations, permanent disability, or retirement before the employee is entitled to a pension. Workers discharged for cause and employees who refuse another job with the company normally forfeit dismissal pay rights, as do workers who voluntarily quit a job.

The amount of payment provided for in dismissal pay arrangements varies directly with the length of service of the employee. The longer the service, the greater the amount of money. Ordinarily a top limit is placed upon the amount that an employee can receive. Although labor agreements vary in respect to the payment formula, as a general rule low-service workers receive one week's wages for each year of service prior to dismissal, with higher than proportional allowances for high-service employees (up to 60 weeks' pay, for example, for 15 or more years of service, and as high as 105 weeks' pay for workers with 25 or more service years).[14]

A problem involving dismissal pay is the situation wherein an employee is subsequently rehired by the company. There is little uniformity

---

[12]U.S. Department of Labor, Office of Welfare and Pension Plans, *Welfare and Pension Plan Statistics, 1960* (Washington, D.C.: U.S. Government Printing Office, 1963), pp. 3–4.

[13]"Severance Pay and Layoff Benefit Plans," *Monthly Labor Review*, LXXXVIII, No. 1 (January, 1965), 27.

[14]*Ibid.*, p. 32.

in collective bargaining contracts relative to the handling of this problem. Actually, a large number of labor agreements which provide for dismissal pay are silent on whether the employee must make restitution to the company upon being rehired or whether he may keep the money paid to him when his employment was originally terminated. Some agreements, however, specifically provide that such an employee must return the money; for example, one telephone industry collective bargaining contract stipulates that such employees must repay to the company any termination payment either in a lump sum or through payroll deduction at a rate of not less than 10 per cent each payroll period until the full amount is paid.

Since the dismissal provision is designed to cushion the effects of employment termination through technological change, merger, and cessation of business (as well as through involuntary retirement due to personal health misfortunes), it is logical to conclude that this benefit, too, will spread in the years ahead. The acceleration of technological and business operations changes in the 1950's and early 1960's was itself responsible for a considerable increase in the dismissal pay statistics in those years: Only 10 per cent of labor agreements had such a provision in 1949.[15] Given the continuing presence of these causative factors, there is little reason to believe that the spread of dismissal pay has run its course.

Reporting Pay

Under the provisions of approximately 90 per cent of the collective bargaining contracts currently in force, employees who are scheduled to work and who do not have instructions from the company *not* to report to their jobs, are guaranteed a certain amount of work for that day or compensation instead of work. Issues involved in the negotiation of reporting pay arrangements are the amount of the guarantee and the rate of compensation, the amount of notice required for the employer to avoid guaranteed payment, the conditions relieving the employer of the obligation to award reporting pay, and the conditions under which such pay must be forfeited by employees.

Labor agreements establish a variety of formulas for the calculation of the amount of the guarantee. Reporting pay ranges from a one-hour guarantee to a full day. About 50 per cent of labor contracts dealing with this issue provide for four hours' pay; approximately 10 per cent call for eight hours' pay. These rates are calculated on a straight time basis.

---

[15]"Dismissal Pay Provisions in Union Agreements, 1949," *Monthly Labor Review*, LXX (April, 1950), 384.

However, under circumstances where workers are called back to work by management outside of regularly scheduled hours, such employees are frequently compensated at premium rates, ordinarily at time-and-one-half the regular rate. Such reimbursement, popularly styled "call-in" pay, might be awarded a worker, if, for example, he is called back to work before he has been off for sixteen hours. Thus, if he regularly works the first shift and is called back under some emergency condition to work the third shift, the labor agreement might require that he be paid at premium rates. In the event that the employee reports for such work only to find that the company no longer has need for his services he will still be entitled to a certain number of guaranteed hours of pay calculated at premium rates.

In most agreements providing for reporting pay an employer is relieved of the obligation to guarantee work or to make a cash payment to employees when he notifies his employees not to report to work. Contracts frequently provide that such notice must be given employees before the end of the worker's previous shift, though in some cases the employer may be relieved of the obligation if he gives notice a certain number of hours before employees are scheduled to work. Eight hours' notice is provided in many labor contracts. In addition, employers are relieved of the obligation to award reporting pay when failure to provide work is due to causes beyond the control of the company. Thus, when work is not available because of floods, fires, strikes, power failures, or "acts of God," in most contracts employers either are fully relieved of the obligation to award reporting pay or the amount of the pay is substantially reduced. Of course, there are many questions of interpretation involved in this situation. For example, does power failure resulting from faulty maintenance relieve the employer of the obligation to award reporting pay? As in so many previous cases, such questions are resolved through the grievance procedure and at times through arbitration.

Under certain circumstances employees forfeit reporting pay. If employees, for example, fail to keep the company notified of change of address, reporting pay is forfeited under many labor agreements. Other forfeitures might result if employees refuse to accept work other than their own jobs, leave the plant before notice is given to other employees not to report to work, or fail to report to work even though no work is available.

Supplementary Unemployment Benefit Plans

One of the most interesting developments in collective bargaining during recent years is the supplementary unemployment benefit (SUB) plan. This new issue of collective bargaining attracted national attention in 1955, when a supplementary unemployment benefit plan was negotiated by the United Automobile Workers and the basic automobile manufacturers, and again in 1956 when the basic steel corporations and the United Steelworkers of America included such a plan in their new labor agreement. There is not much evidence of plans protecting workers' income during periods of unemployment prior to 1955, although a few such arrangements had been established in sectors of the consumer goods industries.

Essentially, SUB plans constitute a compromise between the "guaranteed annual wage" demanded by many unions in the late 1940's and early 1950's, and a continuing management unwillingness to grant such relatively complete job security as the "guaranteed wage" designation would indicate. The plans are geared primarily to two goals: (1) supplementing the unemployment benefits of the various state unemployment insurance systems; and (2) allowing further income to still-unemployed workers after state payments have been exhausted. And they implicitly recognize at least one weakness in the state system: Since the states started paying benefits in the late 1930's, the average ratio of these benefits to average wage levels of employees when working has steadily dropped from approximately 40 per cent three decades ago to somewhat less than 35 per cent today.

About 2.5 million employees are now covered by negotiated supplementary unemployment benefit plans. By far the largest numbers of these are concentrated in the basic auto and steel industries, but such plans are now also in existence in such other widely divergent sectors of the economy as aluminum, glass, farm equipment, retail trade, can, rubber, apparel, printing and publishing, and the maritime industry, and the vast majority of these plans have some major elements of similarity.

All SUB plans, for example, require that an employee have a certain amount of service with the company before he is eligible to draw benefits; the seniority period varies among the different plans—with a one-year requirement in the basic auto and can contracts contrasting with a two-year prerequisite under the steel industry plan and a five-year requirement (the most extreme) under a current agreement between the Minnesota Mining and Manufacturing Company and the Oil, Chemical and Atomic Workers Union. In addition to seniority stipulations, virtually all plans require that the unemployed worker be willing and able to work. The test in this latter connection is, most often, the registration for work by the unemployed worker with a state unemployment service office; for example, under the automobile plan a worker is not qualified to obtain benefits unless he registers for work with the appropriate state office and does not refuse to accept a job deemed suitable under such a state system. Beyond this, the plans invariably limit benefits to workers who are unemployed because of layoff resulting from a reduction in the work force by the company. Workers who are out of work because of discipline, strikes, or "acts of God" cannot draw benefits. Nor can workers whose curtailment of employment is attributable to government regulation or to public controls over the amount or nature of materials or products which the company uses or sells, do so.

Under the most prevalent type of SUB agreement, all employees (including those just hired) start to acquire credit units at the rate of one-half unit for each week in which they work. When they complete enough service to qualify for the benefits (the one to five years cited in the previous paragraph) they are officially credited with these units, which they can then trade off for SUB pay when unemployed up to a maximum unemployment duration. Most plans now have set this maximum at 52 weeks and consequently an automobile or steel industry worker with two years of continuous employment has achieved the maximum amount of SUB coverage. Under about half of the current plans, however, the ratio of credit units to weeks of benefit can be *increased* when the SUB fund falls below a certain level, thereby shortening the duration of benefits.[16] Another common variation is to adjust the ratio in such a way that laid-off workers with long service are protected for a proportionately longer length of time than are shorter-service employees.

Almost universally, employees are entitled to draw benefits only up to the amount of credits that they have established, and can receive no benefits—no matter how large the amount of their credits—during the first week of unemployment, a stipulation which is consistent with the one-week waiting period under most state unemployment insurance plans. In addition, credit units are canceled in the event of a willful misrepresentation of facts in connection with the employee's application for either state or SUB income.

Benefit formulas under most layoff plans set a normal level of payments at 60 to 65 per cent of "take-home" pay (gross pay minus taxes) for all eligible employees. This level comprises payments from both the negotiated benefit plan and the state system. If, for example, a worker whose normal take-home amount is $100 is laid off, a plan which calls for 65 per cent of his take-home pay allows him $65. And if his state unemployment compensation totals $35 weekly, the SUB plan would then pay him the weekly sum of $30 to make up the difference.[17] There

16"Supplemental Unemployment Benefit Plans," *Monthly Labor Review*, LXXXVIII, No. 1 (January, 1965), 24.

17Most SUB plans also stipulate maximum amounts that their beneficiaries can receive in any one week, however. Under the automobile plan, for example, *no* employee can receive more than $50 plus $1.50 for each dependent up to four in any one week. Plans with a flat $40 maximum are common among the Rubber Workers. And in the basic steel agreement the maximum figure is established at $37.50 a week when the affected worker is receiving benefits under a state unemployment system and $60 weekly, plus $1.50 for each dependent up to four, after the state benefits are exhausted.

is some debate even among the most rabid advocates of SUB plans as to whether the level should be pushed beyond this 65 per cent figure, for even at this percentage, several plans have experienced the ironic situation of workers preferring total lay-off to work.

In the past, SUB plans had also to weather another controversy in order to be able to function at all. With the original negotiation of this type of benefit, the question arose as to whether it would be lawful under state unemployment compensation programs for workers to draw *any* benefits from the state during the same week in which they received payment from a privately negotiated plan. Indeed, in the auto plans, it was required that a sufficient number of states officially permit the combination payment to cover two thirds of a particular company's employees before the plan could be effective. Enough states had issued favorable rulings by the end of 1955 to satisfy this requirement. At the present time, forty-four states allow combination payments, five states— Alaska, New Hampshire, New Mexico, South Carolina, and South Dakota —have as yet avoided the issue by taking no stand on it at all, and only Virginia specifically forbids unemployed workers to receive SUB benefits and state compensation in the same weeks. (NOTE: Case No. 7 deals with the related question of benefit entitlement once state unemployment compensation has been *exhausted*.)

To establish the fund for the payment of supplementary unemployment benefits, most plans require that the company—which invariably exclusively finances all SUB plans—contribute a certain amount of money per work hour. Many agreements call for a cash contribution of five cents per hour, although several go as low as two cents and about the same number require ten cents. The payment into this fund most often represents the *maximum* liability of the company, however. Typically a maximum size of the fund is defined and company contributions for any one contractual period stop completely when this limit is reached and maintained: the objectives, aside from relieving the companies of overly rigorous payments, are to prevent too large an accumulation of fund money and to encourage the companies to stabilize their employment levels. On the other hand, when fund finances fall below the stipulated amount—because of SUB-financed payments—the employer must resume payments at the rate required by the plan. In addition, many SUB plans—including most of those negotiated by the Steelworkers— require a further company liability: When the SUB fund reaches the "maixmum" level, companies *continue* to make contributions—first to a Savings and Vacation Plan (to keep *its* benefits fully current) and then once again to the SUB fund—until approximately $250 per employee is accumulated. Only at the latter point do company contributions cease.

The foregoing indicates a number of fundamental characteristics of supplementary unemployment benefit plans of the type currently in force in the basic steel and automobile-manufacturing industries. Such plans are the most common in industry and apply to the vast majority of workers covered by arrangements protecting workers' income during periods of unemployment. In summary, the basic elements of these plans are as follows:

1. They provide a definite and predictable liability against the company.
2. Payments are made solely out of the fund established by the employer contributions.
3. Laid-off employees have the responsibility to accept suitable employment as provided for under state employment service programs.
4. Employees must be eligible to receive state unemployment compensation benefits as a prerequisite to obtaining payments from a supplementary unemployment benefit plan.
5. There is a specified limit to the contributions by the company to the fund.
6. Benefits are paid only to those employees laid off because a company is unable or unwilling to furnish work; such benefits are not available to employees whose employment terminates for any other reason.
7. The total payment to the employee when permissible under state law represents a combination of benefits from a state unemployment compensation system and from the privately negotiated supplementary unemployment benefit plan.

Although plans of this type are the most popular at the present time, another procedure calculated to protect employees' income during periods of unemployment has also been adopted by some companies and unions. This approach establishes for individual workers income security accounts that are financed by company contributions and from which the employee can draw benefits. Such a plan was adopted in 1955 by some glass companies and the United Glass and Ceramic Workers of North America (AFL–CIO). Under this kind of plan the company makes a contribution of $.05 per hour into the employee's account. Once an individual has accumulated a $600 reserve, the contribution is paid into a separate vacation account, from which the worker can draw to supplement regular vacation pay. If the employee is laid off, injured, or sick, he can withdraw from his account up to $30 per week, but not more than 10 per cent of the balance of his account at any one time. Unlike the automobile and steel arrangements, the "glass plan" endows the individual worker with a vested interest in his account. Thus, if the worker is discharged, or is retired, or quits, he receives any balance in his account.

Basic differences are evident in the two types of plans. The automobile and steel plans are based upon a pooled fund, whereas the income security account plan establishes a fund for each employee. Under the glass-plan arrangement there is no integration with state unemployment compensation systems and funds in the individual worker's account may be used independently of the state program; an employee need not be eligible for unemployment compensation to draw upon his account. Finally, whereas the auto and steel plans operate only to provide workers with income for periods of unemployment which stem from the employer's being unable or unwilling to provide an employee with work, the individual income security plan can be used to provide an employee with benefits during periods of unemployment because of illness or injury, or to supplement regular vacation pay. This feature of the plan could make it attractive to workers with high levels of seniority who may never realize any tangible benefits under the supplementary unemployment benefit plans of the kind negotiated in the auto and steel industries.

With the passing of time the impact on the social and economic fabric of the nation of the operation of plans calculated to protect workers' incomes during periods of unemployment will become more evident. Since these plans are still comparatively new and cover a relatively small percentage of the labor force there is insufficient empirical data to determine their effects on the critical elements of the socioeconomic environment. There seems to be little question that they made some contribution to mitigating individual hardship, as well as to maintaining consumer purchasing power, during the general recessions of 1957–1958 and 1960–1961. But additional evidence is needed to establish their impact upon features such as the growth of industry, the level of employment and unemployment, the mobility of labor, the incentive of employees to work, the relations between management and union, the operation and character of state unemployment compensation plans, and technological changes within industry. Much speculation and deductive argument has been advanced in this respect. Unfortunately a large share of the discussion has been initiated on a purely partisan basis and hence has only served to confuse and distort the issues. As in other areas of labor relations, scientific investigation of the effects of this new development of industrial relations is required. Only through such investigation can the impact of the development be measured and evaluated objectively and fairly.

The fact remains, however, that—in strong contrast to virtually every other economic benefit discussed in this chapter—the growth of SUB plans in the decade since their negotiation in the automobile and steel industries has been far from impressive. Most craft unions continue to greet such a device with total apathy, preferring to substitute other economic improvements for its introduction. And seniority protection appears to have thus far satisfied workers in many noncraft industries sufficiently so that SUB has not become a major union demand there. But the continuing hold of SUB upon the several major industries in which it was originally negotiated, and the constant improvement of SUB allowances there, remain facts which cannot be ignored, either in assessing the creativity of the collective bargaining process or in judging the potential impact of this "guaranteed annual wage" compromise should the employment instabilities which have always characterized most industries in which SUB has now been implemented spread to other parts of the economy. If SUB extensions have not been impressive in total, SUB today does exist in sectors where it is needed—namely, in cyclical industries.

A Concluding Word

Whether or not SUB arrangements will ultimately achieve the universality of pension plans, health insurance, paid vacations, and paid holidays (and such various other widespread but considerably lesser benefits as paid time off for obligations stemming from death in the family, jury duty, and voting) thus remains an open question. Yet, *even* in the case of SUB, a broader issue does not. It appears to be all but axiomatic to collective bargaining that *any* benefit, once implemented by the parties, becomes subject through the years to a process of continuous liberalization from the workers' viewpoint. Even supplementary unemployment benefits have undergone this process in the years since 1955, when the automobile industry's maximum of $30 weekly for no more than twenty-six weeks was considered generous.

Many of these benefits continue to allow the same cost advantages to the parties, in terms of both "group insurance" savings and tax minimization, that they did at the times of their various inceptions. Perhaps an even more compelling reason, however, is one which was advanced as early as 1960:

> Both employers and unions have abandoned the code of individualism which calls for "putting it in the pay envelope." In a limited sense paternalism has been revived with unions actively seeking added benefits. . . . Both leisure and benefits are likely to remain attractive relative to wages.[18]

As the new needs and wants have become active, there is little doubt

[18]Sumner H. Slichter, James J. Healy, and E. Robert Livernash, *The Impact of Collective Bargaining on Management* (Washington, D.C.: The Brookings Institution, 1960), pp. 425–26.

that the collective bargaining parties have responded to the challenge.

However, neither for the bargaining parties nor for the nation as a whole is this situation an unmixed blessing. Increasing caution from both management and unions will, in fact, be required as the liberalization process continues, and at least three caveats appear warranted.

In the first place, many improvements in the employee benefit package automatically present potentially unstabilizing sources of grievances which would otherwise be absent. Increasing latitude for employee choice of vacation time, by the incorporation of a "seniority shall govern, so far as possible, in the selection of days" clause, for example, carries far more potential for controversy than a clear-cut statement which rests vacation scheduling exclusively in company hands. So, too, does the spread of the flat monthly pension payment per year of credited service; the question of how many hours or weeks—and under what conditions— constitute such a year is not always easily resolved. Is a suddenly decreed national day of mourning an "act of God," relieving the company of an obligation to grant reporting pay, or do its circumstances compel the employer to pay such monies? Who qualifies as a dependent under an expanded health insurance plan which now accommodates such individuals? The list of such grievance possibilities, further illustrated by the three cases at the end of this chapter, could be extended considerably.

Secondly, *wage* negotiation can never be completely divorced from benefit negotiation. Wage-related *benefits* are immediately increased when wages themselves are increased, and a six-cent-per-hour wage increase might thus conceivably raise total employment costs by considerably more than this amount, because the benefit expenses to the company (in terms of vacation and holiday pay, for example) are *automatically* increased in the process. This labor relations fact of life would hardly be worth citing were it not so often ignored in bargaining rooms, in favor of accommodating only wage increases to increases in productivity (for example) rather than wage increases *plus* wage-related benefit increases. The degree of danger in ignoring these inflationary ramifications, moreover, obviously increases with the increasing value of the benefit itself.

Finally, it is possible that over-all employment has suffered—and conceivably will continue to suffer—from the continuation of the benefit expansion of the type described in this chapter. The evidence thus far is not conclusive. But the increasing cost pressures and personnel administration complexities involved appear to have combined with related factors to push in this direction. Certainly Garbarino, whose exploration of such a possibility for manufacturing employees is perhaps the most thorough of its kind to date, does not dispute this point. He deems it "reasonable to conclude" that the cost and administrative considerations, as well as uncertainty as to future labor requirements and other management problems, have "contributed to minimizing employment expansion without necessarily leading to a major expansion of overtime scheduling."[19]

It is entirely possible that increasing labor-management and (in the case of the last two points) government awareness of these problem areas will result in some slowing down of the continuous liberalization process. Thus far, however, such a deceleration has been notably absent.

DISCUSSION QUESTIONS

1. Which set of arguments as expressed in this chapter's section on pensions carries more weight with you: the case *for* contributory plans, or the case *against* them?
2. "SUB plans of the type negotiated in the automobile and steel sectors are wholly undesirable. They discourage employees in the incentive to work, replace state unemployment compensation systems, discriminate against the worker not represented by a union, place an undetermined but intolerable burden on management, are financially unsound, and can actually cause permanent unemployment among some workers." In the light of your understanding of the character of these SUB plans, evaluate this statement.
3. Paul Pigors and Charles A. Myers have argued that "Management should offer employee benefits and services, not because [it has] to, not only within legal limits, and not as a camouflaged form of bribery, but because such benefits and services are in line with the whole personnel program." Do you agree? Why or why not?

SELECTED REFERENCES

Bloom, Gordon F., and Herbert R. Northrup, *Economics of Labor Relations*, 5th ed. Homewood, Ill.: Richard D. Irwin, Inc., 1965, pp. 613–720.

Garbarino, Joseph W., "Fringe Benefits and Overtime as Barriers to Expanding Employment," *Industrial and Labor Relations Review*, XVII, No. 3 (April, 1964) 426–42.

Ross, Arthur M., "Fringe Benefits Today and Tomorrow," *Labor Law Journal*, VII (August, 1956) 476–82.

Slichter, Sumner H., James J. Healy, and E. Robert Livernash, *The Impact of Collective Bargaining on Management*. Washington, D.C.: The Brookings Institution, 1960, pp. 372–489.

CASE NO. 5

Eligibility for Holiday Pay

(This case involves the requirement that an employee work the last scheduled work day before the holiday to obtain holiday pay.

---

[19] Joseph W. Garbarino, "Fringe Benefits and Overtime as Barriers to Expanding Employment," *Industrial and Labor Relations Review*, XVII, No. 3, April, 1964, 439.

The grievant did *not* work the last day before the holiday because he was laid off on this day. However, he *did* work his last scheduled work day *before* he was laid off. Thus, the decision turns on the meaning of the "last scheduled work day" for purposes of holiday pay.)

This case is centered on a grievance filed by *R*. It is dated June 13, 1961 and provides as follows:

> My week begins Monday thru Saturday and the holiday came on Tuesday. I was told by the Supt. not to report for work on Monday but to come in on Wednesday following the holiday. I came in and worked. The holiday in question was May 30th for which I didn't receive holiday pay. The same incident happened Thanksgiving of last November, also.

Relevant Contractual Language

Provisions of the Labor Agreement which are relevant to this case are cited as follows:

Article V—Holiday Pay: All employees shall receive eight (8) hours pay at their straight time hourly rate for each of the following holidays when no work is performed.
1. Effective May 1, 1959, up to and including April 30, 1960.
   (a) Decoration Day, July 4th, Labor Day, and Thanksgiving Day.
2. Effective May 1, 1960, up to and including April 30, 1961.
   (a) Decoration Day, July 4th, Labor Day, Thanksgiving Day and Christmas Day.
3. Effective May 1, 1961, up to and including April 30, 1962.
   (a) Decoration Day, July 4th, Labor Day, Thanksgiving Day, Christmas Day and New Years Day, provided they meet the following conditions:
4. The Employee would otherwise have been scheduled to work on the holiday if it had been observed as a holiday, and
5. The Employee works the last scheduled work day prior to the holiday and the next scheduled work day after the holiday, and
6. When any holiday specified above falls on a Saturday or Sunday and the Monday following is observed as the holiday by the state or federal government, the Monday shall be deemed to be the holiday.
7. All work performed on the above holidays shall be paid for at the rate of double time.
8. Employees who have not attained the status of regular employees by virtue of their probationary period shall not be entitled to holiday pay listed above.
9. Employees eligible for holiday pay who are subject to layoff, shall be notified by the Employer in writing with a copy to the Union 30 days prior to the holidays listed above of such layoff; employees so notified shall not be entitled to holiday pay; employees not so notified shall be entitled to holiday pay.

Basic Question

The question to be determined in this proceeding is framed as follows: Under the circumstances of this case did the Company violate Article V of the Labor Agreement?

Background

The grievant is employed by the Company as a truck driver. On Friday, May 26, 1961, superintendent *A* instructed the grievant not to report to work until the following Wednesday, May 31. Decoration Day fell on Tuesday, May 30. Pursuant to Company instructions, the grievant did not report to work on Monday, May 29, 1961. His last day of work before Decoration Day was Friday, May 26, and his first day of work following the holiday was Wednesday, May 31. The Company operated on Monday, May 29, during which day other employees of the bargaining unit worked. The grievance arose when the Company refused to pay the grievant holiday pay for Decoration Day.

Position of the Parties

Union

Under the circumstances of this case, the Union claims that the Company violated Article V of the Labor Agreement. It claims that the grievant fulfilled the contractual obligation to qualify for Decoration Day holiday pay within the meaning of Article V.

To support its position the Union argues that May 26 was the grievant's last scheduled work day before Decoration Day, and, therefore, he qualified for pay for this holiday under the meaning of Article V, Section 5, of the Labor Agreement. Thus, the Union states:

> Therefore, the "last scheduled work day" of the grievant, prior to the holiday (Decoration Day) was Friday, May 26, 1961; and since the grievant worked on Wednesday, May 31, 1961, he . . . is entitled to Holiday Pay.

It also points to the negotiations in which the instant holiday pay qualification language was adopted, claiming that "the Union had a specific and definite point that it wanted to negotiate in the holiday clause; it used the word 'scheduled' in a specific and particular sense." It claims that during the negotiations, the employers to the Labor Agreement, including the instant Company, understood this intent and objective of the Union and attempted to introduce language which would have made it more difficult for an employee to qualify for holiday pay. However, the Union avers that its position prevailed and the language which appears in Article V, Section 5, reflects the Union proposal. To support these assertions, the Union introduced a series of documents, designated as Union Exhibits 3 and 4.

Company

On its part, the Company denies that there exists a violation of Article V under the circumstances of the instant case. It claims that words "last scheduled work day" of Article V, Section 5, "means, and should be construed to mean the day immediately before the holiday." Since the grievant did not work on Monday, May 29, he did not qualify for holiday pay, the Company contends.

Further, the Company argues that if Section 5 is not construed in the manner which the Company believes to be correct then "such an interpretation would completely obviate the meaning of Article V, Section 4." On this score, the Company claims that if an employee works the days immediately surrounding a holiday there is the presumption that he would have worked on the holiday. If, however, an employee does not work on the days immediately surrounding a holiday, the presumption is that he would not have worked the holiday. It claims that Section 4 is particularly important since the business is seasonal in character, and, further, the volume of its business and its regularity depends upon the demands by other firms for the use of its trucks. Thus, it states,

As to whether or not there would be employment on any one particular day must require a presumption on the part of the employer. For example, the fact that an employee might be required to work on the Monday preceding a holiday and on the Wednesday following the holiday does not mean there would be work available for him on the Tuesday the holiday fell on. Therefore, it is necessary to set up some standards by which this can be determined in fairness to each employee. Therefore, the language in question raises the presumption that if the employee works on Monday and Wednesday, it is presumed that he would have worked on Tuesday.

. . . Again, we would respectfully invite your attention to the fact that if the employee works the day before the holiday and the day after the holiday, it is presumed that he would have worked the day of the holiday. If he is not scheduled to work on the day before the holiday and on the day after the holiday, then it is presumed he would not have worked on the day that the holiday fell on.

With respect to the negotiation of the holiday pay qualification language, the Company claims that testimony was adduced in the arbitration hearing that the language contained in Article V, Section 5, was understood by both Union and Employer negotiators to require an employee to work "the day before and the day after a holiday" in order to be eligible to receive holiday pay.

On these grounds, the Company requests that the grievance be denied.

Discussion of the Evidence

APPLICATION OF ARTICLE V, SECTION 5: The outcome of this case fundamentally turns on the construction and application of Article V, Section 5, of the Labor Agreement. To be more specific there must be a determination of the meaning of the words "the last scheduled work day prior to the holiday." Does this language require that an employee to be eligible for holiday pay must work the day immediately preceding the holiday? Or do these words mean that the employee qualifies when he works *his* last scheduled work day prior to the holiday even though he does not work the work day immediately preceding the holiday?

In the instant case, R worked on Friday, May 26. He did not work on Monday, May 29, which was the work day immediately preceding Decoration Day. Under the Company theory, the grievant was not qualified because he did not work the last day prior to the holiday. Under the Union theory, R is qualified since he worked on Friday, May 26, which was the grievant's last scheduled work day prior to the holiday in question. He was told by Superintendent A not to report on Monday, May 29.

If the Company's contention is correct, the question arises as to why the parties inserted the word "scheduled" before the words "work day prior to the holiday." If the parties had intended to disqualify any employee from holiday pay if he did not work the last work day immediately preceding a holiday, the question arises as to why they did not adopt language to accomplish this purpose. For example, why did not the parties simply agree to language such as "the employee works the last work day prior to the holiday." On the surface, at least, such language would appear to disqualify any employee who did not work on the last work day immediately preceding a holiday.

History of Negotiations

An explanation for the existence in Section 5 of the word "scheduled" is offered by the Company. In this respect, it makes reference to testimony adduced in the arbitration hearing purporting to show the history of the negotiations which gave rise to Section 5. The burden of this testimony offered by Company witnesses is that despite the existence of the word *scheduled*, Section 5 was adopted by the parties with the intent that employees are required to work the work day prior to a holiday to qualify for pay.

The facts show that the Company offered a proposal for Section 5 which deleted the word "scheduled." This version was not adopted by the parties; and, instead, the one which is currently cited as Article V, Section 5, in the instant Labor Agreement was agreed to by the negotiators. Despite these circumstances, the Company still believes that its basic position is not weakened, since it offered testimony that the parties intended the instant language to mean that an employee to qualify for holiday pay must work the last work day prior to a holiday. In short, with or without the word *scheduled*, the Company believes that the proofs support its basic position.

Company witness, *S*, president of the Company, participated actively in the negotiations. He testified that it was his recollection that there was mutual understanding between the Company and Union negotiators that the words " 'last scheduled work day' mean the day prior to . . . the holiday." His testimony suggests that even though the actual language contains the word *scheduled*, Section 5 was intended to mean that an employee does not qualify if he fails to work the last work day immediately prior to a holiday. Additional Company testimony purports to prove that there was apparent agreement by all concerned that notwithstanding the incorporation of the word "scheduled" in Section 5 an employee still does not qualify for holiday pay unless he works the last working day immediately prior to the holiday.

However, the Company version of the negotiations does not square with that of the Union. Thus, a Union witness, *C*, president of the Union, was also a party to the negotiations. He also testified to the events which led up to the adoption of Article V, Section 5. However, his testimony is poles apart from that offered by Company witnesses. According to *C*, Section 5 was one of the most "hotly" discussed issues of the negotiations. Further, it was his recollection that the Company proposal for Section 5 language which would have deleted the word "scheduled" was rejected by the Union because it feared that such language would disqualify an employee from holiday pay if he were laidoff through no fault of his own on the work day immediately preceding the holiday. He testified that he explained to the Company negotiators that to qualify for holiday pay under the language which was subsequently incorporated in Section 5 "an employee would have to work his last scheduled work day before the holiday."

Thus, we have here testimony which is contradictory on a most crucial feature of this case. There is wisdom in the Company's observation that such "testimony is so contradictory and biased that little weight can be given to either." (Company Post-Hearing Brief, p. 3.) This is indeed a most candid and refreshing statement. It recognizes the most unenviable position in which the Arbitrator finds himself. Further, it suggests that, perhaps, the contending witnesses' memories have been influenced by their partisanship in the instant hearing.

Still, the Arbitrator must, of necessity, apply Section 5 to the facts of this case. He must do the best he can in the light of the entire record. Indeed, if there were agreement between the parties as to their intentions when Section 5 was adopted, there would be no need to arbitrate this case. Undoubtedly, it is because of the different versions of what went on at the negotiations that this case has been stimulated.

"Scheduled" Appears in Section 5

Though the testimony dealing with intent is contradictory, the fact remains that when Section 5 was finally written the word *scheduled* appears in it. About this there is no doubt since it is in the contract. Indeed, if it were not for the contradiction in the testimony cited above, there would be no doubt whatever that an employee qualifies for holiday pay under Section 5 when he works *his* last scheduled work day before the holiday. As the record stands, however, there is some doubt, but such doubt cannot erase the fact that Section 5 does contain the word *scheduled*. Once again, the question arises: If the parties had actually intended to require an employee to work the work day immediately prior to a holiday, why did they use the word "scheduled"? Why did they not simply say that employees had to work the work day immediately prior to the holiday and leave out an inference to the employees' last *scheduled* work day?

It may, of course, be true that there was honest misunderstanding during the give-and-take of negotiations. Perhaps there was confusion as to what the intention of the parties really was. Each party might have left the negotiations with the belief that its version was the one that prevailed.

The Arbitrator, however, has no choice except to read Section 5 in terms of the language which the parties did adopt. If there is doubt as to intent based upon the testimony dealing with the negotiations, there is no doubt about the fact that the parties did agree to the word *scheduled* in Section 5. The word stands therein— plain and unambiguous for all to see.

Consideration of Section 9

Now there is additional contractual language which supports the finding that under Section 5 an employee qualifies for holiday pay when he works his last scheduled work day before a holiday. This language is contained in Section 9 of Article V. Under this provision, an employer who notifies an employee of layoff 30 days prior to a holiday need not pay such an employee for such a holiday *even if the employee works his last scheduled working day prior to a holiday.* Clearly, if the Company's basic position in this case had merit, there would be no need whatsoever for the existence of Section 9. There would be no need since, under the Company's theory, all employees who do not work the last working day immediately prior to a holiday are automatically disqualified. Therefore, there would be no need for the Company to notify an employee of a layoff to be relieved from the holiday pay obligation. Any employee who does not work on the work day immediately prior to a holiday is automatically disqualified. Thus, *R* was laid-off on Monday and so he gets no holiday pay for Decoration Day—so goes the Company's argument.

If this is the accurate construction of Section 5, the question arises as to why the parties put Section 9 into Article V. Certainly, it was not put in the contract just to take up space. Undoubtedly, it was included to give employers some relief from the payment of holiday pay to an employee who would be laid off a long time before a holiday. For example, suppose an employee worked his last scheduled working day on September 15 and is laid off as of this date. He is still on layoff through the month of December. Without Section 9, it could be argued that Section 5 standing alone would guarantee the employee his holiday pay for Christmas Day and New Year's Day. To avoid such a construction, which would appear somewhat questionable under any circumstances, and particularly so in an industry which is seasonal, the parties wrote Section 9 into Article V.

It is stressed that if the Company's construction of Section 5 is correct there would be no need for Section 9. Since the parties did include Section 9, there is an additional basis to find that when they adopted Section 5 they intended the language to mean that an employee qualifies for holiday pay when he works his last scheduled work day before a holiday.

Consideration of Article V, Section 4

Section 4 provides that an employee qualifies for holiday pay when he would have been scheduled to work if it were not for the existence of the holiday. To put it in other terms, an employee does not qualify for holiday pay if he would not have been scheduled to work during the day on which the holiday falls. Thus, July 4 falls on, for example, Tuesday. Employee *X* would not be scheduled on that Tuesday. Consequently, he does not qualify for holiday pay.

The instant Company engages in a business which is seasonal and even during its busy season its volume of business depends upon the demand for its trucks—a demand over which it has no control. Because of this set of circumstances, it is understandable that the Company cannot schedule its employees on a regular basis such as a manufacturing firm can. Certainly this Arbitrator understands that all sorts of factors, including weather, influence the demand for its trucks. Accordingly, it can be expected that the Company's employment practice is subject to fluctuations at any time.

On the basis of these considerations, the Company argues that "as to whether or not there would be employment on any one particular day must require a presumption on the part of the employer." As stated previously, the Company presumes that if an employee works the work days immediately surrounding the holiday, such an employee would have been scheduled on the holiday itself. By the same token, if an employee such as R was not scheduled to work the work day preceding the holiday, it is presumed that he would not have been scheduled on the holiday. Therefore, such an employee is disqualified from holiday pay under Section 4.

Though the record of this Arbitrator demonstrates that he has always given full faith and credit to the rights and prerogatives of management, he simply cannot accept the Company's interpretation of Section 4. What the Company really seeks to do is *to write additional language into Section 4*. Neither by its express language nor by any reasonable inference, does Section 4 establish the "presumption" theory advanced by the Company.

To be sure, the Arbitrator does not pass any judgment on the inherent merits of the "presumption" theory advanced by the Company. Perhaps it would be a wise way to construe Section 4. But it is not the job of any arbitrator to decide a case on the basis of whether action is wise or unwise. His standards are the contract and the proofs and not whether a particular procedure is inherently wise or unwise.

In short, the Arbitrator cannot permit Section 4 to be rewritten in this proceeding to include the "presumption" theory argued by the Company. If he approved the Company action on this basis, would he not be adding to the contract in violation of the scope of his authority as established under Article XIII (d) ?[1]

Frankly, the Arbitrator gave much thought to the Company's "presumption" theory. He recognizes that Company counsel advanced it in a conscientious manner and in good faith. Further, the Arbitrator recognizes that it represents a most important defense for the Company in the proceeding. Nevertheless, after long con-

---

[1] Article XIII, (d), reads: "The Arbitrator may interpret the Agreement and apply it to the particular case presented to him, but he shall have no authority to add to, subtract from, or in any way modify the terms of the parties' Agreement."

sideration, the Arbitrator must conclude that it would be improper to permit Section 4 to be rewritten on the basis argued by the Company.

Evidence Not Conclusive

The record is largely barren of evidence to demonstrate whether *R* actually would have been scheduled on Decoration Day. Whatever evidence that bears on this issue is scant and inconclusive. *R* stands low on the seniority list; he was laid off on Monday, but he returned to work on Wednesday; and he apparently worked about 43 hours the week ending May 27, 1961. (Union Exhibit No. 2.)

Obviously, such evidence is far too meager to establish that *R* would not have been scheduled on Tuesday, May 30. To be sure, if the proofs were clear that the grievant would not have been scheduled on Tuesday, there would be a basis on which to deny the grievance. As stated with reference to Section 9, Section 4 was not put into the contract just to take up space. As with any other provision of the Labor Agreement, it must be given full faith and credit. This Arbitrator does not shut his eyes to any provision of the Labor Agreement. However, for an employee to be disqualified under Section 4, the proofs must demonstrate that the employee would not have been scheduled to work during the work day on which the holiday falls. In the instant case, the proofs fall far short of establishing this, and, therefore, *R* cannot be disqualified under Section 4.

The grievant qualifies under Section 5. Clearly, it would be improper to deprive him of a contractual right under Section 4 unless the proofs were adequate to demonstrate that he would not have been scheduled on Tuesday.

Conclusions

R worked *his* last scheduled work day before Decoration Day. Section 5 does not require that an employee work the work days immediately surrounding a holiday. It requires that the employee work his last scheduled work day prior to the holiday, and his next scheduled work day after the holiday. Further, whatever relief is afforded by the Company from its holiday pay obligation under Section 4 and 9 does not apply in this case. Finally, the proofs do not show that during the negotiations the parties intended that Section 5 be read in a manner which would eliminate the word *scheduled* from its context.

On the basis of these findings, the Arbitrator has no choice except to grant the grievance. He does so in full confidence that he is effectuating the language of Article V of the Labor Agreement.

Award

The grievance of *R*, dated June 13, 1961, is granted on the grounds that under the circumstances of this case the Company violated Article V of the Labor Agreement. Therefore, it is directed that within three working days after the receipt of this award the Company pay *R* for the holiday, Decoration Day, May 30, 1961, in accordance with Article V of the Labor Agreement.

Questions

1. Why is the phrase "last scheduled work day" so important in arriving at a decision in this case?
2. How does the Company show the relationship between Article V, Sections 4 and 5?
3. What do you believe to be the intent of Article V, Section 5?

CASE NO. 6

Disability Benefits

(Under the group insurance policy involved here, employees who are wholly disabled because of illness are entitled to a weekly benefit. However, the plan requires a four-day waiting period before the benefits start, a common enough provision under disability programs. Its chief rationales are to discourage employees from feigning illness and to reduce the costs of the plan. The issue in this case concerns the time at which the four-day waiting period begins.

A key feature of the case is the arbitrator's reliance on "past practice" for his decision. Past practice or customs under a contract is a standard for contractual construction when the language of a labor agreement is ambiguous, or subject to various shades of meaning.)

On April 1, 1963, *S* filed Grievance No. 126 which charges that the Company "violated contract with explanation in plant book, by not counting waiting days from the first day reported to doctor." He claims that under the circumstances of the case, the Company is in violation of Article XXIII, Section 23.1, which states:

The benefits provided by the medical, hospital, and surgical program for employees and their dependents effective August 1, 1962 will remain in effect for the duration of this Agreement.

The Company denied the grievance, and this arbitration has been instituted to determine the controversy between the parties.

Basic Question

The basic question to be determined in this arbitration is framed as follows: Under the circumstances of this case, did the Company violate Article XXIII, Section 23.1, of the Labor Agreement?

Background of Dispute

The fundamental issue in this proceeding is the determination of the method of calculating the waiting period for disability benefits. Under a group insurance policy, carried with the *A* insurance company, employees who are wholly disabled from working are entitled to a weekly benefit. The portions of the Group Insurance Plan pertinent to this proceeding state:

. . . Not more than 52 weeks' benefits will be paid for any one period of disability, and no benefits will be paid for the first four days of any disability due to disease; however, if the Employee is confined as a bed-patient in a legally constituted hospital for at least 24 consecutive hours before the expiration of the four-day waiting period payment of the benefits will begin with the first twenty-four hours of confinement.

During the evening of Friday, January 4, 1963, *S*, the grievant, became sick. He visited a doctor on Saturday, January 5, and was certified that he was totally disabled from performing his duties as of that date. *S* returned to work on January 28. The grievant is regularly scheduled to work five days per week, Monday through Friday.

This dispute centers on the proper method of counting the four-day waiting period as the prerequisite to the obtainment of weekly benefits. The record establishes that the grievant received disability benefits starting on Friday, January 11, the waiting period starting on Monday, January 7. Hence, his waiting period included Monday, Tuesday, Wednesday, and Thursday of the week in question. According to the Union theory, the countdown period should start on Saturday, January 5, the date upon which he was certified as disabled by the attending physician. Hence, under its version, the waiting period should have included Saturday, Sunday, Monday, and Tuesday with the grievant's benefits starting on Wednesday, January 9.

Position of the Parties

Involved in the argument of the parties are the arbitrability of the dispute and the merits of the controversy. According to the Company, the dispute is not within the jurisdiction of this Arbitrator. In this regard it refers to Article X, Section 10.3, of the Labor Agreement which provides, in part, that "the arbitrator will not have the power to add to, subtract from, or modify any of the terms of the agreement. . . ." Its basic contention is that the administration of the insurance plan is not a proper subject for arbitration. Article XXIII, Section 23.1, the Company contends, does not embrace disputes dealing with the interpretation or application of the insurance plan. Therefore, since the instant grievance raises an administrative question, the proper method of calculating the four-day waiting period, the Arbitrator should dismiss it on the grounds of nonarbitrability. It argues that neither the insurance plan nor an explanatory booklet, "The Group Insurance Plan," issued to employees, and relied upon by the Union in support of its case, are parts of the Labor Agreement. Thus, the Company states: ". . . It therefore follows that the arbitrator is not authorized, pursuant to the terms of the contract, to interpret the group insurance plan booklet or the insurance certificate inasmuch as neither document is a part of nor mentioned in the contract between the parties." To buttress its position on the issue of arbitrability, the Company cites arbitration and judicial precedents.

With respect to arbitrability, the Union on its part argues that the Arbitrator may properly under the contract make a determination of the merits of the dispute. It claims that Section 23.1 provides that there shall be no change of benefits under the insurance plan. Since it charges that the method by which the waiting period has been calculated changes the benefits, the merits of the dispute are properly before the Arbitrator. Thus, it argues ". . . It is submitted that BENEFITS under the insurance plan herein have been incorporated into the contract. The Arbitrator has as much right to determine whether or not these benefits have been improperly withheld as he would have to determine whether a proper wage scale was being paid. Such a ruling would in no way 'add to, subtract from or modify any of the terms of this agreement.'" Also, the Union avers that the previously cited booklet, styled the "Group Insurance Plan," hereinafter referred to as the "Insurance Booklet," may properly be used as a basis of a decision in this proceeding. As demonstrated below, the Union relies in part on the Insurance Booklet to defend its position on the merits of the dispute. It believes that the Insurance Booklet may properly be used as a guide for the determination of the correct method for the calculation of the waiting period in question. The Union cites arbitration precedents to support its contention that the dispute is arbitrable.

Contentions Respecting the Merits

With respect to the merits of the case, the parties are also in disagreement. Under the assumption that the insurance plan may be interpreted by the Arbitrator, and under the further assumption that the Insurance Booklet may properly be used as a basis for a determination in this proceeding, the Union emphasizes certain language in both documents. In the first place, it directs attention to the language of the insurance plan which deals with the waiting period. It claims that the phrase contained therein, "the first four days of any disability due to disease," simply means four days, starting from the date of the total disability. In this respect, it argues that the language does not mean the first four scheduled days of work, as the Company avers, but that "the Union's contention (is) that the phrase speaks for itself." Also, the Union directs attention to the Insurance Booklet, which states on page 5 that "the weekly benefit which you (the employee) are entitled to will commence on the first day of disability resulting from accident or on the fifth day of disability resulting from sickness. However, if you are confined in a hospital before benefits for sickness would otherwise begin, payment of the weekly benefit will begin with the first day of confinement." Since there is no qualification of the term *day*, the Union argues that what is meant is simply any day and not a work day.

To support its position relative to the meaning of the word *day* or *days*, as contained in the aforementioned documents, the Union refers to other areas of the contract where the word *days* is used. It argues in this respect that "examination of [the Labor Agreement] shows that whenever the parties describe a period of time by using the word 'day' by itself, it refers to exactly that, 'days' covering not only work days, scheduled work days, but all days." Thereafter, the Union cites 15 instances wherein the contract specifies the word *days* without any qualification. Thus, for example, Section 2.1 states that each employee will become a member of the Union not later than "30 days" following the effective date of the Labor Agreement. In addition, the Union argues that the contract also includes terms, such as "work days," "scheduled days of work," "calendar days," or "working days." Hence, the Union argument is that unless the word *days* is qualified by such terms, the word *days* covers "each and every day of the week and month."

In addition, the Union claims that the method of calculating the waiting period according to the Company theory is "basically unfair." The basis of this allegation involves the procedure of computing the benefits paid to a disabled employee when he is not entitled to a full week's benefits. Normally, a worker receives $65 weekly benefits for a seven-day period of disability. Portions of that weekly benefit, however, are computed by dividing the $65 by seven days. Thus, each day's benefit is calculated at 1/7 of the weekly benefits. To press this point, the Union constructs an example to show what the Union believes to be an inequitable situation if the Company theory of the waiting period is upheld:

Taking a work week Monday through Sunday, an employee may be scheduled on five days from Wednesday through Sunday:

M	T	W	Th	F	S	Su
0	0	x	x	x	x	x

Assuming an employee is disabled for sickness for a week starting Monday, under the Company's argument, he would be paid for only one day that week (Sunday). But, the benefits for that one day would be figured by dividing the weekly benefits by all seven days—including the Monday and Tuesday. The Company has thus used Monday and Tuesday to cut down the daily benefits it pays to an employee (1/7 rather than 1/5), but it refuses to count those same days for the waiting period. They "have their cake and are eating it too."

Another example is presented by the Union to show the "unfairness" of the Company's theory of the waiting period. Thus, "if an employee is scheduled so that he is off the last two days of one work week and off the following two days of the next work week, it is possible for him to be disabled for sickness for EIGHT DAYS before his benefits—under the Company theory—commence." This is the case since under the Company version the four consecutive scheduled days off are not counted as waiting days, and, therefore, the next four scheduled work days constitute the waiting period. In short, the Union argues that scheduled days off under the Company theory do not constitute waiting days, but that the same days off are used to figure daily benefits.

Accordingly, the Union requests that the grievance be granted both because the Company's version of the waiting period violates the Labor Agreement, and because the method is devoid of fairness and equity.

On its part, the Company claims that the grievance should be denied on its merits. A major element of its argument is that the benefit payments to the instant grievant reflects the way the waiting period has been handled in the past. Thus, it avers that "any other interpretation would be in total disregard of an established practice which has been in existence over a period of many years—a practice which has never been questioned by a single employee or the Union until now." To support its position, as based upon past practice, the Company offered as evidence the records of many employees whose claims for weekly benefits, the Company contends, were processed in the same manner as that of the instant grievant.

In addition, the Company refers to a statement in the Insurance Booklet which reads:

The [insurance] plan pays you [the disabled employee] a weekly benefit for periods during which you are disabled and prevented from working as a result of a nonoccupational accident or sickness.

This language, the Company contends, supports its position that scheduled days off should not be counted as waiting days for the payment of disability benefits resulting from sickness.

On these grounds, the Company believes that the grievance should be denied on its merits aside from its position that the grievance is not arbitrable under the Labor Agreement.

Discussion of the Evidence

Arbitrability issue held in abeyance

Two separate issues are involved in this proceeding. The first is the question of the arbitrability of the grievance and the second involves the merits of the claim. In cases wherein the issue of arbitrability is raised, it is customary to deal first with this question before there is consideration of the merits of the particular grievance. If the issue is found to be nonarbitrable, the claim is dismissed and no consideration is given to its merits. If the issue is held arbitrable, a determination is then made as to the merits of the grievance. However, in this proceeding the Arbitrator desires to reverse this sequence and deal first with the merits of the grievance. If *S's* claim is held to have merit, there would then be a determination of the arbitrability of the question. By the same token, if the grievance is denied on its merits, there need be no determination of the question of arbitrability.

Application of insurance plan and insurance booklet

To focus attention on the merits of the grievance, the Arbitrator will assume *arguendo* that the insurance plan and the Insurance Booklet are parts of the Labor Agreement, and, further, that he has the authority to interpret or apply both documents to the facts of this case. In that light, the basic position of the Union rests upon the fact that the words *days* and *day*, as they appear in the insurance plan and the Insurance Booklet are not qualified. Therefore, the waiting period starts on the very day that he *S* was found disabled, January 5.

As the Union argues, in the relevant portion of the insurance plan there is the statement that no benefits will be paid for "the first four days" of any disability due to disease. It does not state four scheduled *working* days as the Company version holds. Also, in the Insurance Booklet, there is the statement that benefits will commence on "the fifth day" of disability resulting from sickness. There is no qualification of the word *day*. As long as the employee is disabled for four days, this period embraces all days, regardless of whether they include work days or scheduled days off. The crux, therefore, of the waiting period is the employee's *disability* and not whether he was scheduled to work during this four-day period.

In short, the Union contends that the pertinent language of the insurance plan and the Insurance Booklet is perfectly clear and unambiguous. Therefore, it requests on this basis the granting of the grievance. Whatever practice that might be involved which would support the Company claim cannot serve to override the clear-cut contractual language.

A Degree of Ambiguity

Now, the Arbitrator understands that when practice and clear-cut contractual language are in conflict the latter standard normally prevails. Accordingly, careful and long consideration has been given to the Union argument that the language involved should constitute the ultimate standard for the determination of the dispute and should supersede any established practice that would tend to establish a construction of the language favorable to the Company's position.

In this respect, the Arbitrator notes as does the Union that the words *days* and *day* as incorporated in the documents in question are not qualified. Also, he notes that in the Labor Agreement the parties frequently did qualify the words *days* and *day* when they desired to give such terms a meaning other than *any* day or days in a week or month. From this point of view, there is considerable merit to the Union's argument that the pertinent language in the documents in question is perfectly clear. In short, the waiting period required under the insurance plan and as explained by the Insurance Booklet includes any and all days from the day upon which an employee is deemed to be disabled.

Nevertheless, the Arbitrator is not fully satisfied that the language in question is as unequivocally clear as the Union would have us believe. The reason for this involves the first sentence on page 5 of the Insurance Booklet which *immediately* precedes that language upon which the Union relies to support its contention that there is no dispute as to the clarity of the meaning of the term *day* or *days* for purposes of this case. Thus, the relevant language of the Insurance Booklet reads as follows:

> The Plan pays you a weekly benefit for periods during which you are disabled and prevented from working as a result of a nonoccupational accident or a sickness.
> The weekly benefit to which you are entitled will commence on the first day of disability resulting from accident or on the fifth day of disability resulting from sickness.

When these sentences are placed in juxtaposition, there is some doubt as to the meaning of the word *day* as contained in the second sentence. Note that the first sentence states that benefits will be paid for periods in which "you are disabled and *prevented from working."* Clearly, on a scheduled day off, an employee is not prevented from working since he would not have worked even if he were not disabled. Thus, an employee does not lose any wages because of a disability which starts on his scheduled day off. From this point of view, therefore, it is reasonable to argue that the waiting period includes only scheduled days of work during which an employee is prevented from working because of a disability. To put it another way, the four-day waiting period would not include nonscheduled working days because on these days the employee would not be prevented from working as the result of a disability.

The Arbitrator does not hold that this analysis necessarily demonstrates that the language involved reflects the unmistakable intent that the waiting period only includes scheduled working days. It is just as reasonable to hold that the unqualified use of the terms *days* and *day* could mean *any kind* of day or days. Still, when one reads the relevant language as a whole, as one must to get the essential meaning of the waiting-period requirement, some doubt is involved as to whether the parties meant scheduled working days or just any kind of days. And if there is some doubt, regardless of its extent, it is proper to determine how the waiting period has been applied in the past. In short, there is *some degree* of ambiguity which properly requires consideration of historical usage.

Past Practice

The four-day waiting period

The evidence clearly establishes a historical practice wherein the countdown for the waiting period did not include scheduled days off. Rather, the practice has been that the waiting period involved only days upon which the disabled employee was scheduled to work. Company Exhibit No. 2 clearly reveals this practice. In this exhibit, there are included the claims of eleven employees all of whom served the same kind of a waiting period as the instant grievant. They were found to be disabled on their days off but these days were not included in the four-day waiting period. Their waiting period began on their first scheduled working day after they were held to be disabled.

There is no need to specify the exact circumstances involved in the processing of each of these claims to demonstrate that their scheduled days off did not count toward the waiting period even though the employees involved were disabled during the nonscheduled working days. The Union does not question the authenticity of this fact. (Transcript, p. 45.) The record clearly establishes that nonscheduled working days of these eleven employees were not counted in the four-day waiting period. (Transcript, p. 46.) Thus:

Q. (By Company Counsel) In all cases, the scheduled days off were not counted for the countdown?

A. (By *M*, Manager of Industrial Relations) That is correct. We started the countdown the first day they would normally be scheduled to work. We didn't count normal days off.

Q. *S* was paid exactly the same as all of these eleven cases?

A. Exactly the same.

In two instances, there was an error in the processing of the claims of disabled employees and scheduled days off were counted as part of the four-day waiting period. These involved the claims of employees *L* (Company Exhibit Number 3) and *R* (Union Exhibit Number 3). However, the error was subsequently discovered and there was an adjustment for the error in the final settlement of their claims. (Transcript, p. 47.)

The record further demonstrates that at no time did any of these employees or the Union file any grievances or otherwise protest against the handling of the waiting period as established by these thirteen employees' claims.

Commencement of payments to hospitalized employees and those involved in accidents

In addition, the Company offered into evidence the claims of thirteen other employees who either were hospitalized or who suffered an accident. (Company Exhibit Number 4.) Under the insurance plan, the four-day waiting period for disability benefits is waived when an employee has an accident or is hospitalized. What is significant with respect to this group of claims is that these employees either suffered an accident or were hospitalized on their scheduled days off, but *their disability benefits did not start until their first scheduled working day following the accident or hospitalization.* They did not begin to draw benefits on their scheduled days off even though they suffered an accident or were hospitalized on such days. Their disability benefits began with their first scheduled working day following their accident or their hospitalization.

Under the Union theory, as propounded in this proceeding, it would follow that payments would begin on the very day of hospitalization or accident whether or not such a day is a scheduled work day. Clearly, the practice does not square with the Union's basic position in this case. The Union does not attempt to refute that payment to employees included within Company Exhibit No. 4 did not begin until their first scheduled working day, and, further, the facts again show that no employee or the Union filed a grievance or registered any other protest to the way the claims of these employees were handled.

Union's Attempt to Explain Away Past Practice

In short, whether one views the historical practice of the payment of claims resulting from disability due to sickness, without hospitalization, or from accidents or hospitalization, the practice as established by the evidence demonstrates that scheduled days off consistently were not included in the waiting period and that benefit payments did not start in the case of accident or hospitalization until the employee's first scheduled work day. It must again be stressed that at no time did the Union or the employee involved in these twenty-six claims file a grievance or otherwise register a protest against the manner in which the claims were processed. Such claims were filed over a five-year period, from 1959 through 1963, and at no time was there a protest.

At no time during the hearing does the Union offer any evidence to refute the practice under which the claims in question were processed. Rather, it seeks to explain away the custom by arguing:

> Considering a unit of at least seven hundred and fifty (750) employees, instances of where this same type of situation has occurred previously are very few. The testimony of the president [of the Union] and the vice-president [of the Union] was without contradiction, that this is the first time a grievance has been filed on this issue, the first time it has come to the Union's attention, and the first instance that the matter has been raised between the Company and the Union. The Company can in no way rely on any argument of "past practice" as that theory is applied to industrial relations. These variations from the clear terms of the contract have not been numerous, and clearly have not been maintained by the Employer with the acquiescence of, or over the objection of, the Union. (Union Post-Hearing Brief, p. 7.)

There are important shortcomings in this explanation calculated to destroy past practice as the basis for a decision in this proceeding. In the first place, the point that the number of claims is not sufficient to establish a practice is entirely without merit. What is important in this respect is that the Union makes no showing whatsoever that scheduled days off were ever utilized in the four-day countdown of the waiting period, or that payments began to hospitalized employees or those suffering an accident when these events took place on an employee's scheduled day off. In short, whatever evidence is available in the record demonstrates that universally the practice has been to exclude nonscheduled work days from the waiting period, and equally with respect to hospitalized employees and those who suffered an accident, such payment did not begin until the employee's first scheduled work day. *Here is a consistent practice covering each and every claim wherein the basic question involved in this proceeding was involved.* To say that the bargaining unit is quite large and that twenty-six claims are therefore not sufficient to establish a practice avoids the basic and unrefuted fact that when this problem has arisen in the past the Company has handled it in exactly the same way as it handled the instant grievant's claim. The argument of the Union would be much more convincing if it showed even *a single instance* in which scheduled days off were used in counting the four-day waiting period, or that payments to hospitalized employees or those disabled because of an accident started on a scheduled day off. The record clearly shows that the Union failed to produce any such evidence. It made an attempt in this direction with the claims of *L* and *R*. However, the evidence shows that these employees' claims were processed in error in the first place, and when the error was discovered, an adjustment in their benefit payments were made.

In the second place, the Arbitrator is not pursuaded by the argument that in the past the Union was not aware that the Company was handling the waiting period problem as it did in the instant dispute, and, therefore, that the practice should not be used as the basis for a decision in this case. What Union counsel would have the Arbitrator believe is that despite a five-year practice which involved twenty-six separate instances, the Union was completely surprised to learn of this custom. There is one theory of contractual construction which could be used to dismiss this argument without further discussion. Thus, a union has the responsibility to use reasonable diligence to discover how a contract is being administered. In considering the record in this case, the Arbitrator frankly does not see why the Union could not have discovered how the waiting period was being handled long before the instant dispute arose if it utilized reasonable diligence. There was no secret as to the procedure; it occurred on twenty-six separate occasions; the Union is presumed to encourage employees to register complaints and questions with it; and the members of the Union are presumed to know of their rights under the insurance plan—indeed, as the Union points out, each employee received the Insurance Booklet which spells out the operation of the benefit. Clearly, the Arbitrator could dismiss the "union awareness" argument outright on the grounds that even if the Union were totally ignorant of the practice, such a consideration does not make the practice any less important for purposes of decision.

There is no need, however, to resolve this issue on those grounds since positive and objective evidence demonstrates that the Union was aware of the method under which the waiting period feature of the insurance plan was being handled. Unrefuted evidence demonstrates that four of the claims included within Company Exhibit No. 4 were actually processed by Union officials. In this respect, *M* testified that "yes, there are four of them. Two by *C*, who was on the grievance committee for many, many years; one by

B, who also has been on the committee a number of times; and one by *D*, who was president of the committee on several occasions." (Transcript, p. 45.) In the light of this evidence, how can Union counsel successfully argue that the practice has not been with the knowledge of both parties to the contract? Here are Union officials themselves who processed claims, but who did not start to draw disability benefits until their first scheduled work day. Thus, *C* was hospitalized on January 28, 1961, a scheduled day off for him. But he did not start to draw disability benefits until January 30, which was his first scheduled work day following his admission to the hospital. *C* was again hospitalized on August 14, 15, and 16, 1962. August 14 and 15 were his scheduled days off. He did not receive disability benefits on these two days. He obtained them for the first time on August 16, his first scheduled work day after his hospitalization. *B* was hospitalized on March 24, 1963, a scheduled day off, and he did not begin to draw disability benefits until March 25, his first scheduled working day after his hospitalization. *D* was hospitalized on January 5, 1963. His scheduled days off fell on January 5 and 6 but he was not paid disability benefits for these two days. He waited until January 7, his first scheduled working day before he started to draw disability benefits.

Here are three union officials who were hospitalized during their scheduled days off, but each of them *waited* until their first scheduled working day following hospitalization before they began to draw disability benefits under the insurance plan. What better evidence is there to show Union knowledge of the practice than the fact that Union officials themselves had processed claims under which the practice was effective? None of them filed a grievance, but accepted as valid the practice in question. Even if it is argued that the application of the practice to rank-and-file union member claims does not constitute evidence demonstrating Union knowledge, a proposition in itself which is highly debatable, the fact remains that Union officials certainly were aware of the practice. Surely, if Union officials have knowledge of the practice, it must follow that the Union itself is aware of it. It becomes almost a matter of common sense to reach this conclusion.

It may be true that the incumbent Union president and vice-president had no knowledge of the practice. (Transcript, p. 34; Transcript, p. 22.) But it cannot be accepted, as argued by the Union, that the instant grievance is the "first time it come to the Union's attention. . . ." Indeed, the matter came to the attention of the Union at the very least when the aforementioned Union officials processed their claims for disability benefits. Any other construction of the evidence in this respect would be entirely unrealistic.

In short, the finding must be that the Union was well aware of the method in which the disability claims were being processed.

Still, no protest was lodged by the Union over a period of five years, during which twenty-six claims were processed which established the practice in question. It is now far too late in the game to argue that there was no "acquiescence" to the practice on the part of the Union. Its failure to file grievances or to otherwise protest against the practice demonstrates such acquiescence beyond any reasonable doubt. This is particularly true, as stated, because Union officers themselves upon four occasions were claimants.

Calculation of Daily Benefits

It is true that employees are paid at a rate of one-seventh of their weekly benefits for each day off. However, it must be stressed that this formula has been used to establish the *amount* of benefit, and does not attach to the calculation of the working period itself. Indeed, in a very adroit way, Union counsel attempts to utilize this formula to establish a practice which would be favorable to his client's case. Thus, he argues that "if any 'past practice' has been shown as being known to both parties, it is in the fact that an employee receives one-seventh of his weekly benefit for each day off. Based on that, both parties knew all seven days counted in establishing the benefits, and it must be assumed that all seven days counted for every purpose." (Union Post-Hearing Brief, p. 7.) The shortcoming of this argument is involved in its very language. It cannot be *"assumed"* that all seven days counted for every purpose. The fact is that the use of the seven-day period, including days off, has been used to establish daily benefits—that is, the amount of the benefits. But this formula which attaches to the *amount* of the payment does not have reference to the practice utilized to determine *when* disability benefits are to start. The practice which the Union attempts to explain away deals with the time at which benefits are to start. It cannot successfully accomplish this purpose by arguing than an employee's scheduled days off are used to calculate the *amount* of the benefits.

At best, the Union herein argues a feature which may have some merit as based upon equity considerations. As it demonstrates, though nonscheduled working days are not counted in the waiting period, they are used to determine the daily benefits paid to disabled employees. Perhaps there is some merit in the Union's argument that such a method is unfair to the employees. Nevertheless, the fact remains that if this situation is inequitable the Union had agreed to it during the five years in which twenty-six claims were processed and paid on the same basis as that of the instant grievant. Under these circumstances, it would be entirely improper for the Arbitrator to upset a well-defined practice on the grounds that the system could be termed inequitable to the disabled employees. The Union had an opportunity to argue this point long before the practice was firmly established as a basis for contractual construction.

Conclusions

What this case really boils down to is the attempt to eliminate through arbitration a practice which the Union now finds burdensome. The parties to this proceeding are seasoned veterans in labor relations and in arbitration. They know full well that arbitration is not the forum to upset an established practice. It is equally well known that contractual language which as in this case is somewhat vague must be applied in the light of its usage. Perhaps if the evidence establishing practice was not a feature in this case, the Arbitrator might have held that the words *days* and *day* as used in the insurance plan and the Insurance Booklet could be interpreted as the Union argues. However, he cannot be blind to the fact that over a period of five years, during which time contracts were negotiated a consistent practice has been established which must provide the fundamental basis for the construction of these terms.

On these grounds the Arbitrator must dismiss the instant grievance on its merits. There is no need, therefore, for the purposes of this case to determine the issue of arbitrability. The fact is that over a period of five years the Company has handled the waiting period under the insurance plan in the same manner as it handled the instant grievant's claim. He was treated exactly the same as were other employees, and for the Arbitrator to upset this procedure at this time would mean to destroy a practice which has been incorporated within the content of the Labor Agreement.

Award

After carefully considering all the evidence, and in his best judgment, the Arbitrator makes the following award:

Grievance No. 126, filed by S on April 1, 1963, is denied on the grounds that under the circumstances of this case the Company did not violate Article XXIII, Section 23.1 of the Labor Agreement.

QUESTIONS

1. How would you handle the Company's contention that the grievance should be dismissed on the grounds of nonarbitrability?
2. Does past practice support the Company or the Union position in this case?
3. Do you believe the Union weakened its case by arguing the equity of the situation?

CASE NO. 7

Supplementary Unemployment Benefits

(This case focuses upon the question of how much in the way of benefits an employee should receive from an SUB plan when his state unemployment compensation benefits are exhausted. Such a situation can easily occur because, whereas the state unemployment compensation programs provide a maximum benefit period of less than fifty-two weeks, SUB programs normally, as we know, now provide a maximum period of fifty-two weeks. While the state benefits are being paid, there is no problem, because the SUB plan will supplement the state benefits. In this case, however, an employee exhausted his state benefits, although he was still eligible to draw benefits from the SUB plan, and the question of how much money he should receive from the SUB plan was ultimately submitted to arbitration. If the SUB plan in question had had a definite statement concerning this problem, there probably would have been no need for arbitration. However, there was *no* clear policy set forth in the plan under discussion. Hence, the dispute and the arbitration.

A five-man arbitration board was established to conduct this arbitration: two company members, two union members, and one of the authors, as Impartial Chairman. Much to the gratification of the last named, both company members and both union members completely supported his decision. Where such tripartite boards are used in arbitration, it is rare for the partisan members to join the Impartial Chairman in a unanimous decision and the chairman was in this case, understandably, quite pleased. He has not always fared so well!)

This dispute was initiated by an appeal of five employees submitted on April 22, 1964. The appeal stated: "We the undersigned wish to file an appeal for supplementary unemployment benefits for the weeks of April 6, 1964 and April 13, 1964. We feel that we should have been entitled to the full amount since we draw nothing from the state." Provisions of the Plan which have relevance to this dispute are as follows:

Article I

14. "Unemployment Insurance" means any system or program, established pursuant to any state or federal law for paying benefits to persons on account of their unemployment under which an individual's eligibility for benefit payments is not determined by application of a "means" or "disability" test, and an "Unemployment Insurance Benefit" means a benefit payable under Unemployment Insurance.

15. "Supplementation" means the receiving by a laid-off Employee of a

Weekly Supplemental Benefit under the Plan for the same week of layoff at approximately the same time and without reduction of Unemployment Insurance because of the payment of the Weekly Supplemental Benefit under the Plan.

Article V, Section 2, Subsection (b) (3)

An applicant shall be eligible for a [SUB] Benefit only if he is laid off from employment in the Bargaining Unit and with respect to the week for which application is made:
has received an Unemployment Insurance Benefit not currently under protest by the Company or was ineligible for such a benefit only because (i) he did not have prior to his layoff a sufficient period of work in employment covered by Unemployment Insurance, (ii) because of a limit under Unemployment Insurance Benefits on the period of time for which Unemployment Insurance Benefits are payable to the applicant;

Article VII, Section 1(a)

The Weekly Supplemental Benefit payable to any eligible applicant commencing after September 1, 1962 shall be the lesser of; (1) An amount which, when added to the applicant's Unemployment Insurance Benefit and other compensation for such week (as defined in Section 2 of this Article) will equal 65% of his weekly after-tax straight-time pay. . . , or (2) thirty dollars.

Article VII, Section 2(a)

"Unemployment insurance and other compensation" for a Week means: the full amount of the UI Benefit, if any, received or receivable by the applicant for such Week (or the estimated amount that would have been received by the applicant for such Week if he had not been ineligible therefor solely as set forth in items (i) and (ii) of Subsection (b) (3) of Section 2, Article V. . . .)

Article VII, Section 2(b)

For purposes of Subsection (a) above, the estimated amount that would have been received by the applicant shall be computed as follows:
(1) For an applicant ineligible for UI Benefits under Section 2(b)(3)(i) of Article V, an amount equivalent to the weekly UI Benefit payable to a person having the same number of dependents as the applicant and having weekly earnings equal to the applicant's weekly straight-time pay as computed under Section 1(b)(1) of this Article throughout the qualifying period under UI.
(2) For an applicant ineligible for UI Benefits under Section 2(b)(3)(ii) of Article V, an amount equivalent of the UI Benefit rate which applied to the most recent Week for which he received UI Benefit.

What this case amounts to is the determination of the Weekly Supplemental Benefit which an employee shall receive from the SUB Trust Fund when the employee is not eligible for state Unemployment Insurance Benefits under specified circumstances.[20] Arti-

[20]These circumstances are those spelled out in Article V, Section 2, Subsection (b)(3)(i) and (ii).

cle VII, Section 1 (a) (1) and (2) establishes the formula of the Plan for Weekly SUB payments. Under its terms, the Weekly SUB payment shall be the lesser of an amount, which when added to the employee's Unemployment Insurance Benefit, will equal 65 per cent of the employee's after-tax straight-time pay, or $30. Suppose an employee is entitled to $50 under the 65-per-cent formula, and assume further that his Unemployment Insurance Benefit is $25. Under these circumstances, the Weekly SUB payment would be $25. Another example demonstrates the importance of the maximum $30 figure established under the terms of the Formula. Suppose 65 per cent of an employee's take home pay is $80, and assume that he receives $36 from the state Unemployment Insurance program. Under these circumstances, the employee's weekly SUB payment would be only $30.

Thus, the Plan contemplates that the amount of money payable to an eligible unemployed employee will be made up of two components—the state Unemployment Insurance Benefit and a Supplemental benefit paid out of the SUB Trust Fund. The SUB payment will be the difference between the amount of money which he draws from the state Unemployment Insurance program and the 65-per-cent figure. To put the arrangement in other terms: first there will be deduction from the 65-per-cent figure of the amount which the employee draws in Unemployment Insurance. Up to a maximum of $30, the SUB Trust Fund will be charged for the remaining amount. This much is rather easy to understand and presents no great problems.

Basic question and position of parties

However, what is the amount of the weekly SUB payment to which an employee is entitled when he is not eligible for state Unemployment Insurance benefits? He is eligible for weekly benefits payable from the SUB Trust Fund, but not eligible for Unemployment Insurance because of state regulations. How much is such an employee entitled to in the form of an SUB payment? This is the crux of the controversy between the Union and the Company members of the Board.

Under the Company construction of the relevant provisions of the Plan, such an employee would receive only that amount of an SUB payment when there is first deducted $36 from the 65-per-cent figure. That is, suppose an employee is entitled to $50 under the 65-per-cent formula. The Company would then deduct $36 from that figure, with the result that the employee receives only $14 from the SUB Trust Fund. In short, the total amount of money which the employee will receive for the week of unemployment would be $14. He does not, of course, actually receive the $36 because, as stated, the employee is not eligible for state Unemployment Insurance benefits. The Company uses the $36 figure to calculate the employee's Weekly Supplemental Unemployment Benefit payment. According to the Union, such an employee should receive a weekly SUB payment of $30.

The Company's policy has been in effect under an agreement reached by the Union and Company members of the Board of Administration on January 17, 1963. At that time, the Board agreed that "an applicant who is eligible for SUB Benefits, but ineligible for UI Benefits, and where such applicant is unable to furnish the required proof of compensation receivable under the UI Plan, his computed SUB Benefit will be based on the assumption that such applicant would have been eligible for $36 weekly UI Compensation." However, the Union members of the Board of Administration now believe that such policy does not square with the basic purpose and intent of the SUB Plan, and argue that "laid-off employees, who are ineligible to draw State UI Benefits, should receive the maximum of $30 per week SUB Benefits." Though the Company members of the Board insist that the current policy agreed to by the Union members should prevail, they do not take the position that this policy should of necessity govern the decision of the Impartial Chairman. Rather, the Company members desire a decision which reflects the language and intent of the Plan. The Chairman would remark in this connection that the Company members in this respect have displayed a most commendable attitude, reflecting the highest standards of maturity and cooperation in labor relations.

Application of provisions

In resolving the conflict between the parties, it is necessary to consider provisions of the Plan which bear upon the question. In this respect, Article VII, Section 2 (a), and Article VII, Section 2 (b) (1) and (2), are of importance. Note that under Article VII, Section 1 (a) (1), the Plan states that for the purpose of determining the SUB payment, such an amount is due the employee which when added to the employee's Unemployment Insurance Benefit "*as defined in Section 2 of this Article*" (Article VII) shall equal 65 per cent of the employee's weekly after-tax straight-time pay. Now, the relevant language of Article VII, Section 2 (a), as it pertains to Unemployment Insurance is this: The *full* amount of the UI benefit, or the *estimated* amount that the employee would have received had he not been ineligible for UI benefits solely because (1) he did not have prior to his layoff a sufficient period of work in employment covered by Unemployment Insurance;[21] or (2) because of a limit under Unemployment Insurance on the period of time

[21]Article V, Section 2, Subsection (b)(3)(i).

for which Unemployment Insurance Benefits are payable to the employee.[22]

That is, when an employee does not receive UI benefits because of these two circumstances, the Plan requires that an estimate be made of the amount that he would have received had he been eligible. Now, the Plan in Article VII, Section 2 (b) (1) and (2), establishes the specific guides under which such estimates shall be computed. What all this means is that an estimate of the amount of the UI benefit is to be made when an employee is not eligible for UI benefits under the aforementioned two circumstances.

After this estimate is made, the question arises as to what to do with such estimate in calculating the amount of SUB payment due the employee under Article VII, Section 1 (a) (1). If the Company's version is accepted, nothing at all is done with the estimate, since, as stated, the Company assumes that the employee would have received $36, the maximum weekly UI benefit which an employee can receive under state law. Thereupon, the Company deducts the $36 from the 65-per-cent figure contemplated by the Plan, and the employee would receive the difference in a SUB payment.

By this time, it should be apparent that the $36 figure does not have validity because under the cited provisions, an *estimate* must be made under the guidelines laid down under Article VII, Section 2 (b) (1) and (2). It is possible that the estimate would equal $36, or that the figure could be less than $36, depending upon the outcome of the formulas established in Article VII, Section 2 (b) (1) and (2), as applied to a particular case.

However, the crucial question is whether the estimated UI Benefits that the employee would have received had he not been ineligible for UI under Article V, Section 2, Subsection (b) (3) (i) and (ii), should or should not be paid to the employee from the SUB Trust Fund. On the grounds that the Trust Fund should be "conservatively" managed, the Company members of the Board believe that the estimated amount is not to be paid to the employee as a SUB payment.

Reasoning of chairman

After careful reflection, the Chairman of the Board cannot support the Company position. At no place in the Plan does one find an express statement establishing that the SUB Trust Fund is not liable for the estimated amount of UI benefits. To the contrary, a meaningful construction of Article VII, Section 1 (a) (1), demonstrates that the SUB Trust Fund is charged with this amount. Note that the provision states that the SUB payment shall be an amount which, when *added* to the applicant's Unemployment Insurance

[22]Article V, Section 2, Subsection (b)(3)(ii).

benefit will equal the 65-per-cent figure. Now, when the employee receives *no actual* UI benefits, it follows that the SUB payment will reflect the amount of UI benefits which the employee would have received had he not been ineligible for UI benefits because of the reasons spelled out in Article V, Section 2, Subsection (b) (3) (i) and (ii). This is the case because the employee is entitled to a SUB payment which will be equal to 65 per cent of his take-home pay. True, when the employee actually receives UI benefits, the amount of SUB benefits would be reduced proportionately. However, if he does not receive any actual UI benefits, the SUB payment must be equal to the 65-per-cent figure or $30, whichever is smaller.

After all, the intent of Article VII, Section 1 (a) (1), is that an employee eligible for SUB benefits will collect 65 per cent of his take-home pay. Normally, the 65 per cent payment will be made up of two parts—the UI Benefit and the SUB payment. The SUB benefit is to be that amount which when *added* to the UI benefit will equal 65 per cent of take-home pay. However, the fact remains that when there is *nothing* to add to in the form of actual UI benefits, the SUB payment must be equal to 65 per cent of take-home pay or $30, whichever is lesser.

The parties took particular care in Article VII, Section 2 (a), to define UI Benefits as the "full amount" received or the "estimated amount" that would have been received except for ineligibility. Then, with additional care, the Plan spells out in particular detail the way that such estimated amount is to be calculated. What is the reason for such meticulous attention to this subject if it were not for the purpose of having the SUB payment include the estimated amount? As the Company argues, the theory of the Plan is to supplement or add to the amount of money which an employee obtains from the state UI Benefit program. It directs the Chairman's attention to the definition of "Unemployment Insurance" and "Supplementation" found in Article I of the Plan. Such definitions, of course, underscore the basic theory of the Plan. The Arbitrator fully understands that its basic structure and concept is the merging of the UI Benefit and the SUB payment to make up a sum equal to 65 per cent of an employee's take-home pay.

Nevertheless, the language of the payment formula does not serve to support the Company's position. Note that the formula requires that the Weekly Supplementary Benefit shall be the smaller of an amount which, when *added* to the UI Benefit, *will equal* 65 per cent of take-home pay, or $30.00. When there is no actual UI Benefit, however, the SUB payment cannot be added to it. Indeed, if the Company theory is carried to its logical conclusion, an employee not eligible for UI Benefits *for any reason* would also be ineligible for an SUB payment. It would appear that under the Company construction of the Plan, an SUB payment can be received by an employee only when there is an actual UI Benefit to supplement. Remove the UI Benefit, and supplementation becomes impossible, and, therefore, an employee, though eligible for an SUB payment, but ineligible for UI Benefits, should not receive any SUB payment. Even the Company concedes, of course, that this was not the intent of the Plan.

Indeed, it is recognized by all concerned that an employee ineligible for UI Benefits because of insufficient work in employment covered by Unemployment Insurance or because he has exhausted his rights under such a program will draw an SUB payment. In short, the parties agree that an SUB payment will be made even if there is no UI Benefit to supplement. Under these circumstances, the benefit formula contemplates that such an employee will be assured the 65 per cent figure or $30, whichever is smaller, and that payment will be made from the SUB Trust Fund.

No other construction appears consistent with the purposes of the Plan and its relevant language. What the Company members of the Board fundamentally argue is that the SUB payment should supplement a nonexistent state UI Benefit. Clearly, there is no actual supplementation under these circumstances. Under the specified reasons for employee UI ineligibility, the SUB payment, in effect, takes the place of the UI Benefit. No supplementation is possible; the parties all agree that some SUB payment is due the employee; and it follows, therefore, that once this concession is made, the SUB payment shall reflect an amount which will equal 65 per cent of the employee's take-home pay or $30, whichever is the smaller.

Under the pay structure existing in the Company, it is almost certain that 65 per cent of any employee's take-home pay will exceed $30. Realistically, therefore, the decision will be that an employee who is ineligible for UI Benefits solely because of the reasons set forth in Article V, Section 2, Subsection (b) (3) (i) and (ii), will receive $30 in Weekly Supplemental Benefits.

As this Opinion demonstrates, the Chairman of the Board of Administration carefully considered the relevant contractual language and the basic intent of the Plan before arriving at a decision. He could do no less in recognition of the trust and confidence reposed in him by the parties. As always, the Chairman was indefatigable in his effort to reach a decision which is proper under the terms of the contract, and one which he can justify in his own conscience. He believes sincerely that his decision is justified by the relevant provisions of the Plan.

Though the Chairman is fully satisfied that his decision is correct, he is certainly aware that the problem presented to him is not easy. The fact that he has spent several days in study, reflection, and writing on the problem is positive proof of its complexity. Through his experience with this case he can well understand why there is a difference of opinion between the parties. However, now that the matter has been settled, the Chairman invites his colleagues on the Board of Administration to join with him in a unanimous decision. He sincerely hopes that this will be done so that all concerned will be further aware of the maturity and the wholesome spirit which prevails in industrial relations within the plant. If, however, a unanimous decision is not possible, the Chairman will fully respect the judgment of the members who disagree with his decision.

Award of Board of Administration

After careful consideration of the relevant provisions of the Supplemental Unemployment Benefit Plan, the Board of Administration makes the following Award:

When an employee is eligible for a Weekly Supplemental Benefit under the terms of the Plan, but ineligible for state Unemployment Insurance Benefits solely for the reasons set forth in Article V, Section 2, Subsection (b)(3)(i) and (ii), of such Plan, such employee shall receive a Weekly Supplemental Benefit in the amount of $30.

QUESTIONS

1. In your own words, state the basic position of the Company and the Union.
2. How do you account for the fact that the company members of the Board approved the chairman's decision, even though the Company denied the Union's claim in the first place?
3. Would you have ruled any differently had you been Impartial Chairman? If so, why?

The modern collective bargaining contract encompasses many issues which do not fall into the general category of wages or "fringe" supplements. Such subjects, rather, deal with the rights and duties of the employer, the union, and the employees themselves. Some of them—such as seniority and discharge—most directly serve to protect the job rights of workers and might be most appropriately thought of as "administrative" concerns. They will be treated in such a manner in Chapter 10.

Other subjects, however, tend to supply the institutional needs of either the labor organization or the particular management—through "compulsory union membership" clauses, for example, or by provisions explicitly allowing the company the right to make decisions for the direction of the labor force and the operation of the plant. These matters will be dealt with in the paragraphs which follow in this chapter.

In considering this institutional dimension of collective bargaining, it must be recognized that the topics which it encompasses can on occasion give the negotiators considerably

9

Institutional issues under

collective bargaining

more trouble than do the wage or fringe issues. There can, indeed, be deeply rooted conflict over basic philosophies of labor relations, the rights of management, and the rights and obligations of unions. And it is, for example, at times infinitely easier to compromise and settle a wage controversy than to resolve a heated difference of opinion as to whether or not a worker should be compelled to join a union as a condition of employment. For all the thorniness of many wage and wage-related issues, some of the longest and most bitter individual strikes have had as their source conflicts dealing with the institutional issues of collective bargaining.

This chapter will inspect, in turn: union membership as a condition of employment, the so-called "checkoff" mechanism, union obligations, and managerial prerogatives.

Union Membership as a Condition of Employment

Prior to the passage of the Wagner Act in 1935, there was essentially only one way in which a union could get itself recognized by an unsympathetic management: through the use of raw economic strength. If the labor organization succeeded in pulling all or a significant part of the company's employees out on strike, or in having its membership boycott the production or services of the company in the marketplace, it stood a good chance of forcing the employer to come to terms. Lacking such economic strength, however, the union had no recourse—even if *all* the company's workers wanted to join it—in the face of management opposition to its presence.

The 1935 legislation, as we know, greatly improved the lot of the union in this regard. It provided for a secret ballot *election* by the employees, should the employer express doubt as to the union's majority status. It also gave the union the exclusive right to bargain for *all* workers in the designated bargaining unit should the election prove that it did indeed have majority support. As Chapter 3 has indicated, these new ground rules for union recognition continue to this day.

Legally fostered recognition has not been synonymous with any assured status for the union as an institution, however. Indeed, in the three decades since the Wagner Act, unions have still been able to find three grounds for insecurity. For one, the law has given the recognized labor organization no guarantee that it could not be dislodged by a rival union at some later date. For a second, there have still been many communication avenues open to antagonistic employers who choose to make known to their employees their antiunion feelings in an attempt to rid themselves of certified unions after a designated interval following the signing of the initial contract. And for a third, the government has not granted recognized unions protection against "free riders"—employees who choose to remain outside the union and thus gain the benefits of unionism without in any way helping to pay for those benefits. Under the law the union clearly has not only the *right* but also the *obligation* to represent all employees in the bargaining unit, regardless of their membership or nonmembership in the union. Unions have particularly feared that the "free-rider" attitude could become contagious, resulting in the loss through a subsequent election (in which nonmembers as well as members can vote) of their majority status and thus of their representation rights.

Consequently, organized labor has turned to its own bargaining-table efforts in an attempt to gain a further measure of institutional security. By and large, such attempts have been successful: by the 1960's, approximately 81 per cent of all contracts contained some kind of "union security" provision.[1]

Such provisions, which are frequently also referred to as "compulsory union membership" devices, essentially are three in number: the closed shop, the union shop, and the maintenance-of-membership agreement.

Brief reference has already been made to each of these mechanisms. A common denominator to all is that in one way or another membership in the union is made a condition of employment for at least some workers. They differ, however, in the timing for the requirement of union membership and in the degree of freedom of choice allowed the worker in his decision about joining the labor organization.

The closed shop and union shop are dissimilar in that under the former the worker must belong to the union *before* obtaining a job, whereas the latter requires union membership within a certain time period *after* the worker is hired. Under a maintenance-of-membership arrangement, the worker is free to elect whether or not he will join the union. Once he does join, however, he must maintain membership in the union for the duration of the contract period or else forfeit his job.

These forms of compulsory union membership can also be viewed as differing with respect to the freedom of the employer to hire workers. Under the closed shop he must hire only union members. This allows the union in effect to serve as the employment agency in most situations, and to refer workers to the employer upon his request. Under union-shop and maintenance-of-membership arrangements, the employer has free access to the labor market. He may hire whomever he wants and the union security provision becomes operative only after the worker is employed.

[1] Theodore Rose, "Union Security and Checkoff Provisions in Major Union Contracts," *Monthly Labor Review*, LXXXII, No. 12 (December, 1959), 1348–51.

A final significant feature of union security is, of course, that it has received considerable attention from both the United States Congress and state legislatures. The laws which both bodies have enacted must be taken into account at the bargaining table, and union security provisions which disregard these relevant public fiats do so only at a definite risk.

As in many other areas of collective bargaining, there are several different approaches to the union security problem. The elasticity of the process is clearly demonstrated in the varied methods which employers and unions have adopted to deal with the issue.

The *closed shop*, obviously the most advantageous arrangement from labor's point of view, appeared in 33 per cent of the nation's agreements in 1946.[2] Prohibited for interstate commerce by the Taft–Hartley Act of 1947, it visibly decreased in its frequency in the years immediately thereafter and an elaborate study of 1,716 collective bargaining contracts which was conducted by the Bureau of Labor Statistics in 1954 revealed that by the latter year less than 5 per cent of all agreements researched contained such a provision.[3] No exhaustive investigation on the subject has been conducted since 1954, but there is reason to suspect that the closed shop's decline is somewhat exaggerated in the Bureau's figures. Not only was the study confined primarily to agreements governed by the Taft–Hartley Act and hence not completely representative, but—as Slichter, Healy, and Livernash could argue even in the 1960's—"many enterprises subject to the Taft–Hartley Act, which nominally have the union shop, in fact have the closed shop either because the employer finds it advantageous or because the union is too strong for the employer and dictates the terms of the contract."[4] Even some industries subject to Taft–Hartley, moreover, have refused to accept the law's closed-shop verdict—notably building construction, which bluntly flouted it until 1959, when the Landrum-Griffin Act recognized the special characteristics of that sector and officially allowed it a stronger form of union security which approximates the closed shop.

Nonetheless, there can be no denying that closed-shop arrangements received a severe setback with the passage of Taft–Hartley, and that presumably at least the bulk of the closed-shop provisions which continue in force have been negotiated by companies and unions which are not within the scope of the national labor law.

[2]Theodore Rose, "Union Security Provisions in Agreements, 1954," *Monthly Labor Review*, LXXVIII, No. 6 (June, 1955), 646.

[3]*Ibid.*

[4]Sumner H. Slichter, James J. Healy, and E. Robert Livernash, *The Impact of Collective Bargaining on Management* (Washington, D.C.: The Brookings Institution, 1960), p. 29.

With the decrease in usage of the closed shop, the *union shop* became the most widespread form of union membership employment condition. After being part of only 17 per cent of all contracts in 1946,[5] it appeared in about 57 per cent of all labor agreements in 1954 and probably is contained in well over two thirds of all contracts today.

The *maintenance-of-membership* arrangement, originating in the abnormal labor market days of World War II, is still fully legal, but is utilized relatively infrequently. After appearing in about one quarter of all contracts in 1946, it had steadily lost ground in the 1950's and only 7 per cent of all contracts studied in 1958–1959 made provision for it.[6] Much of the loss was undoubtedly absorbed by the gains of the union shop, which maintenance-of-membership employers, having already taken *this* step toward accommodating the union, have rarely resisted very adamantly.

Two other brands of union security, both relatively infrequent, constitute compromises between the union's goal of greatest possible security and the management's reluctance to grant such institutional status. Under the *agency shop*, nonunion members of the bargaining unit must make a regular financial contribution—usually the equivalent of union dues—to the labor organization, but no one is compelled to join the union. The money is, in fact, at times donated to recognized charitable organizations. Nonetheless, the incentive for a worker to remain in the "free-rider" class is clearly reduced in this situation, and the union thus gains some measure of protection. The *preferential shop* gives union members preference in hiring, but allows the employment of nonunionists and its efficacy seems to depend on how the parties construe the word *preference*.

Though the straight union shop thus appears to be the most popular form of union security, some employers and unions have negotiated variations of this species of compulsory union membership. Under some contracts employees who are not union members when the union shop agreement becomes effective are not required to join the union. Some agreements exempt employees with comparatively long service with the company. Under other contracts old employees (only) are permitted to withdraw from the union at the expiration of the agreement without forfeiting their jobs. Under this arrangement a so-called "escape period" of about fifteen days is included in the labor contract. If an employee does not terminate his union membership within the escape period, he then must maintain his membership under the new arrangement. Newly hired workers, however, are required to join the union.

[5]Theodore Rose, "Union Security Provisions in Agreements, 1954," *op. cit.*
[6]Theodore Rose, "Union Security and Checkoff Provisions in Major Union Contracts," *op. cit.* Part of the decline is, however, not entirely real: some arrangements have adopted the name of "union shop" but modified the latter in practice to equate or nearly equate to maintenance of membership.

Whether the straight union shop or modifications of it are negotiated, the Taft–Hartley law forbids an arrangement which compels a worker to join a union as a condition of employment, unless thirty days have elapsed from the effective date of the contract or the beginning of employment (whichever is later). In administering this section of the law the National Labor Relations Board has held that the thirty-day grace period does not apply to employees who are already members of the union.[7] However, it interprets the provision literally for workers who are not union members on the effective date of the contract or who are subsequently employed. Thus, in one case a union-shop arrangement was declared unlawful because it required workers to join the union on the twenty-ninth day following the beginning of employment.[8] Another union security arrangement was held to be illegal because it compelled employees to join the union if they had been on the company's payroll thirty or more days: in invalidating this latter agreement, the Board ruled that it violated the law because it did not accord employees subject to its coverage the legal thirty-day grace period for becoming union members *after* the *effective date* of the contract.[9]

Whereas some negotiators have adopted variations of the straight union shop, others have devised a number of alternatives to the maintenance-of-membership arrangement. Only at the termination of the agreement are employees under most maintenance-of-membership arrangements permitted to withdraw from the union without forfeiting their jobs, and usually only a fifteen-day period is provided at the end of the contract period during which time the employee may terminate his union membership. But many agreements have a considerably less liberal period of withdrawal, from the worker's viewpoint, and some contracts allow more than the modal fifteen days. If an employee fails to withdraw during this "escape" time, he must almost invariably remain in the union for the duration of the new collective bargaining agreement.

Under some labor agreements, maintenance-of-membership arrangements also provide for an escape period after the *signing* of the agreement to permit withdrawals of existing members from the union. Other agreements do not afford this opportunity to current members of the union but restrict the principle of voluntary withdrawal to newly hired workers.

Still another variation of maintenance of membership was concluded in the basic steel industry in the early 1950's. Under this arrangement the contract required each new employee to sign an application for

[7]*Charles Krause Milling Co.* (1951), 97 NLRB 336.
[8]*Chesler Glass Co.* (1950), 92 NLRB 1016.
[9]*Continental Carbon, Inc.* (1951), 94 NLRB 1026.

membership in the union upon being hired. Such an employee, however, had the option of canceling the application between the fifteenth and thirtieth day of employment. If the application was not canceled during this period, the employee was required to remain in the union as a condition of employment.[10]

These modifications are fully consistent with the law in all but the 19 "right-to-work" states, which ban any form of compulsory union membership, but certain other arrangements are not. Reference has already been made to the terms of Taft–Hartley under which an employee cannot lawfully be discharged from his job because of loss of union membership unless he loses his membership in a union because of nonpayment of dues or initiation fees. In spite of the existence of an arrangement requiring union membership as a condition of employment, expulsion from a union for any reason other than nonpayment of dues or initiation fees *cannot* result in loss of employment. The National Labor Relations Board will order the reinstatement of an employee to his job with back pay where this feature of the law is violated. Depending upon the circumstances of a particular case, the Board will require the employer or the union, or both, to pay back wages to such an employee.

The Board has, in fact, applied a literal interpretation to this feature of Taft–Hartley. In one case[11] the Board has held that a worker actually does not have to *join* a union even though a union-shop arrangement may be in existence. His only obligation under the law is his willingness to tender the dues and initiation fees required by the union. In this case three workers were willing to pay their union dues and initiation fees but they refused to assume any other union-related obligations, or even to attend the union meeting at which they would be voted upon and accepted. As a result the union had secured the discharge of these workers under the terms of the union security arrangement included in the labor agreement. The Board held that the discharge of workers under such circumstances violated the Taft–Hartley law, ruled that both the union and the company engaged in unfair labor practices, and ordered the workers reinstated in their jobs with full back pay.

The "right-to-work" laws themselves, of course, serve as formidable obstacles to union security arrangements in the primarily Southern and Southwestern states in which, through 1966, they remained on the books. On the other hand, not only has their effect on labor relations in these states been highly debatable, but in its 1965–1966 sessions the United States Congress came close to repealing the relevant Taft–Hartley Act

[10]After 1956, the basic steel labor agreement adopted a union security formula which requires all current union members to remain in the union and makes union membership compulsory for all newly hired workers.

[11]Union Starch and Refining Co. (1949), 87 NLRB 779.

passage permitting the enactment of such state laws (Section 14b),[12] and there was at the time of this writing some likelihood that the repeal would ultimately be enacted.

Were Congress to remove Section 14b, this action would nullify all "right-to-work" laws as far as these laws apply to interstate commerce because of the *federal pre-emption* doctrine, which forbids states to pass laws in conflict with a federal statute. And in this event the "right-to-work" laws existing in Alabama, Arizona, Arkansas, Florida, Georgia, Iowa, Kansas, Mississippi, Nebraska, Nevada, North Carolina, North Dakota, South Carolina, South Dakota, Tennessee, Texas, Utah, Virginia, and Wyoming would have application only in the area of *intra*state commerce. They would cease to have any effect upon firms engaged in interstate dealings.

That this would be the case is made evident by a 1956 decision of the United States Supreme Court, although the decision dealt with the railroad industry—governed, as are the airlines, by the Railway Labor Act and not Taft–Hartley. In 1951, Congress enacted an amendment to the Railway Labor Act which legalized union security arrangements in the industries covered by the statute. In addition, the amendment specifically overrode state laws regulating or prohibiting union security arrangements to the extent that these laws applied to the railroad and airline industries. The 1956 decision of the Supreme Court dealt with the question of whether the Nebraska right-to-work law could apply to these industries. In a unanimous decision, the high court held that the state law could *not* prohibit employers and unions in the railroad and airline industries from negotiating union security clauses on the ground that the federal statute takes precedence over the state law.[13] It is safe to assume that such a precedent, although directly dealing with a different law than Taft–Hartley, would be sustained in the event of repeal of 14b.

Regardless of the fate of "right-to-work" legislation, however, it seems very likely that the question of whether union security provisions should be negotiated in labor agreements will remain a controversial one for some time to come—among the general public and some direct parties to collective bargaining, if not among the large segment of unionized industry which has already granted such union security.

This controversy actually contains three major elements: morality, labor relations, and power.

[12]The repeal measure passed the House by a 20-vote margin, but a filibuster led by Senator Everett M. Dirksen of Illinois prevented the bill from being formally considered by the Senate. AFL–CIO officials, nonetheless, claimed that as many as 56 senate votes, or more than the majority needed, would have been forthcoming in favor of repeal had the measure been brought to a vote.

[13]*Railway Employees Department* v. *Hanson*, (1956), 351 Sup. Ct. 225.

Whether or not it is *morally* right to force an employee to join a union in order to be able to work is not an easy issue to resolve. Unions and supporters of unionism often argue that it is not "fair" to permit an employee to benefit from collective bargaining without paying dues, given the fact that the union must under the law represent all workers in the bargaining unit. And the argument is not without logic. Improvements obtained in collective bargaining *do* benefit nonunion members as well as union member employees, and the union *is* compelled by law to represent nonunion bargaining unit employees even in the grievance procedure in the same fashion as it has the duty to handle grievances of union members. On the other hand stands the equally plausible argument that employees should not be forced to join a union in order to work. Such compulsion seems to many people to be undemocratic, immoral, and unjust. Almost everyone, however, has different ideas on what is "morally" correct in this controversy. Indeed, even the clergy has been drawn into the fight, and its members have exhibited the same lack of unanimity in their opinions as have other people. If these stewards of God are not certain what is morally correct, how can college professors make a judgment which will once and for all resolve the moral issue?

Some observers claim that union security is the key to *stability in labor relations*. It is argued that a union which operates under a union shop arrangement will be more responsible and judicious in the handling of grievances and in other day-to-day relations with its employers because of its guaranteed status. Again, there is some strength to this argument. At times, conflict between union members and nonunion employees does hamper the effective operation of the plant, and on this basis, some employers may welcome an arrangement to force all employees to join the union, to preclude such conflicts. Moreover, unions can also claim that in the absence of a union security provision, the union officers must spend considerable time in organizing the unorganized and keeping the organized content so that they will not drop out of the union. Proponents of this position justifiably declare that if union officers are relieved from this organizational chore, they can spend their time in more constructive ways which will be beneficial not only to the employees but also to the company.

On the other hand, other debators point out with equal justification that unions which *do* enjoy a union security arrangement sometimes use this extra time to find *new* ways to harass the company. The solution to *this* particular controversy appears to an outsider to depend upon the character of the union involved and on its relationship with the employer. Clearly, no one would blame an employer if he resisted granting the union shop to a union which had traditionally engaged in frequent wildcat strikes, continually pressed grievances which had no merit and, in short, sought to harass management at every turn.

At times, finally, employers and unions themselves argue along morality and labor relations lines to conceal a different purpose—their respective desires for *power* in the bargaining relationship. It is self-evident that the union *does* have more comparative influence in the negotiation of labor agreements and in its day-to-day relationship with the employer when it operates under a union shop. And, by the same token, the employer has more comparative influence when employees need not join the union to work and may terminate their membership at any time. Or, in short, the parties may speak in terms of morality merely as a smokescreen to conceal an equally logical but less euphemistic power issue.

But "power" still remains a rather nebulous term. Depending upon the assumptions one makes, a union could have infinitely more "power" than a company, and the *reverse* would be true under a different set of assumptions and circumstances. Given this elusiveness, as well as the unhappy connotations often placed on the word, it is perhaps not surprising that the verbal controversy over union security continues to be waged along the other lines described as well as those of "power."

The Checkoff

Checkoff arrangements are included in the large majority of collective bargaining contracts. This dues collection method, whereby the employer agrees to deduct from the employee's pay the latter's monthly union dues (and in some cases also his initiation fees, fines, and special assessments) for transmittal to the union, has obvious advantages for labor organizations, not only in terms of time and money savings but also because it further strengthens the union's institutional status. For the same reasons, many managers are not enthusiastic about the checkoff, although some have preferred it to the constant visits of union dues-collectors to the workplace. Once willing to grant the union shop, however, employers have rarely made a major bargaining issue of the checkoff *per se*. And the growth of this mechanism has been remarkably consistent with that of the union security measure: where in 1946 about 40 per cent of all labor agreements provided for the checkoff system of dues collection, by 1954 this percentage had increased to about 75 per cent[14] and the figure is, as we know, approximately 80 per cent today.

Taft–Hartley, as was also pointed out earlier, regulates the checkoff as well as union security: Under the law the checkoff is lawful only on

[14] Theodore Rose, "Union Security Provisions in Agreements," *op. cit.*, p. 657.

written authorization of the individual employee. It is further provided that an employee's written authorization may be irrevocable for only one year or for the duration of the contract, whichever is shorter.

Soon after the Taft–Hartley law was enacted the question arose as to the lawfulness of a collective bargaining provision under which an employer deducts initiation fees, special assessments, and fines as well as regular monthly membership dues. In addition, a question was raised as to whether it was required under the national law that each employee personally sign a new authorization card each year. On May 13, 1948, the Assistant Solicitor General of the United States issued an opinion which has served to clarify these questions somewhat.[15] He ruled that the term *membership dues*, as utilized in the law, includes initiation fees and assessments as well as regular periodic dues. On the other hand, he made no reference to fines assessed against union members for the violation of union rules. The Assistant Solicitor General further offered as his opinion the ruling that checkoff arrangements which provide an employee the annual opportunity to rescind a written authorization did not appear to be a "willful" violation of the Taft–Hartley law. This meant that arrangements between employers and unions which give such an opportunity to employees but which do not actually involve the signing of a new authorization each year are valid.

As a result, many checkoff provisions now allow for the deduction of initiation fees and assessments as well as for regular monthly membership dues. In addition, it is a common practice in industry for employees to sign one authorization card. However, under the latter arrangement, both the collective bargaining contract and the authorization card clearly state that the employee has an annual opportunity, usually lasting for 15 days, to rescind his written authorization. If he does not avail himself of his opportunity, the authorization card remains in force for another year.

Checkoff provisions frequently deal with matters other than the specification of items that the company agrees to deduct. Some arrangements specify a maximum deduction that the company will check off in any one month, require each employee to sign a new authorization card in the event that dues are increased, indemnify the company against any liability for action taken in reliance upon authorization cards submitted by the union, require the union to reimburse the company for any illegal deductions, and provide that the union share in the expense of collecting dues through the checkoff method. Not all these items, of course, appear in each and every checkoff arrangement; many labor agreements, however, contain one or more of them.

[15]"Coverage of Checkoff Under Taft–Hartley Act," *Monthly Labor Review*, LXVII (July, 1948), 42.

From the foregoing, it appears rather clear that though the checkoff is an important issue of collective bargaining, it does not normally constitute a crucial point of controversy between employers and unions. It does not contain the features of conflicting philosophy which are involved in the union security problem, falls far short of other problems of collective bargaining as a vexatious issue between the parties, and has rarely by itself become a major strike issue since the stakes are not that high. As a matter of fact, though the checkoff serves the institutional needs of the union, employers often find some gain from the incorporation of the device in the collective bargaining agreement. This would be particularly true where the labor contract contains a union security arrangement. Not only does the checkoff obviate the previously noted need of dues collection on company premises with the attendant impact upon the orderly operation of the plant, but it avoids the need of starting the discharge process for employees who are negligent in the payment of dues. Frequently, without a checkoff, an employee who must belong to a union as a condition of employment will delay paying his dues, and the employer and union both are then faced with the task of instituting the discharge process, which is most commonly suspended when the employee (faced with loss of employment) pays his dues at the last possible minute. The checkoff eliminates the need for this wasted and time-consuming effort on the part of busy employer and union representatives.

Even when the union shop is not in effect, moreover, the checkoff need not necessarily be given permanent status. The employee obligates himself to pay dues for one year only, and if he desires to stop the checkoff he may do so during the "escape period." But, under any circumstances, if the management believes that the union with which it deals is so irresponsible as not to deserve the checkoff, it need not agree to it as its part of the renegotiated contract, and the mechanism is consequently also "revocable" from the company's point of view.

Union Obligations

The typical collective bargaining contract contains one or more provisions establishing certain *obligations* on the part of the labor organization. By far the most important of these obligations involves the pledge of a union that it will not strike during the life of the labor agreement. Most employers will, in fact, refuse to sign a collective bargaining contract unless the union agrees that it will not interrupt production during the effective contractual period.

The incorporation of a no-strike clause in a labor agreement means that all disputes relating to the interpretation and the application of a labor agreement are to be resolved through the grievance and arbitration procedure in an orderly and peaceful manner, and not through the harsh arbiter of industrial warfare. The pledge of the union not to strike during the contract period stabilizes industrial relations within the plant and thereby protects the interests of the employer, the union, and the employees. Indeed, a chief advantage that employers obtain from the collective bargaining process is the assurance that the plant will operate free from strikes or other forms of interruption to production (slow-downs, for example) during the contract period.

Companies and unions have negotiated two major forms of no-strike provisions. Under one category, there is an *absolute and unconditional* surrender on the part of the union of its right to strike or otherwise to interfere with production during the life of the labor agreement. The union agrees that it will not strike for any purpose or under any circumstances for the duration of the contract period. Employers, of course, obtain maximum security against strikes by this approach to the problem.

Under the second major form, the union can use the strike only under certain *limited* circumstances. For example, in the automobile industry the union may strike against company-imposed production standards. Such strikes may not take place, however, before all attempts are made in the grievance procedure to negotiate production standard complaints. Other collective bargaining contracts provide that unions can strike for any purpose during the contract period but only after the entire grievance procedure has been exhausted, when the employer refuses to abide by an arbitrator's decision, or when a deadlock occurs during a wage-reopening negotiation. The union cannot strike under any other conditions for the length of the contract.

In the vast majority of cases, labor organizations fulfill their no-strike obligations, just as most unionized companies fulfill all their contractually delineated responsibilities. However, in the event that violations do take place, employers have available to them a series of remedies. In the first place, under the terms of the Taft–Hartley law employers can sue unions for violations of collective bargaining contracts in the United States district courts. And although judgments obtained in such court proceedings may be assessed only against the labor organization and not against individual union members, additional remedies are provided for in many collective bargaining contracts. Under some of them, strikes called by a labor union in violation of a no-strike pledge terminate the entire collective bargaining contract. In others, the checkoff and any agreement requiring membership as a condition of employment are suspended.

In addition, the employer may elect to seek penalties against the instigators and the active participants or either group in such a strike. Many contracts clearly provide that employees actively participating in a strike during the life of a collective bargaining contract are subject to discharge, suspension, loss of seniority rights, or termination of other benefits under the contract, including vacation and holiday pay. The right of an employer to discharge workers participating in such strikes has been upheld by the United States Supreme Court.

Finally, arbitrators usually will sustain the right of employers to discharge or otherwise discipline workers who instigate or actively participate in an unlawful strike or slowdown. Such decisions are based upon the principle that the inclusion of a no-strike clause in a labor agreement serves as the device to stabilize labor relations during the contract period and as a pledge to resolve all disputes arising under the collective bargaining contract through the orderly and peaceful channels of the grievance procedure.

At times, strikes and other interruptions to production that are not authorized by the labor organization occur. These work stoppages, commonly known as "wildcat strikes," are instigated by a group of workers, sometimes including union officers, without the sanction of the labor union. Under many labor agreements, the employer has the right to discharge such employees or to penalize them otherwise for such activities

A special problem has been created by the Taft–Hartley law in reference to wildcat strikes. Under this law a labor union is responsible for the action of agents even though the union does not authorize or ratify such conduct.[16] Thus, an employer may sue a union because of a wildcat strike even though the union does not authorize or ratify the work stoppage. As a result of this state of affairs, unions and employers have negotiated the so-called "nonsuability clauses" which were discussed in Chapter 3. Under these arrangements, the company agrees that it will not sue a labor union because of wildcat strikes provided that the union fulfills its obligation to terminate the work stoppage. Frequently, the labor contract specifies exactly what the union must do in order to free itself from the possibility of damage suits. Thus, in some contracts containing nonsuability clauses, the union agrees to announce orally and in writing that it disavows the strike, to order the workers back to their jobs, and to refuse any form of strike relief to the participants in such work stoppages.

Other features of some collective bargaining contracts also deal with

[16]Section 301 (e), states: ". . . For purposes of this section, in determining whether any person is acting as an 'agent' of another person as to make such other person responsible for his acts, the question of whether the specific acts performed were actually authorized or subsequently ratified shall not be controlling."

strike situations. Under many labor agreements, the union agrees that it will protect company property during strikes. To accomplish this objective, the union typically pledges itself to cooperate with the company in the orderly cessation of production and the shutting down of machinery. In addition, some unions agree to facilitate the proper maintenance of machinery during strikes even if achieving this objective requires the employment of certain bargaining unit maintenance personnel during the strike. Finally, it is not uncommon for unions to agree in the labor contract that management and supervisory personnel entering and leaving the plant in a strike situation will not be interfered with by the labor organization.

Many collective bargaining contracts place other obligations upon unions extending well beyond the area of strikes and slowdowns. Under many agreements, for example, the union obligates itself not to conduct on company time or on company property any union activities that will interfere with the efficient operation of the plant. The outstanding exception to this rule, however, involves the handling of grievances: Meetings of union and company representatives which deal directly with grievance administration usually are conducted on company time. Some agreements also permit union officials to collect dues on company property where the checkoff is not in existence. And another exception found in many contracts involves the permission given to employees and union officers to discuss union business or to solicit union membership during lunch and rest periods.

Another frequently encountered limitation of union activity on plant property involves restrictions of visits to the company by representatives of the international union with which the local is affiliated. Still another denies unions permission to post notices in the plant or to use company bulletin boards without the permission of the company. Where the union is allowed to use bulletin boards, many labor contracts specify the character of notices that the union may post: notices are permitted, for example, only when they pertain to union meetings and social affairs, union appointments and elections, reports of union committees, and rulings of the international union. Specifically prohibited on many occasions are notices which are controversial, propagandic, or political in nature.

Managerial Prerogatives

That collective bargaining is in many ways synonymous with limitations on managerial authority is an observation which was offered on the earliest pages of this book. A fundamental characteristic of the process is restriction on the power of the company to make decisions in the area of employer–employee relations, and much of the controversy about collective bargaining grows out of this factor. On the one hand, the labor union seeks to limit the authority of management to make decisions when it believes that such restrictions will serve the interests of its members or will tend to satisfy the institutional needs of the union itself. On the other hand, the responsibility for efficiency in operation of the enterprise rests with management. The reason for the existence of management, in fact, is the over-all management of the business, and executives attempt to retain free from limitations those functions which they believe are indispensable for the successful operation of the business. Since the responsibility for efficiency of the enterprise rests upon the shoulders of management and not of the union, companies feel that they must retain for themselves the authority to make certain decisions free from control of the bargaining process. Consequently, controversy in collective bargaining occurs when the desire of unions to achieve an objective through the bargaining process is in conflict with the determination of management to exercise a particular function on a unilateral basis.

The problem is, moreover, hardly disposed of simply because most union leaders assert—and normally, in good faith—that they have no intention of interfering with the "proper functions of management." Years of witnessing official union interest expand from the historical wages and hours context into such newer areas as those outlined in this portion of the book have led managers understandably to conclude that what is "proper" for the union depends on the situation and the values of the union membership.

Nor do employers find much consolation in the fact that the managerial decision-making process is already limited and modified by such economic forces as labor market conditions, by such laws as those pertaining to minimum wages, and by the employee-oriented spirit of our society. If unionism is not by any means the only restriction on company freedom of action in the personnel sphere, it is nonetheless a highly important one for companies whose employees live under a union contract.

Beyond this, finally, the controversy is hardly *confined* to the personnel area, for managers can point to numerous (although proportionately infrequent) instances of strong union interest in such relatively removed fields as finance, plant location, pricing, and other "proper" management functions. In recent years, for example, some railroad unions have constantly blamed their employers' high degree of bonded indebtedness for depriving railroad workers of "adequate" wage increases; legal representatives of the Ladies' Garment Workers as well as those of several other unions have become familiar faces in courtrooms, to protest plant relocations of their unions' employers; and the United Automobile Workers' interest in the pricing of cars is now all but taken for granted in automobile industry bargaining rooms (although the UAW's freely offered advice on this subject has yet to be accepted by the automobile manufacturers). Given the present state of the government's "legal duty to bargain" provisions, as Chapter 3 has indicated, no one can assert with complete confidence that such examples will not multiply in the years ahead.

In many ways, in fact, ramifications of the subject extend far beyond the two parties to collective bargaining. There is justification, indeed, for arguing that the "managerial rights" issue really pivots upon the broader question of what the appropriate function of labor unions in the life of our nation should be.

Managements have frequently translated their own thoughts on the subject into concrete action. Approximately one half of all labor agreements today contain clauses that explicitly recognize certain stipulated types of decisions as being "vested exclusively in the Company."[17] Such clauses are commonly called "management prerogative," "management rights," or (more appropriately, to many managers), "management security" clauses.

Fairly typical of management prerogative provisions is the following, culled from the 1964–1967 agreement of a large Midwestern durable goods manufacturer:

> Subject to the provisions of this agreement, the management of the business and of the plants and the direction of the working forces, including but not limited to the right to direct, plan, and control plant operations and to establish and to change work schedules, to hire, promote, demote, transfer, suspend, discipline, or discharge employees for cause or to relieve from duty employees because of lack of work or for other legitimate reasons, to introduce new and improved methods or facilities, to determine the products to be handled, produced, or manufactured, to determine the schedules of production and the methods, processes, and the means of production, to make shop rules and regulations not inconsistent with this agreement and to manage the plants in the traditional manner, is vested exclusively in the Company. Nothing in this agreement shall be deemed to limit the Company in any way in the exercise of the regular and customary functions of management.

Some rights clauses, by way of contrast, limit themselves to short general statements. These are much more readable than the above, but considerably less specific (for example, "the right to manage the plant and to direct the work forces and operations of the plant, subject to the

---

17See, for example, "Management Rights Provisions in Major Agreements," *Monthly Labor Review*, LXXXIX, No. 2 (February, 1966), 171.

limitations of this Agreement, is exclusively vested in, and retained by, the Company.")

No matter which way management injects such clauses into the contract, however, two industrial relations truisms must also be appreciated: (1) the power of the rights clause is always subject to qualification by the wording of every other clause in the labor agreement; and (2) consistent administrative practices on the part of the company must implement the rights clause if it is to stand up before an arbitrator.

According to one point of view, moreover, the inclusion of such a clause in a labor agreement is *unnecessary* and, of course, many agreements do not make any reference to managerial rights. This practice of omission is often based upon the belief that the employer retains all rights of management which are not relinquished, modified, or eliminated by the collective bargaining contract. Thus, in the absence of collective bargaining, according to this view, the employer has the power to make *any* decision in the area of labor relations that he desires (subject to considerations of law, the market place, etc.). This right is based upon the simple fact that the employer is the owner of the business. For example, the employer's right to promote, demote, lay off, and rehire may be limited by the seniority provisions of the collective bargaining contract. And the contract may stipulate that layoffs be based upon a certain formula. However, to the extent that such a formula does *not* limit the right of the employer to lay off, it follows that management may exercise this function on a unilateral basis.

This concept of management prerogatives is sometimes called the *"residual theory"* of management rights. That is, all rights "reside" in management except those which are limited by the labor agreement or conditioned by a past practice. Where a management embraces the residual theory, it most commonly takes a stiff attitude at the bargaining table relative to union demands which would tend further to limit rights of management. With more elements of an "Armed Truce" than an "Accommodation" philosophy, it views the collective bargaining process as a tug of war between the management and the union—management resisting further invasions by the union into the citadel of management rights, which are to be protected at all costs as a matter of principle.

Such companies are not particularly concerned with the merits of a union demand. *Any* demand which would impose additional limitations on management must be resisted. For example, such a management, regardless of the merits of a particular claim, would typically resist the incorporation of working rules into the labor agreement—rules dealing with such topics as payment to employees for work not actually performed, limitations on technological change or other innovations in the operation of the business, the amount of production an employee must turn out to hold a job, and how many men are required to perform a job. One can also safely predict that a residualist management would strongly resist any demand that would limit its right to move an operation from one plant to another, shut down one plant of a multiple-plant operation, subcontract work, or compel employees to work overtime. In addition, such a management would quite likely try aggressively when the occasion seemed appropriate to *regain* "rights" which it had previously relinquished.

Indeed, today many employers *are* striving to reclaim the right to make unilateral determinations of working rules. The 116-day steel strike of 1959, as well as many other important strikes of recent years, was waged because management desired to erase from the bargaining relationship working rules to which it had agreed in previous years. It is understandable why labor organizations resist these attempts of management: With the elimination of working rules, employees could more easily be laid off, for example. Since automation and changing market demands constitute in many relationships constant threats to job security, it is no mystery why some unions would rather strike than concede on this point.

The opposing view of the theory of residual rights is based upon the idea that management has responsibilities other than to the maximization of managerial authority. It proceeds from the proposition that management is the "trustee" of the interests of employees, the union, and the society, as well as of the interests of the business, the stockholders, and the management hierarchy. Under the *"trusteeship theory,"* a management would invariably be willing to discuss and negotiate a union demand on the merits of the case, rather than reject it out of hand because the demand would impose additional limitations on the operation of the plant. Such a company would not necessarily *agree* to additional limitations, but it would be completely amenable to discussing, consulting, and ultimately negotiating with the union on any demand that the latter might bring up at a collective bargaining session. Exhibiting an attitude of "Cooperation," the trusteeship management does not take the position that the line separating management rights from that of negotiable issues is fixed and not subject to change. Rather, it attempts to balance the rights of all concerned with the goal of arriving at a solution that would be most mutually satisfactory. As such, the "trusteeship" and "residual" theories are poles apart in terms of management's attitude at the bargaining table and even in the day-to-day relationship between the company and the union.

There is no "divine right" concept of management in the trusteeship theory, a statement which cannot be made for the residualist camp. No better summary of the differences between the two theories on this score has ever been made than that offered a decade ago by UN Ambassador

Arthur J. Goldberg, then General Counsel of the United Steelworkers of America:

> . . . Too many spokesmen for management assume that labor's rights are not steeped in past practice or tradition but are limited strictly to those specified in a contract; while management's rights are all-inclusive except as specifically taken away by a specific clause in a labor agreement. Labor always had many inherent rights, such as the right to strike, the right to organize despite interference from management, police powers, and even courts; the right to a fair share of the company's income even though this right was often denied; the right to safe, healthful working conditions with adequate opportunity for rest. Collective bargaining does not establish some hitherto nonexisting rights; it provides the power to enforce rights of labor which the labor movement was dedicated to long before the institution of arbitration had become so widely practiced in labor relations.[18]

It is impossible to determine how many companies follow the residual theory of management rights and how many follow the trusteeship theory. Cross-currents are clearly at work: The previously mentioned management attempt to regain work-rule flexibility, and the equally visible trend to more employee-centered management which was described in Chapter 1. The relative infrequency of Cooperation philosophies would, however, indicate that trusteeship managements remain in the distinct minority. Moreover, there is no universal truth as to which would be a *better* policy for management to follow, or whether some compromise between the two might form the optimum arrangement. The answer to this problem must be determined by each company in the light of the climate of the particular labor relations environment.

Conclusions

If unions and management are viewed as institutions, as distinct from the individuals whom they represent, the issues considered in this chapter take on special meaning. Institutions can survive long after individuals have perished, and in a real sense the problems of union security, union obligations, and management rights are related to the *survival* of the bargaining institutions. Union security measures preserve the union *per se* (although in so doing they may also allow it to do a better job for the members of the organization.) Similarly, to survive and function as an effective institution, management must be concerned with its prerogatives to operate the business efficiently. It must also be concerned

[18]"Management's Reserved Rights under Collective Bargaining," *Monthly Labor Review*, LXXIX, No. 10 (October, 1956), 1172.

with union obligations as *these* might affect its continued effectiveness.

In principle, therefore, the devices of collective bargaining which feed the institutional needs of the union and the firm are cut from the same cloth. They are designed to assure the long-run interests of the two organizations. The objectives of labor unions and companies are quite different, but the fact remains that to carry out their respective functions both need security of operation. Business operates to make a profit, and thus must be defended against encroachments of organized labor which might unreasonably interfere with its efficiency as a dynamic organization in the society. And although firms clearly differ in their philosophical approach to this problem, as witness the sharp differences between the residual and trusteeship concepts of management rights, the typical management position is the fundamental one that the business unit must be permitted to operate as efficiently as possible within the collective bargaining relationship. Its insistence upon management prerogatives stands as a bulwark of defense in this objective.

But unions *also* justify themselves as institutions on the American scene in their attempting to protect and advance the welfare of their members, and union security arrangements are an important avenue toward the realization of *this* objective. Although there may be philosophical objections to compulsory union membership, there cannot be any question that union security arrangements serve the long-run survival needs of organized labor.

If we view in retrospect the labor relations environment over the years, the conclusion appears irrefutable that business and unions have been relatively successful in reconciling these fundamental objectives, however much the verbal controversies continue to rage. Businesses which have engaged in collective bargaining relationships have by and large not only been able to survive but have often flourished. Many of the most influential and prosperous firms in this country have, as we know, been highly unionized for years. Likewise, organized labor has not only survived but has grown appreciably in strength over the years, the contemporary decline in union membership being accountable chiefly from causes other than management destruction. Moreover, if institutional survival and growth of unions is measured by the quality of employee benefits, one would have to conclude that in most relationships unions have succeeded in defending and promoting the welfare of their members. Although the objectives of the two institutions are quite different, and although occasional major impasses are reached by unions and managements in their bargaining on these issues, meaningful protection for both organizations has been provided in the vast majority of unionized industry.

DISCUSSION QUESTIONS

1. Arguing in favor of "right-to-work" laws, a publication of the National Association of Manufacturers has expressed the view that "No argument for compulsory unionism—however persuasive—can possibly justify invasion of the right of individual choice." Do you agree or disagree? Why or why not?
2. "From the viewpoint of providing maximum justice to all concerned, the agency shop constitutes the optimum union security arrangement." To what extent, if any, do you agree with this statement?
3. Which of the two management prerogative concepts, residual or trusteeship, do you personally tend to favor, and why?
4. Evaluate the opinion of former Steelworker Union president David J. Mc-Donald that "nothing could be worse than to have . . . management appease the union, and nothing could be worse than to have the union appease management," relating these remarks to the areas of management rights and union security.

SELECTED REFERENCES

Chandler, Margaret K., *Management Rights and Union Interests.* New York: McGraw-Hill Book Company, 1964.

"Management's Reserved Rights Under Collective Bargaining," *Monthly Labor Review,* LXXIX, No. 10 (October, 1956).

Rose, Theodore, "Union Security and Checkoff Provisions in Major Union Contracts," *Monthly Labor Review,* LXXXII, No. 12 (December, 1959), 1348–51.

Stone, Morris, *Managerial Freedom and Job Security.* New York: Harper & Row, Publishers, 1963.

Provisions relating to seniority, discipline, employee safety, and the various other "administrative" areas of the labor relationship have, as in the case of institutional provisions, the common characteristic of falling into the noneconomic classification of collective bargaining. It should not, however, be concluded that they do not have a profound influence upon the economic operation of the plant or the economic status of the employees.

The character of a seniority clause, for example, can have a vital impact upon the efficient operation of the productive process. Similarly, the protection afforded an employee as a result of the discharge clause can be of much greater importance than any of the rights he enjoys as a result of the negotiation of wage rates or fringe benefits. It matters little to the worker who has been discharged for an obviously unfair reason that the wages called for by the labor contract are very generous.

Moreover, at the present time the problem of automation rivals the importance of most wage issues for many collective bargaining relationships. In a real sense, in fact, the

10

Administrative issues under

collective bargaining

adjustment to automation through contract negotiations cuts across the entire gamut of bargaining. Currently, the overriding concern of many employees and unions is with job security, a posture resulting from the fact that each day many hundreds of jobs are eliminated by innovations in the technological structure of industry. Already there has been mention of union demands which are rooted at least partially in the automation problem: early retirement of workers, severance pay, and supplementary unemployment benefit programs, for example. As will be demonstrated, many administrative demands of unions also flow from worker fears that jobs are vulnerable because of automation.

In short, as important as the negotiation of economic issues may be, one cannot ignore these nonwage administrative issues of collective bargaining. Both are interwoven in the contemporary labor relations environment and to ignore or slight either—or, clearly, the institutional area of the contract, as well—would represent a distortion and an incomplete picture of present-day labor relations in the United States.

The following discussion indicates the nature of these problems, the manner in which employers and unions handle them in collective bargaining, and recent trends in administrative clause negotiations.

Seniority

The principle of seniority, under which the employee with the greater length of company or company subunit service receives increased job security (and, commonly, greater entitlement to employee benefits), is not a new one for American industry. The railroads and printing trades, for example, have emphasized it for many decades.

For at least four reasons, however, seniority has received increasing stress in labor contracts over the past twenty-five years.[1] In the first place, both management and employee representatives have become convinced that there is a certain amount of justice to the arrangement, especially in terms of work contraction or recall opportunities after layoffs. Secondly, the application of seniority is an objective one, calculated to avoid arbitrariness in the selection of personnel for particular jobs and consequently less irksome for the labor negotiators to deal with than alternative devices. Thirdly, the employee benefit programs which have mushroomed in these years have been geared almost exclusively to seniority—often, to make them more acceptable to the companies by restricting the number of employees entitled to the benefits. And fourthly,

---

[1]For an excellent full description, see Sumner H. Slichter, James J. Healy, and E. Robert Livernash, *The Impact of Collective Bargaining on Management* (Washington, D.C.: The Brookings Institution, 1960), pp. 104–41.

outside agencies, notably government labor boards and impartial arbitrators, have tended to weigh seniority heavily in their decisions.

Almost every labor agreement now includes some seniority formula, and this practice has become a deeply imbedded feature of the collective bargaining process. It is a chief method whereby employees obtain a measure of security in their jobs. It also limits the freedom of management to direct the labor force and influences considerations of plant efficiency. A seniority structure which approaches the ideal would be one which affords protection to employees in their job rights and at the same time does not place unreasonable restrictions on the right of management to make job assignments without sacrificing productivity and efficiency in the plant. This objective can best be realized to the extent that a seniority system is constructed to fit a particular plant environment. It must be tailored to fill the requirements of the technology, the kinds of jobs, the skills and occupations of the employees, and the character of labor relations of a specific company. A seniority formula that might be desirable in one industrial situation might not be suitable to another plant environment. In addition, perhaps no other phase of the collective bargaining relationship demands so much of company officials and union leaders in terms of common sense, good faith, and reciprocal recognition of the problems of management, the labor organization, and the employees.

As a result of the nature of the seniority principle, many problems are inherent in the formulation and application of a seniority structure. Among the major problems, beyond the crucial determination of the phases of the employment relationship which are to be affected by the length-of-service principle, are: establishment of the unit in which employees acquire and apply seniority credits; identification of circumstances under which employees may lose seniority; determination of the seniority status of employees who transfer from one part of the bargaining unit to another or who leave the bargaining unit altogether; and the fixing of certain exceptions to the seniority system. As can be expected, these problems are handled in a multitude of fashions in collective bargaining relationships. Some labor agreements, moreover, attempt to cover all of these issues and some deal with only certain ones of them.

Virtually all labor agreements, for example, provide that seniority play a part in the determination of layoffs, in rehiring, and in promotions. But, as discussed below, the same labor agreement might use one seniority system to govern layoffs and rehiring and a different one in connection with promotions (where considerations of ability and physical fitness are often as important as, and in many cases more important than, length of service). Where a fixed shift system exists in a plant, labor agreements may permit workers their choice of shifts on the basis of seniority, and factors such as personal convenience, wage or hour differentials, and the kind of job itself may dictate the senior worker's choice in this respect. Under other contracts, however, seniority plays no role in shift assignments.

Units for seniority

There are three major systems relating to the unit in which an employee acquires and applies his seniority credits: company- or plant-wide, departmental or occupational, and a combined plant and departmental seniority system.

Under a *company- or plant-wide seniority system,* the seniority status of each employee equals his total service with the firm. Thus, transfers from job to job within the establishment or transfers from one department to another have no effect on an employee's seniority standing. Subject to other features of the seniority structure, an employee under the company- or plant-wide system will apply his seniority for purposes covered by the seniority system on a strictly company- or plant-wide basis. In actual practice this system is not used in companies in which it would be necessary for an employee to undergo a considerable training period when he takes a new job to replace a worker with less seniority. It is practicable only for companies where the jobs are more or less interchangeable. A company-wide system obviously gives the greatest protection to employees with the longest length of service. On the other hand, depending upon the other features of the seniority structure, it could serve as a deterrent to the efficiency and productivity of the plant.

Under *departmental or occupational seniority systems,* separate seniority lists are established for each department or occupational grouping in the plant. If such a system does not have any qualifications or limitations, an employee can apply his seniority credits only within his own department or occupation. Such a system facilitates administration in large companies employing a considerable number of workers. It minimizes the opportunity for large-scale displacement of workers from their jobs in the event of layoffs or discontinuation of particular jobs because of technological innovations, or because of permanent changes in the market for the products of the company. On the other hand, additional problems arise as the result of the use of this kind of seniority system. If layoffs in one department become necessary or if certain jobs in such a department are permanently discontinued while other departments are not affected, a state of affairs could develop wherein employees with long service in a company would find themselves out of a job while employees with less seniority were working full time. In addition, under a strict departmental seniority structure, transfers between departments tend to be discouraged because a transfer could result in complete loss of accumulated seniority.

As a result of the problems arising from a strict company or departmental seniority system, many companies and unions have negotiated a number of plans combining these two types of seniority structures. Under a combination system, seniority may be applied in one unit for certain purposes and exercised in another unit for other purposes. Thus, seniority may be applied on a plant-wide basis for purposes of layoffs, whereas department-wide seniority is used as the basis of promotion. A variation of this system is to permit employees to *apply* their seniority only within the department in which they are working, but to *compute* such seniority on the basis of total service with the company. In addition, although the general application of seniority is limited to a departmental basis, employees laid off in a particular department may claim work in a general labor pool in which the jobs are relatively unskilled and in which newly hired employees start out before being promoted to other departments. At times a distinction is drawn between temporary layoffs resulting from lack of business or material shortages and permanent layoffs resulting from changes in technology or permanent changes in the products manufactured by the company. Under the former situation seniority may be applied only on a departmental basis, or seniority might not govern at all (as in autos), whereas under the latter circumstances employees have the opportunity to apply their seniority on a plant-wide basis. Other variations of the combination system are utilized within industry as determined by the circumstances of a particular plant.

Limitations upon seniority

Regardless of the type of system under which seniority credits are accumulated and applied, many collective bargaining agreements place certain limitations and qualifications upon length of service as a factor in connection with layoffs. Possibly as many as one third of all agreements in existence may include such limitations. In some cases, seniority systems provide for the retention of more senior employees only when they are qualified to perform the jobs which are available. In considerably fewer labor agreements, a senior employee will be retained in the event of layoffs in a plant only when he is able to perform a job available "as well as" other employees eligible for layoff.

Although a large number of labor agreements permit employees scheduled for layoff to displace less senior employees, limitations on the chain displacement or "bumping" process are also included in many labor agreements. Employers, unions, employees, and students of labor relations recognize the inherent disadvantages of seniority structures which permit unlimited bumping. Such disadvantages are manifested in many ways. Bumping could result in serious obstacles to plant efficiency and productivity to the detriment of all concerned, could cause extreme uncertainty and confusion to workers who might be required to take a number of different jobs as a result of a single layoff, and could result in serious internal political problems for the labor organization.

For these reasons, careful limitations usually are placed on the bumping process. Many labor agreements allow an employee to displace a less senior worker in the event of a layoff only when the former employee has a minimum amount of service with the company. Other contracts circumscribe the bumping process by limiting the opportunity of a senior employee to displacement of a junior worker from a job that the employee with longer service has already held. Under this system, the worker comes down in the same fashion that he went up the job ladder. Under other seniority systems the area into which the employee may bump is itself limited. Thus, it may be stipulated that employees can bump only on a departmental or divisional basis, or can displace workers only within equal or lower labor grades. In addition, the objective of limiting the displacement process is achieved by permitting the displacement of only the *least* senior employee in the bumping area and not of any other less senior employees.

Most labor agreements provide for rehiring in *reverse* order of layoffs —the last employee laid off is the first rehired. In addition, laid-off employees are given preference over new workers for vacancies that arise anywhere in the plant. However, such preferences given employees with longer service are frequently limited to the extent that the employee in question is competent to perform the available work. In this connection the problem of the re-employment of laid-off workers becomes somewhat complicated when a straight departmental seniority system is used. In such a case, although a labor agreement might provide for the rehiring of workers in the reverse order of layoffs, production might not be revived in reverse order to the slack in production and thus employees with shorter service might be recalled to work before employees with greater seniority. To avoid such a state of affairs, some labor contracts provide the older employee in terms of service with the opportunity of returning to work first, provided he has the ability to carry out the duties of the available job.

Length of service as a factor in promotion is of less importance than it is in layoffs and rehiring, and in only a relative handful of contemporary labor agreements is length of service the *sole* factor in making promotions. The incidence is low because all parties to collective bargaining realize that a janitor, for example, in spite of many years of service in this position, is not qualified to be promoted to, say, a tool- and die-maker's job. But if such a criterion is rarely the sole factor in the assignment of workers to higher-rated jobs, the vast majority of labor agreements now require that seniority along with other factors be given *consideration*. In many contracts seniority governs promotions when the senior employee is "qualified" to fill the position in question. Under other collective bargaining agreements seniority becomes the determining criterion in promotions when the senior employee has ability and physical fitness for the job in question "equal to that" of all other employees who may desire the better job. Under the latter seniority structure, length of service is of secondary importance to the ability and physical fitness factors, however.

In practice, management makes the decision about which worker among those bidding for the job gets the promotion and in the vast majority of cases this decision of the company is satisfactory to all concerned. This is the case many times because the senior employee *is* best qualified for the job in question or because the company is completely willing to give preference to him when ability differences among employees are not readily discernible. At times, however, when the company passes over a senior employee in favor of an employee with shorter service in making a promotion, the union may protest the action of the company through the grievance procedure. For example, the union may argue that the senior employee bidding for the better job has equal ability to that of the worker whom the company tapped for the promotion. The problem in such cases is to evaluate the comparative abilities of the two workers. Such a determination involves the study and appraisal of the entire work record of both workers. Consideration here is usually given to such items as the previous experience of the workers on the actual job in question or on closely related jobs; the education and training qualifications of the workers for performing the job in question; production records of the employees; and absenteeism, tardiness, and accident records when relevant. Ordinarily, such disputes are resolved between the union and the company on the basis of these considerations. At times, however, the parties are still in disagreement and the matter is then most often referred to an impartial arbitrator who will make the decision in the case. (NOTE: Case No. 8 deals with such an arbitration. An employee had the length of service for a promotion, but was denied it by the company on the grounds that he lacked the necessary ability for the better job.)

Seniority in transfers

Another seniority problem involves the seniority status of employees who *transfer* from one department to another. As stated above, interdepartmental transfers do not create a seniority issue under a straight plant-wide seniority system. To the extent that seniority is acquired or applied on a department-wide basis, however, the problem of transfers becomes important to employers, unions, and employees: Reference has been made to the fact that interdepartmental transfers are discouraged when employees lose all accumulated seniority upon entering a new department. Some contracts deal with this problem by allowing a transferred employee to retain his seniority in his old department, while starting at the bottom of the seniority scale in the new department; under these circumstances such an employee would exercise seniority rights in his old department in the event he were laid off from his new department. Some contracts even permit such an employee to further accumulate seniority for application in his old department in the event that he is laid off from his new department. Another approach to the problem permits the transferred employee to carry his seniority acquired in the old department to the new department. This is a common practice where the job itself is transferred to a new department, where the job or the department itself is permanently abolished, or upon the merging of two or more departments.

Still another seniority problem arises under the circumstances of an employee's transferring entirely *out of the bargaining unit*. This issue is particularly related to the seniority status of workers who are selected by management to fill foremen's jobs. There are three major approaches to this problem. Under some contracts a rank-and-file employee who takes a supervisory job simply loses accumulated seniority. If for some reason his supervisory job is terminated and he desires to return to a job covered by the collective bargaining contract, he is treated as a new employee for purposes of seniority. Another method is to permit such an employee to retain all seniority credits earned earlier when he serves as a foreman. Under this latter approach, if the employee transfers back to the bargaining unit, he returns with the same number of seniority credits as he had when he left. Finally, under some contracts, an employee taking a supervisor's job accumulates seniority in the bargaining unit while he serves as a foreman. If he returns to the bargaining unit, he comes back not only with the seniority credits that he acquired before he took the supervisory job, but with seniority credits accumulated while he served as a foreman. Rank, at times, does have its privileges.

Obviously, the seniority status of foremen is not a problem when management fills its supervisory posts by hiring outside the plant. On the other hand, the problem is a real one when the company elects to fill such jobs from the rank and file. It is apparent that a worker with long seniority in the bargaining unit would hesitate to take a foreman's job if he would lose thereby all his accumulated seniority. In recognition of this situation many employers and unions have agreed that workers promoted from the bargaining unit to supervisors' jobs at least may retain the seniority they accumulated while covered by the labor agreement. Whatever approach unions and companies take to this problem, it generally would be desirable to spell out the method in the labor agreement. Confusion, uncertainty, and controversy could arise when the contract is silent on this issue.

Exceptions to the seniority system

Under many collective bargaining contracts there is provision for some *exemptions* from the normal operation of the seniority structure. One of these involves the issue of "super-seniority" for union officers. Some companies and unions have agreed that designated union officers may have a preferred status in the event of layoffs. Such employees are protected in employment regardless of their length of service with the company. They are entitled to such consideration strictly by virtue of the union office which they hold, however, and lose their super-seniority status when their term of office is terminated.

One obvious problem involved in the negotiation of a super-seniority clause is the designation of the employees who are to have this status. Frequently, labor agreements limit this protection to the comparatively major local union officers. If too many employees are covered by a super-seniority status, the effective and fair operation of the seniority structure might be prevented. In any event it is common practice to specify exactly which officers of the union are to be included under the super-seniority clause.

Another problem concerns the bumping rights of employees protected under such an arrangement. Contracts usually are clear as to just what job or jobs such employees are entitled to when they are scheduled for layoff. In addition, it is common practice to make clear the rate of pay that the employee will earn in the new job. Thus, if a worker protected by super-seniority takes another job which pays a lower rate than his regular job to avoid layoff, the contract specifies whether or not he will get the rate of the job that he is filling or the rate of his regular job. Obviously, when these problems *are* resolved in the labor agreement, there is less chance for controversy during the hectic atmosphere of a layoff itself.

Some labor agreements also permit management to retain in employment during periods of layoff a certain number of non–union-officer employees regardless of their seniority status. Such employees are designated as "exceptional," "specially skilled," "indispensable," or "meritorious" in collective bargaining contracts. As in the case of super-seniority, problems growing out of this exception to the seniority rule normally are resolved in the collective bargaining contract. Problems in this connection involve the number of employees falling into this category, the kind of jobs that they must be holding to receive such preferential status, their bumping rights (if any), and the rate of pay they shall earn in the event that they are retained in employment in jobs other than their regular ones.

Another general exception to the normal operation of a seniority system involves newly hired workers. Under most labor agreements such workers must first serve a probationary period before they are protected by the labor agreement. Such probationary periods are frequently specified as being from about thirty to ninety days, and during this period of time the new worker can be laid off, demoted, transferred, or otherwise assigned work without reference to the seniority structure at all. However, once such an employee serves out his probationary period, his seniority under most labor agreements is calculated from the first day of hire by the company.

Under the terms of many collective bargaining contracts, employers may lay off workers on a *temporary* basis without reference to the seniority structure. Such layoffs are for short periods of time and result from purely temporary factors, such as shortages of material, power failures, and the like. It is, of course, vital in this connection that the labor agreement define the meaning of temporary layoff. At times, contracts incorporate the principle that employers may lay off without reference to seniority on a temporary basis but fail to specify what is meant by the term "temporary layoff." Some agreements define the term as any layoff for less than five or even ten working days. Other contracts, however, specify that the seniority structure must be followed for any layoff in excess of twenty-four hours. Whatever time limit is placed on the term, the labor agreement should specify the duration of a temporary layoff. By this means, a considerable amount of future argument will be avoided. Of course, once the temporary layoff period has been exhausted, a laid-off employee can then exercise his seniority rights in accordance with the seniority structure of the labor agreement.

Finally, virtually all seniority structures specify circumstances under which an employee *loses* his seniority credits. All employees should fully understand the exact nature of these circumstances and the significance of losing seniority credits. Under the terms of most collective bargaining contracts an employee loses his seniority if he is discharged, voluntarily quits, fails to notify the company within a certain time period (usually five working days) of his intentions to return to work after he is recalled by the company after a layoff, fails to return to work after an authorized leave of absence, neglects to report to work within a certain period of time (usually ninety working days) after discharge from military service, or is laid off continuously for a long period of time, usually from about twenty-four to forty-eight months.

A concluding comment

However qualified it may be in particular situations, there can be no denying the current acceptability of the seniority criterion in regulating potential competition among employees for jobs and job status. The traditional arguments that seniority fosters laziness, rewards mediocrity, and crimps individual initiative are no longer automatically brought into play by managers to oppose this length-of-service criterion. And the on-balance benefits of seniority, both in improving employee morale and in minimizing administrative problems, are no longer seriously questioned by progressive companies, *if* length of service is limited by such other factors as ability when these are meaningful. Although it is probably true that in general a seniority system tends to reduce the efficiency of the plant operation to some extent, if care is taken to design a system to the needs of the particular company, and if length of service *is* appropriately limited in its application, the net loss to plant efficiency is normally not very noticeable.

Beyond this, many would argue that efficiency, despite its obvious importance, should not be the only goal of American industry. The advantages of providing a measure of job security to employees, and thereby relieving them of the frustrations of discrimination and unfair treatment, cannot be easily quantified. But human values have become the increasing concern of modern management, and the judicious use of seniority clearly serves the human equation.

Discharge and Discipline

In the absence of a collective bargaining relationship, an employer may discharge or otherwise impose penalties upon an employee without any limitations except those imposed by law. An employee may be discharged for any reason, or, indeed, for no reason. The power of discipline in a nonunion situation remains fully and completely in the hands of the employer.

Once a collective bargaining relationship is established, however, the employer's prerogative to discipline employees is invariably limited by the labor agreement. The nature of such a restriction is not that the company loses its right to discharge or otherwise discipline employees;

rather, it is that the employer's right in this connection is restricted to the extent that he can inflict discipline on employees only for sufficient and appropriate reasons.

Thus, most collective bargaining contracts contain the general statement that an employee can be discharged only for "just cause." And the critical interpretation of "just cause" is accomplished through industrial practice, through the results of the grievance procedure existing in the particular plant, through common sense, and through arbitration decisions.

Frequently companies and unions agree that a particular infraction by an employee constitutes a proper reason for discharge and there is no litigation on the issue. On the other hand, in many cases the employer and the union are in disagreement as to whether an offense by an employee constitutes a valid basis for discharge. Under these circumstances, the issue is discussed and debated between the company and the union in the grievance procedure. If the parties fail to reach an agreement through this process, the dispute is frequently submitted to an arbitrator for final decision.

It is understandable that a large percentage of arbitration cases involve discharge. Discipline, of course, is required to run an efficient business. If every worker were free to do what he wanted, the productive process could hardly be carried out effectively; such a state of affairs would operate to the distinct disadvantage of the employees, the employer, and the union. Accordingly, the right of the employer to discipline becomes an indispensable prerequisite to the operation of a successful business. On the other hand, to the worker and to his family, the loss of a job by discharge is very serious. Not only does it result in the loss of a man's immediate livelihood, but the stigma of discharge is likely to make it more difficult for an employee to find another job. From this point of view, a discharge has much more serious consequences to the worker and his family than does a permanent layoff. In addition, a discharged employee frequently loses part of his coverage under most state unemployment compensation laws. Thus, because the implications of discharge are so profound, this feature of collective bargaining has frequently proven both highly challenging and quite controversial for both labor relations parties.

Although the majority of contracts contain only the previously noted general and simple statement that discharge can be made only for "just cause" (or "proper reason"), many labor agreements list one or more specific grounds for discharge: violation of company rules, failure to meet work standards, incompetency, violation of the collective bargaining contract (including in this category the instigation of or participation in a strike or a slowdown in violation of the agreement), excessive absenteeism or tardiness, intoxication, dishonesty, insubordination, wage garnishments, and fighting on company property. Labor agreements which list specific causes for discharge normally also include a general statement that discharge may be made for "any other just or proper reason."

In addition, many contracts distinguish between causes for immediate discharge and employee offenses which require one or more warnings. For example, sabotage or willful destruction of company property may result in immediate discharge, whereas a discharge for absenteeism may occur only after a certain number of warnings. In recognition of the fact that not all employee infractions are grave enough to warrant discharge, lesser forms of discipline are imposed at times under collective bargaining relationships. Into this category fall oral and written reprimand, suspension without pay for varying lengths of time, demotion, and denial of vacation pay. Frequently, union and management representatives in the grievance procedure will agree upon a lesser measure of discipline even though the employer presumably has the grounds to discharge an employee for a particular offense. At times the union and the employee in question will be willing to settle a case on these terms rather than risk taking the case to arbitration.

A very large number of collective bargaining contracts specify a distinct procedure for discharge cases. Many of them require notice to the employee and the union before the discharge takes place. Such notification generally is required to contain the specific reasons for the discharge. A hearing on the case is also provided for in many labor agreements and in this respect the typical labor agreement requires not only the presence of the worker in question and an appropriate official of the company, but also a representative of the labor organization. Frequently, collective bargaining agreements provide for a suspension period before the discharge becomes effective. The alleged advantage of this latter procedure is that it provides for an opportunity to cool tempers and offers a period of time for all parties to make a careful investigation and evaluation of the facts of the case.

Part of the procedure for discharge cases is provided for in the general grievance procedure of the collective bargaining contract. As suggested, almost every labor agreement provides for appeal of discharge cases and this appeal is taken through the regular grievance procedure, since the appeal is looked upon as a grievance. If, for example, the labor agreement provides that the employee or the union must appeal a discharge within a certain number of days, such appeal must be made during this period or the discharge may become permanent regardless of the merits of the case. Likewise, a company which neglects its obligation to give an answer to the appeal within the stipulated number of days may find that it has lost its right to discharge a particular worker regardless of the justice of the situation.

Frequently, labor agreements also provide that a discharge case has a priority over all other cases in the grievance procedure. Some of them even waive the first few steps of the grievance procedure and start a discharge case at the top levels of the procedure. In these arrangements, companies and unions recognize the fact that it is to the mutual advantage of all concerned to expedite discharge cases. The worker wants to know as quickly as possible whether or not he has a job in the plant. The company also has an interest in the prompt settlement of a discharge case because of the disciplinary implications involved and because labor agreements normally require that the company award the employee loss of earnings where a discharge is withdrawn.

From the foregoing, it should be clear that under a collective bargaining relationship, the employer does not lose his right to discipline or discharge. What is involved, however, is that it is more difficult for management to exercise this function. There must be just cause, a specific procedure must be followed, and, of course, management must have the *proof* that an employee committed the offensive act.

If cases do go to arbitration, in fact, the arbitrator will be particularly concerned with the quality of proof that management offers in the hearing. The occasions on which employers have lost discharge cases in arbitration because the evidence which they have presented is not sufficient to prove the case for discharge are many in number. At times, the company's case against the employee has simply been poorly prepared; at other times, the management has not been able to assemble the proof despite the most conscientious of company efforts (one difficulty in this latter regard, as all arbitrators are well aware, is that employees dislike to testify against other employees who are charged with some offense).

If the arbitrator did not demand convincing proof before sustaining discipline, however, the protection afforded employees by the labor agreement would be worthless. The same situation prevails in our civil life, wherein juries have freed criminals because the state has not proven its case. Such courses of action reflect one of the most cardinal features of our system of justice, the presumption that a man is innocent until proven guilty, and this hallmark of our civil life plays no less a role in the American system of industrial relations. Though this situation has undoubtedly resulted in the reinstatement to their jobs with full back pay for employees who are in fact "guilty," it is beyond argument that an employer bears the obligation to prove charges against employees whom it has displaced. In the absence of such an obligation, this most important benefit allowed employees under a collective bargaining contract, protection against arbitrary management treatment, is obviously negated. (NOTE: Case No. 9 at the end of this chapter involves the discharge of two employees under a collective bargaining contract.)

Safety and Health of Employees

Few people would argue that employees do not have a real interest in the area of industrial safety and health. After all, it is the worker and his family who suffer the most devastating consequences of neglect in this area, in terms of accidents, sickness, and even death. And although most employers can sincerely claim that they, too, are deeply interested in safe and healthy working environments, such concern cannot restore to life a man killed on the job, restore his limbs, or succor his family when an employment-caused accident or illness disables an employee for long periods of time. Indeed, this consideration is at the root of a long-standing policy of the National Labor Relations Board that safety and health demands of unions are mandatory subjects of collective bargaining. Thus, employers must bargain on these issues even though company working conditions are also subject to the many safety regulations imposed by federal and state statutes.

Not surprisingly, then, most collective bargaining contracts contain explicit provisions relating to the safety and health area, although such provisions take one of two routes depending upon the particular contract.

On the one hand, many contracts merely state in *general* terms that the management of the plant is required to take measures to protect the safety and health of employees. At times the term *measures* is qualified by the word *reasonable*. When a contract contains such a broad and general statement, the problem of application and interpretation is obviously involved and disagreements between the company and union in this regard are commonly resolved through the regular grievance procedure, or by the operation of a special safety committee.

The second category of contracts provides a *detailed and specific* listing of safety and health measures which obligate the company. Thus, many agreements stipulate that the company must provide adequate heat, light, and ventilation in the plant; that it will control drafts, noise, toxic fumes, dust, dirt, and grease; that it will provide certain safety equipment, such as hoods, goggles, special shoes and boots, and other items of special clothing; and that it is responsible for placing guards and other safety devices on machines. In addition, under many contracts, the company must provide first-aid stations and keep a nurse on duty. Of course, whether or not a collective bargaining contract contains safety rules, a company must comply with the state safety and health laws applicable to its plant.

Many labor agreements impose obligations on employees and unions as well as on employers in the matter of safety. Such provisions recognize the fact that safety, despite the individual employee's crucial stake in it, is a joint problem requiring the cooperation of the company, employees, and the union. Under many labor agreements, employees must obey safety rules and wear appropriate safety equipment, and employees who violate such rules are subject to discipline. In some labor agreements the union assumes the obligation of educating its members to comply with safety rules and procedures of the plant. And some labor agreements in the interest of safety also establish a joint union–management safety committee. Many of these committees serve as advisory bodies on the general problem of safety and health. Other committees, however, have the authority to establish and enforce safety and health rules, allowing the union a considerably more active role.

Production Standards and Manning

Certainly one of the most important functions of management is that of determining the amount of output that an employee must turn out in a given period. So important is this area to management's objective of operating an efficient plant that employers will at times suffer long strikes to maintain this right as a unilateral one.

It is easy to understand why employers have such a vital interest in production standards. To the degree that employees increase output, unit labor costs decline. With declining labor costs, employers make a larger profit, or else they can translate lower labor costs into lower prices for their products or services with the expectation of thereby increasing the total volume of sales and strengthening the financial position of the company.

There is still another way to look at production standards in the operation of the firm. If employees produce more, the employer will have to hire commensurately fewer additional employees, or may even be in a position to lay off present employees on a temporary or permanent basis. Indeed, with a smaller labor force, the management could also save on the number of foremen needed to supervise the work of its employees.

Production standards are thus directly related to the manning of jobs, or to the question of how many employees are needed to carry out a specific plant assignment. But even where contractual commitments or past practices obligate the company to assign a certain minimum number of workers to a given operation at all times, significant economies can be realized by management if it is able to impose higher production standards upon this inflexible crew.

If the interest of management in production standards is understandable, however, it is no less understandable that employees and their union representatives have an equal interest in ensuring "reasonableness" and "fairness" in this phase of the firm's operation. Before the advent of unions, employers could require employees to produce as much as management directed. Failure to meet these production standards could result in the summary dismissal of the employee. At times, employees suffered accidents, psychological problems, and a generally shortened work life in meeting the standards of the employer. And although modern and enlightened management does not normally impose production standards that employees cannot reasonably attain, unions and employees are nonetheless still vitally concerned with the amount of production that an employee must turn out in a given length of time because of the patent ramifications for job opportunities and union membership.

There is no simple solution to the problem of how much an employee must produce to hold his job or to earn a given amount of pay. At times, the determination of a solution is purely subjective in character: A foreman or superintendent's individual judgment is the criterion adopted to resolve the problem. To this, unions argue that the judgment of employees or labor union officers is as good as that of the management representatives.

More sophisticated methods of determination are available, but these techniques, too, are hardly so perfect or "scientific" as to end the controversy. Such techniques fall under the general title of time and motion studies. That is, having been shown the most efficient method of performing a job, so-called "average" employees who are presumably thus working at "average" rates of speed are timed. From such a study, management claims that the typical employee in the plant should at least produce the average amount in a given period. Where incentive wage systems are in effect, as we know, the employee receives premium pay for output above the average. However, production standards are important even when employees are paid by the hour, since failure to produce the average amount could result in employee discipline of some sort—ranging from a reprimand to discharge, with the intervening levels such as a suspension or a demotion to a lower-paying job. Unions are far from convinced that time and motion studies constitute the millenium in the resolution of the production standards problem. They claim that the studies are far from scientific, since they still involve human judgment, and that employees who are timed are often far better than "average" (and that the rate of speed of the studied employees is consequently unrealistically fast).

With few exceptions (most notably in the garment industries), unions have pressed for an effective means of *review* of employer establishment of production standards, rather than toward seeking the right to establish such standards initially. Organized labor has generally believed that employee and union institutional interests are served as effectively, and without the administrative and political complexities of initial standard establishment, if there is a union opportunity for *challenge* of the management action either through arbitration or by the exercise of the right to strike *during the contractual period* in the event of unresolved production standards disputes.

Some unions have historically preferred the right to strike to arbitration in this area. The United Automobile Workers has, for example, steadfastly refused to relinquish its right to strike over production standards disputes, and although the UAW now agrees to arbitration on virtually all other phases of the labor agreement, it is adamant in its opposition to the arbitration of standards. The international neither distrusts arbitrators nor challenges their professional competency. Rather, it believes that a union cannot properly prepare and present a case in arbitration which can successfully challenge production standards. It contends that the problems are so complicated, the proofs so difficult to assemble, and the data so hard to present in meaningful form that arbitration is not the proper forum to resolve production standards disputes. In essence, it claims that employers have an advantage in any arbitration dealing with production standards, and the union does not intend to turn to this process because it would jeopardize the interests of its members.

On the other hand, most unions have now agreed to the arbitration of production standards. Beyond reflecting the general contemporary acceptance of the arbitration process itself, this course of action has behind it a highly practical reason: Frequently, production standards are protested by only a small group of employees in the plant. For example, the employer may have changed (because of improved technology, equipment, or methods) the standards in one department, but left unaltered at least temporarily the standards in all other departments. Without arbitration, the only way in which the affected employees could seek relief would be for the entire labor force to strike—at times, a politically inopportune weapon for the union to use because the employees in the other departments are satisfied and do not care to sacrifice earnings just to help out employees in a single department. Arbitration avoids this situation, while still allowing a final and binding decision on the grievance of the protesting employees.

There is, however, probably no area of labor relations wherein management and organized labor still stand any further apart than in production standards. There is no magical solution to such controversies when they arise. Standards lie at the heart of the operation of the plant, and are vital to the basic interest of the employees and unions. To say that they should be established "fairly" and "resonably" is a most idle statement to make, falling in the category of "we should all love our mothers." In the give and take of day-to-day operations, wherein production standards may be changed, deep and bitter circumstances are perhaps even *bound* to arise. The stakes are very high, and as long as management seeks efficiency and the union seeks to protect the welfare of its employees, there exists no easy solution to the problem. Certainly nothing approaching a panacea for it has yet been discovered by the parties to collective bargaining.

At least, however, if companies and unions fully recognize the apparent inevitability of standards disputes, the fact that no dispute in this area will perhaps ever be settled in such a way that all involved in it will be fully satisfied, and the high degree of sensitivity of this labor relations issue, at least the point of realism will have been reached. Once these basic propositions are understood, the parties are in a position to fashion workable production standards compromises without jeopardizing the broader collective bargaining relationship.

Automation

As stated at the beginning of this chapter, the problem of automation cuts across much of the contemporary collective bargaining process. Most of the methods which the private parties have employed to ease the adjustment to this new technology are administrative and institutional in nature, insofar as they deal with the job rights of workers, the institutional needs of labor organizations, and the rights of management in directing the work force. But such previously discussed "economic" issues as severance pay, pension-right vesting and supplemental unemployment benefits also are increasingly being geared to cushioning the labor-saving and displacement effects of automation. It is thus quite unrealistic to view this problem as falling exclusively within one descriptive category. Indeed, one is fully justified in looking at this final portion of the chapter as a synthesizer of many current trends in collective bargaining, providing the capstone of the "administrative" segment but actually extending well beyond it.

Broadly defined, automation is the control of the elements of production through a system of automatic devices which integrate the entire productive process. Not only is the human hand not needed, but the process also makes less necessary a major feature which distinguishes human beings from animals: judgment. Automated computers are now able to determine optimally what product to produce in the first place, the color and design of the product, where the goods should be sold, and even the pricing of the product.

Even today, automation affects, to some extent, almost all segments of the work force. Although the industrial blue-collar worker, and particularly the unskilled and semiskilled factory worker, has thus far been hardest hit, examples abound to show the impact of automation, even at this relatively early stage in its history, in other sectors of the economy. In railroading, for example, robot track-laying equipment and the automatic handling and dispatching of freight cars have made many jobs obsolete. The same can be said of many forms of retail trade, as symbolized by one mail-order house in which a computer now handles 90,000 tallies each day, keeping an automatic inventory record of the 8,000 items sold by the firm in the process. Nor has government employment been immune from automation's inroads: The 450 United States Treasury clerical workers who were in the mid-1960's replaced by a computer designed to accommodate the 350 million checks issued by the federal government every year are far from unique among the casualties of automation in that sector.

The fact remains, however, that the blue-collar worker in mass production industry—unionism's strongest bastion—has been the most visible victim of the advent of automation. In the modern automobile plant, 154 engine blocks now run through the production line in one hour, requiring 41 workers; under older methods, the same amount of production required 117 men. In the typical automated radio-manufacturing establishment, only two employees produce 1,000 radios per day, where standard hand assembly required a labor force of 200. And, perhaps most dramatic of all, fourteen glass-blowing machines, each operated by a single worker, today produce 90 per cent of all glass light bulbs used in the United States, as well as all the glass tubes used in radio and television sets except for the picture tubes![2]

For all these labor displacement and related skill rating and wage payment effects, there are clearly offsetting advantages offered by automation. Certainly, the automating *employer* benefits, either by gaining a competitive edge or by closing a competitive gap, in making this form of technological change. Of far more general benefit, national living standards are raised immensely by the increased productivity allowed. It is now estimated, for example, that the average family income in the United States at constant dollars will be $15,000 annually in the year 2000, up from $6,720 today.

There are, moreover, still other advantages to automation: greater safety, resulting from the use of modern methods of materials handling and from the elimination of other hazardous jobs; a frequent improvement in product quality, since the automatic machine has little room for human error; and even an improved defense posture for the nation,

[2]Edward B. Shils, *Automation and Industrial Relations* (New York: Holt, Rinehart & Winston, Inc., 1963), p. 179.

modern methods of warfare having as their common denominator an automation base. Most important of all, it can be argued with considerable justification that every one, *in the long run*, benefits from the needs and wants created by improved technology. There are infinitely more men working in the automobile production and servicing industries than there ever were blacksmiths, for example. And the number of employees associated with the telephone industry vastly exceeds the highest labor force totals ever achieved by the town-crier profession.

All these arguments, however, are of small consolation to the employee actually being displaced or threatened by automation. Just as logically, he can echo the irrefutable statement of Lord Keynes that "in the long run, we are all dead." And he can often balance the fact that automation has generally improved working conditions by pointing to undesirable features of the problem which have an impact upon the workers in the plant: greater isolation of employees on the job, with less chance to talk face to face with other workers and supervisors; a greater mental strain, particularly since mistakes can now be much more costly; the deterioration of social groups, since it requires considerably less teamwork to run the modern operation; and the fact that jobs in the automated plant (or office) are fast becoming much more *alike*, with less on-the-job variety also often the case, and attendant psychological and social implications stemming from this situation.

But most worrisome of all to the industrial worker is the threat of displacement, or at least of severe skill requirement downgrading, through *future* automation. The results of one employee survey with which the authors are personally familiar showed almost three quarters of all respondents replying in the negative as to whether they believed that "automation is a good thing for workers" (and many of them added that the new methods constituted a "real job threat"). Such findings have been echoed in countless other studies.

The fears appear to be well grounded. If automation undeniably creates new jobs and even industries, the possibility remains that at the present time automation is destroying more jobs than it creates. Even placing all government and private estimates at their rock-bottom minima, it is likely that 4,000 jobs are eliminated *each week* in this manner. And however many of the displaced are ultimately reabsorbed into the employed labor force, the increasing skill requirements of an automated world leave little room for at least the unskilled worker to join their ranks: at the time of this writing, with a national rate of unemployment seemingly inflexibly fixed in the 3.5 to 4.5 per cent range, the rate for unskilled workers had steadily exceeded 12 per cent in recent years.

Thus, if by far the greatest *organizational* problem of unions involves the organization of the white-collar sector in the face of the automation-caused changing complexion of the work force, within the *current arena of collective bargaining,* organized labor—both as the blue-collar worker's representative and for its own institutional preservation—has inevitably been forced toward the promotion of *measures minimizing job hardship for blue-collar workers.*

Accordingly, unions have in recent years pushed hard, and with much success, for several devices geared explicitly to cushioning the employment impact of automation. In addition to such previously discussed areas as SUB, pension vesting, severance pay, extended vacation periods, and early retirement provisions (which have frequently been negotiated for reasons other than adjustment to automation), several such devices deserve attention.[3]

(1) *Advance Notice of Layoff or Shutdown:* Such advance notice, impracticable for management in the case of sudden cancellation of orders and various other contingencies, is far more feasible where automation is involved, since many months may be required to prepare for the automated equipment and processes. An increasing number of agreements now call for notice considerably in excess of the few days traditionally provided for in many contracts, with most of the liberalizations now providing for three to twelve months.

Managements independently have often agreed with the advisability of such liberalization—to maintain or improve community images, to dispel potentially damaging employee rumors, and, frequently, because of a desire to develop placement and training plans for displaced workers. Very often, in fact, the actual notice given by management exceeds that stipulated in the contract. There seems to be little doubt, however, that unions have been instrumental in inserting longer advance-notice provisions in some contracts—as in portions of the meat-packing and electronics industries—which might otherwise not have modified traditional practices.

(2) *Adoption of the "Attrition Principle":* An agreement to reduce jobs solely by attrition—through, in other words, deaths, voluntary resignations, retirements, and similar events—by definition gives maximum job security to the present jobholder, although it does nothing to secure the union's long-run institutional interests. As a compromise, it has appealed to many employers as an equitable and not unduly rigorous

[3]Much of the following exposition is based upon information provided in a comprehensive 1964 review by the United States Department of Labor's Bureau of Labor Statistics, *Methods of Adjusting to Automation and Technological Change.* See also Edward B. Shils, *op. cit.,* and Gerald G. Somers, Edward L. Cushman, and Nat Weinberg, eds., *Adjusting to Technological Change* (New York: Harper and Row, Publishers, 1963).

measure. Managements have proven particularly amenable to this arrangement when the voluntary resignation rate is expected to be high, when a high percentage of workers is nearing retirement age, or when no major reduction of the labor force is anticipated in the first place (and the number of jobs made obsolete by automation is consequently small to begin with). In other cases, unions have been the major force behind introduction of the principle—usually, however, with some modifications more favorable to the union as an institution placed upon it. Thus, the current agreement between the Order of Railroad Telegraphers and the Southern Pacific Railroad places an upper limit of 2 per cent upon the jobs which can be abolished for any reason in a given year. Good faith is obviously required in such cases as the latter, however: as Bok and Kossoris comment,

> If [employers] are bound to follow attrition by agreement, temptation may arise to hasten the departure of employees by imposing more onerous working conditions or otherwise making the job less attractive. Further controversy may result if the agreement does not answer such questions as whether employees must agree to transfer or to accept more demanding positions and assignments in order to remain on the payroll.[4]

(3) *Retraining*: An expanding but unknown number of bargaining relationships now provide opportunities for displaced employees to retrain for another job in the same plant or another plant of the same company. The same protection is also increasingly being extended to employees for whom changes in equipment or operating methods make it mandatory to retrain in order to hold their current jobs. Often such retraining opportunity, which is most commonly offered at company expense, is limited to workers who meet certain seniority specifications. General Electric workers, for example, must have at least three years of continuous service in order to qualify. At other times, preference but not a promise for retraining is granted senior workers, as in one Machinist Union contract which provides that such employees "shall be given preference for training on new equipment, provided they have the capabilities required."

Where such provisions have significantly mitigated displacement, not unexpectedly, they have been implemented by companies whose operations have been expanding in areas other than those causing the initial displacement. "Retraining for *what?*" is a meaningful question when such expansion is not in evidence, or at least is not highly likely. Lack of employee self-confidence or lack of worker intelligence levels which are sufficient to meet the new skill requirements have also been known

4Bureau of Labor Statistics, U.S. Department of Labor, *Methods of Adjusting to Automation and Technological Change, op. cit.*, p. 5.

to make the retraining opportunity an essentially valueless one for employees permitted to utilize it. Yet, there is much to be said for retraining in the absence of such adverse factors; as the Personnel Director of Inland Steel has stated,

> . . . Retraining makes maximum use of manpower and contributes to the long-range security of the individual. . . . We think this is smart because it minimizes resistance to change, enables us to get up production faster than when people fear they won't keep their jobs, and gives us a quicker return on our investment.[5]

(4) *Automation Funds:* Ironically, the several "automation funds" which have sprouted in a variety of industries in the recent past do little or nothing to aid employees who are actually displaced. They do, however, tend to make it easier for management to implement change, both by gaining the cooperation of the *retained* workers and by strengthening the union's institutional status through providing benefits for present and future union members. Such funds as those negotiated by the United Mine Workers, American Federation of Musicians, West Coast Longshoremen, New York Longshoremen, United Packinghouse Workers, and Amalgamated Meat Cutters with various employers are essentially devices for sharing the savings of automation with retained employees—through such means as free medical care, guaranteed weekly pay provisions, early retirement allowances, and lump sum "bonus payments."

In addition to the political and public relations advantages which they allow to the various unions, there are specific advantages in the funds from management's point of view. Kennedy believes that perhaps the major such advantage

> . . . is that it impresses more strongly on the employees the reason for the benefits which they are reciving. When the benefits are paid from an "automation" fund, it is clear that they are being paid out of the savings of automation and that the employees are expected to cooperate with the automation process in return for such benefits. On the other hand, when the savings of automation are shared through higher wage rates or through improved fringe benefits without a fund, the service of the benefits as well as the reason for giving them may not be so evident in the beginning and are much more easily forgotten with time.[6]

On such a pragmatic basis, automation funds can probably be expected to continue their spread.

(5) *Restrictions on Subcontracting:* "Subcontracting," the term

---

[5] *Wall Street Journal* (August 23, 1961), p. 6
[6] Thomas Kennedy, *Automation Funds and Displaced Workers* (Boston: Graduate School of Business Administration, Harvard University, 1962), pp. 351–52.

which stands for arrangements made by a company (for reasons such as cost, quality, or speed of delivery) to have some portion of its work performed by employees of another company, obviously can have major work-opportunity ramifications for the first company's employees. There is probably no completely integrated company in the nation, and some measure of subcontracting has always been accepted by all unions as an economic necessity. But when the union can argue that union member employees *could* have performed the subcontracted work, or that such work *was* previously done by bargaining unit employees, it can be counted upon to do so. And when disputes do arise over this issue, they are, as Chapter 4 has pointed out, often of major dimensions. In the face of automation-caused job insecurity, there has been an observable recent trend toward union control over many types of subcontracting; the battle has tended to move from open interunion competition to the union–management bargaining table.

So thorny is the subcontracting problem that more than 75 per cent of all major contracts still make no direct reference to it in a special contractual section. But an increasing number of contracts are incorporating in various of their other sections (ranging from union recognition clauses to seniority articles) or in separate "memoranda of understanding" certain limitations on the procedure.

The limitations are of several kinds: (1) agreements that subcontractors will be used *"only"* on special occasions (for example, "where specialized equipment not available on company premises is required," "where peculiar skills are needed") ; (2) no-layoff guarantees to present employees (as in "no Employee of any craft, which craft is being utilized by an Outside Contractor, shall be laid off as long as the Outside Contractor is in the plant doing work that Employees in such craft are able to do") ; (3) provisions giving the union veto power over any or all subcontracting; and (4) requirements that the company prove to the union that time, expense, or facility considerations prevent it from allowing present employees to perform the work.

Slichter, Healy, and Livernash have summed up the present situation as follows:

> [Unlike many other collective bargaining areas] subcontracting remains an area of conflict in labor relations. Where adjustment has been achieved by the adoption of workable contract language, it has usually had the effect of limiting management's flexibility to a considerable extent. Seldom has explicit language been adopted affirming management's right to subcontract without challenge from the union. The trend has been in the opposite direction. . . .[7]

[7]Sumner H. Slichter, James J. Healy, and E. Robert Livernash, *op. cit.*, pp. 315–16.

Only when more adequate solutions to the problems of automation are formulated can one expect the conflict in this area to abate.

(6) *Other Measures:* Unions have also unilaterally attempted to minimize the administrative, institutional, and other problems of automation through increasingly successful if still limited bargaining table campaigns for: (a) shorter work weeks, often with a prohibition against overtime work when qualified workers are on layoff or where the overtime would result in layoffs; (b) the requirement of joint labor–management consultation prior to the introduction of any automated change; (c) the overhauling of wage structures with job upgrading to reflect the "increased responsibility" of automated factory jobs; and (d) special job and wage provisions for downgraded workers, to minimize income losses suffered by such workers, or to offset these entirely. In addition, unions have in some cases sought to facilitate new employment through the development of their own training, placement, and referral services. And, perhaps most visibly, they have often waged highly ambitious political lobbying campaigns (both on the international and AFL–CIO levels) for: a vast array of employment-generating public works programs; far-reaching tax programs and expanded social security benefits (to increase consumer purchasing power and lessen the burden on those most likely to be displaced) ; and innovative federal and state training programs.

As judged by short-run goals—the insertion of the various contract provisions within labor agreements and, in the latter case, the enactment of the lobbied-for legislation—unions have achieved a considerable measure of triumph. And the fact that they have frequently been aided in such campaigns by increasingly social-minded employers in no way detracts from this success. Although union aggressiveness and creativity has varied widely, there can be no denying that many unions have considerably alleviated the burdens of automation for many workers. (NOTE: Many cases involving job opportunities in newly automated establishments have been the subject of arbitration decisions. One such case, in which the company hired new employees who were obviously well qualified to maintain automated equipment rather than give one of these jobs to its own employee who had sought it, forms the basis of Case No. 10.)

Yet, neither singly nor in combination have these measures, or the host of other automation-adjustment methods cited earlier, provided anything approaching a full solution for the basic problems with which they deal. The displacement and displacement threats continue, now actually in accelerated form, as automation continues to prove that it is both a blessing and a curse for society. Indeed, a case can be made that a vicious circle is involved: Virtually all these measures increase labor costs for the companies concerned, giving the employer even further motivation for automating, and often thus causing the represented employees to lose jobs all the more rapidly.[8]

There appears to be rather general agreement among all segments of our society on at least three relevant points, however. First, most of us concede that automation is a product of society. It is not caused only by individuals, single firms, or groups of firms, but rather it is an expression of our cultural heritage, of our educational system and of our group dynamics. As such, unlike other problems affecting collective bargaining it requires not only a private (labor–management) solution but a supplementary public (government) one. Second, we are essentially in agreement that no single group should bear the entire burden of automation. Rather, we admit that we should all bear the burden by making sure that the benefits of the increased productivity allowed by automation are shared by all. Without such a philosophical basis, automation would mean that some would make spectacular gains, and others would shoulder the full burden. We do not want automation to divide the nation into the "haves" and the "have nots." Third, we share general unanimity that this is a time for daring innovation in social dynamics and social engineering and that, although the problem is great, we fortunately have within our capacity the power to deal with the issues within a system of free enterprise. Since old methods will not work, we must innovate and pioneer.

The increasing attention being given to automation at the bargaining table (and by the bargaining parties in the public arena) can thus be viewed as recognition of a great but not necessarily insurmountable challenge.

A Concluding Word

The mutual accommodations and adjustments to the hard issues of collective bargaining which the parties have displayed in regard to wages, employee benefits and institutional issues is no less in evidence when one inspects the current status of the administrative issues in our labor relations system. Management has increasingly recognized the job-protection and working-condition problems of the industrial employee and has made important concessions in these areas. At the same time, however, there has been reciprocal recognition on the part of unions that the protection of the employee cannot be at the expense of the destruction of the business firm. The axiom that employees cannot receive any protection from a business which has ceased to exist appears to have been

---

[8]This is, of course, true only if the costs are incurred in any event. If they occur *only* if one automates, they reduce the saving and in some cases could make automation unprofitable.

fully appreciated by all but the extreme recalcitrants of the labor movement, and workable compromises have been possible with respect to the areas of seniority, discipline, and the various other dimensions discussed in this chapter no less than in the case of previous topics.

Clearly there is considerable room for future progress, and on occasion the conflicts between the parties on the administrative issues can be very serious. Production standards and subcontracting remain two highly visible sticking-points. And strikes do, of course, at times result. There should be no illusion that the sensitive matters of collective bargaining are adjusted *without* painful struggle. Such an observation would not be realistic and would run contrary to the contemporary scene. Even standing alone, however, this chapter demonstrates rather irrefutably that managers and unionized employee representatives have increasingly recognized each other's position. It offers additional evidence of the growing maturity of the American labor relations system.

DISCUSSION QUESTIONS

1. It has been generally agreed that the increased use of the seniority concept in industrial relations has lessened the degree of mobility among workers. What can be said (a) for, and (b) against, such a consequence?
2. "The typical labor agreement's disciplinary procedures contain as many potential advantages for management as they do for unions and workers." Comment.
3. Jack Barbash has commented that "Management's perception of technological change is producing an offensive strategy; the union's perception is in general producing a defensive strategy." Confining your opinion to automated changes, do you agree?
4. The several devices noted in the last section of this chapter constitute the major existing avenues for minimizing employee resistance to automation. Can you suggest other measures which might be utilized in an attempt to realize this goal?

SELECTED REFERENCES

Kennedy, Thomas, *Automation Funds and Displaced Workers*. Boston: Graduate School of Business Administration, Harvard University, 1962.

Phelps, Orme W., *Discipline and Discharge in the Unionized Firm*. Berkeley: University of California Press, 1959.

Shils, Edward B., *Automation and Industrial Relations*. New York: Holt, Rinehart and Winston, Inc., 1963.

Slichter, Sumner H., James J. Healy and E. Robert Livernash, *The Impact of Collective Bargaining on Management*. Washington, D.C.: the Brookings Institution, 1960, pp. 104–371, 624–662.

Somers, Gerald G., Edward L. Cushman and Nat Weinberg, editors, *Adjusting to Technological Change*. New York: Harper & Row, 1963.

U.S. Department of Labor, Bureau of Labor Statistics, *Methods of Adjusting to Automation and Technological Change*. Washington, D.C.: U.S. Government Printing Office, 1964.

CASE NO. 8

Seniority and Promotions

(Arbitration cases such as this one are particularly difficult because frequently the evidence supporting the respective positions of the parties is not clear-cut or overwhelming. Nonetheless, controversies in which a promotion formula combines length of service and ability qualifications are common in arbitration and the following case therefore may be regarded as representative of a major source of arbitration.)

On February 8, 1961, the grievant, *P*, filed the following grievance,

> *R* was given a job as PBX-Repairman. I was not consulted as to whether I wanted the job or not. My seniority runs from April 16, 1956. This is a violation of the Agreement between the Company and the Union, Section 21, page 22, paragraph 21.1. I expect to be awarded the job of PBX-Repairman which *R* holds. *R's* seniority runs from September 25, 1956.

Having failed to resolve the grievance in the Grievance Procedure, the parties have instituted this arbitration to determine the dispute.

Basic Question

During the arbitration hearing the parties agreed that the following constitutes the question to be determined by the arbitrator: Did the Company violate Section 21, paragraph 21.1, in the promotion of employee *R*, junior in service to employee *P*, to the job classification of PBX-Repairman?

Contractual Language

Both parties cited contractual language during the hearing and in their post-hearing briefs:

21.1. Seniority shall be given first consideration in a promotion to a job on a higher wage guide in the same exchange and work group (Plant Craft, Plant Clerical, Traffic Control, Commercial) when the individual has the necessary qualifications to efficiently and effectively perform the work.

Background of Dispute

On January 29, 1961, the Company promoted *R* to the job of PBX-Repairman. For pay purposes this job falls in Group 7. The case centers on *P's* claim that he should have been assigned this job.

For purposes of the Labor Agreement, *P's* seniority date is April 16, 1956, and that of *R* is September 25, 1956. Both employees were originally hired as Linemen, a job which falls in Group 4. Subsequently, the grievant was promoted to the job styled Combination-man, a Group 6 job. He was promoted to this job about 2½ years after he was hired and was serving in this job when the circumstances of this case arose. *R* was promoted to Storekeeper, a Group 5 job, and held this job until the Company promoted him to PBX-Repairman.

Position of the Parties

Union

The Union alleges that under the circumstances of this case the Company violated Paragraph 21.1 of the Labor Agreement. At the heart of the Union's case is the contention that under this provision the Company is obligated to promote employees on the basis of seniority. Thus, it stated: "It is apparent that this paragraph in short provides that promotions be by seniority." The Union claims that "the language of Paragraph 21.1 is clear and unambiguous. It means just what it states," and advises that "in construction of contracts, the language is to be given its usual and ordinary meaning . . . (and) Courts have repeatedly ruled that where a contractual relation exists by virtue of a written contract expressed in clear and unambiguous language, the Courts will not look further to construe it." Applying this construction of Paragraph 21.1 to the facts of the instant case, the Union's position is that since *P* has greater seniority than *R*, the grievant should have obtained the PBX-Repairman job. Therefore, the Company violated Paragraph 21.1 because it failed to promote on a seniority basis, the Union claims.

It argues that Paragraph 21.1 does not require the senior employee "to have experience so as to be able to efficiently and effectively perform the work. The only requirement stated is that the employee has the *necessary qualifications to efficiently and effectively perform the work.*" If the employee has the qualifications to perform the work, the promotion becomes effective immediately. If, however, he does not have the necessary qualifications to perform the work, the Union avers that "the presumption [is] that he is to receive subsequent training." Thus, in either case, the Union holds that the senior employee is guaranteed the promotion. If he has the qualifications, he obtains the promotion immediately. If he does not have the qualifications, the Union argues that the intent of the relevant provision of the Labor Agreement presumes that the Company will train the senior employee to perform the duties of the job.

Although the Union believes that the literal and plain language of Paragraph 21.1 requires the Company to promote on the basis of seniority, it offers additional arguments to support this position. It argues that the change in the seniority language which occurred with the execution of the 1953 Labor Agreement is evidence of the validity of this position. Thus, "the Company insisted on showing the history of the Promotion and Reclassification Section 21. In so doing it introduced contracts dated May 16, 1952, May 17, 1953, and the August 30, 1959, contract. A studied review of these contracts actually supports the Union's position."

Beyond the contention that the language *per se* of Paragraph 21.1 requires promotion by seniority alone, the Union claims that the Company failed to adhere to standards laid down in this provision of the contract when it promoted R. In this respect, the Union claims that the Company promoted R when it compared his qualifications with those of P. It argues that Paragraph 21.1 makes "no mention . . . of comparison of qualifications of employees with other employees. That provision was eliminated in the 1953 contract." That the Company used the comparison method to promote R, the Union urges, is made evident by the testimony of B:

> We declared in that conference that they were not qualified because "qualified" implies that he is fit—able to take over the duties without training. This was not their case. We determined that R had the majority of the qualifications that were necessary—the majority over the two applicants or candidates.

In addition, the Union avers that Paragraph 21.1 not only precludes qualification comparison between employees, but also forbids the Company from choosing "the best qualified employee" for the promotion. Further, it rejects the contention that the Company has "any right to unilaterally establish factors to be used in the determination as to whether an employee has the qualifications to efficiently and effectively perform the work."

The Union alleges that in by-passing P, the Company "acted arbitrarily and in lack of good faith." This allegation is based upon the Union's assessment of the procedure which the Company used in the selection. On the assumption that the promotion was based on the comparison of the qualifications between the two employees in question, the Union alleges that it was "done without an adequate determining principle; not governed by any fixed rules, procedures, or standards." The Union also alleges that the Company made the selection without determining the facts, and since it did not ascertain the facts, it could not make a fair decision. In summary, on this issue of procedure, the Union states "in comparing qualifications of individual employees for the purpose of determining who is best qualified for promotion, exacting ground rules must not only be established but must be known and followed by those who are required to grade or evaluate employee qualifications. To do otherwise would make a mockery of a promotion clause and destroy the morale of the employee group."

Finally, the Union cited other arbitration decisions in support of its position.

On these grounds the Union requests that the grievance be granted.

Company

On its part the Company argues that it did not violate the Labor Agreement under the circumstances of this case. The Company's position is that seniority is a basis for promotion only when an employee has the necessary qualifications to efficiently and effectively perform the work of the job. In this respect, it states as follows: "It is also the Company's position that the language contained in the present Agreement clearly provides that the Company should consider seniority first only when the individual has the necessary qualifications tu efficiently and effectively perform the work." *P*, the Company contends, did not have the qualifications to perform the job effectively and efficiently, and, therefore, he does not have the right to the promotion. It claims that the change in the seniority language in 1953 provides the Company with full authority to determine the qualifications of employees for jobs which are to be filled by promotion. Since this change, the Company alleges that "the Union no longer shares in the determination of qualifications." In the instant case the Company determined the qualifications needed for the job in question, and further determined that *P* did not have these qualifications. Therefore, the grievant did not have the right for the promotion under the Labor Agreement, the Company avers.

Finally, the Company argues that it provided *P* with opportunities to obtain the technical qualifications for the job in question, but "the record shows he did not take advantage of them." In this respect the Company refers to a Company-sponsored course, "Fundamentals of Electricity," offered at *V* University. *P*, the Company points out, did not enroll in this course though he was selected to attend.

Discussion of the Evidence

Seniority and paragraph 21.1

At the heart of this proceeding is the determination of whether the language and intent of Paragraph 21.1 requires promotions strictly on the basis of seniority: does Paragraph 21.1 require promotions on a straight and strict seniority basis? A basic position of the Union is that promotions are to be made on a strict seniority basis: "it is apparent that this paragraph in short provides that promotions be by Seniority." If, in fact, Paragraph 21.1 requires promotions on a straight seniority basis, there need be no further inquiry into the merits of this case. P had seniority over R, and if the Union position is correct, the grievance must be granted forthwith.

In making this determination, it is worthwhile to determine the development of the current language of Paragraph 21.1. It was first adopted in the contract negotiated in 1953. In the 1952 contract the promotion policy was incorporated in Paragraph 22.1 and Paragraph 22.1–1.

22.1. Seniority shall be given first consideration in promotions and reclassifications within the bargaining unit when the individuals have equal and sufficient qualifications to efficiently and effectively perform the work.

22.1–1. Tests and/or other methods of determining qualifications may be used by the Company after review by the certified Union Representative.

In the 1953 contract the parties eliminated former Paragraph 22.1–1, and changed Paragraph 22.1 to read as follows:

Seniority shall be given first consideration in a promotion to a job on a higher wage guide in the same group (Plant Craft, Plant Clerical, Traffic, Commercial) when the individual has the necessary qualifications to efficiently and effectively perform the work.

In the current (1960) Labor Agreement, the promotion language is contained in Paragraph 21.1, as cited previously.

Now, for purposes of this case it is of crucial importance to notice that in the 1953 and current labor agreements, the parties did not eliminate the standard of qualifications for employees who are being considered for promotion. Though it is true that changes were made—elimination of Paragraph 21.1–1 and the "equal and sufficient" language—the parties did not intend that promotions be awarded on a strict seniority basis. Without belaboring the point, it is plain that the parties have agreed to give seniority first consideration when the individual *"has the necessary qualifications to efficiently and effectively perform the work."* It is quite clear from this language that seniority is to govern promotions *after* an assessment is made of the employee's qualifications.

Clearly, if the parties had intended to promote employees strictly on the basis of seniority, they would not have included the qualification phrase in Paragraph 21.1. If this were their intention, why did not the parties agree to a statement such as this: "Seniority shall be the only consideration in the making of promotions."

Note that Paragraph 21.1 does not state that seniority shall be the *only* consideration. It states that it shall be the *first* consideration *when* an employee has the necessary qualifications to perform the job. Thus, it conditions seniority with a qualification determination. Certainly, the language which the parties adopted is a far cry from language which would require promotions *strictly and only* on a length-of-service basis. In short, the Arbitrator simply cannot find in the current language of Paragraph 21.1, or in its development, that the parties agreed to a straight seniority system for promotions.

A fair and reasonable reading of the language precludes any such finding. In the last analysis, what the Union would have the Arbitrator do is to shut his eyes to the qualification phrase of Paragraph 21.1 and stop reading the provision after the word "Commercial." This would be as much an improper procedure for the Arbitrator to follow as in another case to read out of the contract language which protects some job right of an employee. No arbitrator who desires to justify the trust placed in him may ignore language in a collective bargaining contract.

Past practice

Indeed, this Arbitrator's analysis of the contractual language is buttressed by evidence dealing with the experience of the parties. At times, the way in which the parties to a contract apply it is of great significance in the construction of its terms in arbitration. That the Arbitrator is aware of the importance of "past practice" is made evident by the fact that upon occasion he has decided cases based upon the practice of the parties.

In the instant case, there is evidence that seniority has not been used invariably as the basis for promotion. Undoubtedly, there have been many occasions in which the senior employee obtained the promotion over a junior service employee who may have been considered. In fact, it is probably safe to conclude that there have been many more cases wherein senior employees have obtained promotions over junior service employees than the reverse.

However, what is of importance is that there have been instances wherein the Company has promoted junior service employees over senior employees. If the Union's position is to have merit, there should not be a single instance since 1953 wherein senior employees have been deprived a promotion in favor of junior employees. If the Union is correct in its basic position that Paragraph 21.1 means that the senior employee is guaranteed the promotion regardless of his qualifications, how does one explain away the instances wherein this has not occurred?

A Company witness testified that in August, 1959, he was promoted to the job of PBX-Repairman, the same job involved in the instant case. He testified that prior to the obtaining of the promotion he asked the Company for and received literature dealing with the elements of electricity. He also testified that there were more senior employees than he who did not get the job. True, this witness testified that the senior men whom he by-passed "did not want the job at that time," but still it is somewhat significant and revealing that here we have a junior employee by-passing senior employees in a promotion.

Further, Supervisor *B* testified *without contradiction*, that in October, 1959, three senior men who indicated interest in promotions did not receive them. Of great significance is the fact that one of these employees filed a grievance, but it was rejected by the Company and the case was apparently dropped. The Arbitrator would not conclude on the basis of this single instance that the Union had necessarily agreed with the Company that promotions need not be awarded on the basis of seniority, but again what is significant is that here we have another instance which is consistent with the Arbitrator's analysis that Paragraph 21.1 does not guarantee promotions on the basis of seniority. If these few instances do not add up to what arbitrators would hold as a binding "past practice," it follows nevertheless that there is evidence which is *consistent* and *not inconsistent* with the Arbitrator's judgment.

Qualifications of grievant

The upshot of the previous discussion is simply that the grievant is not entitled to be promoted to the PBX-Repairman job merely because he has greater seniority than the employee whom the Company promoted. He would be entitled to the job if he had the "necessary qualifications to efficiently and effectively perform the work" of the job in question when the promotion was made. If the evidence demonstrates that he possessed the necessary qualifications, he would have the contractual right to the promotion. If, on the other hand, the evidence shows that *P* lacked the necessary qualifications, it will be required to dismiss his complaint.

The job in question is styled PBX-Repairman. In Exhibit 1, page 45, of the Labor Agreement there appears the following statement:

PBX-REPAIRMAN
Installation and maintenance of PBX or PABX systems and stations that require inside wiring only.

Of course, if the basic position of the Union were upheld, it would not be necessary to inquire into the qualifications of the grievant to fill the job in question since under that theory *P* would automatically be entitled to the promotion. Since the Arbitrator has rejected such an interpretation of Paragraph 21.1, it becomes necessary to assess the qualifications of the grievant in terms of the job in question.

In this connection *B's* testimony relative to essential qualifications for the PBX-Repairman job becomes of vital importance. He was questioned at great length as to these qualifications, and on this issue was subjected to a most searching cross-examination on the part of Union Counsel. At certain points his testimony is not clear and precise. Such shortcomings have been pointed out in the Union's post-hearing brief and duly considered by the Arbitrator.

Nevertheless, *B* pointed out in clear fashion the basic qualifications of the job: ". . . In the first place, it is that the fundamentals, or familiarity with the fundamentals of electricity is basic. This is the thing that all the rest of the man's knowledge rounds on. Whether he has any knowledge or familiarity with it or whether he doesn't would make a great deal of difference;" and his answer to the following question is precise:

Q. For the specific job of a PBX-Repairman, what is one of the most important factors, looking at it over-all either technical or nontechnical?

A. Knowledge or familiarity with the fundamentals of electricity and circuitry.

Of great significance is the fact that at no point was such testimony challenged or contradicted. In short, the Arbitrator must conclude that a most basic qualification for the job in question is knowledge of the fundamentals of electricity and circuitry. If this were not *the* basic qualification, it would have been expected that *B's* testimony in this respect would have been refuted and challenged. As the record shows, there was much testimony as to the nontechnical factors involved in the job and reference to some technical factors. All these factors, however, must be subordinated to the uncontradicted testimony that knowledge of the fundamentals of electricity and circuitry is the outstanding qualification required of an employee aspiring to the job of PBX-Repairman. *It is emphasized that B's testimony in this respect went unchallenged and uncontradicted.*

Now, the question arises as to the right of the Company to assess the qualifications of the grievant in terms of the basic qualification of the job in question. It is a well recognized principle of labor relations, underscored by countless arbitration decisions, that unless a contract provides to the contrary, the employer has the right to make the initial determination of the qualifications of employees. Thus, when a contract

. . . is silent as to how and by whom the determination of qualifications is to be made, management is entitled to make the initial determination, subject to challenge by the union on the grounds that the management's decision was unreasonable under the facts, or capricious, arbitrary, or discriminatory . . . even where the contract makes the employer the sole judge [of qualifications], arbitrators have held that management's action must not be unreasonable, capricious, arbitrary, or discriminatory.

In reviewing the entire record, the Arbitrator finds that the judgment of the Company was correct in determining that the grievant did not have the "necessary qualifications to efficiently and effectively perform the work" of the job in question. Reference is again made to the uncontradicted evidence that knowledge of the fundamentals of electricity and circuitry constitute the basic qualification for the PBX-Repairman job. P testified as to his duties as a Combination-man: "We install telephones, maintain the lines, and maintain the telephones on the premises; trouble shoot and do repair work." However efficiently the grievant performed these duties, the fact remains that there is no evidence that he possessed the knowledge of the fundamentals of electricity and circuitry at the time the promotion was made. In short, at no place in the entire record is there any statement, or even a strong inference, that P possessed such knowledge.

There is no need to belabor this point. There was no protest to B's statement that a most basic qualification was a knowledge of electricity and circuitry. The record is completely barren of evidence demonstrating that the grievant possessed such knowledge.

Neither does the evidence demonstrate that the Company discriminated against the grievant. Whatever his reasons, the fact remains that the grievant refused to attend a Company-sponsored course called "Fundamentals of Electricity." The course was started originally on September 10, 1960, and terminated on January 26, 1961. It was held on the campus of V University. Because the first course was oversubscribed by the employees of the Company, a second one was offered from January 3, 1961, and ended on May 25, 1961. Classes met two days a week for one hour and a half. Tuition for the course amounted to $26, with the Company paying $18 and the employee $8. Also, the Company did not reimburse the employee for travel or for his dinner. The grievant was selected for the first course, but refused to attend because of family reasons. He lives ten miles from the site of the V campus.

It is true, of course, that the course was voluntary and the Union stresses this point. Still the fact is that forty-three employees enrolled in the first course even though it was voluntary. In fact, since there were spaces for only fifteen employees, the second course was arranged. That there is no grounds for a charge of discrimination against the grievant is made evident by the fact that P was one of the original fifteen employees selected for the first course. Moreover, the voluntary character of the course does not erase that fact that the grievant did not possess the knowledge of electricity that he would have undoubtedly obtained had he attended the course.

Finally, a charge of discrimination against the grievant under the circumstances of this case cannot stand because the record does not prove that all PBX-Repairmen are promoted from the Combination-man classification. *B* testified *without contradiction* that they (PBX-Repairmen) may be "laterally promoted, if I can use that term, from a Cable Splicer classification, and they may again make a lateral movement from Switchmen's classification. They might even come from the ranks of our engineers." Apparently it is true that Combination-men are frequently promoted to the job of PBX-Repairman. As stated, *R*, a former Combination-man, was promoted to the job, though it should be recalled that *R* obtained and received material from the Company dealing with the fundamentals of electricity. Further, it is noted that *P* testified that during the past two years, three Combination-men were promoted to PBX-Repairmen. Still the fact remains that there was no refutation of *R's* aforementioned testimony. Clearly, if the proof were clear-cut and convincing that *all* PBX-Repairmen were promoted from the Combination-man classification, there would be a strong basis to find that the Company discriminated against the grievant. However, since there is no such proof, a finding of discrimination against the grievant on these grounds would not be warranted.

Company procedure

The obligation of the Arbitrator is to determine whether or not *P* has the contractual right to the job of PBX-Repairman under the terms of Paragraph 21.1 of the Labor Agreement. On the basis of the entire record the finding is that he does not have this right. Though he has greater seniority credits than the employee whom the Company promoted, the evidence does not show that he has the necessary qualifications to efficiently and effectively perform the work associated with the job in question. Undisputed evidence demonstrates that a most essential qualification of the job is the knowledge of the fundamentals of electricity and circuitry. Nothing in the record demonstrates that *P* possessed this qualification at the time that the promotion was made. For this reason, the Arbitrator cannot grant this grievance.

There is the temptation to compare the qualifications of *R* and *P*. However, such a comparison is not to be made under the terms of Paragraph 21.1. When the parties executed their 1953 contract, they struck from their promotion policy the requirement to compare the qualifications of employees who are candidates for promotion. Consequently, the Arbitrator has no right or inclination to compare the qualifications of the two employees in question. Under the 1952 contract, such a comparison would be in order, and, indeed, required under Paragraph 21.1 of that contract. Such a procedure is not permitted under the instant Labor Agreement.

The Arbitrator notes that the Company apparently did compare the qualifications of the two employees before the promotion was made. That this was done is made clear by the testimony of *B*:

> We decided in that conference that they were not qualified because "qualified" implies that he is able to take over the duties without training. This was not their case. We determined that *R* had the majority of the qualifications that were necessary—the majority over the two applicants or candidates.

To the extent that the Company did compare the qualifications, it engaged in a procedure which is not called for by the terms of the Labor Agreement. The Arbitrator agrees fully with the Union that in Paragraph 21.1 "no mention is made of comparison of qualifications of employees with other employees," and "nor does the paragraph state that the employee must be the best qualified employee."

However, after due consideration, the Arbitrator cannot find for the grievant on the grounds that the Company engaged in a practice which is not called for by the Labor Agreement. The fact still remains that *P* did not have the necessary qualifications for the job in question within the meaning of Paragraph 21.1 at the time that the promotion was made. By far, this is the outstanding feature of the case, and the gap in the grievant's qualifications cannot be remedied on the grounds that the Company did compare his qualifications with those of *R*. Had the record demonstrated that the grievant possessed the necessary qualifications, he would, of course, have been entitled to the job.

During the Arbitration hearing the Union had every opportunity to enter into the record the qualifications of the grievant. At no place in the entire record is there any evidence whatsoever that the grievant possessed knowledge of the fundamentals of electricity and circuitry. And it should be stressed once again that there was no challenge, refutation, or contradiction to the testimony that a most basic qualification of the job in question was the knowledge of the fundamentals of electricity and circuitry. In the light of this analysis, the Arbitrator would not be applying or interpreting the language and intent of Paragraph 21.1 properly if he awarded the job to the grievant. In his judgment this would be an incorrect approach on the basis of the entire record even though he frankly admits that the Company procedure in comparing the qualifications of the two employees is not consistent with the language of Paragraph 21.1.

Undoubtedly, the Union would have the Arbitrator put the grievant on the job on the basis of this Company error. Without minimizing this Company shortcoming, the Arbitrator believes he would do more violence to the language and intent of Paragraph 21.1 if he granted the grievance on this basis than to deny the grievance while fully being aware of the Company's improper procedure. Clearly, the balancing of equities, and the determination to reach a decision which clearly reflects the intent of the parties is a frequent chore of arbitrators. In the instant case there is the problem of balancing of the equities in the light of the intended use of Paragraph 21.1. After all, the error of the Company did not attach to the essence and meaning of Paragraph 21.1. It was correct in its judgment that the grievant did not possess the necessary qualifications. Thus, its error was procedural and not substantive.

QUESTIONS

1. Why did the Arbitrator refuse to compare the qualifications of the grievant and R for the job in question?
2. Would you have granted the grievance on the grounds that the company did make such a comparison?
3. What sort of contractual language would have assured the grievant the right to the PBX-Repairman job?

CASE NO. 9

Discharge

(Case No. 9 is an arbitration case involving the discharge of employees under collective bargaining agreements. Though the facts of the case are rather bizarre, it still contains the customary issues involved in a discharge case. It should make very interesting reading, but the student should pay particular attention to the elements of proof which are required in disciplinary cases. Not only must a company rule under which an employee is disciplined be fair and reasonable, but the employer must be able to *prove* that the employee performed the act cited by the company as grounds for discharge. In this case, the arbitrator, as he must in all cases involving discipline, paid close attention to the proof, even though the act which gave rise to the discharge was somewhat out of the ordinary.)

This case has been initiated by the filing of grievances by A and B. A filed his grievance on August 8, 1961, such grievance stating as follows:

Protest of discharge dated 8–4–61. I feel this discharge was too severe disciplinary action.

I don't think the charge was severe enough to warrant this type of disciplinary action.

I feel that my record with the Company should be considered.

Therefore, I am requesting to be reinstated without loss of seniority and with full back pay.

B filed his grievance on August 7, 1961, such grievance stating as follows:

B, clock no. _____, was discharged by management on August 4 at twelve hundred hours (12.00).
Request restoration to his job with full back pay.

Having failed to resolve the grievances in the Grievance Procedure, the parties have instituted this arbitration to determine the dispute.

Relevant Contractual Language

Articles of the Labor Agreement which are relevant to this case provide as follows:

ARTICLE III

Section 1. "The Management of the Business of the Employer and the direction of its Personnel, including the right to hire, discipline, or discharge employees for just cause, to transfer, promote them or lay them off and to maintain discipline, order, and efficiency in its plants are the sole responsibility of the Employer, providing the exercise of such rights does not conflict with the provisions of the Agreement.

Section 2. "The type of products to be developed or manufactured, the location of the plants, the schedules of development of production, the methods, processes, and means of conducting its business are the employer's prerogatives.

ARTICLE XIII

Section 1. "Employees are subject to discharge or dicliplinary action for just cause. Where any discharge or disciplinary action is taken and the affected employee feels he has been unjustly dealt with, he may submit his case to the Grievance Committee for review of the Employer and it shall be settled according to the Grievance Procedure as provided in this agreement. If it is found that the employee was unjustly discharged or disciplined, he shall be reinstated without loss of seniority and with such back pay as shall be determined by the parties.

Section 2. "If a Grievance concerning a discharge or disciplinary action is not filed in writing within two (2) work days from the date of such action, then the action taken shall be considered final and the case closed.

Section 3. "In case of a discharge or disciplinary action, the Employer will notify the Steward of the Department involved as soon as possible."

Basic Question

At the outset of the arbitration hearing, the parties submitted the following question to be determined by this Arbitrator: Was the discharge of *B* and *A* for just cause?

The background

B, age 39, had completed two years' four months' service with the Company before he was discharged whereas A, age 41, had completed four years' seven months' service when he was discharged. At the time of the discharge B was classified as a Unit Assembler. At one time this employee served as a Steward of the Union. When he was discharged, A was serving as a Maintenance Man.

The discharges resulted from an altercation between the employees on August 3, 1961. It is alleged by the Company that B provoked the disturbance by committing a "very distasteful act" on the person of A, and that after the act was done, A in turn struck B. On August 4, a meeting was held on the situation. The following persons attended the meeting: the grievants; H, General Foreman; S, Stock Room Foreman; C, Assistant General Foreman; and the Vice President of the Union, L. At the close of the meeting, the Company discharged the two employees.

Position of the Parties

Company

The Company contends that both employees were discharged for "just cause" within the meaning of the contract. It claims that B instigated the altercation by "committing a very distasteful act, one that is not consistent with the safe and decent behavior of employees. An act of this kind could cause serious injury under certain circumstances." Hence, the Company claims that B's discharge was justified because he provoked the disturbance. With respect to A, the Company claims that he had other "recourses to stop this unpleasant horseplay. He should have reported such conduct to his supervisor, which he did not do, but took matters in his own hands and used physical violence." Thus, the Company believes that A, though not the instigator of the altercation, deserves discharge because he should have reported the incident to supervision rather than striking B.

Further, the Company claims that there is in force in the plant "a well-known and strictly enforced policy of the Employer" that employees instigating or participating in a fight or disturbance on Company premises are subject to discharge.

On these grounds, the Company requests that the Arbitrator deny the grievance.

Union

On the grievants' side, the Union argues that the discharges were not for just cause within the meaning of the Labor Agreement. It points out that discharge is a "capital punishment" and that the

Company did not prove that the employees deliberately engaged in a fight. It claims further that "the right of an employee to defend himself from attack should not be ignored."

It characterizes the disturbance between the employees as "an accident that happened between the two employees." Thus, it was not a "fight," but an "accident," and, therefore, the discharges were not warranted. In addition, it directs attention to the record of the employees, specifically alleging that in the meeting of August 4, a Company representative voluntarily stated that "*A* was a good employee."

A part of the Union's case rests upon the procedure under which the employees were discharged. It points out that the stewards of the department in which the employees worked were not notified of the discharges within the meaning of Article XIII, Section 3. Further, it claims that the meeting of August 4 was not a true meeting to discuss the merits of the case, but rather the "Management had their minds made up before the meeting of August 4."

On these grounds the Union requests that the grievance be granted.

Discussion of the Evidence

The disturbance of August 3

The circumstances of this case occurred on August 3, 1961, in the shipping area in the Company's plant. On this day *B* was serving as a truck driver. *A* was repairing a high-lift fork truck. Apparently either he or a supervisor told *B* to obtain and deliver a quantity of distilled water which was needed for the aforementioned truck's battery. *B* obtained the water and placed it on the dock. Thereupon, *B* left the area to either pick up or deliver some mail.

When he returned to the shipping area, he apparently believed that the water was not where he placed it. To determine whether it was still on the dock, *B* walked toward the shipping dock. It was in this vicinity that *A* was repairing the truck. To get to the dock, *B* squeezed between the fork lift truck and *A*. The immediate location of the fracas was a narrow passage.

Up to this point the facts are not in dispute. However, the record becomes somewhat contradictory after this time. *A* testified that when *B* came between him and the truck he, *B*, grabbed *A's* person in the area of the buttocks. In slang, but descriptive language, the allegation is that *B* "goosed" *A*. Thereupon *A* hit *B*.

A does not deny that he hit *B*. But *B* denies that he committed the aforementioned act. *B* testified on this point as follows: "I went over to *A* and placed my right hand on his shoulder to get his attention. I stepped between *A* and the lift truck and possibly brushed him and he hit me."

In reply to the question as to what *B* did with his left hand, *B* first testified that "I possibly could have brushed him with my left hand." Upon being queried further as to what he did with his left hand, *B* then testified: "I do recall what I did with my left hand—I placed it on my stomach to push my stomach in."

The disturbance was witnessed by *S*, Stock Room Foreman. He happened to be standing in the shipping area when the incident occurred. He testified as follows: "I was in the shipping area along with the grievants on August 3. I was standing about 6 feet from them. *B* walked up to *A* and put one hand on his shoulder and 'goosed' him with the other. *A* struck him."

Though the presence of *S* at the scene of the disturbance was not denied by either of the grievants, *B* testified that the foreman was not standing in a position so as to get an accurate picture of the circumstances. The burden of *B's* testimony in this respect is that *A*, standing in front of *B*, and between *B* and *S*, obscured *S's* vision to the extent that the foreman could not have seen what *B* did with his left hand. Thus, *B* testified: "*S* was there—I don't know what he saw. But he was standing in front of *A*. I don't see how he could have seen my left hand move."

Evaluation of the evidence: B's role in the disturbance

If *B's* version of the affair is accepted at face value, *A* struck him without provocation. As such, *B* is completely guiltless, and if anyone should be discharged, it is *A*. It would be difficult for this Arbitrator to believe that *A*, a mature man with a spotless record in the Company, and particularly with the complete absence of any evidence demonstrating that he hit anyone else, would strike *B* just because *B* brushed against him. Such a finding just does not seem reasonable to this Arbitrator.

Certainly, it must have been that *A* had a stronger provocation to hit *B* than merely being brushed either by *B's* left hand or by his stomach. Added to this is the testimony of *S*. Clearly, he had no motivation except to relate the circumstances as he saw them. Indeed, Foreman *S* did not even report the incident to his management. The discharges were touched off when *B* himself told the Assistant General Foreman, *C*, on August 3 of the affair so that a medical report could be filled out. Apparently *A* struck *B* very hard causing much pain to *B*. In short, if *S* desired to get the grievants into trouble, he would have reported the incident. Instead, he did not come forward with his testimony until such time as an investigation was touched off by *B* himself.

It is difficult to find that *S* was not telling an accurate story. Even *B* testified that he *B* "did not know" what *S* saw. His testimony was that he believed that the foreman was not in the position to determine the accuracy of what happened. Even though *A* stood between S and B, this does not necessarily mean that he did not have a good view of what B did with his left hand. After all, the foreman was only standing six feet from the grievants at the time of the incident.

The Arbitrator, therefore, accepts the testimony of S. There is no reason to dispute it since there is no basis to believe that the foreman had any motivation except to tell an accurate story. Hence, there is the testimony of A and S that B did "goose" A. There is not a scrap of evidence demonstrating that their testimony constitutes a kind of a conspiracy to get B in trouble. It is stressed that the foreman remained silent until an official investigation was touched off by B's report to the Assistant General Foreman. Likewise, A did not report the incident, though he testified that B committed a very distasteful act to his person. Such conduct on the part of the foreman and A does not add up to a plot designed to jeopardize B.

Events of August 2

In addition, there are the circumstances of the preceding day. A testified that B on August 2 "goosed" him. A testified that after this incident he told B: "This is mine, God-damn it; keep your hands to yourself." With respect to the August 2 circumstances, B testified that "if A warned me, I did not hear the warning" and that "I never 'goosed' A before." What impressed the Arbitrator concerning the circumstances of August 2 is that the record shows that B's testimony was first "if A warned me, I did not hear it." After this was stated, B then denied the act. If, in fact, B had not committed the act on August 2, is it not reasonable to believe that he would have immediately denied the act? Why did he first state that "if A warned me, I did not hear it?"

Of course, this discharge was not motivated by the circumstances of August 2. There was no report of this incident before the matter was brought to a head by the events of August 3. It becomes important only to the extent that there is some evidence, though admittedly not 100 per cent perfect, that B had "goosed" A before August 3.

Seriousness of B's act

In the light of the entire record, the Arbitrator finds that B did "goose" A on August 3. In his defense, B testified that "what happened was not a fight—not horseplay—it was not premeditated." If it were neither of these things, B concludes that his discharge was not justified.

The Arbitrator does not find any need to clarify the act of B in some neat category. He does not have to find that it constitutes fighting or an immoral act or innocent horseplay. The fact is that what *B* did do was to provoke a disturbance. The best evidence of the disturbance is the blow which *A* struck. If there is a fixed principle in arbitration, it is that professional and seasoned arbitrators invariably uphold the right of a company to assure that its plant is a safe place to work. Scores of decisions demonstrate that experienced arbitrators hold that a company's premises are for work and not for fighting, horseplay, and the like. Whatever job protection is afforded by a contract does not normally extend to employees who endanger the lives and physical well-being of other employees by provoking fights or disturbances. This is such a fixed principle of arbitration that there is no need to cite precedents.

However one classifies *B's* act, the fact remains that he could have caused serious injury to *A* and to himself. As will be developed below, the Arbitrator believes that *A's* blow was a psychological reflex action. Thus, what if *A* held a lethal weapon in his hand at the time, such as a tie-rod or some other piece of metal? Conceivably, *A* could have hit *B* with such an instrument causing him serious injury. Or what if *A* had jumped and hit himself against some solid object, or fallen and caused serious injury. People are of different psychological makeup and react differently to stimuli.

Thus, *B's* act could have resulted in serious injury to himself and/or to *A*. At the minimum, the evidence does show that *B* was struck and was injured. About this, there is no speculation. It is of little importance whether or not the action was premeditated. That no more serious injury resulted is indeed fortunate.

The Company has the right to take prudent action to assure that its premises are a safe place to work. It has the right to assure that production is carried out free from horseplay and/or fighting. Further, employees have the right to work in a climate free from disturbances occasioned by horseplay and fighting. Indeed, the Company would be derelict in its duty to its employees if it did not act positively to assure that the work process is carried out in a climate free from harm resulting from employee provocations, horseplay, and fighting.

On the basis of these observations, the Arbitrator finds that *B's* discharge was for just cause within the meaning of the contract. At the minimum, his action was innocent horseplay. Still, what he did do was to create a disturbance which was inimical to the safety of himself and other employees.

A's role in the disturbance

The Company discharged *A* because he struck *B*. To support this action, the Company points out that it has been its policy to discharge employees for fighting regardless of the degree of guilt and provocation. Hence, the Company feels that no exception should be made in this case. *A* should have reported *B's* conduct to supervision without resorting to violence, the Company adds.

In general, the policy of disciplining all employees engaging in an altercation is sound because frequently the situation is so confused that it is impossible to determine the shades of guilt and responsibility of the participating employees. Further, the rule makes sense since at times employees, though provoked, will engage in violence far beyond that which is necessary to defend themselves from bodily harm. Further, the Arbitrator agrees that an employee, though provoked, should make every reasonable attempt to avoid further conflict. The plant is for work and is not a battleground to test courage, manhood, and the like. In short, as far as humanly possible, employees have the responsibility to minimize disturbances resulting from fighting or horseplay.

The Arbitrator has tried to support by these observations his opinion that the aforementioned Company policy in principle and as a general rule is correct. It tends to accomplish the objective of making the plant a safe and efficient place in which to carry out production.

Still, the policy cannot be applied automatically under all circumstances. There must be some assessment of the merits of a particular case. Suppose, for example, an employee without any provocation takes a lethal weapon in his hand to use against a second employee. This employee defends himself by striking the first employee. Certainly, under such circumstances it cannot be argued successfully that both employees should be discharged.[1]

Admittedly, this hypothetical example is not parallel to the circumstances of the instant case. *B* did not strike *A* in the common-sense meaning of the term. *A's* blow probably was not necessary to defend himself from further bodily harm. The evidence, however, is crystal clear that *B* provoked the disturbance by engaging in an act which even the Company states is "very distasteful." In short, there is no question as to who provoked the disturbance. It was *B*. Added to this is the nature of the provocation. As stated, people act differently to the same kind of stimulus. To some people, being "goosed" would not be of serious consequences—it could be laughed off as a big joke. To other persons, like *A*, this is very serious because of psychological considerations. The Arbitrator sincerely

---

[1]A policy to the effect that all employees participating in a plant disturbance are to be discharged regardless of shades of guilt has not been upheld under all circumstances by professional and experienced arbitrators. Thus: "Occasionally, apparently despairing of applying precisely just penalties to combatants in accordance with their degree of guilt, management sometimes tries to apply a general rule that all participants in a fight will be discharged, or otherwise disciplined equally, without regard to who started it or who inflicted more damage. Even this course of action has not been altogether successful." Lawrence Stessin, *Employee Discipline* (Washington, D.C.: Bureau of National Affairs, 1960), p. 94.

believes that the blow which *A* struck was an automatic reflex to the stimulus. *B* triggered the blow by his act.

The Company is correct in stating that it would have been better for *A* to have reported *B's* conduct to supervision instead of striking him. However, the Arbitrator believes that the application of the stimulus so enraged *A* that he was not capable of rational action. There is no evidence that *A* has ever struck another employee, or anyone else for that matter. Hence, under ordinary circumstances, it could be expected that *A* even under provocation would have reacted in a nonviolent manner. But what we have here is a kind of provocation which causes irrational conduct on the part of some people.

Further events of August 2

From these considerations, the Arbitrator believes that *A* should not be discharged. However, the fact is that *A* testified that *B* "goosed" him on August 2. Thus, the Arbitrator believes that *A* should have reported the incident of August 2 to Management, though the Arbitrator is fully aware that employees do not normally like to inform on each other. This, however, is beside the point since the objective should be a safe place to work. *A* was aware on August 2 that *B* had engaged in conduct which was very disturbing to him. He had the opportunity to report the situation to Management.

Thus, even if one argues that the blow which *A* struck on August 3 was an impulsive act, beyond his control, the same analysis does not apply for August 2. There was sufficient time for a proper report to be made to Management. After all, the enforcing of discipline in the plant is the responsibility of the Company.

In short, there is some guilt which *A* bears. He had the opportunity to make a report which would undoubtedly have staved off the circumstances of August 3. However distasteful it might have been for *A* to report *B* to Management, the fact is that he should have followed this course of action.

Still, on the basis of the entire record, the Arbitrator does not believe that *A* should be discharged for his part in the disturbance. By the time the parties will receive this award, *A* shall have been separated from the Company for a period of about four months. Thus, this period of time is a sufficiently long disciplinary period for *A* to have suffered for his failure to take prudent action on August 2. Further, this penalty should demonstrate to all concerned that this Arbitrator is of the conviction that employees have the duty to avert disturbances as far as humanly possible. In short, this suspension period, and not discharge, is the proper penalty for the part which *A* had in this affair.

Procedure Considerations

The Union contends that the Company did not follow the correct procedure at the time that the discharges were effected. To be sure, a company is obligated to follow contractual and reasonable procedures as a prerequisite to discipline even if the discipline on the merits is warranted. Specifically, the Union claims that the Company did not notify the Stewards of the grievants in accordance with Article XIII, Section 3, and that the meeting held on August 4 was not carried out in a spirit to get at the facts of the case. Note that the Union charges that the Management had "made up its mind before the meeting."

With respect to the lack of notice to the Stewards, the Union raises an important point. Certainly, this Arbitrator requires that a company honor the language of a labor agreement to which it has agreed. Should the Arbitrator order the reinstatement of both employees to their jobs with full back pay because the Company did not notify the Stewards as promptly as Section 3 implies? After due consideration, the Arbitrator does not believe that this would be the proper course of action under the circumstances of the case.

The obvious purpose of the notification requirement is to enable the Union to provide adequate representation to disciplined employees. By early and quick notification, the Union can more adequately defend the employees who have been discharged or otherwise disciplined. Though the Company did not comply with the technical meaning of Section 3, the fact is that vice president T participated in the August 4 meeting. Thus, there was present a ranking officer of the Union whose status is higher than the stewards. Certainly, he was in as good a position to represent the grievants as was a steward. In short, if the essence and meaning of Section 3 is to provide Union protection and representation to the grievants, the presence of the Union vice president fulfilled this objective. Note that the Union does not argue that T was not able to offer the grievants adequate protection in the August 4 meeting. Rather, its position is that there was a technical violation of Section 3. In short, the Union's position here is not substantive but technical. It might have been another matter if the evidence demonstrated that T for some reason did not provide the grievants with the same substantive protection as their stewards would have. No evidence of this sort is in the record.

In the second place, when the Company received the grievance a few days after the discharges, the stewards in question had been informed of the discipline because they signed the grievances. Thus, between August 4 and August 8 stewards S and E were informed of the discipline. Their signatures appear on the grievances. To be sure, the essence of Section 3 is that there should be notification to stewards before the elapse of three to four days. The Arbitrator takes full cognizance of this consideration.

Still the fact remains that there was Union representation for the grievants in the August 4 meeting in the person of vice president *T*, and between this date and the dates on which the grievances were filed, the stewards were notified. For these reasons, the Arbitrator finds that there was substantial compliance with Section 3. Though there may not have been technical compliance, there was substantive compliance, and, therefore, the Arbitrator does not believe that justice under the contract would be done if he used a technicality to reinstate employees.

With respect to the meeting itself, the Arbitrator has no way of knowing whether the Company had "made up its mind" before the session. It is impossible to make such a determination on the basis of the story. Though *B* testified that the "facts were not brought to light that it was not a fight, it was not horseplay, it was not premeditated," the Arbitrator does not find that he was not permitted to speak at the meeting. Certainly, not even *B* testified that he was muzzled at the meeting. Further, *B* testified that he was put in a position of either calling *A* a "liar or forfeiting his job," stating that he "did not make it a practice to call anyone a liar." Frankly, the Arbitrator does not understand this line of reasoning. According to the record, *A* stated in the meeting that *B* had "goosed" him and that he hit him. If *A* did not have his facts straight on August 4, it was up to *B* to correct the record. The Arbitrator does not see how *B* was put in an unfavorable position in the August 4 meeting because of the desire of the Company to get the straight story from both of the grievants.

The Arbitrator does not believe that *B* did not obtain a fair hearing at the meeting as alleged by him. As stated, he had an opportunity to present his side of the story. If he tended to shield *A* by his reluctance to tell what he believed to be the truth, this was his choice and not that of the Company. Frankly, what the Arbitrator believes to be the basis of *B's* allegation of not getting a fair hearing is that the Company refused to put the same assessment on the facts as *B* did. It was not that there was a dearth of facts at the meeting—it was that *B* believes that the Company's interpretation of the facts is in error. However, the latter consideration is a far cry from a situation where a company arbitrarily refused a disciplined employee the opportunity to tell his side of the story.

Conclusion

Thus, the Arbitrator rejects the contention that the discharges should be put aside because of the way in which the August 4 meeting was conducted. Indeed, what is very curious to this Arbitrator is that vice president *T* did not appear at the arbitration hearing to corroborate the allegation that the meeting was not conducted in a fair manner. No explanation was offered for his absence, and the only ones who testified to the alleged unfairness of the meeting were the grievants themselves, and particularly, *B*. Perhaps the meeting was not conducted with all of the dignity and fairness of an arbitration hearing, but the Arbitrator does not find the necessary proof that the grievants could not tell their side of the affair.

Award

Grievance of *B*:

The grievance of *B* dated August 7, 1961, is denied on the grounds that he was discharged for just cause within the meaning of the Labor Agreement.

Grievance of *A*:

The grievance of *A* dated August 8, 1961, is granted to the extent that upon the receipt of this award the Company is directed to reinstate him on his job, without back pay, but without penalty to his seniority rights, on the grounds that under the circumstances of this case his discharge was too severe a penalty within the meaning of Article III and Article XIII of the Labor Agreement.

QUESTIONS

1. Do you believe that the arbitrator was wrong in suspending *A*? Why or why not?
2. Will this decision tend to impair the company's rule against fighting?
3. Would you have sustained the discharge of *B* if it did not cause a disturbance in the plant?

CASE NO. 10

Automation: Hiring from Outside to Fill Job Vacancy

(As in this case, it is sometimes cheaper for management to hire capable workers "off the street" to fill the jobs created by automation, rather than to fill the new jobs with current employees who may need training. Here, the new job was a result of the building of a new plant which contained a great deal of automated equipment. To fill it, the company hired new employees who were clearly well qualified for the positions. It rejected its own employees because of alleged shortcomings as far as *their* qualifications were concerned. Part of the case presented here by the company to defend its action against the grievance was that its own employee, the sole bidder for the job in question, had failed a test testing his aptitude for the job.

The case, of course, has grave implications, since depending upon the decision the basic interests of all concerned will be seriously affected. As in any arbitration case, however, the arbitrator must be guided by the language of the labor agreement bearing on the filling of job vacancies, and by the evidence which is relevant to the dispute.)

On October 30, 1961, *W* filed the following grievance:

I bid on a "maintenance helper" job classification and was turned down. Article VI, Section 10 of the contract states "the employee having the greatest seniority and who is capable and best qualified shall receive the job."

No man with greater seniority has bid for the job.

I have worked as a "maintenance helper" before at the plant. Therefore I see no reason why I can't do so in the future.

Having failed to resolve the grievance, the parties instituted this arbitration to determine the dispute.

Contractual Language

The following provisions of the Labor Agreement have been cited by the parties as relevant to this dispute:

ARTICLE VI

Section 1. Seniority rights shall prevail, subject to the ability of each employee to perform the work required. In the case of layoff, employees will be laid off in the reverse order of their seniority. Any controversy over the seniority standing of any employee on the seniority list shall be submitted for the grievance procedure.

Section 2. It is understood that seniority shall be departmental, subject, however, to the provisions in this section. In the event of a severe or unusual recession in the Company's business, disputes relating to the order of layoff of senior employees shall be subject to the grievance procedure.

    b. The employee claiming the right to a junior employee's job must have actually performed the job satisfactorily at this plant at a prior time.

    d. No probationary period for training will be granted to any senior employee claiming the right to a junior employee's job.

    e. The employees who remain to fill the available jobs must be able to perform the work as satisfactorily as the employee replaced.

Section 4. Casual labor may be employed for the performance of unskilled work in all departments throughout the plant. For the purpose of determining seniority, the provisions governing temporary employees shall apply to casual labor.

Section 10. An open job shall be defined as any job that requires additional personnel. Open jobs shall be filled in the following manner.

    a. Upon request the Personnel Office will furnish a list of all open jobs to the Union. Such list must be posted on all bulletin boards throughout the plant for three working days at the end of which time the job becomes closed.

b. Those employees desiring to do so may make applications on their own time for an open job by filling out an application during the time the job is open. Such employees will remain on their present jobs until called by the Personnel Office or Plant Superintendent, when they shall be interviewed for such jobs in order of seniority.

c. The employee having the greatest seniority who is capable and best qualified shall receive the job.

d. Employees bidding on a job in another department (interdepartmental bids) shall be based on plant seniority.

e. In event there is an opening in a higher classification within a department, departmental seniority shall prevail in bidding for the opening.

f. If an employee bids into another job or department he shall retain his previous departmental seniority for a period of one year. The reason being, protection in event the employee is not suited for the new job or abolishing of the new job.

ARTICLE VII

Section 5. The arbitrator may interpret the Agreement and apply it to the particular case presented to him but he shall, however, have no authority to add to, subtract from, or in any way modify the terms of this Agreement or any agreements made supplementary hereto. The decision of the arbitrator shall be final and binding upon both parties.

ARTICLE XX

Section 5. The supervision and control of all operations and the direction of all employees are vested solely in the Company. The Union, upon request, shall be informed fully concerning the reasons for layoffs, demotions, discharges, and transfers, and may submit the same for review in the manner provided for the submission of grievances.

Basic Question

The basic question to be determined in this proceeding is framed as follows: Under the circumstances of this case, was the grievant, *W*, entitled to the job of Maintenance Helper under the applicable provisions of the Labor Agreement?

Background

On October 17, 1961, the Company posted the following job for bid:

OPEN JOB BULLETIN

October 17, 1961

MAINTENANCE HELPER

2 Required

Age: 21–30 years

Education: High School graduate, or equivalent in practical experience. High School training should include several semesters in Manual Training.

Must be able to pass mechanical and other aptitude tests.

Should be in sound physical health.
Must furnish set of basic hand tools.
Start—$2.17 per hour
After 90 days—$2.22 per hour
After 1 year—$2.27 per hour

W was the only employee who bid on the job. Apparently a second employee also bid on it, but it appears that he withdrew his bid. Thus, for purposes of this case, the fact is that *W* was the only bargaining unit employee who bid for the job, which had been created by the building of a new plant using a variety of automated equipment.

W is forty-six years old, holds five years' seniority with the Company, and completed five years of grammar school, though the Navy considered him as having had the equivalent of eight years' schooling. He is classified as a Yardman and Clean-Up man in the Extraction Department.

On October 24, 1961, the Company administered a test, accepted in evidence as Company Exhibit No. 4, to the grievant. It was composed of five parts—four parts written and one part motor. *W* obtained a score of 1.2. According to the Company, a passing score is 2.0. Subsequently, the Company hired four new employees to fill the job in question. These employees also took the test and scored 2.0 or higher.

The Maintenance Helper classification was negotiated in the current Labor Agreement for the first time. Its starting rate is $2.17 per hour. For the first time the parties also established a classification in the instant contract called "Casual and Temporary Employees Labor Pool for Use in All Departments in Plant." This classification, hereinafter referred to as "Casual Employees," provided for a starting rate of $1.99.

The Maintenance Helper job is located in the Maintenance Department. This Department includes, beyond the new classification, the following jobs: Group A (Specialist), $2.73; Group B (General Repair), $2.48; Oilers, $2.49; and Painters, $2.48.

The dispute arises because the Company turned down the grievant's application for the job.

Position of the Parties

Union

It is the Union's basic contention that *W* is entitled to the job within the meaning of Article VI. The Union charges that the Company violated the contract by not giving the job to the grievant, and instead hired a number of men from the outside. Thus: "Instead of permitting the man who bid for the job, the Company hired a number of men from the outside on the basis of a testing system." With respect to the test, the Union argues that it did not agree to any testing system; that the Company did not have the right to exclude the grievant from the job on the basis of the test; and that even if the Company had a right to give tests, the particular test administered to the grievant was not a "good test."

In addition, the Union claims that the grievant has the qualifications to fill the job in question, and to buttress this contention it points to the work experience of the grievant. Thus, it states: "With reference to the testimony, despite any test that they gave the man, he has actually done work of a type that a helper has done in the past."

On these grounds the Union requests that the grievant be put on the job in question and be awarded retroactive pay.

Company

On its part the Company contends, of course, that there is no violation of the Labor Agreement. In support of this fundamental position, it offers a series of arguments. It claims that the grievant does not have the qualifications to fill the job in question. It argues that the name of the job "Maintenance Helper" is deceptive, and that the job actually requires "certain and definite mechanical skills and aptitudes. The job requires competence or aptitude in all of the relevant job duties . . . not in just some of them." On this point the Company urges that the classification in question was negotiated to provide a source for additional Class "A" and Class "B" Maintenance Men:

> It was emphasized that the building of a new feed mill underway at the plant required a build-up of the maintenance force, and because it was difficult to get mechanics with experience in the feed industry, that this classification was established for new mechanics in the department that were not thoroughly acquainted with the various types of machinery and processes in the plant. And as vacancies appeared or were created in the top two classifications in the Maintenance Department, it is expected that employees in the "maintenance helper" group would qualify for promotion.

To buttress its position that the Maintenance Helper job is one requiring important mechanical skills, and not one of a "flunkey assistant," the Company points to the fact that the Casual Employees classification was established in the same negotiations that gave rise to the Maintenance Helper classification. Thus:

> It is not reasonable to assume that such a job would be established to work in each department where needed and that a classification for additional unskilled labor would be established just for the Maintenance Department. . . . The undisputed testimony was that the purpose of this

classification was to have a group of unskilled laborers available for use in any department if they were needed. Now it is not reasonable to assume that the Company would establish such a classification as this to be used in all departments and then create a separate one just for the Maintenance Department and for the same purpose to be called "maintenance helper."

With respect to the qualifications of the grievant, the Company argues that he failed the test; that he was demoted from two jobs because of his deficiency in arithmetic (emphasizing in this connection that the job of Maintenance Helper requires a knowledge of math); that W has never performed the work which the new job requires; and that his application blank does not contain any evidence of previous mechanical aptitude or experience. Thus, it concludes on this point: "even without the tests, there was no doubt that W was unqualified for the job. But the tests served in an objective manner to bolster this conclusion. They also afforded W an objective means to demonstrate if he had the necessary aptitudes and capabilities for the job."

With respect to the test, the Company believes that it has the right to administer the test given to the grievant. It claims that "the labor agreement between the parties does not prohibit the use of tests in determining capabilities and qualifications; most Arbitrators . . . would disagree . . . that the Company had no right to administer tests without the Union's consent"; that the test is an objective method to determine whether employees have capabilities and qualifications for a job; and that the kind of test which the Company used in this case was "designed to test for the things required on this job. . . ."

Finally, the Company points to Article VI, and in particular to Section 10c, and states: "the grievant met only one of the requirements for the job; namely, seniority. He is not capable and does not have the ability or qualifications to perform the job satisfactorily." Thus, the Company's contention is that the grievant does not have the right to the job under Article VI because he is not "capable" of performing it.

On these grounds the Company requests that the grievance be denied.

Discussion of the Evidence

Analysis of Article VI, Section 10

It is not disputed that the job in question was declared open for bid and that W was the only bidder. The Company decided he was not capable for the job, and used as the basis of its decision his failure to pass the aforementioned test, its assessment of his other qualifications and experience, and its determination of the requirements of the Maintenance Helper job. After reaching this decision, the Company hired new employees from the outside to fill the job. Therefore, the crucial problem in this case is the determination of whether the grievant had the right to the job under Article VI of the Labor Agreement.

At the crux of this case is the filling of a job vacancy. In Article VI, Section 10, the parties have agreed as to the exact method to be used in the filling of job vacancies. The right of the grievant to the job in question must be established in terms of Section 10. Here we have a carefully drawn up plan which reflects the basic intent of the parties in this respect. Article VI contains ten separate sections dealing with the seniority problem. But it is in Section 10 that the parties have precisely established the method of filling job vacancies, and have further established whatever rights an employee has to an open job on the basis of seniority. Therefore, it is plain that this dispute must turn upon the correct application of Section 10 to the circumstances of this case.

In its opening statement, Section 10 provides that "an open job shall be defined as any job that requires additional personnel." It then states that "open jobs shall be filled in the following manner." Note the word *shall*, which the parties have agreed to in this respect. By using this clear-cut word, the parties obviously intended that job vacancies cannot be filled in any manner except as provided for in the subsequent provisions of Section 10. *In short, Section 10 provides the exclusive and only method for the filling of job vacancies.* No other method can be used. There is no need to belabor this point, since the words "shall be filled" are unambiguous and unequivocal. It permits of no departure from the procedure laid down in Section 10.

What is this procedure which binds the Company, the Union, the employees, and, of course, the Arbitrator? Subsection (a) provides that upon request of the Union, the Personnel Office will furnish a list of all open jobs, such list to be posted on the plant's bulletin boards for three working days. At the end of three working days, the job is closed. This obviously means that interested employees have three working days to bid on open jobs. If an employee does not bid within this time period, he forfeits any claim to the open job.

What does Section 10 provide for after a job opening is posted for bid? The answer to this question is established in subsection (b). It states that "those employees" desiring to do so may make application for the job. When the bids are closed, the Personnel Office or Plant Superintendent will interview the applicants in order of seniority. Thus, "such employees will remain on their present jobs until called by the Personnel Office or Plant Superintendent, when they shall be interviewed for such jobs in order of seniority."

The important question, of course, is who among the bidders is successful. What standards are incorporated in Section 10 upon which this determination shall be made? In this respect, subsection (c) is crucial. It provides that the successful bidder will be "the employee having the greatest seniority who is capable and qualified . . ." In short, the Company must pick the employee with the greatest seniority who is capable and best qualified. By the same token, it does not mean that the employee with the greatest seniority is guaranteed the job. Certainly, Section 10 (c) does not provide for a straight and automatic seniority system. Under proper circumstances, a junior service employee may be selected over a senior service employee.

The word "capable" in subsection (c)

The heart of the Company's case is that since it deemed W not capable for the job it was not required to honor his bid. Thus, what the Company argues is that under Section 10 it may reject any and all bids for an open job when it believes any or all employees making application for a job are not capable or qualified to fill it. In the instant case, the Company believes that it was not required to select the grievant for the job because "he is not capable and does not have the ability or qualifications to perform the job satisfactorily." Thus, the basis of the Company's case, of course, rests upon the word *capable* that is found in subsection (c). In short, the Company would ignore the remaining provisions of Section 10 and base its case upon the single word *capable*. Once the determination is made that a bidder or bidders is or are not capable, the remaining provisions of Section 10 are inoperative.

In all sincerity, the Arbitrator cannot accept this kind of construction of Section 10, though he acknowledges that the Company has assumed its position in a conscientious manner and in good faith. He cannot accept it because the Company argues a construction which is not consistent with the language of Section 10 when regarded as a whole. The intent of the parties relative to the filling of vacancies can only properly be deduced from Section 10 when it is regarded as a whole and not from only one word which appears in it. This conclusion reflects a cardinal principle of arbitration to the effect that the true intent of contract language cannot be deduced from a single word or phrase but from the entire scope of language which applies to the problem under consideration. As stated in Elkouri's standard volume on arbitration, *How Arbitration Works*, 1960, pp. 207–208:

> It is said that the primary rule in construing a written instrument is to determine, not alone from a single word or phrase, but from the instrument as a whole, the true intent of the parties and to interpret the

meaning of a questioned word or part with regard to the connection in which it is used, the subject matter and its relation to all other parts or provisions.

Similarly, Sections or portions cannot be isolated from the rest of the agreement and given construction independently of the purpose and agreement of the parties as evidenced by the entire document. . . . The meaning of each paragraph and each sentence must be determined in relation to the contract as a whole. This standard requiring the agreement to be construed as a whole is applied very frequently.

Thereupon, Elkouri cites many arbitration cases decided by several distinguished and professional arbitrators to underscore these statements.

Section 10 when regarded as a whole

Why does the Company's construction appear in variance with the intent of Section 10 when the language is regarded as a whole? The answer to this question is very simple. When the language is regarded as a whole, it becomes unmistakably clear that it was the intent of the parties that job vacancies will be filled from among those employees who bid upon the open job. Consider the following elements of Section 10: It contemplates in subsection (b) that employees will bid on the job; thus, it states "those employees" desiring to occupy the job will make application. Then immediately below, in subsection (c), it states "the employee having the greatest seniority who is capable and best qualified shall receive the job." Now to which employee does the term *the employee* refer? Obviously, it refers to *an* employee of *"those employees"* who bid on the job in accordance with the procedures established in subsection (b). Thus, to the extent that subsection (c) establishes a capability and qualification test to condition seniority, it establishes those standards in terms of "those employees" who bid on the job in the first place. In short, subsection (c) establishes the procedure of selecting an employee who "shall receive the job" in terms of "those employees" who originally bid on the job. Even the words *best qualified* which appear in subsection (c) contemplate a contest between the bidders on the job. This means that the person with the greatest seniority will get the job provided he is "best qualified" among the bidders. Thus, once again, we are driven to the conclusion that the Company must fill the job from among those employees who bid on the job in the first place.

Of course, if there are no bidders, the Company is free to fill the job by hiring new employees. But if there is a bidder, or bidders, the Company, under Section 10, is obligated to fill the job with such employees before going outside the plant. In the instant case, of course, new employees have no right to bid on vacant jobs since

Section 10 contemplates that only employees who have established seniority may bid on such jobs. Section 10 does not establish a qualification or capability contest between bargaining unit employees and outsiders. Rather, it sets up such a contest between those bargaining unit employees who have bid upon a vacant job.

In short, the intent of Section 10 when the language is viewed as a whole is that job vacancies are to be filled by bargaining unit employees who bid on the jobs. There is only one possible way to affirm the Company's position and that is to ignore one word of Section 10 and read it complete apart from all its other provisions. To be sure, the Arbitrator did consider whether this would be a proper method to apply Section 10. After long and hard deliberation, he is of the judgment that to affirm the Company's position on these grounds would place a construction upon Section 10 not contemplated by the language of the provisions when regarded as a whole. This is not to say that at times arbitration decisions may not turn on one word or phrase. But what is important in this proceeding is that it would be entirely improper to base a decision on one word when Section 10 taken as a whole shows that the parties intended to fill vacant jobs from those employees who bid on the job in the first place.

Absence of practice

It would be reasonable to expect that, if Section 10 means what the Company would like it to mean, there would be some practice to support its construction. However, there is absolutely nothing in the record to show that in the past the Company by-passed bargaining unit employees who bid on a job and filled the vacancy from the outside. The instance wherein the Company apparently filled a skilled electrician's job from the outside is not pertinent because no bargaining unit employee bid on the job when it was posted. Under such circumstances, the Company, of course, can hire from the outside.

Surely, if the Company's construction of Section 10 were valid it can be expected that at some time job vacancies would have been filled from the outside after bargaining unit employees bid on the job. In the absence of such evidence, it can only be held that in the past job vacancies were filled by selecting an employee from those employees who bid on the job.

Of course, it may be perfectly true that the Company had no need to go to the outside after bargaining unit employees bid on the job because one or more of the bidders for a vacant job was capable and qualified to handle the vacancy. In this respect, the Arbitrator notes that the job in question is a new one and, consequently, it is possible that for the first time the Company believed it necessary to by-pass bargaining unit employees and hire from the outside. Still, it does appear somewhat curious to this Arbitrator that there is no actual practice in the past to show that the Company filled jobs from the outside after bargaining unit employees bid on the vacancies. The absence of such evidence buttresses the Arbitrator's conviction that the intent of Section 10 is to fill job vacancies from the employee who bid on the jobs.

Negotiation of current labor agreement

Further, there is nothing in the negotiations which resulted in the adoption of the Maintenance Helper classification which changes this judgment. Even if it be conceded that the Company established this classification to provide a source for Maintenance Men to man the new feed mill, and so informed the Union, the fact still remains that there is not one scrap of evidence to show that there was any mutual intention to waive the requirements of Section 10 in filling the vacancies. If it were the idea of the Company that it could depart from Section 10 to fill the job in question from the outside and by-pass bargaining unit bidders, there is, of course, no evidence whatsoever that the Union agreed to any such program.

In this connection, the Arbitrator has taken note of the establishment of the "Casual Employees" pool in the same negotiation. On this point, the same basic observation holds. Thus, even if it be conceded that the establishment of this classification tends to prove that the Maintenance Helper job requires more than rudimentary skills, the fact remains that there still is no showing that the Maintenance Helper job was to be filled apart from the requirements of Section 10.

The Arbitrator has searched the record very carefully on this point, and at no place is there any evidence whatsoever that there was an agreement that the new job could be filled from the outside after bargaining unit employees bid on the job. Mr. S, Plant Manager, testified that a Union representative stated: "you mean an apprentice classification," after S established the character of the classification which he was attempting to put into the contract. But this statement did not show by any stretch of the imagination that the Union agreed to a future policy where the Company could by-pass bargaining unit bidders and fill the job in question from the outside.

Indeed, these observations underscore the Arbitrator's conviction that the language of Section 10 precludes the filling of jobs from the outside when bargaining unit employees bid on the vacancy. If the parties intended to place the job in question into a separate category, and free it from the requirements of Section 10, they would have adopted suitable language in the Labor Agreement. Instead, what we have in the contract is the mere listing of the new job along with its rate of pay in Appendage "A" of the Labor

Agreement, and without any qualifications whatsoever so as to isolate the job from the operation of Section 10.

Irrelevant considerations

As a result of these considerations, the Arbitrator finds that the Company violated the language and intent of Article VI, Section 10 when it refused to select the grievant for the job in question. He was the only bidder, and, therefore, the Company was obligated to place him in the job. The Company was without the authority to fill the job from the outside when a bargaining unit employee bid on the job.

Because of the grounds upon which the decision has been reached, other issues in this case become irrelevant. It is not that they are not important; rather, it is that the Arbitrator has no need to deal with them; and, since there is no need to deal with them for purposes of this case, it would be entirely improper for him to resolve them. An arbitrator goes out of bounds if he decides issues which are not pertinent to the reaching of a decision in a particular case. Once a decision is reached, an arbitrator has no right to roam through the record and decide issues which are not pertinent to his decision even though these latter issues are inherently important.

Thus, the Arbitrator finds no need to establish the content of this new job, and the skills required to perform the job. The parties were miles apart on this issue. The Union believes that the job in question is a routine job requiring low level skills for its effective performance. On the other hand, the Company contends that the new job is a highly skilled mechanic's job requiring great skill and capability to perform it. As stated, it is the Company's contention that the new job is a source for additional Maintenance Men who will be required to run the new feed mill. Further, the parties are poles apart on the qualifications of the grievant to fill the job. The Company, of course, believes that W is completely unqualified to fill it, and to buttress this position presented a number of items, including his demotion from two jobs which required a knowledge of arithmetic, and his failure to pass the written and motor test. On the other hand, the Union presented items which it believes show that the grievant has the capability to fill the new job. On these issues, the Arbitrator need pass no judgment, since, as stated, W was the only bidder on the job, and under the provisions of Section 10 he was entitled to it.

A good share of the testimony of the parties and their arguments related to the aforementioned written and motor test. The Company contends that it has the authority to require the grievant to take the test, and that it has the right to disqualify W from the job (at least in part) because he failed the test. The Union charges that the Company did not have the right to give *W* the test, and that even if it did have the right, the test was not a valid one.

The Arbitrator finds that the test issue is not relevant to his decision, and it would be improper for him to decide these questions. Nothing in his decision relates or is intended to relate to whether the Company has the right to administer such tests to bargaining unit employees, or whether, if it has such a right, the test is valid to ascertain the capabilities of an employee bidding on the job in question. These questions would properly arise in a proceeding when there would be a determination between employees who have established seniority and who have bid on a job vacancy. As stated, Section 10 (c) does not establish a qualification contest between bargaining unit employees and outsiders. It sets up a contest of this sort between bidders who have already established seniority. Thus, the issues involving the test would be pertinent, and would have to be decided by the Arbitrator, if they were germane to a case involving the determination of the qualifications of employees who have established seniority and who have bid on a job.

Perhaps the parties will be disappointed that the issues involving the test have not been resolved in this proceeding. To be sure, the Arbitrator is also somewhat disappointed that he cannot deal with these issues. They are, indeed, important and challenging. Nevertheless, these personal predilections must not overcome the hard fact that there is no need to deal with them for purposes of this case.

Conclusions

It is the Arbitrator's decision that the grievant will be put in the Maintenance Helper classification. However, he shall not award him any back pay because the original grievance did not make any claim for money. This is far too late in the game for the grievant to claim retroactive pay. As the Company states, the Arbitrator "is completely without authority to award back pay since a request for the same is not included in the grievance. It seems almost unnecessary to argue that the Arbitrator cannot award something that is unclaimed." This argument makes sense, since the absence of a back pay claim on the part of the grievant when he wrote his grievance indicates that when the grievance was being processed in the Grievance Procedure it was contested only on the basis of whether the grievant had the right to the job. There is no evidence showing that claim for retroactive pay was made prior to the time that Union Counsel made it at the arbitration hearing. Who knows whether or not the grievance might have been compromised short of arbitration if both issues—*W's* right to the job and to back pay—had been part of the grievant's complaint.

If the Company is disappointed in this decision, the fact is that the Arbitrator has no choice in the matter. As amply demonstrated, Article VI, Section 10 establishes the *exclusive* procedure for the filling of vacancies. If this is not a wise or desirable procedure, the parties have the opportunity to change it in negotiations. But it cannot be changed in arbitration which is a judicial and not a legislative forum. The Company and Union are fully aware that this Arbitrator does not read employee rights into labor contracts which have not been negotiated by the parties. They are aware that he has denied many grievances when employee's claims are not supported by contractual language or a clearly defined practice. Moreover, as these parties know by experience, this Arbitrator is fully aware of Management rights and in many cases he has denied grievances when the conduct of Management has not been limited by the contract.

All these considerations were fully kept in mind as the Arbitrator worked on this case. He does not adopt certain standards for decision for one case only to adopt different standards to decide another case. The clear fact is that the grievant had a right to the job under Article VI, Section 10 of the contract. Its language clearly establishes the intent of the parties when they adopted it; and nothing in the practice of the parties or in the negotiations out of which the job was established alters the firm conviction of the Arbitrator that Section 10 requires that the Company fill vacancies from those employees who bid on a job vacancy before going to the outside. *W* bid on the job, and since he was the only bidder, he is entitled to it.

Award

On the basis of the evidence, and in his best judgment, the Arbitrator makes the following award:

1. The grievance filed by *W* dated October 30, 1961, is granted on the grounds that the company violated Article VI, Section 10, of the Labor Agreement.
2. Within three (3) working days, the Company is directed to place the grievant on the job of Maintenance Helper.

QUESTIONS

1. How would *you* have decided the case? Justify your decision with cogent arguments.
2. Whatever your decision may be, what effect would it have on the Company's testing program?
3. Assume that you held for the Union; how would that decision affect future decisions to automate the plant?

part four

SOME FINAL THOUGHTS

The productive potential of the United States depends upon many factors, including the status of employer–employee relations. Our nation has been extremely fortunate in being endowed with a highly favorable natural environment for the encouragement of the productive process. Its virtually inexhaustible stores of natural resources, advantageous geographic location, and population growth constitute a sound basis for an expanding and dynamic economy. Despite these considerations, the fact remains that the fruitfulness of the productive process of our nation depends fundamentally upon the creativeness of the managerial function, the economic and political system in which business and labor operate, and the industry and the spirit of the labor force. Other nations which have not attained the level of industrial development of the United States can match to an extent our natural resources. Few people, however, equal the vigor and the creativeness of the American people in implementing the productive process. In the last analysis, the level of the standard of living of a nation depends not so much upon its stores of iron ore, coal, oil,

Concluding statement

and the like, as upon the motivation and the energy of its people, and the system of government and economics within which the productive process is accomplished.

A fundamental if implicit thesis of this volume has been that an important prerequisite for the increasing productivity of the American nation is the status of its employer–employee relations. Since we are a nation practicing free enterprise, what has thus far remained (despite a highly visible trend to increasing government interest in labor relations) an essentially private employer–employee relationship is by far the dominant characteristic of the industrial relations environment. The character of this relationship determines to an important extent our productive capabilities. A wholesome labor relations environment that encourages maximum efforts of labor and management will do much toward improving our standard of living. In contrast, the productive process will be obstructed to the extent that the employer–employee relationship is implemented in a hostile framework. From this it follows not only that the best interests of employers and employees are dependent upon the establishment of a harmonious industrial relations climate, but that the entire nation likewise has a real stake in the accomplishment of this objective.

In retrospect the evidence is clear that collective bargaining relations in the United States have improved remarkably over the years. It is well to recall in this connection that widespread collective bargaining is a comparatively recent development in this country. The earliest unions date from 1800, and unionism can hardly be viewed as a new phenomenon, but even 35 years ago only a relatively few employers and employees were involved in the process, virtually none of the vital industries of the nation were characterized by collective bargaining, and unionism had not yet penetrated the major mass-production sectors. During the period of growth of collective bargaining, union–employer relations in these industries were far from satisfactory and not conducive to high levels of industrial productivity. Since the process was new and virtually untried, there was much distrust and suspicion on both sides of the bargaining table. Many employers questioned the methods and the ultimate objectives of labor unions and in general aggressively resisted the development of unions. In some cases unions moved too fast in their development and failed to take into consideration the legion of problems involved in establishing collective bargaining within new industries. On a number of occasions, labor–management relations deteriorated into prolonged and violent strikes resulting in loss of life, in physical injury, and in destruction of company property. It may be argued with some validity that these events probably were unavoidable because of the newness of the collective bargaining process. Such happenings might be regarded as the "growing pains" of a new and potentially important area. Notwithstanding these considerations, the fact remains that some of the history of the development of industrial relations—particularly prior to the 1930's but even as late as World War II—is not pleasant to recall.

With the passage of time, labor relations handled under the collective bargaining process have improved enormously. As noted earlier, violence during strikes has virtually disappeared from the American industrial scene. To appreciate this, one has only to compare the bloody Memorial Day, 1937, Little Steel incident with the automobile industry strikes in the fall of 1964. In the steel industry strike ten lives were lost, scores of people suffered serious physical injury, and there was severe damage to property. In the automobile strikes only token picket lines were manned by the union, and there was no violence and no damage to property. The latter strikes were so "civilized," indeed, that some of the companies involved in it supplied power for the TV sets viewed by employees serving on "picket-line duty."

The virtual demise of the role of violence is, however, only one of many developments attesting to the greatly improved state of labor relations in recent years. The earliest pages of this volume indicated that there has been similar progress along almost every basic labor–management dimension, and it is hoped that by this point in the book the reader stands in fundamental agreement. The facts show not only that in an overwhelming number of instances the parties have been able to negotiate under a strike deadline without reaching a stalemate, but that with respect to unauthorized, or "wildcat," strikes the record is similarly impressive. Instead of resorting to industrial warfare as the means of adjusting and settling disputes arising over the interpretation and application of an existing contract, employers and unions settle these problems through the grievance and arbitration procedure, thereby lending considerable further stability to their relationships.

Running through the preceding pages are testimonials to other types of success—from a stress on considerably more informed bargaining sessions to the attainment of a far larger measure of contracts that constitute "good compromises," and from the almost complete disappearance of "Conflict" philosophies to the great growth of "Accommodation" (if not "Cooperation") ones.

Indeed, under some management–union relationships there is now a genuine feeling of mutual trust and respect between the parties. Although contract negotiations, grievances, and arbitration cases are treated with vigor by both the company and the union, the problems are handled within a general framework of friendliness and of bilateral trust and confidence. It is obvious that such a state of development of industrial relations fosters high levels of productivity, profits, wages, and quality of product. It means that all parties to the collective bargaining process, including the public, derive benefit.

Such progress in labor relations did not develop by accident. There are cogent reasons for the great strides that have been made in the union–management relationship. Developments in management and union attitudes, in philosophy, and in procedures have been responsible for this trend.

On the part of companies, there is general acceptance, even if this is in many cases given begrudgingly, of the process of collective bargaining. In contrast to the state of affairs three decades ago, the typical management of the late 1960's has no open quarrel with the existence of collective bargaining. However much it might prefer a nonunionized work force (and however greatly it might continue to oppose the union in theory) it is now preoccupied with the practical problem of *getting along with* its labor organization on a day-by-day basis, while preserving at the same time those managerial prerogatives needed to operate an efficient and productive enterprise. Many companies operating under collective bargaining contracts sincerely believe that the protection of job rights of their employees by a labor agreement is desirable. Though at times protection of job rights obtained through collective bargaining might diminish plant productivity, most companies and unions have found the collective bargaining contract sufficiently elastic to accommodate the objectives of both efficiency of production and the protection of job rights. The pliability of the collective bargaining process has thus far provided chances for the reconciliation of both objectives and it is to be suspected that even the thorny problems of automation will ultimately be resolved in the same way (although, here, most likely in conjunction with government actions).

In addition, many companies have taken a realistic approach to the institutional character of unionism. They are aware that to an extent the collective bargaining process tends to supply the needs of the union as an institution, as well as to provide the mechanism whereby the terms of employment of workers are established. Many contractual provisions are agreed to by management on the theory that a union secure in its status may be more judicious in its behavior at the bargaining table and in grievance negotiations.

Management's recognition of the problems and needs of employees likewise is an important element in the establishment of sound relations under collective bargaining. Relations between companies and unions are bound to be more harmonious as management exhibits a genuine understanding of the problems confronted by the individual employee. A union will tend to be more aggressive and attempt to impose more limitations on the managerial function to the extent that a company, through its general behavior and personnel policies, demonstrates an unsympathetic attitude toward employees' problems and objectives. Indeed, one major reason for the establishment and the expansion of unions is that in the past some companies did not give sufficient attention to the needs of employees. At present the evidence is quite clear that the business community in general is vitally concerned with the welfare of its workers. One of the primary bases of the science of personnel management is the development of techniques and procedures which have at their core the sympathetic consideration of employee problems. In many companies the needs of employees are given equal weight and attention with the problems of finance, production, sales, and quality control. And executives are, in fact, assigned to personnel departments to no small extent because of their ability to understand sympathetically employees' problems and their capability to deal with employees on the basis of sound human relations. This development means that a solid foundation exists for more harmonious relations between companies, unions, and employees.

There is also a growing tendency on the part of industry to place the operation of labor relations in the hands of qualified and professional managers. There is scarcely a major company in existence that has not established a department to handle labor relations and personnel problems. More important, in many companies the industrial relations department has equal prestige and status with any other division or department within the enterprise. Such a development likewise fosters better relations at the bargaining table. But because collective bargaining negotiations and the administration of labor agreements constitute a most difficult and highly responsible job, it is necessary that companies entrust such a function to executives who are qualified in terms of training, motivation, skill, and personality. Companies which delegate these duties to unqualified personnel or impose the duties as additional responsibilities on already busy executives cannot expect to acquire a labor relations climate conducive to high levels of productivity.

It is also noteworthy that companies are increasingly conducting classes and other training programs involving the problems of contract administration for *first-line supervisors*. This appears an indispensable part of a sound company industrial relations program. Frequently, grievances arise because first-line supervision has not been adequately trained in the principles of labor relations and in the meaning and application of the collective bargaining contract. With the growth of the science of industrial relations, and particularly as this is cast within the framework of collective bargaining, it is imperative that a company's labor relations program be executed and administered correctly by all levels of supervision. To the extent that this has been recognized by the business community, the cause of harmonious and sound labor relations has been proportionately advanced.

Not only does the evidence, finally, reveal that employers in increasing numbers are giving sympathetic understanding to the problems of employees and unions: There is also a growing awareness by *union* members and their leaders of the problems of management. At present many union leaders, although they are representatives of organizations that are above all political, are fully conscious of the fact that in the last analysis the welfare of employees depends upon the economic prosperity of the firm. The leaders understand further that the collective bargaining process is conditioned by the economic framework surrounding the particular negotiations, and that the over-all economic character of a firm or an industry relative to its competitive position, sales, profits, capital equipment, expansion requirements, and quality of production necessarily determines the economic benefits which can be provided to employees. There is increasing awareness that a company has obligations not only to its employees but also to its investors, management, and customers. These considerations do not mean that unions are less militant in collective bargaining. Negotiations are not conducted in a tea-party atmosphere. What these observations do mean is that labor relations generally improve to the degree that collective bargaining negotiations are based upon factual information and rationality, and carried on in a general atmosphere of reciprocal recognition of problems and in a spirit of genuine good faith and mutual respect. Clearly, guesswork, emotionalism, preconceived notions of equity, and intransigence, whether displayed by a company or a union in collective bargaining negotiations, are not conducive to good labor relations.

Collective bargaining literally means the joint determination of the terms of employment. The process does not *create* the problems of the employment relationship; issues such as wages, hours and overtime, vacations, holidays, discipline, job classification, promotions, and employee safety and health exist with or without collective bargaining. Problems growing out of the employment relationship must be solved, in one way or another. In the absence of collective bargaining they are handled and determined by the employer on a unilateral basis. His decisions in this respect are final; they have as their frame of reference his own standards of fairness and are limited only by the marketplace and the law.

But if collective bargaining does not create the problems of the employment relationship, it *does* establish a definite procedure wherein they are handled and resolved. Employers and employees, through their respective representatives, negotiate the terms of employment and provide the mechanisms by which these terms can be administered throughout the contractual duration. Whatever deficiencies remain in the present system, the considerable progress which has been made in the past few decades augurs well for the future productive potential of the nation, assuming only that we can exercise sufficient patience in having our expectations for collective bargaining translated into action.

appendix

The purpose of this problem is to familiarize students with the negotiation of a labor contract. The problem is strictly a hypothetical one and does not pertain to any actual company or union. It is designed to test in a practical way the student's understanding of the issues of collective bargaining studied during the semester and the strategy of the bargaining process. The strategy and techniques of negotiations are treated in Chapter 5 and the issues of collective bargaining are dealt with primarily in Chapters 7 through 10. Before the actual mock negotiation, the student should carefully reread these chapters.

Mock negotiation problem

Procedure and Ground Rules:

1. Class will be divided into Labor and Management negotiation teams. Each team will elect a chairman at the first meeting of the team.
2. Teams will meet in sufficient number of planning sessions to be ready for the negotiations. Each participant will be required to engage in necessary research for the negotiation.
3. In the light of the following problem, each team will establish *not more* than 8 items *nor less* than 6 which it will demand. *All demands must be based upon the problem. No team will be permitted to make a demand which is not based upon the problem.* For purposes of this problem a union wage demand and all fringe issues, if demanded, will be considered as only *one* (1) demand.
4. Each team should strive to negotiate demands which it believes to be most important. This requires the weighing of the alternatives in the light of respective needs of the group the team is representing.
5. Compromises, counterproposals, trading, and the dropping of demands to secure a contract will be permitted in the light of the give and take of the actual negotiations.
6. Each team should strive sincerely and honestly in the role playing to do the best job possible for the group which it represents. This is a *learning* situation and to learn there must be sincere dedication to the job ahead.
7. *Absolutely no consultation with any of the other teams, regardless of whether Company or Union, will be permitted. Each team must depend entirely upon its own resources.*
8. Chairmen should coordinate the planning of each team, decide on the time and place for planning sessions, and assign work to be done to members of the team. Chairmen, however, are not to do all the talking in the actual negotiations. To maximize the learning situation, each member of the team should positively participate in the negotiations.
9. There must either be a settlement of all issues in the negotiation or a work stoppage. *No extension of the existing contract will be permitted.* It is a question of either settlement or work stoppage.
10. Someone on each team should keep track of the settlements. Do not write out the actual contractual clauses agreed to. It will suffice only to jot down the substance of agreements.
11. There will be a general discussion of the problem after the negotiation. Each team chairman or his representative will make a brief statement to the entire class as to the final outcome of the problem.

Herein follows the problem upon which the demands will be based and which provides the framework for the negotiation. *Read the prob-*

lem very carefully to assess the situation. Base your demands only upon this problem.

Representatives of the Auto Products Corporation of Indiana and representatives of Local 5000 of the Auto-Metal Workers National Union are in the process of renegotiating their collective bargaining contract. The time of the negotiations is the present. Accordingly, the parties in the negotiation are conditioned by current conditions with respect to the law of labor relations, economic conditions, and patterns of collective bargaining. The present contract terminates at the close of today's negotiation. (Instructor should set date of mock negotiation and time that contract expires).

The Company, which was founded in Indianapolis in 1920, has steadily grown in size. In 1920, it employed 425 production and maintenance workers and at present about 3,800 such workers are employed. Except for the depression years of 1929–1933 the financial structure of the Company has been relatively good: In the last fiscal year, the sales of the Indianapolis plant amounted to $56,000,000 (compared to $52,000,000 in the previous year); the Company earned $4,500,000 net profits after taxes; and its total assets amounted to $35,000,000, including an inventory of unsold goods of $6,500,000.

The Company manufactures a variety of auto accessory parts. Such products include auto heaters, oil pumps, fan belts, rear view mirrors, and piston rings. About 65 per cent of company sales are to the major basic auto companies; 25 per cent to auto repair facilities; and the rest to the government.

The employees of the Company were not formed into a union until 1937. In that year, as a result of the campaign to organize the mass production industries, the Union established itself. It was victorious in an NLRB election and the certification as a result of the election was awarded to Local 5000 on January 17, 1937. From that date, Local 5000 has represented the production and maintenance workers of the Company.

The first collective bargaining agreement between the Company and Local 5000 was signed on June 14, 1937.

Only one strike has taken place since the Union came into the picture; it occurred in 1940. The issues of the strike were the Union's demands for union shop, increased wages, and six paid holidays. The strike lasted six weeks, and when it terminated, the Union obtained for its members a four-cent hourly wage increase, retroactive to the day of the strike (the Union had demanded seven cents), and four paid holidays. The Union failed in its attempt to obtain any arrangement requiring membership in the Union as a condition of employment. The current contract does not include a "checkoff". At the time of these negotiations all but 350 workers in the bargaining unit are in the Union.

The average wage in the plant is $2.90 per hour. The plant involved in the negotiations is located in Indianapolis, but the Company also operates a plant in Little Rock, Arkansas, which produces the same items. It was built in 1960, and now employs 1,500 workers. Efforts to organize the southern plant have not been successful. The average rate in the nonunion plant is $1.75 per hour. During the last eight months 300 employees in the Indianapolis plant have been laid off. It is no secret that the reason for this has been the increase of output in the Arkansas plant.

The Company works on a three-shift basis, paying a three-cent premium for the second and third shifts, although it customarily operates only two shifts, and only on occasion operates the third shift. Employees work a standard 40-hour work week. On the first two shifts the Company operates all its departments, which means an equal division of the labor force on the two shifts. When it operates a third shift, it operates only the departments needed to fill pressing orders. In the last three years it operated a third shift only on 70 working days.

In general, the relations between the Management and the Union have been satisfactory, although there have, of course, been the usual disagreements. However, in the last year there have been two "wildcat" strikes, participated in by some of the workers in the Oil Pump Department. In both cases the Union disclaimed all responsibility for the strikes and alleged that it did what it could to get the workers back to their jobs. The first wildcat strike lasted two days and the second, four days. There is an absolute no-strike clause in the present contract, and the Company threatened to sue the Union for damages under the terms of the Taft–Hartley Law, the Company claiming that the first violation of the contract cost it $75,000 in damages, and the second, $185,000. However, the Company finally decided not to sue. No one was disciplined because of the strike.

The existing contract contains a standard grievance procedure, and provides for arbitration of all disputes arising under the contract, except for those pertaining to production standards. Management has the unilateral right to establish production standards. During the last contractual period (three years) 275 grievances were filed by employees protesting against "unreasonably" high production standards. As required by the contract, the Company negotiated the production standard grievances, but the Union did not have the right to appeal to arbitration, or to strike over them. The management rights clause states in effect that the Company retains all rights except as limited by other provisions of the labor agreement.

Provided in the contract are a series of fringe benefits: six paid holidays; a pension plan which is better than industry pattern; a very good hospitalization and surgical benefits insurance plan; and a vacation plan wherein employees receive one week's vacation for one year of service and two weeks for five or more years of service. The total costs of all these fringe benefits amount to 63 cents per hour. The current contract does not require that employees retire when eligible for pension.

The seniority clause provides for promotions to be based on length of service and ability. During the contract period, twenty-one grievances were filed by employees who protested against the Company filling jobs

with junior service employees. The Company's position in these grievances was that the junior employees had more ability than the senior
employees. Five of these grievances went to arbitration, the Company
winning four of them and the Union winning one. Promotions are bid
for on a departmental basis.

The seniority area of the existing contract also provides for plant-wide
application of seniority credits for layoffs and recalls. During the recent
period in which many layoffs occurred because of declining sales, the
Company, as required by the contract, laid off many junior employees
rather than senior employees because of the plant-wide system. Foremen
have complained to Management and the Union that in many cases the
junior employees who have been laid off were more efficient employees
than the senior employees who had to be retained. The foremen requested
Management to take action in the next negotiation to remedy this
situation.

In addition, the current contract provides that an employee whose job
goes down, or whose job is pre-empted by a senior employee, may bump
any junior employee provided he has the qualifications to fill the job.
During the layoff periods the Company complains that this situation has
caused a great deal of expense because of an unreasonable amount of
displacement. The existing contract further provides for "super-seniority"
for the sixty Union stewards and other Union officials, but this provision
protects the stewards and Union officials only from layoffs.

Last year, the stewards spent on the average about ten hours each per
week on grievance work for which they were paid by the Company.
There are no limitations on stewards' performing such grievance work.
Foremen have complained that some stewards are "goofing off," using
"Union business" as a pretext not to work. All stewards deny what the
foremen say. In fact, the stewards claim that it is the unreasonable attitude of foremen that provokes grievances and complaints. Also, the
stewards claim that there cannot be a true measure of their time on the
basis of the number of written grievances filed (a total of 185 were filed
last year) since a good share of their time is spent discussing grievances
on an oral basis with employees and supervisors before a written grievance is filed. There is no record showing how many of these oral discussions ended problems without written grievances being filed.

Last year, because of an unexpected order from the government, the
plant worked overtime for a period of two weeks. Under the existing
contract, the Company has the right to require overtime. About 200
employees refused to work overtime, and only did so because the Company threatened to fire them if they refused. It has been rumored that
these 200 employees have been causing a lot of trouble in the Union
about this overtime affair. In addition, the Company has the right to
select the employees to work overtime and some employees have claimed
that foremen are not being fair and are giving their personal friends the
opportunity to earn the extra money and discriminating against the
other employees.

For many years each skilled tradesman has worked only within his trade. There are five trades hired: mechanics, carpenters, tool and die workers, plumbers, and electricians. Five months ago the Company required a mechanic to do a job normally performed by a plumber. The employee and Union filed a grievance, and the case went all the way to arbitration. The Arbitrator sustained the position of the Union on the basis of the "past practice" principle. Altogether the Company hires about 175 skilled tradesmen. Their average rate is $3.47 per hour. Skilled tradesmen have been affected by the current layoff. Twenty-five of them are laid off. They charge that the Company has been subcontracting out skilled work which could be done in the shop. Under the current contract, there is no restriction on the Company's right to subcontract.

The existing contract contains an "escalator" clause, providing for the adjustment of wages in accordance with changes within the Consumer Price Index and provides for a one-cent increase in wages for each 0.5 point change in the CPI. During the last three years in which the existing contract has been in force, the employees received a twelve-cent increase in wages as a result of the "escalator." In addition, the employees received four-cents an hour increase in each of the two previous years. This latter increment resulted from the operation of the so-called "annual improvement" feature of the contract. The current $2.90 average wage rate in the plant includes the increases from the escalator and annual improvement factors.

The present contract was negotiated for a three-year period. Both sides indicated during the contractual period that they may want to move away from this long-term arrangement in the future for a variety of reasons. However, there is no assurance that this attitude indicated a sincere position on the part of the parties, or merely expression of a possible bargaining position.

With respect to the current layoffs, the facts show that of the 300 employees laid off, 75 had exhausted their benefits under the Indiana Unemployment Compensation Act. The present contract does not provide for a supplementary unemployment benefit program.

Automation has been a problem in the Company for a period of several years. About 250 workers have been permanently separated because of automation. Union and Management meetings to deal with the problem during the past several years have proven fruitless. Previous discussions have centered around the rate of automation, the problem of the displaced employees, training of employees for the jobs created by automation, and seniority systems. All indications are that the next wave of automation will cost about 390 bargaining unit jobs. Part of the rumor is that the Company intends to hire employees from the outside to run these new machines. The 250 employees who have been permanently separated are in addition to the current 300 employees who are on layoff because of the southern situation.

There has been considerable controversy over the problem of temporary transfers. Under the existing contract, the Company may not transfer an employee to a job not in his current classification unless there is an emergency. Even then the Union must agree that an emergency exists before an employee can be transferred to a job on a temporary basis.

There also is a problem involving "working rules." These include: a fifteen-minute rest period every four hours, no change in the number of employees to jobs unless the job technology is substantially changed, paid lunch periods for scheduled or unscheduled overtime that exceeds four hours, and paid "wash-up" time for ten minutes prior to quitting time. The Company contends that these "working rules" are costing it a lot of money. Whenever this issue has been brought up in the past, the Union has refused any change.

Company records show that: 60 per cent of the workers have seniority of from thirty days to ten years; 30 per cent have more than ten years and less than twenty years; and 10 per cent have more than twenty years. The average age of the employees in the plant is thirty-nine. About 20 per cent of the bargaining unit are women; and 15 per cent are Negroes. In the past, Negroes by custom have been restricted to janitor and common labor jobs.

During the last several weeks, most employees have been wearing buttons and arm-bands stating: "We want total job security." A few days ago the company posted many large signs stating: "The best way to achieve job security is through more production. Go! Go! Go!" Now, the union wants these signs taken down on the grounds that they are causing fear and confusion among its members. In addition, the union found out that the posters were printed in a nonunion shop.

(For the Instructor)

How to Use Mock Negotiation Problem

We have used the preceding mock negotiation problem with great success for several years. Students are uniformly enthusiastic about the problem, and there exists a friendly rivalry among the students during the weeks preceeding the negotiation. Here are some suggestions on how to use the problem most effectively:

1. The class should be divided into union and management negotiation teams about the middle of the semester. Each management and union team should include from three to five students. The teams could be selected in random fashion, but a better method is to distribute the better students among the different teams: by the middle of the semester the instructor should have a good idea of the capability and the potential of the students. Each student should be assigned to a specific team, and each team should elect a chairman as rapidly as possible.
2. The teams should be instructed to conduct the research necessary in order to collect the data and arguments to be presented at

the negotiation. The instructor should advise students where the information can be found. The more helpful sources include: the *Monthly Labor Review*, of the U.S. Department of Labor; the Bureau of National Affairs' *Collective Bargaining Negotiations and Contracts*; special reports of the United States Department of Labor; existing collective bargaining contracts; the AFL-CIO *Federationalist*; the *AFL-CIO News*; publications of the American Management Association and other management sources; *Labor Law Journal*; *Industrial and Labor Relations Review*; *Business Week*; and the *New York Times* and *Wall Street Journal*.

3. Experience has shown that each team should meet in its private planning sessions about five times for about two to three hours for each session before the negotiation. This is in addition to research conducted on an individual basis. Because of the time involved, the negotiation could be used instead of the traditional term paper.

4. The instructor may, if he desires, attend some of the planning sessions, although in recent years we have not been doing this on the grounds that the full responsibility for planning should be assumed by the students. If visits are made, the instructor should not shape the over-all strategy of the team but merely consult with the team on particular problems.

5. We have found that the negotiation session should last about four hours. It could be held on an evening or a Saturday morning. Announce the date well in advance of the actual negotiation—at least six weeks.

6. The negotiation should be held toward the end of the semester so that the students can use the knowledge gained during the semester. We have usually scheduled the exercise during the second to the last week of the semester.

7. The number of negotiations depends upon the number of students in the class. In one semester, the class included sixty-six students, and, hence, there were six negotiations going on simultaneously. Be sure to arrange for the rooms in which the negotiations are to be held well in advance of the exercise. If possible, the room should be of the conference type, though any room will do provided that chairs can be arranged around a table so that the teams face each other.

8. The instructor should visit each negotiation and his time should be divided equally among the groups. If some technical problem arises during the negotiation, the instructor should deal with the issue. Other than this, the instructor should remain silent as he observes the negotiation. *Do not give any help to any team while the negotiation is underway.* At times, we have had management and organized labor representatives visit the negotiations. Uniformly they have been impressed with the success of the students and their competency at the bargaining table.

9. The teams should be instructed that the sessions must end promptly at the specified time. If the negotiations are to end at 10 P.M., they should end at 10 P.M. Do not extend the time

since to do so would result in lack of uniformity for the different teams.

10. When the negotiations are over, all students should meet in one room for a wrap-up session. Each chairman should report on whether there was a strike or settlement; the major difficulties and problems of the negotiation; and other highlights of the negotiation. The chief purpose of this session, however, is for the instructor to make observations based on his visits to the negotiations. This session should not exceed forty-five minutes. This meeting is usually charged with emotion, some horseplay, and friendly criticism of each other by the students. If there is not a definite time limit, it could go on indefinitely. In the instructor's analysis, the students should be treated kindly. They have worked hard and deserve congratulations and a pat on the back. Remember that this is their first experience and mistakes will be made. These should be pointed out, but in a strictly impersonal manner.

11. Other suggestions are that: (1) some arrangements should be made for the students to have coffee during the negotiations; (2) if possible, smoking should be permitted; (3) to pacify the janitorial staff, the rooms should be cleared of debris, and chairs and tables rearranged when the negotiations are ended; (4) the instructor should permit some poetic license during the actual negotiation, but cut off a student or a team which invents too much; and (5) he should not discourage some of the fun which the students develop during the negotiations.

Index